Anglo-Saxon Studies 33

OLD AGE IN EARLY MEDIEVAL ENGLAND

Anglo-Saxon Studies

ISSN 1475-2468

GENERAL EDITORS
John Hines
Catherine Cubitt

'Anglo-Saxon Studies' aims to provide a forum for the best scholarship on the Anglo-Saxon peoples in the period from the end of Roman Britain to the Norman Conquest, including comparative studies involving adjacent populations and periods; both new research and major re-assessments of central topics are welcomed.

Books in the series may be based in any one of the principal disciplines of archaeology, art history, history, language and literature, and inter- or multi-disciplinary studies are encouraged.

Proposals or enquiries may be sent directly to the editors or the publisher at the addresses given below; all submissions will receive prompt and informed consideration.

Professor John Hines, School of History, Archaeology and Religion, Cardiff University, John Percival Building, Colum Drive, Cardiff, Wales, CF10 3EU, UK

Professor Catherine Cubitt, School of History, Faculty of Arts and Humanities, University of East Anglia, Norwich, England, NR4 7TJ, UK

Boydell & Brewer, PO Box 9, Woodbridge, Suffolk, England, IP12 3DF, UK

Previously published volumes in the series are listed at the back of this book

OLD AGE IN EARLY MEDIEVAL ENGLAND

A CULTURAL HISTORY

Thijs Porck

THE BOYDELL PRESS

© Thijs Porck 2019

All Rights Reserved. Except as permitted under current legislation no part of this work may be photocopied, stored in a retrieval system, published, performed in public, adapted, broadcast, transmitted, recorded or reproduced in any form or by any means, without the prior permission of the copyright owner

The right of Thijs Porck to be identified as the author of this work has been asserted in accordance with sections 77 and 78 of the Copyright, Designs and Patents Act 1988

First published 2019
The Boydell Press, Woodbridge
Paperback edition 2021

ISBN 978-1-78327-375-1 hardback
ISBN 978-1-78327-634-9 paperback

The Boydell Press is an imprint of Boydell & Brewer Ltd
PO Box 9, Woodbridge, Suffolk IP12 3DF, UK
and of Boydell & Brewer Inc.
668 Mt Hope Avenue, Rochester, NY 14620–2731, USA
website: www.boydellandbrewer.com

A CIP catalogue record for this book is available
from the British Library

The publisher has no responsibility for the continued existence or accuracy of URLs for external or third-party internet websites referred to in this book, and does not guarantee that any content on such websites is, or will remain, accurate or appropriate

Contents

Illustrations	vi
Acknowledgements	vii
Abbreviations	ix
Introduction	1
1 Definitions of Old Age	16
2 Merits of Old Age	52
3 Drawbacks of Old Age	76
4 *frode fyrnwitan*: Old Saints in Anglo-Saxon Hagiography	110
5 *hare hilderincas:* Old Warriors in Anglo-Saxon England	135
6 *ealde eðelweardas*: *Beowulf* as a Mirror of Elderly Kings	177
7 *gamole geomeowlan*: Old Women in Anglo-Saxon England	212
Conclusion	232
Bibliography	237
Index	264

Illustrations

1. Adoration of the Magi on the Franks Casket (© Trustees of the British Museum) — 26
2. The Three Patriarchs as the three ages of man (© The British Library Board. Harley 603) — 29
3. Abraham and his servants on their way to free Lot in Prudentius' *Psychomachia* (© The Parker Library, Corpus Christi College, Cambridge) — 140
4. An elderly warrior to the left of Patientia in Prudentius' *Psychomachia* (© The Parker Library, Corpus Christi College, Cambridge) — 141
5. Abraham meets the king of Sodom in the Old English Hexateuch (© The British Library Board. Cotton Claudius B. iv) — 142
6. War of the Kings in the Old English Hexateuch (© The British Library Board. Cotton Claudius B. iv) — 143
7. Illustration of Psalm 7 in the Harley Psalter (© The British Library Board. Harley 603) — 144
8. Elderly warriors on the Bayeux Tapestry (Details of the Bayeux Tapestry, 11th century, by special permission of the City of Bayeux) — 147

The author and publisher are grateful to all the institutions and individuals listed for permission to reproduce the materials in which they hold copyright. Every effort has been made to trace the copyright holders; apologies are offered for any omission, and the publisher will be pleased to add any necessary acknowledgement in subsequent editions.

Acknowledgements

"As soon as a man recognizes that he has drifted into age, he gets reminiscent. He wants to talk and talk; and not about the present or the future, but about his old times" (Mark Twain, 'Frank Fuller and My First New York Lecture', 1897). This book was written during the formative years of my academic life and would not have been possible without the generous help of many individuals.

First and foremost, I would like to express my sincerest gratitude to my teacher and mentor, Rolf H. Bremmer Jr, for his support, inspiration and advice on all matters of language and life, ranging from Old English inflections to proper table manners. Further thanks are due to various colleagues at Leiden University, past and present, for their support, encouragement and advice: Wim van Anrooij, Luisella Caon, Marcelle Cole, Rosanne Hebing, Krista Murchison, Nienke Venderbosch, Geert Warnar and Katinka Zeven. I also thank my students for making teaching Old English my dream job, joining me for film nights and field trips, and trusting me with the supervision of their theses.

The book has benefitted from the comments of the anonymous reviewers, as well as various individuals who have generously read draft versions of individual parts: Wim van Anrooij, Berber Bossenbroek, Rolf H. Bremmer Jr, Kees Dekker, Peter Hoppenbrouwers, Manfred Horstmanshoff, Susan Irvine, Jenneka Janzen, Miriam Jones, Christina Lee, Gerard Limburg, Jodie Mann, Krista Murchison, Gale Owen-Crocker, Henk Porck, Christine Rauer and Jenny Weston. Parts of this book were presented at conferences in Brussels, Leeds, Leiden, Manchester and Granada; I would like to thank the organisers and participants for their insightful remarks and questions. I also owe a debt of gratitude to my editorial assistant Amos van Baalen who carefully proofread this entire book and helped with the index. All remaining mistakes are, of course, my own.

Writing this monograph would also have been impossible without the support of various institutions and organisations. The Leiden University Centre for the Arts in Society, first of all, has provided me with stability and administrative support. The staff of the British Library and the Parker Library have been particularly helpful in guiding me through the process of acquiring permissions for the reproduction of images. I would also like to thank the staff at Boydell and Brewer, especially Rob Kinsey and Caroline Palmer, for their patience, advice and support for the project.

On a more personal note, I thank my parents, Breca and Cnut (for life, love and indifference, respectively), and anyone else who has read this preface looking for their own names but has now discovered I accidentally left them out (I apologise). Last but not least, my heartfelt thanks go to Laura Limburg, who has been by my side for the last fifteen years and keeps me healthy and sane. While 'growing old' may be a daunting prospect, she makes 'growing old together' something to look forward to!

Abbreviations

ÆCHom I	*Ælfric's Catholic Homilies: The First Series*, ed. P. Clemoes, EETS ss 17 (Oxford, 1997) (cited by homily and line number)
ÆCHom II	*Ælfric's Catholic Homilies: The Second Series*, ed. M. Godden, EETS ss 5 (London, 1979) (cited by homily and line number)
ÆLS	*Ælfric's Lives of Saints*, ed. W. W. Skeat, EETS os 76, 82, 94, 114 (London, 1881–1900) (cited by text and line number)
Archiv	*Archiv für das Studium der neueren Sprachen und Literaturen*
ASE	*Anglo-Saxon England*
ASPR	Anglo-Saxon Poetic Records
Assmann	*Angelsächsische Homilien und Heiligenleben*, ed. B. Assmann (Kassel, 1889) (cited by homily and line number)
Battle of Maldon	'The Battle of Maldon', ed. and trans. D. G. Scragg, in *The Battle of Maldon, AD 991*, ed. D. G. Scragg (Oxford, 1991)
Bazire and Cross	*Eleven Old English Rogationtide Homilies*, ed. J. Bazire and J. E. Cross (Toronto, 1982) (cited by homily and line number)
Bede, *HE*	*Bede's Ecclesiastical History of the English People*, ed. and trans. B. Colgrave and R. A. B. Mynors (Oxford, 1969; rpt. 1992) (cited by book and chapter)
Beowulf	*Klaeber's Beowulf*, ed. R. D. Fulk, R. E. Bjork and J. D. Niles, 4th ed. (Toronto, 2008)
BGdSL	*Beiträge zur Geschichte der deutschen Sprache und Literatur*
BHL	*Bibliotheca Hagiographica Latina*, ed. Bollandists, 2 vols (Brussels, 1899–1901)
Blickling Homilies	*The Blickling Homilies of the Tenth Century*, ed. R. Morris, EETS os 58, 63, 73 (London, 1874–80) (cited by homily and page number)
CCCC	Cambridge, Corpus Christi College
CCSL	Corpus Christianorum, Series Latin
DOE	*Dictionary of Old English: A to H online*, ed. A. Cameron, A. C. Amos, A. diPaolo Healey *et al.* (Toronto, 2016), http://www.doe.utoronto.ca/index.html

DOML	Dumbarton Oaks Medieval Library
EETS	Early English Text Society (os= Original Series; ss = Supplementary Series)
Fontes Anglo-Saxonici	*Fontes Anglo-Saxonici Project*, ed. Fontes Anglo-Saxonici: World Wide Web Register, http://fontes.english.ox.ac.uk/
Gneuss and Lapidge	H. Gneuss and M. Lapidge, *Anglo-Saxon Manuscripts: A Bibliographical Handlist of Manuscripts and Manuscript Fragments Written or Owned in England up to 1100* (Toronto, 2014)
HA	*The Heroic Age: A Journal of Early Medieval Northwestern Europe*
JEGP	*Journal of English and Germanic Philology*
Ker	N. R. Ker, *Catalogue of Manuscripts Containing Anglo-Saxon* (Oxford, 1957)
Klinck, *OEE*	*The Old English Elegies: A Critical Edition and Genre Study*, ed. A. L. Klinck (Montreal, 1992)
MLN	*Modern Language Notes*
Napier	*Wulfstan; Sammlung der ihm zugeschriebenen Homilien nebst Untersuchungen über ihre Echtheit*, ed. A. S. Napier (Berlin, 1883) (cited by homily, page and line number)
NQ	*Notes and Queries*
ODNB	*Oxford Dictionary of National Biography* (Oxford, 2004), http://www.oxforddnb.com
PASE	*Prosopography of Anglo-Saxon England*, http://www.pase.ac.uk
PL	Patrologiae cursus completus, series Latina, ed. J.-P. Migne, 221 vols (Paris, 1855–1864) (cited by volume and column)
RES	*Review of English Studies*
S	P. H. Sawyer, *Anglo-Saxon Charters: An Annotated List and Bibliography* (London, 1968)
Shippey, *PoW*	*Poems of Wisdom and Learning in Old English*, ed. and trans. T. A. Shippey (Cambridge, 1976)
SiP	*Studies in Philology*
Vercelli Homilies	*The Vercelli Homilies and Related Texts*, ed. D. G. Scragg, EETS os 300 (London, 1992) (cited by homily and line number)

Unless otherwise noted, all translations from Old English and Latin are my own. All Bible quotations refer to the Latin Vulgate and the translations are the Douay-Rheims translation.

Introduction

Sussex, England, over twelve hundred years ago. A young man named Cuthman led a desolate life; poor and homeless, he had to take care of his paralysed, widowed, elderly mother. To move around Cuthman carried his mother on a special barrow, which he suspended over his shoulders by means of a rope. One day, the rope broke and Cuthman had to replace it with plaited elder twigs. Some nearby mowers saw the incident and mocked his misfortune. Instantaneously, the mocking mowers were punished by a sudden tempest, which drove them from their field and ruined their crops. By this sign, Cuthman realised that God was on his side and he resolved to build a church wherever the rope substitute happened to break next. Reports differ as to what happened afterwards. According to one version of the story, the rope of elder twigs broke at Steyning, Sussex, where Cuthman's church still stands.[1] A second, more sensational version has Cuthman rid himself of his burdensome mother by hurling the elderly woman and her barrow down a hill; he then built his church wherever she crash-landed.[2]

The two versions of Cuthman's story raise several questions: was Cuthman's mother's survival into old age unique in Anglo-Saxon England, and would she have been respected for her old age or would she have been regarded as a burden? These two questions relate to two persistent presumptions with regard to old age in past societies: there were few to no elderly in the past, and those who did grow old were highly respected for their 'rarity value'.[3] In this introduction, these two presumptions will be considered within the context of early medieval England, c.700–c.1100. The first is touched upon only in this introduction, while the second is directly related to the overall topic of this book: the Anglo-Saxon cultural conceptualisation of old age.

The answer to the question of whether many people grew old in Anglo-Saxon England depends, in the first place, on how old age is

---

[1] G. R. Stephens and W. D. Stephens, 'Cuthman: A Neglected Saint', *Speculum* 13 (1938), 448–53.
[2] S. Crawford, '*Gomol is snoterost*: Growing Old in Anglo-Saxon England', in *Collectanea Antiqua: Essays in Memory of Sonia Chadwick Hawkes*, ed. M. Henig and T. J. Smith (Oxford, 2007), 53–9. The original source of the story, the *Vita s. Cuthmanni* (BHL 2035), does not contain this second version. This *vita* has been related to the mid-eleventh-century revival of Anglo-Latin hagiography, see J. Blair, 'Saint Cuthman, Steyning and Bosham', *Sussex Archaeological Collections* 135 (1997), 186–92.
[3] P. Thane, *Old Age in English History: Past Experiences, Present Issues* (Oxford, 2000), 1.

defined. Gerontologists generally work with two different definitions. The first, 'chronological age', considers people old when they have lived for a specific number of years.[4] This threshold of old age is defined differently in various cultures and even within a single community the chronological onset of age can be set anywhere between forty and seventy years of age, though the age of sixty appears most commonplace.[5] A second definition concerns 'functional age'; people are considered old when they are no longer able to perform certain communal functions or, in the case of women, lose the ability to give birth.[6]

Taking the chronological definition of old age as a point of departure, it can easily be demonstrated that several Anglo-Saxons lived for a considerable number of years. The oldest Anglo-Saxon I have been able to identify was a monk called Egbert, who fell mortally ill along with his brother Æthelhun in the year 664. Feeling the hour of death upon him, Egbert implored God to allow him more time to make amends for his sins. When Egbert returned to his brother, the latter rose from his bed, crying: "O frater Ecgbercte, O quid fecisti? Sperabam quia pariter ad uitam aeternam intraremus; uerumtamen scito, quia quae postulasti accipies" ['Brother Egbert, what have you done? I hoped that we should both enter into eternal life together; but you are to know that your request will be granted'].[7] Æthelhun died the next day, but it would take Egbert sixty-five more years to make his journey hence; he died in the year 729, at the age of ninety.

Egbert's story was recorded by the Venerable Bede (c.673/4–735) in his *Historia ecclesiastica gentis Anglorum* [Ecclesiastical History of the English People] (731). In the same work, Bede also reports the great ages at which other men and women passed away, such as Archbishop Theodore of Tarsus (88) and Abbess Hild of Whitby (66).[8] Of others, such as Bishop John of Beverley and Archbishop Berhtwald and the missionary Willibrord, Bede merely indicates that they retired, died or lived to a venerable old age; Hildelith, abbess of the Barking nuns, is even said to have passed away "ad ultimam senectutem" [extremely old].[9] Bede's collection of bishops and abbesses can be supplemented

---

[4] See, e.g., P. Johnson, 'Historical Readings of Old Age and Ageing', in *Old Age from Antiquity to Post-Modernity*, ed. P. Johnson and P. Thane (London, 1998), 4.
[5] J. T. Rosenthal, *Old Age in Late Medieval England* (Philadelphia, 1997), 1; S. Shahar, 'Old Age in the High and Late Middle Ages: Image, Expectation and Status', in *Old Age*, ed. Johnson and Thane, 43; S. Shahar, *Growing Old in the Middle Ages: 'Winter Clothes Us in Shadow and Pain'* (London, 1997), 13.
[6] See, e.g., M. M. Sheehan, 'Afterword', in *Aging and the Aged in Medieval Europe*, ed. M. M. Sheehan (Toronto, 1990), 204–5; S. Lewis-Simpson, 'Old Age in Viking-Age Britain', in *Youth and Age in the Medieval North*, ed. S. Lewis-Simpson (Leiden, 2008), 244–50.
[7] Bede, *HE*, III.27.
[8] Bede, *HE*, IV.23, V.8.
[9] Bede, *HE*, V.6, V.11, V.23, IV.10.

Introduction

by the names of inhabitants of early medieval England for whom the *Oxford Dictionary of National Biography* (*ODNB*) has recorded life dates which indicate that they died at the age of sixty or over, as listed below.[10]

List 1. Names, titles and life dates of elderly individuals in early medieval England found in *ODNB*

1. Ælfflæd (654–714), abbess of Strensall-Whitby
2. Ælfric of Eynsham (c.950–c.1010), homilist and abbot
3. Æthelwold (904/9–984), abbot of Abingdon and bishop of Winchester
4. Alcuin (c.740–804), abbot of St Martin's, Tours, and royal adviser
5. Benedict Biscop (c.628–689), abbot of Wearmouth and scholar
6. Bede (673/4–735), monk, historian, and theologian
7. Berhtwald (c.650–731), archbishop of Canterbury
8. Boniface (672x5?–754), archbishop of Mainz, missionary
9. Ceolfrith (642–716), abbot of Wearmouth and Jarrow
10. Eadgifu (b. in or before 904; d. in or after 966), queen of the Anglo-Saxons
11. Ecgberht (639–729), church reformer
12. Edward ('the Confessor') (1003x5–1066), king of the English
13. Eilmer (b. c.985, d. after 1066), pioneer of man-powered flight
14. Hadrian (630/7–709), abbot of St Peter's and St Paul's, Canterbury
15. Hild (614–680), abbess of Strensall-Whitby
16. Ingulf (c.1045–1109), abbot of Crowland
17. Lul (c.710–786), archbishop of Mainz
18. Stephen of Ripon (fl. c.670–c.730), priest
19. Theodore of Tarsus (602–690), archbishop of Canterbury and theologian
20. Walburg (c.710–779?), abbess of Heidenheim
21. Wilfrid (c.634–709/10), bishop of Hexham
22. Willibrord (657/8–739), abbot of Echternach
23. Wulfstan (c.1008–1095), bishop of Worcester

---

[10] For a helpful overview of Anglo-Saxon and related entries in the *ODNB*, see H. Foxhall Forbes *et al.*, 'Anglo-Saxon and Related Entries in the *Oxford Dictionary of National Biography* (2004)', *ASE* 37 (2008), 183–232.

The list clearly demonstrates that several Anglo-Saxons lived long lives, even if with its clerical bias the list is probably far from representative of early medieval England as a whole. More systematic and quantifiable approaches to establishing the number of chronologically old people in Anglo-Saxon England are impossible, however, since the birth dates of individuals were seldom recorded and medieval sources in general rarely mention the age of individuals involved.[11] In fact, according to one of the leading demographers in the field of old age studies, Peter Laslett, it is extremely hard to find any demographical information about the presence of old people in England for the period before 1540; he even argues that the information for the period 1540–1990 is not sufficient for a full, complex analysis.[12]

Despite this lack of viable sources, historians have challenged the notion that elderly people were particularly rare in the Middle Ages. Peter Stearns, for instance, claimed that the idea of a limited number of elderly in the pre-industrial past is based on a "misconstruction of preindustrial demography": the low life expectancy in past societies has been misinterpreted as an average age at death. In fact, Stearns argues, people had a good chance of becoming old once they had lived through early childhood.[13] Shulamith Shahar draws the same conclusions for the Middle Ages and posits that the elderly made up 5 to 8 per cent of the population.[14] Pat Thane, an authority on the history of old age in England, argues that the elderly 'probably' made up about 9 per cent of the population during the entire Middle Ages.[15] Although such estimates are hard to back up with statistical evidence, it is reasonable to assume, along with Joel Rosenthal, that "the actual presence of aged men and women was encountered at virtually all social levels and in all social settings".[16]

---

[11] Cf. H. Cayton, 'Some Contributions from the Written Sources', in *East Anglian Archaeology Report No. 9: North Elmham. Vol. 2*, ed. P. Wade-Martins (Gressenhall, 1980), 303–7, who, using a sample of 200 individuals mentioned in chronicles, estimates an average age at death of 57.7 years, but also discusses the drawbacks of using documentary sources of this kind.

[12] P. Laslett, 'Necessary Knowledge: Age and Ageing in the Societies of the Past', in *Aging in the Past: Demography, Society and Old Age*, ed. D. I. Kertzer and P. Laslett (Berkeley, 1995), 9–10.

[13] P. N. Stearns, *Old Age in Preindustrial Society* (New York, 1982), 5.

[14] S. Shahar, 'The Middle Ages and Renaissance', in *The Long History of Old Age*, ed. P. Thane (London, 2005), 79.

[15] P. Thane, 'Old Age in English History', in *Zur Kulturgeschichte des Alterns: Toward a Cultural History of Aging*, ed. C. Conrad and H.-J. von Kondratowitz (Berlin, 1993), 19.

[16] Quoted in A. Classen, 'Old Age in the Middle Ages and the Renaissance: Also an Introduction', in *Old Age in the Middle Ages and the Renaissance: Interdisciplinary Approaches to a Neglected Topic*, ed. A. Classen (Berlin, 2007), 13.

Introduction

Applying the second definition of old age, functional age, to Anglo-Saxon England is equally problematic. If a person is considered old when they are no longer able to perform certain social functions, insight must be gained into the 'experience of aging': what was it actually like to be old and how and when did people operate within their communities? This actual experience of aging is difficult to study, if only because a person's way of life depended on a wide array of additional circumstances, such as social and economic class, nutrition, gender, environment, health and religious status.[17] Any attempt to reconstruct the socio-historical reality of old age will, inevitably, result in a collection of highly contradictory experiences, each influenced by the individual circumstances of the elderly persons under discussion.[18] In addition, Anglo-Saxon sources are not particularly well suited to studying the experience of aging: demographic information is scarce and archaeological and osteological evidence can be hard to interpret.[19] Moreover, no sufficient number of (auto-)biographies of old people from early medieval England have survived for a viable reconstruction of the experience of aging in this period.[20]

The impracticalities of applying the chronological and functional definitions of old age, mentioned above, do not mean that the topic of old age cannot be studied within an Anglo-Saxon context. A third definition of old age, 'cultural age', sees old age as a cultural construct, built up out of a society's expectations, mentalities and ideas, as reflected in, and defined by, the society's cultural heritage.[21] This cultural construct of old age is often considered to be separate from demographic trends and actual experience of old age; the image of old age is not only based on daily perception and actual experience, but

---

[17] *The Cultural Context of Aging: Worldwide Perspectives*, ed. J. Sokolovsky, 2nd ed. (Westport, 1997), xxv.
[18] Johnson, 'Historical Readings', 15.
[19] On the difficulties of interpreting bio-archaeological information, see, e.g., Lewis-Simpson, 'Old Age in Viking-Age Britain', 246–7; C. Lee, 'Body and Soul: Disease and Impairment', in *The Material Culture of Daily Living in the Anglo-Saxon World*, ed. M. Clegg Hyer and G. Owen-Crocker (Exeter, 2011), 307. New methods are being developed, however, which may improve the identification and study of bodily remains of elderly individuals, see C. Cave and M. Oxenham, 'Identification of the Archaeological "Invisible Elderly": An Approach Illustrated with an Anglo-Saxon Example', *International Journal of Osteoarchaeology* 26 (2016), 163–75; C. Cave and M. Oxenham, 'Sex and the Elderly: Attitudes to Long-Lived Women and Men in Early Anglo-Saxon England', *Journal of Anthropological Archaeology* 48 (2017), 207–16.
[20] There is, however, some epistolary source material, notably the letters by Alcuin and Boniface, which is discussed in chapters 2 and 3 below.
[21] W. A. Achenbaum, 'Foreword: Literature's Value in Gerontological Research', in *Perceptions of Aging in Literature. A Cross-Cultural Study*, ed. P. von Dorotka Bagnell and P. S. Soper (New York, 1989), xiv; Thane, 'Old Age in English History', 5–6.

also on literary *topoi*, older stereotypes and clichés.[22] It is this cultural construction of old age, as reflected by the cultural heritage of early medieval England, that is the main topic of this book.

Modern Western society has been characterised as 'gerontophobic': old age is commonly associated with a decline in physical aptitude, as well as an increase in dependency and loneliness. For many, growing old is a daunting prospect and, as a result, it is often described in negative terms.[23] This bleak view on old age in the present has led to the somewhat romantic idea that 'the past' was wholly different; back then, the elderly "had a rarity value" and "were culturally more valued and respected than in the present".[24] However, historians have been keen to point out that a negative outlook on old age is nothing new. From Classical Antiquity onwards, there has been an ambivalent attitude towards the elderly: they were respected for their wisdom and experience, but simultaneously shunned, pitied and held up as a reminder that everyone will eventually suffer the same, miserable fate of senescence.[25]

Despite the general trend in old age studies of denouncing overly positive associations with old age in the past, some scholars have singled out the early medieval period in England as a time in which old age was held in high esteem. John Burrow, for instance, asserted that the Anglo-Saxons preferred old age above all other age categories, since it was associated with an increased sagacity and piety: '[I]f we were to follow Philippe Ariès in supposing that every period of history favours or privileges one among the ages of man, the only possible

---

[22] A. Janssen, *Grijsaards in zwart-wit. De verbeelding van de ouderdom in de Nederlandse prentkunst (1550–1650)* (Zutphen, 2007), 14; D. G. Troyansky, 'The Older Person in the Western World: From the Middle Ages to the Industrial Revolution', in *Handbook of the Humanities and Aging*, ed. T. R. Cole, D. D. van Tassel and R. Kastenbaum (New York, 1992), 40–1; Rosenthal, *Old Age in Late Medieval England*, 5. For an opposite view, see M. Sandidge, 'Forty Years of Plague: Attitudes toward Old Age in the Tales of Boccaccio and Chaucer', in *Old Age in the Middle Ages*, ed. Classen, 373; cf. G. Minois, *History of Old Age from Antiquity to the Renaissance*, trans. S. Hanbury Tenison (Oxford, 1989), 11.

[23] E.g., R. Freedman, 'Sufficiently Decayed: Gerontophobia in English Literature', in *Aging and the Elderly: Humanistic Perspectives in Gerontology*, ed. S. F. Spicker, K. M. Woodward and D. D. van Tassel (Atlantic Highlands, 1978), 49–61.

[24] Thane, *Old Age in English History*, 1. Cf. C. Gilleard, 'Old Age in the Dark Ages: The Status of Old Age During the Early Middle Ages', *Ageing & Society* 29 (2009), 1065, "survival into old age was a rare but frequently revered attainment".

[25] For studies on the appreciation of old age through time, see, e.g., *Zur Kulturgeschichte des Alterns*, ed. Conrad and von Kondratowitz; Thane, *Old Age in English History*; *Long History*, ed. Thane. For studies on the Middle Ages in particular, see Shahar, *Growing Old* and contributions to *Aging and the Aged*, ed. Sheehan and *Old Age in the Middle Ages*, ed. Classen.

Introduction

choice for the Anglo-Saxon period would be *senectus*.'[26] Ashley Amos, who studied a number of words for 'old' in Old English, drew a similar conclusion; the vocabulary for growing old mainly had positive connotations for the Anglo-Saxons.[27] Sally Crawford, while offering a balanced analysis of the status of elderly individuals on the basis of archaeological finds, noted that "[a]ccording to the literary evidence, the later Anglo-Saxon period was the golden age for the elderly".[28]

However, the idea of the Anglo-Saxon period as a golden age for old age is incongruent with the many negative remarks about senescence found in contemporaneous sources. Although some Old English texts attest to the idea that age and experience make an old person wise and worthy of respect, others abound in concerns about ungodly elderly and feature graphic descriptions of the physical drawbacks associated with old age, such as the loss of hair and teeth. Indeed, senescence is often presented as a destructive force, leaving the elderly passive, physically inept and on the verge of death. More dramatically, aging was even associated with the torments of Hell and the author of a homily in the late tenth-century Vercelli Book described it as "helle onlicnes" [a prefiguration of Hell].[29]

Two article-length studies on the conceptualisation of old age in Anglo-Saxon England have tried to redress the balance and have argued for a more nuanced view. In his discussion of various stages of the life cycle in Old English literature – "not as a reflection of an historically accurate reality, but as an expression of the Anglo-Saxon social outlook on matters of age" –,[30] Jordi Sánchez-Martí briefly notes an ambivalent attitude towards old age. A long life was associated with respectable wisdom, but also approached with some reservations, especially on account of its connection to physical decline. Similarly contrasting representations of old age are identified by Philippa Semper, who has focused mostly on Old English heroic poetry and Anglo-Saxon hagiography.[31]

---

[26] J. A. Burrow, *The Ages of Man: A Study in Medieval Writing and Thought* (Oxford, 1986), 109.
[27] A. C. Amos, 'Old English Words for Old', in *Aging and the Aged*, ed. Sheehan, 95–106. The same selection of Old English words is reviewed in H. Bouwer, *Studien zum Wortfeld um eald und niwe im Altenglischen* (Heidelberg, 2004). For a complete analysis of the semantic field of old age in Old English, see T. Porck, 'Growing Old among the Anglo-Saxons: The Cultural Conceptualisation of Old Age in Early Medieval England', unpublished PhD dissertation, Leiden University, 2016.
[28] Crawford, '*Gomol is snoterost*', 59.
[29] *Vercelli Homilies*, hom. 9, lines 84–5.
[30] J. Sánchez-Martí, 'Age Matters in Old English Literature', in *Youth and Age*, ed. Lewis-Simpson, 205.
[31] P. Semper, '*Byð se ealda man ceald and snoflig*: Stereotypes and Subversions of the Last Stages of the Life Cycle in Old English Texts and Anglo-Saxon Contexts',

Extending the nuanced approaches of Sánchez-Martí and Semper, this monograph is the first book-length study to focus on how the Anglo-Saxons considered, appreciated and imagined old age. By studying the early medieval English cultural record within its appropriate context, this book seeks to do justice to the complexity, diversity and ambivalence of the perceptions and representations which, together, make up the Anglo-Saxon cultural conceptualisation of old age.

Cultural conceptualisations: A theoretical framework

History is like a semi-submerged frog. In his short story "The Secret History of Eddypus, the World-Empire" (1901–2), Mark Twain made the following observation:

> One of the most admirable things about history is, that almost as a rule we get as much information out of what it does not say as we get out of what it does say. And so, one may truly and axiomatically aver this, to-wit: that history consists of two equal parts; one of these halves is statements of fact, the other half is inference, drawn from the facts. To the experienced student of history there are no difficulties about this; to him the half which is unwritten is as clearly and surely visible, by the help of scientific inference, as if it flashed and flamed in letters of fire before his eyes. When the practised eye of the simple peasant sees the half of a frog projecting above the water, he unerringly infers the half of the frog which he does not see. To the expert student in our great science, history is a frog; half of it is submerged, but he knows it is there, and he knows the shape of it.[32]

Twain's description of the academic study of history may strike the present-day historical scholar as controversial. Few academics today claim to generalise "unerringly" beyond what the sources tell them, given the limitations of the source material itself and the temporal and cultural differences that separate the scholar from his object of research. Nevertheless, using what might be called "scientific inference", in so far as this term covers the plethora of academic methods available to historians, they can argue for a plausible interpretation of what their sources have to say about the topic they are interested in.[33] Contradictory to Twain's assumptions, however, this enterprise is not without "difficulties". Following Twain's analogy of a frog-

---

in *Medieval Life Cycles: Continuity and Change*, ed. I. Cochelin and K. E. Smyth (Turnhout, 2013), 287–318.

[32] M. Twain, *The Science Fiction of Mark Twain*, ed. D. Ketterer (Hamden, 1984), 191.

[33] For an effective and sensible defence of the cultural historian's ability to reconstruct a viewpoint of people in the past and an answer to the 'Postmodern Challenge' regarding the unattainability of objective truth about the past, see R.

catching peasant, the "experienced student of history" nowadays first needs to describe accurately the type of amphibious creature they are pursuing, define the advantages and limits of their method of seizing it, and the properties of the puddle it is in, as well as reflect on the value of catching it in the first place. The paragraphs below present the theoretical framework I have used in this book, by defining what is meant by 'cultural conceptualisation', outlining the methodological approach, reviewing the limits of the research material in terms of its applicability to answering the main question, and ascertaining the overall purpose of the book.

Cultural conceptualisation is a term coined by the cognitive linguist Farzad Sharifian. It denotes "[t]he ways in which people across different cultural groups may construe various aspects of the world and their experiences. These include people's view of the world, thoughts, and feelings."[34] Sharifian explains that cultural conceptualisations, such as the behaviour expected of an old person or the idea of old age, are "distributed representations across the minds in a cultural group".[35] Members of a cultural group typically share physical proximity, speak the same language, engage in similar rituals and interact with each other; through this interaction, cultural conceptualisations are constantly negotiated and renegotiated. Ultimately, an idea that may have originated in an individual mind spreads across an entire cultural group and becomes part of this group's collective view of the world.[36] In this sense, a cultural conceptualisation may be said to form part of a community's *mentalité* as defined by Aaron Gurevich:

> *Mentalité* implies the presence of a common and specific intellectual equipment, a psychological framework shared by people of a given society united by a single culture enabling them to perceive and become aware of their natural and social environment and themselves. A chaotic and heterogeneous stream of perceptions and impressions is converted by consciousness into a more or less ordered picture of the world which sets its seal on all human behaviour.[37]

Cultural conceptualisations may be manifested and reflected in various types of cultural artefacts, including language, dance, gesture, poetry and narratives.[38] For cultural historians, cultural conceptualisation is

---

D. Hume, *Reconstructing Contexts: The Aims and Principles of Archaeo-Historicism* (Oxford, 1999); cf. R. J. Evans, *In Defence of History*, rev. ed. (London, 2000).

[34] F. Sharifian, *Cultural Conceptualisations and Language: Theoretical Framework and Applications* (Amsterdam, 2011), 39.
[35] Sharifian, *Cultural Conceptualisations*, 5.
[36] Sharifian, *Cultural Conceptualisations*, 3–17.
[37] A. Gurevich, 'Historical Anthropology and the Science of History', in *Historical Anthropology of the Middle Ages*, ed. J. Howlett (Cambridge, 1992), 4.
[38] Sharifian, *Cultural Conceptualisations*, 12.

a helpful notion, since it allows them to see a homily or a poem not merely as the product of the experience and context of an individual author but also as reflective or constitutive of a collective mentality. As such, the works of Ælfric of Eynsham, while shaped by patristic traditions, his own personal background and monastic surroundings at the turn of the eleventh century, can be analysed as exhibiting, or forming, the worldview of the broader cultural group to which he belonged.

Naturally, ideas are not shared evenly among all members of a cultural group and idiosyncracies may arise from differences in age, gender and social class, to name but a few factors of importance. Sharifian explains that "cultural conceptualisations appear to be heterogeneously distributed across the minds of a cultural group".[39] Put differently, members of the same community need not share exactly the same ideas about something like old age, and it is possible to encounter slight differences in the way something is conceptualised by an individual. In reality, individuals "show various degrees of knowledge about their conceptualisations"; consequently, an analysis of cultural conceptualisations at the group-level ideally extends to multiple individuals and multiple forms of discourse.[40] Cultural historians, then, should not restrict their analysis to a single author or a single genre of texts; they should also expect their sources to reflect the complexity, diversity and richness of cultural ideas that arise from generations of human interaction.

In order to establish the cultural conceptualisations of a group, Sharifian advocates an ethnographic or cultural anthropological approach.[41] The disciplines of cultural anthropology and history have a long past of mutual attraction.[42] Part of the practical appeal of anthropology for the historian is its value as a source of thought-provoking analogies, as the historian John Tosh explains:

> The findings of anthropology suggest something of the range of mentalities to be found among people who are acutely vulnerable to the vagaries of climate and disease, who lack 'scientific' control of their environment, and who are tied to their own localities – conditions which obtained in the West during most of the medieval and early modern periods.[43]

---

[39] Sharifian, *Cultural Conceptualisations*, 21.
[40] Sharifian, *Cultural Conceptualisations*, 12–13.
[41] Sharifian, *Cultural Conceptualisations*, 12–13.
[42] See, e.g., M. de Jong, 'The Foreign Past: Medieval Historians and Cultural Anthropology', *Tijdschrift voor Geschiedenis* 109 (1996), 326–42; Gurevich, 'Historical Anthropology'.
[43] J. Tosh, *The Pursuit of History: Aims, Methods and New Directions in the Study of Modern History*, 4th ed. (Harlow, 2006), 295.

Introduction

For the study of old age, for instance, the identification of old women as 'culture bearers' in anthropological studies of various traditional societies is an interesting concept that the historian may wish to borrow in order to see to what extent this observation also holds for the past (see chapter 7 below). More broadly, anthropology teaches historians to view past societies as both similar and different to their own. In the past, people had emotions and feelings, they organised their society and expressed their thoughts in writing and art, and trying to understand the culture of those societies is like "trying to understand a group of foreigners somehow dropped in our midst".[44] However, as Tosh rightly points out, cultural historians cannot approach their evidence in exactly the same manner as anthropologists do; they always have to recognise the limitations of their source material.[45]

The sources considered in the various chapters of this book cover a wide range of cultural material, ranging from encyclopaedic texts, to visual arts, homilies, wisdom poetry, hagiography and heroic literature. Each of these types of evidence reflects or transmits cultural conceptualisations in its own way and must be studied in its own specific historical and cultural setting. This varied cultural record calls for a multidisciplinary approach that differs per source type considered. Specifically, an analysis of homiletic material requires placing these texts in the context of religious and theological traditions that Anglo-Saxon homilists generally followed, or, occasionally, consciously departed from; any study of heroic poetry must show an awareness of the broader Germanic heroic tradition to which poems such as *The Battle of Maldon* and *Beowulf* belong; and so on. Much of the methodological framework with respect to the validity and usability of the source material is reserved for the individual chapters, since it is not efficient to discuss here in detail the diverse nature of all the sources discussed in this book.

However, a general observation with regard to the representativeness of the Anglo-Saxon material considered is in order here. With few exceptions, all the documents and artefacts that date back to this period originate from only a small portion of the early medieval English community: the learned, well-to-do members of the clergy and nobility. Texts, for instance, have come down to us in manuscripts produced in monasteries, often at the behest of high-ranking members of the secular and religious aristocracy. The Anglo-Saxon cultural conceptualisation of old age demarcated in this book, therefore, reflects the mindset only of this restricted cultural group and

---

[44] B. J. Malina, *The New Testament World: Insights from Cultural Anthropology*, 4th ed. (Louisville, 2001), 24.
[45] Tosh, *Pursuit of History*, 295–8.

cannot lay absolute claim to representing what went on in the minds of ordinary people, such as farmers, peasants and washerwomen.[46] There are further restrictions with regard to the source material. For instance, many of the artefacts that circulated in the early Anglo-Saxon period itself have been lost; materials from the later period, on the other hand, have survived in greater numbers, again affecting the representativeness of the cultural record for the entirety of the period under consideration, c.700–c.1100. Additionally, the age of the author, whether anonymous or named, is in the great majority of cases unknown. Thus, while one's perception of growing old is likely to have been influenced by the tally of one's own years, this aspect cannot be taken into account for the early medieval sources under scrutiny in this book.[47] Within these limitations, however, I hope to demonstrate that it is possible to form an idea of how the proportion of Anglo-Saxons represented by the cultural material from early medieval England conceptualised old age.

A cultural-historical reflection on old age as proposed here serves at least two purposes. On the one hand, as Gurevich has noted, "[h]istory as a discipline cannot successfully fulfil its social function if it does not pose the vital questions of the present to the culture of the past".[48] The greater awareness of societal aging and the rise of 'ageism' in the twenty-first century create a need for contrastive or parallel images of how people in the past viewed old age and the elderly.[49] In addition, this book hopes to contribute to the academic field of medieval studies in general and Anglo-Saxon studies in particular by providing a new 'hermeneutic lens'.[50] An awareness of old age raises questions about sources that have hitherto been left unasked and calls attention to aspects formerly ignored. For instance, this book, for the first time, calls attention to the importance of old age in the poem *Beowulf* and comes to a new reading that touches upon the purpose of the poem as a mirror of elderly kings (see chapter 6). There is much that can still be learnt about medieval and Anglo-Saxon society, for one thing, by surveying how they viewed the older members of their community and, for another, by analysing the multifaceted way they conceptualised old age. In the end, history may be a partly visible frog, but it is

---

[46] Similar restrictions apply to source material from earlier periods, see, e.g., H. Brandt, *Wird auch silbern mein Haar: Eine Geschichte des Alters in der Antike* (Munich, 2002), 13.

[47] P. Thane, 'The Age of Old Age', in *Long History*, ed. Thane, 27, provides the example of the German poet Goethe, whose successive versions of *Faust* show an increasing appreciation of old age as the author himself grew older.

[48] Gurevich, 'Historical Anthropology', 14–15.

[49] Thane, 'Age of Old Age', 9–29.

[50] Cf. Classen, 'Old Age in the Middle Ages', 15.

Introduction

worth noting that completely new frogs are discovered every year by those who know what to look for.[51]

In order to establish the Anglo-Saxon cultural conceptualisation of old age, this book is subdivided into seven chapters, each of which is outlined briefly below.

Chapter 1 closely considers how Anglo-Saxon scholars and artists defined old age in relation to other stages of the life cycle. Encyclopaedic notes, homilies and visual arts featured various schematic representations of the human life span, ranging from three to six 'ages of man'. This chapter provides an overview of all such attestations in the Anglo-Saxon cultural record. In doing so, I challenge the claim, made by Isabelle Cochelin, that early medieval scholars on the life cycle typically subdivided old age into a 'green' old age, when someone could still be healthy and active, and a 'grey' old age, during which physical decrepitude would set in.[52] As a rule, this subdivision was not made by Anglo-Saxon commentators, who, instead, typically represented old age as a single stage that began at the age of fifty and was mainly characterised by bodily decline. In order to fully appreciate these Anglo-Saxon notions of the place of old age in the human life cycle, the aspect of 'transfer of knowledge' is taken into account: where did the Anglo-Saxons get their ideas from and how did they adapt their sources?

The next two chapters focus on the ways Anglo-Saxon homilists and poets reflected on the assets and liabilities of old age. Chapter 2 takes into account how the potential merits of old age – respect, wisdom and spiritual superiority – were represented, while chapter 3 reviews and weighs the depiction of the physical, social and emotional drawbacks that could come with the years. The two main text types under consideration in these two chapters – homilies and wisdom poetry – each in their own way reflect circulating ideas about the advantages and disadvantages of growing old, extending from the accumulation of valuable experience to the loss of bodily aptitude. Both chapters re-evaluate Burrow's claim that the Anglo-Saxons preferred old age above all other age categories, by showing that Anglo-Saxon authors were well aware that the merits of old age were not for everyone and that old age did not automatically demand social respect or grant profitable wisdom. By contrast, the detrimental effects of age were seen as almost inescapable.

Chapter 4 is the first of four chapters that focus on specific groups in Anglo-Saxon society, taking into account the notion that the

---

[51] K. Mathiesen, 'Seven New Species of Miniature Frogs Discovered in Cloud Forests of Brazil', *The Guardian*, 4 June 2015.
[52] I. Cochelin, 'Introduction: Pre-Thirteenth-Century Definitions of the Life Cycle', in *Medieval Life Cycles*, ed. Cochelin and Smyth, 11.

consequences of old age depended on various social variables, including an individual's social standing, way of life and gender. Specifically, chapter 4 considers elderly saints and the *topos* of senescence as found in Anglo-Saxon hagiography. As such, the chapter covers mostly new ground by calling attention to a neglected element in various saints' lives: recurring themes that hagiographers used to shape the story of their subjects' senectitude. In all, these saints' lives reveal how Anglo-Saxon hagiographers and their audiences anticipated the challenges posed by old age and how, ideally, a saint would answer those challenges. Senescent saints, often high-ranking members of the clergy, set a standard that was hard to meet for mere mortals: to exhibit the merits of old age, despite suffering from the physical vicissitudes of growing old.

Similar behaviour was expected of the elderly warriors found in Old English heroic poetry – the subject of chapter 5. The chapter initially establishes the historical presence of old men on the Anglo-Saxon battlefield by surveying archaeological, pictorial and documentary evidence. It then considers the representation of veteran warriors in such poems as *The Battle of Maldon*, *Genesis* and *Beowulf*, within the context of the broader Germanic heroic tradition to which these poems belong. Like the old saint, the elderly warrior was expected to persevere despite being physically less able to do so, making himself useful not merely by providing advice or encouraging the troops but also by taking a leading role in the vanguard.

Chapter 6 discusses the application of the ideal of the elderly warrior to elderly warrior-kings. A king's physical inability to fulfil his royal responsibilities in his later years was a real political problem in the early Middle Ages and, as will be shown in this chapter, it turns out to be one of the main topics of *Beowulf*, albeit mostly overlooked by the ever-expanding scholarship on the poem. By focusing on how the *Beowulf* poet calls attention to the problems of old age, I suggest a novel reading of the epic poem as a mirror of elderly rulers. In his presentation of the aged kings Hrothgar and Beowulf, the poet juxtaposes two models of elderly kingship: a passive, diplomatic model, represented by the former, and an active, heroic model embodied by the latter. In an excursus, I suggest that this reading of *Beowulf* may hold a clue to the identification of an elderly royal patron of the poem.

Chapter 7 comprises a first foray into the study of the status of old women in Anglo-Saxon England. Due to a general lack of poetic representations of and explicit comments on old women in the cultural record, the chapter may seem something of an anomaly in the book. Rather than analysing the way these old women were represented by Anglo-Saxon writers, this chapter focuses on how the status of these women might be reconstructed on the basis of how their lives and actions have come down to us in chronicles, letters and wills. Despite the fragmented and anecdotal nature of the evidence, it is nonetheless possible to establish that the transition to old age for these women did not necessarily entail reduced social status, as has been suggested for early medieval women in general.

The concluding chapter, finally, synthesises the most noteworthy results of the analysis of the cultural conceptualisation of old age in Anglo-Saxon England and briefly considers possible routes for future research. By surveying the early medieval English attitudes towards old age and the elderly, this book provides an insight into how Anglo-Saxons imagined the final stages of their lives and what they expected from senior members within their communities. As the seven chapters below will demonstrate, Anglo-Saxon poets, scholars and homilists associated senescence with the potential for wisdom and pious living, but they also anticipated various social, psychological and physical repercussions of growing old. The attitude towards elderly men and women – whether they were saints, warriors or kings – was equally ambivalent. Far from a historically unique 'golden age for old age', the Anglo-Saxon period was a time in which senescence was approached with mixed feelings. Naturally, old age was defined relatively to other stages of life, which is why, in the first chapter, we turn to how Anglo-Saxon scholars defined senescence within the human life cycle.

1

Definitions of Old Age

What goes on four legs in the morning, on two legs at noon, and on three legs in the evening? The answer to this ancient 'Riddle of the Sphinx' – a human being, who crawls on all fours as a baby, walks on two legs as an adult and walks with a cane in old age – is possibly the most well-known example of a schematic division of the life cycle into different phases.[1] Such divisions of life into from three to twelve distinct 'ages of man' are frequently found in texts and visual art works, from Antiquity to the present day.[2] These textual and visual schemes help to reveal how people conceptualised their lifespan and how they defined old age in relation to other phases of life. In this chapter, I look at how Anglo-Saxon authors and artists divided the life cycle into different phases and what these divisions may reveal about their conceptualisation of old age.

Following the publication of three fundamental books on the medieval life cycle in 1986,[3] most treatments of the ages of man in medieval thought have concentrated on the later Middle Ages.[4] In 2013, Cochelin presented an overview of the schematic periodisations of the human lifespan found in texts from the Christian West up to the year 1200.[5] Within her sample of eighty texts, Cochelin found that thirty-four texts dating from between the sixth century to the year 1120 showed remarkably less variation than those of earlier and later dates. On the basis of these thirty-four texts, Cochelin then established a 'universal' life cycle definition:

---

[1] *Anthropology and the Riddle of the Sphinx: Paradoxes of Change in the Life Course*, ed. P. Spencer (London, 1990). In this form, the Riddle of the Sphinx is first referred to in Sophocles' *Oedipus Rex* (429 BC); I am indebted for this information to Manfred Horstmanshoff (Leiden University).

[2] *Long History*, ed. Thane.

[3] Burrow, *Ages of Man*; M. Dove, *The Perfect Age of Man's Life* (Cambridge, 1986); E. Sears, *The Ages of Man: Medieval Interpretations of the Life Cycle* (Princeton, 1986).

[4] E.g., *Ages of Woman, Ages of Man: Sources in European Social History, 1400–1750*, ed. M. Chojnacka and M. E. Wiesner-Hanks (London, 2002); M. Goodich, *From Birth to Old Age: The Human Life Cycle in Medieval Thought, 1250–1350* (Lanham, 1989).

[5] Cochelin, 'Introduction: Pre-Thirteenth-Century Definitions', 1–54.

between the sixth and the early twelfth centuries, the life cycle can contain three, four, five, six or seven ages, because the three main phases, *pueritia, iuuentus*, and *senectus*, can each be divided into two and, exceptionally for *senectus*, even into three ages. A life cycle of three is comprised of the three main phases; one of four means that one of the three phases has been subdivided and so on. Whatever the number of subdivisions, we are still facing one unique, if very flexible, way of conceiving the ages of man.[6]

Furthermore, she noted that the life cycle definition dating from this period was characterised by a "subdivided old age" into a young or 'green' old age, during which someone could still be active and healthy, and a 'grey' old age, when physical decrepitude set in.[7] Cochelin also remarked that this systematic division of *senectus* into two stages was less common in Late Antiquity and the later Middle Ages, during which "*senectus* was more often perceived as just one long old age, from its lower age limit, often around forty nine, to its end, death".[8]

Given that Cochelin's overview included only four Anglo-Saxon texts and did not take into account visual representations of the ages of man,[9] the question remains whether this proposed universal life cycle definition, with its underlying tripartite structure and its subdivided old age, reflects early medieval English attitudes towards the human life cycle. In order to test Cochelin's conclusions, I provide in this chapter a complete overview of all the attestations of the ages of man in the Anglo-Saxon cultural record.[10] In addition, I establish at what age Anglo-Saxon commentators considered someone old: how did they define the 'threshold of old age'? Throughout the chapter, the aspect of 'transfer of knowledge' is taken into account: where did these authors and artists get their ideas from and how did they adapt their sources?[11]

---

[6] Cochelin, 'Introduction: Pre-Thirteenth-Century Definitions', 11.
[7] For this distinction, see also Thane, 'Old Age in English History', 31–2; Thane, 'Age of Old Age', 22.
[8] Cochelin, 'Introduction: Pre-Thirteenth-Century Definitions', 14.
[9] Cochelin, 'Introduction: Pre-Thirteenth-Century Definitions', 24, 27–8, discusses Bede's *De temporibus* (c.703) and *De temporum ratione* (c.725), the *Commentaria in s. Joannis euangelium* by Alcuin (d. 804) and the work of Byrhtferth of Ramsey (d. c.1020).
[10] Excluding here the more allusive references to the human life cycle in Old English poetry, for which, see: H. Soper, 'Reading the Exeter Book Riddles as Life-Writing', *RES* 68 (2017), 841–65.
[11] Unless otherwise noted, the information about the Latin sources used for Old English texts is derived from *Fontes Anglo-Saxonici*.

The ages of man in Anglo-Saxon thought

While the medieval English conceptualisations of the human life cycle are relatively well-studied,[12] John Burrow's seminal work *The Ages of Man* remains the only study that seriously discusses the Anglo-Saxon period. With respect to the sources dating from this period, Burrow claimed that he had "probably missed no major evidence".[13] Nevertheless, Burrow's overview was incomplete and he had overlooked a number of representations of the ages of man found in Old English and Latin texts as well as in the visual arts. Below, I discuss each of these representations, alongside the ones that were dealt with by Burrow. The order in which the various texts and works of art appear below is prompted by the number of phases imposed on the human lifespan, rather than their dates of composition. Following this overview, the results will be considered in the light of Cochelin's conclusions as outlined above.

Two ages of man

In his classic study of the representations of the life cycle, Franz Boll noted that the most simple division of life is a dichotomy between youth and old age, a contrast which stems from analogy with other sets of antipodes, such as day and night, summer and winter, and life and death.[14] In Old English, the contrastive word pairs *eald and geong* 'old and young' and *geong and eald* 'young and old' are frequently attested.[15] These antonymic pairs turn out to be mainly used with the sense of 'everyone', as in the following description of the victims of death in the Old English prose life of St Guthlac: "se rica and se heana, se gelæreda and se ungelærda, and geong and eald, ealle hi gelice se stranga dead forgripeð and nymð" [rich and poor, learned and unlearned, and young and old, strong death overwhelms and takes them all equally].[16]

Occasionally, the youth–age contrast was appealed to within the context of similar pairs of antonyms, as in the Old English gnomic poem *Maxims II*:

---

[12] Sears, *Ages of Man*; Dove, *Perfect Age*; Goodich, *From Birth to Old Age*.
[13] Burrow, *Ages of Man*, 1, n. 2.
[14] F. Boll, 'Die Lebensalter. Ein Beitrag zur antiken Ethologie und zur Geschichte der Zahlen', in *Kleine Schriften zur Sternkunde des Altertums*, ed. V. Stegemann (Leipzig, 1950), 161–2.
[15] *DOE*, s.v. *eald*, sense I.A.1.b; *DOE*, s.v. *geong*, sense I.A.1.a.viii.
[16] *Das angelsächsische Prosa-Leben des heiligen Guthlac*, ed. P. Gonser (Heidelberg, 1909), 160.

Definitions of Old Age

God sceal wið yfele,   geogoð sceal wið yldo,
lif sceal wið deaþe,   leoht sceal wið þystrum,
fyrd wið fyrde,   feond wið oðrum.[17]

[Good must be against evil, youth against old age, life against death, light against darkness, army against army, one enemy against the other.]

This contrast between youth and age will be discussed in more detail in chapters 2 and 3.

The twofold division of life is also found in an exegetical context. For instance, Ælfric (c.950–c.1010) used this bipartite scheme to explain Matt. 8:11 ("And I say to you that many shall come from the East and the West, and shall sit down with Abraham, and Isaac and Jacob in the kingdom of Heaven") in his homily for the third Sunday after the Epiphany:

Đurh eastdæl magon beon getacnode þa ðe on geogoðe to gode bugað. for þan ðe on eastdæle is þæs dæges angin. Đurh westdæl sind getacnode þa ðe on ylde to godes þeowdome gecyrrað for þan ðe on westdæle geendað se dæg.[18]

[By the East may be signified those who turn to God in youth, because in the East is the start of the day. By the West are signified those who in old age turn to the service of God, because in the West the day ends.]

Ælfric probably took this equation between east and west and the two ages of man from a homily by Haymo of Auxerre (d. 865/866).[19] Ælfric himself can be credited for adding the connection with the start and beginning of the day, although this was a commonplace.[20]

While the frequent occurrence of the contrast between youth and age might suggest that the two ages of man was a dominant theory of the life cycle in Anglo-Saxon thought, it is more likely that the Anglo-Saxons referred to youth and old age as two extremes of a more complex spectrum of life. These more intricate schemes of life call for

---

[17] *Maxims II*, ed. and trans. Shippey, *PoW*, lines 51–3.
[18] *ÆCHom I*, hom. 8, lines 162–5.
[19] Haymo, *Homiliae de tempore*, hom. 19: "ab oriente, qui ab ipsa infantia vel pueritia Deo servit: ab occidente, qui in senectute vel decrepita aetate ad Dei servitutem convertitur" [from the east, he who from his very infancy or childhood serves God: from the west, he who is converted to the service of God in his old age or the age of decrepitude]. PL 118, col. 145c. On the use of Haymo by Ælfric, see J. Hill, 'Ælfric and Haymo Revisited' in *Intertexts: Studies in Anglo-Saxon Culture Presented to Paul E. Szarmach*, ed. V. Blanton and H. Scheck (Tempe, 2008), 331–48; C. L. Smetana, 'Ælfric and the Homiliary of Haymo of Halberstadt', *Traditio* 17 (1961), 457–69. For Ælfric's use of Haymo in this particular passage, see M. Godden, *Ælfric's Catholic Homilies: Introduction, Commentary and Glossary*, EETS ss 18 (Oxford, 2000), 66.
[20] Boll, 'Lebensalter', 162.

a more detailed analysis than the twofold divisions discussed above, since they stem from various intellectual traditions, ranging from biblical exegesis to the medical theory of the humours.

Three ages of man

Boll described the division of the life cycle into youth, middle age and old age as a natural development out of the two-age system, whereby the additional second or middle age always represents "die Spitze der Pyramide" [the top of the pyramid].[21] This triadic scheme is often associated with *De anima* and the *Ars rhetorica* by Aristotle (384–322 BC), but these works were probably not directly known in Anglo-Saxon England.[22] Instead, those Anglo-Saxons who commented on a threefold division of the life cycle mostly derived their inspiration from biblical exegesis.

Bede (673/674–735), for example, related the three ages of man to Christ's Parable of the Three Vigils (Luke 12:36–8). In this parable, Christ compared his disciples to servants who await their lord's return from a wedding feast during three vigils. Bede's commentary runs as follows:

> Prima quippe vigilia primaevum tempus est, id est pueritia. Secunda, adolescentia vel iuuentus, quae auctoritate sacri eloquii unum sunt, dicentis: Laetare iuuenis in adolescentia tua; tertia autem, senectus accipitur. Qui ergo vigilare in prima vigilia noluit custodiat vel secundam, ut qui converti a pravitatibus suis in pueritia neglexit ad vias vitae saltim in tempore iuuentutis evigilet. Et qui vigilare in secunda vigilia

---

[21] Boll, 'Lebensalter', 163–5.

[22] In the former work, Aristotle argued that all living things go through phases of *augmentum* 'growth', *status* 'status, stasis' and *decrementum* 'decay'; in the latter, he described the emotions and moral qualities of *iuuenes* 'youthful people', people *in statu* 'in their prime' and *senes* 'elderly people'. Quoted in Burrow, *Ages of Man*, 5–10, 191–4. Aristotle's *De anima* and the *Ars rhetorica* are not mentioned in J. D. A. Ogilvy, *Books Known to the English, 597–1066* (Cambridge, MA, 1967), M. Lapidge, *The Anglo-Saxon Library* (Oxford, 2006) or Gneuss and Lapidge. See also J. J. Campbell, 'Knowledge of Rhetorical Figures in Anglo-Saxon England', *JEGP* 66 (1967), 2. However, Ælfric may have used the *De anima* in one of his homilies, see R. M. Fera, 'Metaphors for the Five Senses in Old English Prose', *RES* ns 63 (2012), 723, n. 69.

Another champion of the threefold division of life was Isidore of Seville (c.560–636), who linked the three ages of man to various triads, such as the three animals usually found in fables – the lion (youth), the goat (adolescence) and the snake (old age) –, the three heads of Cerberus and a team of three horses associated with the dead. *Isidorus Hispalensis: Etymologiae XI*, ed. F. Gasti (Paris, 2010); *Isidore of Seville's Etymologies*, trans. P. Throop (Charlotte, 2013) I.xl.4, XI.iii.33, XVIII.xxxvi.2. None of these Isidorian triadic schemes of life appear to have been used by Anglo-Saxon authors for whom the *Etymologiae* was certainly available, see, e.g., Ogilvy, *Books Known*, 167; Lapidge, *Anglo-Saxon Library*, 311.

noluit tertiae vigiliae remedia non amittat, ut qui in iuuentute ad vias vitae non evigilat saltim in senectute resipiscat.²³

[Indeed, the first vigil is the youthful time, which is childhood. The second, adolescence or youth, which according to the authority of the sacred word are the same, saying: 'Rejoice, O young man, in your adolescence' (Eccles. 11:9). The third, moreover, is accepted to be old age. Therefore, whoever does not want to be awake during the first vigil, should observe the second, so that whoever has neglected to turn away from vices in childhood, is at least watchful of the ways of life in the time of youth. And whoever does not want to be alert during the second vigil, may they not let go of the remedies of the third watch, so that whoever is not watchful of the ways of life in youth, at least recovers their senses in old age.]

Bede's commentary, which explains that it is never too late to turn to a Christian way of life, was copied verbatim from a homily by Pope Gregory the Great (c.540–604).²⁴

Ælfric drew heavily on Bede or Gregory for a similar explanation of the Parable of the Three Vigils in his homily for the Common of a Confessor.²⁵ Like Bede and Gregory, Ælfric compared the three vigils to the three ages of man: "cildhade" [childhood], "weaxendum cnihthade" [growing youth/adolescence] and "forweredre ylde" [worn-out old age]. He then continued:

> Se ðe nolde wacian   on ðære forman wæccan,
> swa ðæt he on cildhade   gesohte his drihten
> and mid godum bigengum   hine gegladode,
> wacie he huru   on þære oðre wæccan
> and his mod awrecce   of middaneardlicum gedwyldum,
> forþan ðe he nat þone timan,   ðe his drihten cymð.
> Gif hwa ðonne bið,   þe hine sylfne forgyt
> on þam twam wæccum   and wunað on his leahtrum,
> warnige he þonne,   þæt he huru ne forleose
> þa ðriddan wæccan,   þæt he ne forwurðe mid ealle,
> ac huru on his ylde   of ðam yfelan slæpe
> his ærran nytennysse   ardlice arise
> and mid soðre gecyrrednysse   gesece his drihten
> and on godum weorcum   wunige oð ende.²⁶

---

²³ Bede, *In Lucam evangelium expositio*, ed. D. Hurst, CCSL 120 (Turnhout, 1960) IV, 257, lines 1139–58. Cf. Burrow, *Ages of Man*, 68.
²⁴ Gregory, *Homiliae in evangelia*, ed. R. Étaix, CCSL 141 (Turnhout, 1999), trans. D. Hurst, *Gregory the Great: Forty Gospel Homilies* (Kalamazoo, 1990), hom. 13, lines 74–82.
²⁵ Assmann, hom. 4. Cf. Burrow, *Ages of Man*, 68–9. For the sources of this particular homily, see M. Clayton, 'Of Mice and Men: Ælfric's Second Homily for the Feast of a Confessor', *Leeds Studies in English* ns 24 (1993), 7.
²⁶ Assmann, hom. 4, lines 67–83.

[He, who did not wish to keep awake during the first vigil, so that he sought his Lord in childhood and made him happy with good practices, let him at least keep awake during the second vigil and drive away his heart from worldly errors, because he does not know the time when his Lord will come. If, then, there is anyone who forgets himself during the two vigils and persists in his vices, he should take warning that he at least will not miss the third vigil, so that he will not perish completely, but at least in his old age will quickly arise from his bad sleep, his former ignorance, and with true conversion will seek his Lord and accustom himself to good works, until the end.]

Ælfric's admonition to accustom oneself with good deeds and his reference to "yfelan slæpe" [bad sleep] may have been inspired, in part, by a third source, a homily by Haymo of Auxerre. Similarly to Ælfric, Haymo used the terms "somnum torporis a se excutiat" [he should discard from himself the sleep of apathy] and "in bono opere se exerceat" [he should occupy himself with the performing of good deeds].[27]

Ælfric used the tripartite division of the life cycle again when he discussed the three different types of death in his sermon for the octave of Pentecost:

Mors acerba, mors inmatura, mors naturalis; ðæt is on Englisc, se bitera deað, se ungeripoda deað, and se gecyndelica. Se bitera deað is gecweden þe bið on cildum, and se ungeripoda deað, on geongum mannum, and se gecyndelica, þe becymð þam ealdum.[28]

[*Mors acerba, mors inmatura, mors naturalis*. That is in English: the bitter death, the immature death and the natural death. The bitter death is called that which happens to children, and the immature death happens to young people and the natural one comes to the elderly.]

Ælfric based this passage on Julian of Toledo's *Prognosticon futuri saeculi*: "Tria sunt genera mortis, id est acerba, inmatura, naturalis. Acerba infantium, inmatura iuuenum, matura, id est naturalis, senum" [There are three kinds of death, that is the bitter one, the immature one and the natural one. The bitter one for the children, the immature one for the young, the mature one, that is the natural one, for the elderly].[29]

The Anglo-Saxon homilist responsible for Blickling Homily XIV changed the fourfold structure of his Latin source into a division of life

---

[27] Haymo, *Homiliae aliquot de sanctis*, hom. 10, PL 118, cols. 788b–9c. This use of Haymo is discussed neither by Hill, 'Ælfric and Haymo', Smetana, 'Ælfric and the Homiliary' nor Clayton, 'Of Mice and Men'.

[28] Ælfric, *Homilies of Ælfric: A Supplementary Collection*, ed. J. C. Pope, EETS os 259–60 (Oxford, 1967–8), hom. 11, lines 112–17.

[29] M. McC. Gatch, *Preaching and Theology in Anglo-Saxon England: Ælfric and Wulfstan* (Toronto, 1977), 134, lines 17–18. The text from the *Prognosticon futuri saeculi* cited here derives from a series of excerpts compiled by Ælfric himself.

Definitions of Old Age

into three phases. This homily describes the birth of John the Baptist. John's aged parents Elizabeth and Zachary had spent their entire lives without sin; their "yldo" [old age], according to the homilist, was no different from their "iugoþ" [youth] and "midfyrhtnes" [middle age]:

> Ac hie wæron gemyndige ealra Godes beboda, 7 on ælce wisan hie wæron þære godcundan æ swiþe gehyrsume. 7 nu seo heora iugoþ 7 seo midfyrhtnes butan æghwylcum leahtre gestanden, hwylc talge we þonne þæt seo yldo 7 se ende þæs heora lifes wære ne se fruma swylc wæs?[30]

> [But they were mindful of all of God's commandments, and they were very obedient to Divine Law in every way. And now their youth and middle age stand without any sin, how can we consider that their old age and the end of their life were not like the former?]

As Giuseppe D. De Bonis has demonstrated, this passage is a rendering of a sermon by Peter Chrysologus (d. 450), which compared Elizabeth and Zachary's "senectus" [old age] to their "pueritia" [childhood], "adolescentia" [adolescence] and "iuventus" [youth].[31] In other words, the Blickling homilist preferred a threefold division of the life cycle over a division into four ages of man.

Yet another tripartite division of the life cycle is found in a scribal interpolation in the homily 'De temporibus Anticristi' by Archbishop Wulfstan (d. 1023).[32] The interpolation concerns Simon Magus's magic contest with the apostles Peter and Paul and describes Simon's skills in shape-shifting:

> 7 ða het æt nyhstan se casere feccan þæne symon to him. 7 þa ða he him to com 7 him ætforan stod, þa ablende he þurh deofles cræft swa þæs caseres eagan 7 ðæra þe him mid wæron þæt heom ðuhte oðre hwile þa hy hine beheoldon þæt he wære swylce hit cild wære þæt hy on locedon; oðre hwile eft swylce he medemre ylde man wære; 7 oðre hwile swylce he eald geðungen man wære; 7 swa on mænige wisan he hiwode þurh drycræft fela leasbregda.[33]

---

[30] *Blickling Homilies*, hom. 14, pp. 161, 163.
[31] G. D. De Bonis, 'The Birth of Saint John the Baptist: A Source Comparison between Blickling Homily XIV and Ælfric's Catholic Homily I.xxv', in *Hagiography in Anglo-Saxon England: Adopting and Adapting Saints' Lives into Old English Prose (c.950–1150)*, ed. L. Lazzari, P. Lendinara and C. Di Sciacca (Barcelona, 2014), 262–3.
[32] According to Bethurum, the interpolation was not written by Wulfstan himself. Wulfstan, *The Homilies of Wulfstan*, ed. D. Bethurum (Oxford, 1957), 132, n. 70. J. C. Pope, review of Wulfstan, *Homilies*, ed. Bethurum, *MLN* 74 (1959), 338–9, argues, however, that the interpolation is Wulfstan's. This attestation is not discussed in Burrow.
[33] Wulfstan, *Wulfstan's Eschatological Homilies*, ed. and trans. J. T. Lionarons (2000), http://webpages.ursinus.edu/jlionarons/wulfstan/Wulfstan.html; Wulfstan, *Homilies*, ed. Bethurum, does not include the interpolation.

[And then at last the Emperor had Simon brought to him. And when he came and stood in front of him, then through the devil's power he blinded the Emperor's eyes and those of the people with him, so that they thought at one time, when they looked at him, that he was like a child whom they looked at; a second time again as if he were a middle-aged man; and another time as if he were a distinguished, old man; and so in many ways he practiced deception through sorcery.]

The specific order "cild" [child] – "medemre ylde man" [middle-aged man] – "eald geðungen man" [distinguished old man] in relation to Simon Magus's magical transformations is not found in the source of this passage, the apocryphal *Passio sanctorum apostolum Petri et Pauli*. The *Passio* gives the sequence "puer" [child] – "senior" [old man] – "adolescentior" [young man]:

> qui ingressus coepit stare ante illum et subito mutare effigies, ita ut fieret subito puer et posthaec senior, altera uero hora adolescentior. mutabatur sexu, aetate, et per multas figuras diaboli ministerio bachabatur.[34]

[After coming and standing (before Nero), he suddenly began to change faces, such that he suddenly became a boy and after that an old man, but in another moment a younger man. He was changed in sex and age, and through many forms he was raging in the service of the devil.]

Two other Old English adaptations of this apocryphal story are closer to the source than the interpolation in Wulfstan's homily. Blickling Homily XV, like the *Passio*, starts with the sequence "geong cniht" [young boy] – "eald man" [old man], after which there is a gap in the manuscript.[35] Ælfric, in his homily on the Passion of Peter and Paul, gave the same order for the first two shifts, "cnapa" [boy] – "harwenge" [grey-haired man], added a third, "on wimmannes hade" [in the guise of a woman], and then ended the sequence, like the *Passio*, with "on cnihthade" [in youth].[36] Thus, while Simon Magus's shape-shifting act is dealt with in various Old English homilies, the sequence of childhood–middle age–old age in the interpolation in Wulfstan's homily is unique and may be a conscious attempt of its author to model the original sequence of Simon Magus's physical changes on the pattern of the three ages of man. As such, the interpolation attests to the widespread

---

[34] *The Ancient Martyrdom Accounts of Peter and Paul*, ed. and trans. D. L. Eastman (Atlanta, 2015), 236–7. For the use of the *Passio sanctorum apostolum Petri et Pauli* in medieval England, see A. Ferreiro, *Simon Magus in Patristic, Medieval and Early Modern Traditions* (Leiden, 2005), 201–20.
[35] *Blickling Homilies*, hom. 15, p. 175.
[36] *ÆCHom I*, hom. 26, lines 172–4.

Definitions of Old Age

popularity of the threefold division of the life cycle in Anglo-Saxon England.

Another apocryphal story that has often been linked to a threefold division of the life cycle is the Adoration of the Magi.[37] Since Matt. 2:1–12 describes the Magi merely as wise men who have come to worship the Christ child and give him their gifts, all additional information, including their names, number, dress, origins and age, derives from apocryphal traditions.[38] From the sixth century onwards, the Three Magi were described or depicted as representations of the three ages of man.[39] A clear, textual example that may have been known in Anglo-Saxon England is offered by the ninth-century *Collectanea Pseudo-Bedae*, a florilegium of riddles and encyclopaedic material. The *Collectanea* was once ascribed to Bede, but its most recent editors argue that "the majority of its localizable contents originated either in Ireland or England, or in an Irish foundation on the continent".[40] In the text, the Three Magi are described, respectively, as an old man, a beardless youth and a mature, fully bearded individual:

> Magi sunt, qui munera Domino dederunt: primus fuisse dicitur Melchior, senex et canus, barba prolixa et capillis, tunica hyacinthina, sagoque mileno, et calceamentis hyacinthino et albo mixto opere, pro mitrario uariae compositionis indutus: aurum obtulit regi Domino. Secundus, nomine Caspar, iuuenis imberbis, rubicundus, milenica tunica, sago rubeo, calceamentis hyacinthinis uestitus: thure quasi Deo oblatione digna, Deum honorabat. Tertius, fuscus, integre barbatus, Balthasar nomine, habens tunicam rubeam, albo uario <sago>, calceamentis milenicis amictus: per myrrham filium hominis moriturum professus est.[41]

> [The Magi are those who gave gifts to our Lord: the first is said to have been Melchior, an old man and white-haired, with a long beard and locks, wearing a blue tunic, an apple-green cloak, shoes of mixed blue and white work, and a Phrygian cap of varied make: he brought gold to the Lord as his king. The second, named Caspar, was a beardless youth, red-haired, dressed in a green tunic, a red cloak, and blue shoes; he honoured God with frankincense as an offering worthy of God. The third was swarthy, fully bearded, called Balthasar, with a red tunic, and clad in a white variegated cloak and green shoes; through his gift of myrrh he avowed that the Son of Man was to die.]

---

[37] Sears, *Ages of Man*, 91–4.
[38] For an overview, see G. Schiller, *Iconography of Christian Art* (London, 1971) I, 94–114.
[39] Schiller, *Iconography*, 101.
[40] M. Lapidge, 'The Origin of the *Collectanea*', in *Collectanea Pseudo-Bedae*, ed. and trans. M. Bayless and M. Lapidge (Dublin, 1998), 12.
[41] *Collectanea*, ed. and trans. Bayless and Lapidge, nos. 52–4.

Fig. 1. Adoration of the Magi on the Franks Casket, front panel (detail).

Parallels of this description of the Three Magi in terms of the three ages of man are mainly found in Irish sources,[42] but also in the *Wessobrunn Prayer* manuscript, a ninth-century Bavarian copy of an unknown, Anglo-Saxon manuscript.[43] Hence, this Latin text may have circulated in early medieval England as well, even though differentiation in age among the Magi is not found in any text in Old English. The earliest mention of the Magi in Old English is in the ninth-century *Old English Martyrology*, where they appear as three "tungolcræftegan" [astronomers], but no further information on their ages is provided.[44] Similarly, although Ælfric referred to the Magi in three different homilies, he never connected them to the three ages of man.[45] Be that as it may, the link between the wise men visiting Christ and a tripartite division of the human life cycle does feature in various works of Anglo-Saxon art.

Depictions of the Three Magi as young, middle-aged and elderly are found on two Anglo-Saxon whale-bone carvings. The first of these objects is the front panel of the Franks Casket, an early eighth-century

---

[42] *Collectanea*, ed. and trans. Bayless and Lapidge, 211–13; cf. M. McNamara, *The Apocrypha in the Irish Church* (Dublin, 1975), 54–6.

[43] Munich, Bayerische Staatsbibliothek, clm. 22053 (c.790, Wessobrunn Abbey). A facsimile and edition of the passage about the Magi is reproduced in U. Schwab, *Die Sternrune im Wessobrunner Gebet* (Amsterdam, 1973), 99–100. On the use of an Anglo-Saxon manuscript by the Bavarian scribe, see G. A. Waldman, 'Excerpts from a Little Encyclopaedia – the *Wessobrunn Prayer* Manuscript Clm. 22053', *Allegorica* 2 (1977), 9.

[44] *The Old English Martyrology*, ed. and trans. C. Rauer (Cambridge, 2013), no. 12.

[45] See the discussion in U. Nijst, 'The Magi in Anglo-Saxon England', in *Feestnummer aangeboden aan prof. dr. Aurelius Pompen O.F.M. op zijn zestigsten verjaardag* (Tilburg, 1939), 129–37.

whale-bone box kept in the British Museum, London.[46] On this panel, the Magi are placed in single file and can easily be identified by a runic inscription which reads "ᛗᚫᚷᛁ" [MÆGI]. The artist differentiated the Three Magi in age through their posture and the length of their beards: the Magus nearest to the infant Christ is depicted as kneeling on one knee and has the longest beard of the three, the second stands up straight and has a slightly less prominent beard, while the third, standing furthest away from Christ, is beardless (fig. 1). A second whale-bone carving, dated to the eleventh century and kept in the Victoria and Albert Museum, London, depicts the Three Magi in a similar way, although here the beardless Magus appears second in line.[47] The Anglo-Saxon provenance of this second piece is disputed, since it has been variously ascribed to England, northern France and northern Spain.[48]

The Anglo-Saxon illuminator of the Bury St Edmunds Psalter also depicted the Three Magi as the three ages of man.[49] This drawing of the Adoration of the Magi is placed in the margin of Ps. 71:10–11 ("The kings of Tharsis and the islands shall offer presents: the kings of the Arabians and of Saba shall bring gifts and all kings of the earth shall adore him: all nations shall serve him"), a text which is often associated with the scene. In this illustration, the differentiation in age is again borne out by their posture and beards: one is young and beardless, the second has a beard and stands, while the third, eldest Magus has a beard and he kneels down at the feet of Mary.[50]

---

[46] For a recent description of the scenes on the Franks Casket, see R. Abels, 'What Has Weland to Do with Christ? The Franks Casket and the Acculturation of Christianity in Anglo-Saxon England', *Speculum* 84 (2009), 549–81, esp. 558, n. 17.

[47] Victoria and Albert Museum, London, no. 142-1866.

[48] For a discussion of the different views, see J. Beckwith, *The Adoration of the Magi in Whalebone* (London, 1966), 31–3; P. Williamson, *Medieval Ivory Carvings: Early Christian to Romanesque* (London, 2010), 359–60. Beckwith ascribes the piece to the area around the English Channel, while Williamson favours northern Spain.

[49] Rome, Vatican City, Biblioteca Apostolica Vaticana, Reg. lat. 12 (s. xi$^{2/4}$, prob. Canterbury, Christ Church; the 'Bury St Edmunds Psalter'). Gneuss and Lapidge, no. 912. Apart from two studies on its marginal illustrations, this manuscript has received little scholarly interest. R. M. Harris, 'The Marginal Drawings of the Bury St Edmunds Psalter (Rome, Vatican Library, MS Reg. Lat. 12)', unpublished PhD dissertation, Princeton University, 1960; A. Heimann, 'Three Illustrations from the Bury St Edmunds Psalter and Their Prototypes. Notes on the Iconography of Some Anglo-Saxon Drawings', *Journal of the Warburg and Courtauld Institutes* 29 (1966), 39–59. A description of the drawings in the manuscripts can also be found in T. H. Ohlgren, *Insular and Anglo-Saxon Illuminated Manuscripts: An Iconographic Catalogue, c. A.D. 625 to 1100* (New York, 1986), 44–6.

[50] Bury St Edmunds Psalter, 78v. The manuscript has been digitised and this folio can be accessed at: http://digi.vatlib.it/view/MSS_Reg.lat.12/0166. The

Old Age in Early Medieval England

There may have been yet a fourth Anglo-Saxon depiction of the Three Magi as the three ages of man. The Antwerp Sedulius, a ninth-century Carolingian manuscript of Caelius Sedulius' *Carmen Paschale*, contains a miniature of the Adoration of the Magi, in which the Three Magi are differentiated in dress, beard and age, in the order youth–middle age–old age.[51] The miniatures of this manuscript have been shown to reflect a now lost Anglo-Saxon, possibly Northumbrian, eighth-century exemplar.[52] Hence, this Anglo-Saxon exemplar may also have contained the depiction of the Magi as representing the three ages of man.[53]

A final, visual rendition of the three ages of man is found in the Harley Psalter.[54] The Harley Psalter is one of three medieval English psalters based on the Utrecht Psalter, in which each psalm is introduced by a line drawing that provides a literal interpretation of the text.[55] Around the year 1000, the Utrecht Psalter was in Christ Church, Canterbury, and demonstrably influenced a number of English artists there: in addition to the Harley Psalter, the Eadwine Psalter and the Paris Psalter were modelled on the Utrecht Psalter.[56] Despite the reliance of these three psalters on a common exemplar, each manuscript is commonly seen as a reflection of the culture and period of production.[57] In the illustration introducing Psalm 104, the artist of the Harley Psalter followed his Utrecht exemplar and drew three figures, holding scrolls (fig. 2). The figures probably represent the Three Patriarchs,

---

architectural enclosure of the scene reveals an interesting parallel with the carving in the Victoria and Albert Museum.

[51] Antwerp, Museum Plantin-Moretus, M. 17.4 (s. ix, Liège; the 'Antwerp Sedulius'), 14v.

[52] J. J. G. Alexander, *Insular Manuscripts, 6th to the 9th Century* (London, 1978), 83, pl. 291. See also: Lapidge, *Anglo-Saxon Library*, 26–7.

[53] Two further Anglo-Saxon manuscripts, London, British Library, Add. 49598 (s. x² [971x984], Winchester; the 'Benedictional of St Æthelwold'), 24v; Rouen, Bibliothèque municipale, 274 (Y.6) (1014x1023, prov. (and origin?) Canterbury, Christ Church; the 'Sacramentary of Robert of Jumièges'), 37, depict the Magi as three identical, beardless men. Gneuss and Lapidge, nos. 301, 921. The illustrations are reproduced in E. G. Millar, *English Illuminated Manuscripts from the Xth to the XIIIth Century* (Paris, 1926), pls. 5, 12.

[54] London, British Library, Harley 603 (s. x/xi or xi¹, Canterbury, Christ Church; the 'Harley Psalter'). Gneuss and Lapidge, no. 422.

[55] Utrecht, Universiteitsbibliotheek 32 (820x835, Hautvillers Abbey; the 'Utrecht Psalter'). For an introduction to this manuscript, see F. Wormald, *The Utrecht Psalter* (Utrecht, 1953).

[56] Cambridge, Trinity College Library, R.17.1 (1155x1170, Canterbury, Christ Church; the 'Eadwine Psalter'); Paris, Bibliothèque nationale de France, lat. 8846 (1180x1200, Canterbury, Christ Church; the 'Paris Psalter'). W. Noel, 'The Utrecht Psalter in England: Continuity and Experiment', in *The Utrecht Psalter in Medieval Art: Picturing the Psalms of David*, ed. K. van der Horst, W. Noel and W. C. M. Wüstefeld (Tuurdijk, 1996), 121–65.

[57] Noel, 'Utrecht Psalter in England', 121–2.

Definitions of Old Age

Fig. 2. The Three Patriarchs as the three ages of man. Harley Psalter, 52v.

Abraham, Isaac and Jacob, whose covenants with God, here depicted in the form of scrolls, are all described in the Psalm.[58] The Three Patriarchs are differentiated for age; the first has a slightly crooked posture and a white or grey beard, the figure in the middle has a full, black beard, while the last, representing youth, has no beard at all. To my knowledge, the depiction of the Three Patriarchs as the three ages of man is unparalleled in Christian iconography and is only found in the Harley Psalter, the Eadwine Psalter and their exemplar, the Utrecht Psalter.[59] Depicting the patriarchs as the 'three ages of man' could be an attempt by the illuminators to show that the message of the Psalm applied to everyone: young, middle-aged and old.

A textual attestation of the three ages of man that, uniquely, is unrelated to biblical exegesis features in the mid-ninth-century Book of Cerne.[60] The Book of Cerne is a prayer book containing a collection

---

[58] For the identification of the three figures as Abraham, Isaac and Jacob, see the commentary for Psalm 104 in K. van der Horst and F. Ankersmit, *The Utrecht Psalter: Picturing the Psalms of David*, CD-ROM (Utrecht, 1996); W. Noel, *The Harley Psalter* (Cambridge, 1995), 87, interprets these three figures as "possibly three of His prophets upon whom the story is hung".

[59] Harley Psalter, 52v; Eadwine Psalter, 185r; Utrecht Psalter, 60v. The Paris Psalter has a different illustration for this Psalm.

[60] Cambridge, University Library, MS L1.1.10 (c.820x840, Mercia; the 'Book of Cerne'). Gneuss and Lapidge, no. 28.

of texts for private devotion and meditation, including seventy-four Latin prayers, many of which occur in other manuscripts.[61] Prayer 8, 'Confessio sancti penitentis' [the confession of the holy penitent], one of the seven prayers that are unique to the Book of Cerne,[62] mentions the three ages of man:

> pro hoc confiteor uobis quaecumque feci in puerile aetate uel in iuuentute uel in senectute – et sepe peccaui in multis rebus multum deum inritaui.[63]

> [I confess to you that which I committed in the age of childhood or in maturity or in old age – and I have often sinned and greatly angered God in many things.]

These lines form part of a long list of potential sins which a penitent could recite during confession, which means that the prayer was probably intended as a liturgical text for the administration of penance.

As I have argued elsewhere, this prayer is closely related to three Old English prayers with which it probably shared a common, Latin source, but the prayer in the Book of Cerne is the only one to feature the three ages of man.[64] The parallel passage in a longer version of the prayer, in a tenth-century manuscript,[65] lists sins committed in four distinct phases of life:

> Ic eom anddetta for eall þæt unriht þe ic æfre gefremede on minum cildhade oððe on minre geogoðe oððe on minre strengðe oððe on minre ylde þe æfter fulwihte agylte 7 on manegum þingum swiðe gode abealh.[66]

> [I acknowledge all the injustice which I have ever done in my childhood or in my youth or in my strength or in my old age, which I committed after baptism and with many things greatly angered God.]

A shorter version of the prayer, added to an eleventh-century manuscript,[67] only lists childhood and old age, as two extremes of the entire spectrum of life:

---

[61] For the Book of Cerne, see M. P. Brown, *The Book of Cerne: Prayer, Patronage and Power in Ninth-Century England* (London, 1996), esp. 136–43 (for the prayers).
[62] A. J. Frantzen, *The Literature of Penance in Anglo-Saxon England* (New Brunswick, 1983), 88, notes that this prayer "appears in no other manuscript yet known"; cf. T. Porck, 'Two Notes on an Old English Confessional Prayer in Vespasian D. xx', NQ ns 60 (2013), 493–8.
[63] Book of Cerne, 47v, lines 15–17, ed. A. B. Kuypers, *The Prayer Book of Aedeluald the Bishop, Commonly Called the Book of Cerne* (Cambridge, 1902), 92–5.
[64] Porck, 'Two Notes'.
[65] London, British Library, Cotton Vespasian D. xx (s. x med). Ker, no. 212; Gneuss and Lapidge, no. 395.
[66] H. Logeman, 'Anglo-Saxonica Minora, I', *Anglia* 11 (1889), 101–2, lines 54–7.
[67] London, British Library, Cotton Tiberius C. i (1070x1100, Sherborne). Ker, no. 197; Gneuss and Lapidge, no. 376.

Definitions of Old Age

Ic eom andetta þara þe ic of cildhade oð þas ieldo þe ic æfter fulwihte agylte 7 on manegum ðingum swiðe gode abealh.[68]

[I acknowledge those (sins) which I committed from childhood to old age, after baptism, and with many things verily offended God.]

The third Old English prayer related to prayer 8 in the Book of Cerne leaves out the passage altogether.[69] The common origin of these four prayers is unknown and it is impossible to determine what the source text reads regarding the division of the life cycle. Nevertheless, the differences in the extant versions suggest, at the very least, that while the Anglo-Saxon writers may have differed in opinion as to whether a twofold, threefold or fourfold division was the most suitable way to define the life cycle, none of them felt the need to divide old age into two phases, in contrast to what would have been expected from the research by Cochelin.

The examples mentioned above reveal that the threefold division of the life cycle enjoyed widespread popularity in Anglo-Saxon England from an early period onwards and was represented in both word and image. With the exception of the prayer in the Book of Cerne, all attestations of the three ages of man stem from biblical exegesis and work on the analogy of various biblical or apocryphal triads, such as Christ's Parable of the Three Vigils, the Three Magi and the Three Patriarchs.

Four ages of man

While the tripartite scheme of life stems in general from biblical exegesis, a life cycle divided into four parts has its major roots in natural philosophy. The Greek philosopher Pythagoras (c.570–c.495 BC) is credited with the idea that a man's life can be divided into four stages, analogous to the four seasons in the course of a year.[70] Later, this Pythagorean tetradic life cycle was related to other sets of four, such as the elements and the humours.[71] This interrelation between the various sets of four made the scheme appealing for two Anglo-Saxon authors in particular: Bede (673/674–735) and Byrhtferth of Ramsey (fl. c.986–c.1016).

The first Anglo-Saxon attestation of a distinction between four ages of man is found in Bede's *De temporum ratione* (c.725), a work on the

---

[68] Logeman, 'Anglo-Saxonica Minora', 99, lines 86–8.
[69] This text is edited in R. Fowler, 'A Late Old English Handbook for the Use of a Confessor', *Anglia* 83 (1965), 1–34; see also Porck 'Two Notes', 495.
[70] *The Four Seasons of Human Life: Four Anonymous Engravings from the Trent Collection*, ed. H. F. J. Horstmanshoff et al. (Rotterdam, 2002), 40–1.
[71] Sears, *Ages of Man*, 9–16.

Table 1. Bede's scheme of physical and physiological fours

Qualities	Moist and hot	Hot and dry	Dry and cold	Cold and moist
Season	Spring	Summer	Autumn	Winter
Elements	Air	Fire	Earth	Water
Ages of man	*infantes*	*adolescentes*	*transgressores*	*senes*
Humours	Blood	Red choler	Black choler	Phlegm

reckoning of time.[72] Here, Bede explains how the four ages of man correspond to four other sets of 'fours': the seasons, the qualities, the elements and the humours. He begins by noting how the four seasons can be understood in terms of the four qualities: spring is moist and hot, summer is hot and dry, autumn is dry and cold and winter is cold and moist. In the same way, the four qualities combine to form the four elements: air, fire, earth and water. Analogous to the four seasons, the human life cycle also consists of four phases and Bede distinguishes between *infantes* 'children', *adolescentes* 'young people', *transgressores* 'the middle-aged' and *senes* 'the elderly'.[73] Each of these phases is linked to the same qualities as its corresponding season and each is governed by one of the four humours: blood governs childhood, red choler governs youth, black choler governs maturity and old age is governed by phlegm (see table 1). Bede then outlines the typical behavioural characteristics that these dominating humours produce within human beings. The elderly dominated by phlegm, for example, are made "tardos, somnolentos, obliuiosos" [slow, sleepy, and forgetful].[74]

Cochelin interpreted Bede's unusual term *transgressores* as referring to the stage of life starting at forty-nine and hence she hypothesised that Bede here presents a subdivision of old age into two phases.[75] This hypothesis is improbable, however, given that *adolescentia* in most other medieval definitions of the life cycle ends at the age of twenty-eight and rarely directly precedes the onset of old age.[76] Moreover, Byrhtferth of Ramsey, who based his discussion of the four ages on Bede, interprets Bede's *transgressores* as representing *iuuentus*, the stage which typically precedes old age: "Colera nigra (id est melancholia) in transgressoribus uiget (id est qui <in> iuuentute sunt)" [Black choler (that is, melancholy) flourishes in those in a state of transition (that is, those in their

---

[72] Bede, *De temporum ratione*, ed. C. W. Jones, *Opera didascalica*, CCSL 123 B (Turnhout, 1977), trans. F. Wallis, *Bede: The Reckoning of Time* (Liverpool, 2012), ch. 35. Cf. Burrow, *Ages of Man*, 12–16.
[73] Bede, *De temporum ratione*, ed. Jones, trans. Wallis, ch. 35.
[74] Bede, *De temporum ratione*, ed. Jones, trans. Wallis, ch. 35.
[75] Cochelin, 'Introduction: Pre-Thirteenth-Century Definitions', 24.
[76] Cochelin, 'Introduction: Pre-Thirteenth-Century Definitions', 3–5.

Definitions of Old Age

manhood)].⁷⁷ Thus, Bede's rendition of the four ages more probably presents old age as a single, undivided phase of life.

Not all of Bede's sources for his scheme of the physical and physiological fours have been identified. Bede probably derived the basic scheme of the four qualities, humours and seasons from Isidore of Seville's *De natura rerum*.⁷⁸ The origin of his information on the dominant humours for each of the four ages, however, is still uncertain. According to Faith Wallis, Bede's source is possibly the *Epistola ad Pentadium* by Vindicianus (c.632–c.712).⁷⁹ Vindicianus' letter seems an unlikely direct source, however, since it differs from Bede's text in some crucial aspects, such as the fact that it posits two dominating humours for each of the four ages rather than one.⁸⁰ In addition, Vindicianus describes a different effect of phlegm on the elderly: "flegma facit homines corpore compositos, vigilantes, intra se cogitantes, cito adferentes canos in capite, minus audaces" [phlegm makes people calm in their body, watchful, thinking to themselves, quickly bringing grey hairs on their heads, less daring].⁸¹ Bede's remark on the slow, sleepy and forgetful elderly may have been based on an alternative source or, possibly, his personal experience.

As noted above, Byrhtferth, an Anglo-Saxon monk who lived at Ramsey Abbey, made use of Bede's tetradic scheme. Byrhtferth's rendition of the physical and physiological fours in his *Manual* or *Enchiridion* (1012–1020), a computational handbook, is the earliest known version of this doctrine in English:⁸²

> Butan þissum þingum þe we sprecende synt, synt geswutelunga and gehwylcnyssa and twelf winda naman, and synt þa feower timan amearcod, lengten, sumor, hærfest and winter, and eac þa gelicnyssa, þæt ys cildhad and cnihtiugoð and geþungen yld and swyðe eald yld.

---

⁷⁷ Byrhtferth, *Byrhtferth's Enchiridion*, ed. and trans. P. S. Baker and M. Lapidge, EETS ss 15 (London, 1995), I.1, lines 112–13.
⁷⁸ Bede, *De temporum ratione*, trans. Wallis, 101, n. 319.
⁷⁹ Bede, *De temporum ratione*, trans. Wallis, 101, n. 319.
⁸⁰ "[F]legma in pueris cum sanguine ab ineunte aetate usque in annos XIIII, exinde cholera rubea dominatur cum parte sanguinis in iuuenibus usque ad annos XXV. exinde usque in annos XLII maxima pars sanguinis dominatur cum cholera nigra. exinde usque ad summam aetatem sicut in pueris flegma dominatur moriente autem homine haec omnia revertuntur in sua loca" [Phleghm, with blood dominates in children from an early age even to 14 years of age, from that time red choler dominates with a part of blood in the young people until 25 years of age. From then until the age of 42 the major part is dominated by blood, with black choler. From then to a certain time, just like in children, phlegm also dominates the dying man, all these things return to their places.]. Vindicianus, *Epistola ad Pentadium*, ed. V. Rose, *Theodori Prisciani Euporiston libri III* (Leipzig, 1894), 487–9; cf. Burrow, *Ages of Man*, 15, n. 2.
⁸¹ Vindicianus, *Epistola*, ed. Rose, 489.
⁸² Cf. Burrow, *Ages of Man*, 15–18.

Lengtentima and cildiugoð geþwærlæcað, and cnihtiugoð and sumor beoð gelice, and hærfest and geþungen yld geferlæcað, and winter and yld ateoriað.[83]

[Apart from these things we are discussing, there are significations, and qualities, and the names of the twelve winds, and the four seasons are written down – spring, summer, autumn and winter – and also the similitudes – childhood, adolescence, manhood and very old age. Spring and childhood correspond, and adolescence and summer are alike, and autumn and manhood keep each other company, and winter and age decline together.]

Byrhtferth followed Bede in linking old age to winter, water, and the humour phlegm:

Hiemps ys winter; he byð ceald and wæt. Wæter ys ceald and wæt; swa byð se ealda man ceald and snoflig. Flegmata (þæt byð hraca oððe geposu) deriað þam ealdan and þam unhalan.[84]

[*Hiems* is winter; it is cold and wet. Water is cold and wet; likewise an old man is cold and rheumy. Phlegm (mucus or a head-cold) harms the old and infirm.]

Although Byrthferth follows Bede closely, he describes the elderly as cold and rheumy, rather than slow, sleepy and forgetful, drawing out the analogy with winter, water and phlegm.

Byrhtferth further expanded on the theory of the four ages of man in a complex diagram that survives in two twelfth-century computational manuscripts.[85] The diagram is known as 'Byrhtferth of Ramsey's diagram of the physical and physiological fours', although Byrhtferth himself called it *De concordia mensium atque elementorum* [On the concord of the months and elements]. With this diagram, Byrhtferth shows how various elements of the universe (months, seasons, elements, ages of man, wind directions) are all related to each other: "the diagram is about *concordia*, the way apparently different aspects of the physical universe figure each other, expressing God's perfection in the perfect symmetry of His creation".[86] Like the *Enchiridion*, the diagram relates the four ages of man to the four seasons, the four contraries and the

---

[83] Byrhtferth, *Enchiridion*, ed. and trans. Baker and Lapidge, I.1, lines 117–23.
[84] Byrhtferth, *Enchiridion*, ed. and trans. Baker and Lapidge, I.1, lines 131–3. Byrhtferth repeated the links between the four ages, contraries, elements and seasons in his fourth book: IV.1, lines 72–84.
[85] London, British Library, Harley 3667 (s. xii$^{2/4}$, Peterborough), 8r; Oxford, St John's College 17 (1102–1113, Thorney Abbey), 7v.
[86] Byrhtferth, *De concordia mensium atque elementorum. On the Concord of the Months and the Elements. Also Known as his Diagram of the Physical and Physiological Fours*, ed. P. S. Baker, http://web.archive.org/web/19961025235309/http://www.engl.virginia.edu/OE/Editions/Decon.pdf. Cf. Burrow, *Ages of Man*, 16–8.

Definitions of Old Age

four elements. In addition, the diagram adds the number of years at which each age ends: *pueritia* or *infantia* ends after fourteen years, *adolescentia* after twenty-eight years, *iuuentus* ends after forty-eight years and *senectus* ends after seventy or eighty years.

The age limits for Byrhtferth's first three ages may have been derived from Isidore of Seville, who comments on them in two of his works, each describing a sixfold division of the life cycle. In his *Differentiae*, Isidore distinguishes between *infantia* (ending at the age of seven), *pueritia* (fourteen), *adolescentia* (twenty-eight), *iuuentus* (forty-nine), *senectus* (seventy-seven) and *senium* (not limited to a particular number of years).[87] In his *Etymologiae*, Isidore mentioned the same scheme, but the fourth age, *iuuentus*, ends at the age of forty-eight and the fifth, *aetas senioris* or *grauitas*, at the age of seventy.[88] Byrhtferth's age limit

---

[87] Isidore, *Differentiae*, II.19: "Prima hominis aetas infantia, secunda pueritia, tertia adolescentia, quarta iuuentus, quinta senectus, sexta senium. Duae primae aetates singulis annorum terminantur hebdomadibus, propter simplicem vitam. Nam infantia septimo anno finitur, quartodecimo pueritia, dehinc sequens adolescentia duabus constat hebdomadibus propter intellectum et actionem. Quae duae nondum erant in pueris, et porrigitur haec aetas a quinto decimo anno usque ad XXVIII. Post haec succedens iuuentus tribus hebdomadibus permanet, propter tria illa, intellectum et actionem, corporisque virtutem. Ista aetas a XXVIII anno exoritur, et quadragesimo nono consummatur, quando et in feminis partus deficit. Porro senectus quatuor hebdomadibus completur propter accedentem illis tribus animi et corporis grauitatem. Incipit enim haec aetas a quinquagesimo anno, et septuagesimo septimo terminatur. Ultima vero senium nullo certo annorum tempore definitur, sed solo naturae fine concluditur" [The first age of a person is infancy, the second is childhood, the third is adolescence, the fourth manhood, the fifth old age, the sixth feebleness. The first two ages are each terminated by a seven-year period, because of their simple life. For infancy is finished in the seventh year, childhood in the fourteenth. After this, adolescence follows, consisting of two seven-year periods for the sake of understanding and rationality. These two qualities did not yet exist in childhood, and this age stretches from the fifteenth year to the twenty-eighth. Coming after this, manhood lasts for three seven-year periods on account of three things: understanding, action, and the strength of the body. This age starts from the twenty-eighth year and finishes in the forty-ninth, a time when, in women, giving birth ceases. Furthermore, old age is completed by four seven-year periods because of the approaching heaviness in mind and body in the three areas of understanding, action, and strength. This age begins from the fiftieth year and ends in the seventy-seventh. The end of feebleness is defined by no particular period of years, but concludes solely with the end of nature]. PL 83, cols. 81b–c, trans. P. Throop, *Isidore of Seville's Synonyms and Differences* (Charlotte, 2012).

[88] Isidore, *Etymologiae*, XI.ii, 2–6, 6–8: "Prima aetas infantia est pueri nascentis ad lucem, quae porrigitur in septem annis. Secunda aetas pueritia, id est pura et necdum ad generandum apta, tendens usque ad quartum decimum annum. Tertia adolescentia ad gignendum adulta, quae porrigitur usque ad uiginti octo annos. Quarta iuuentus, firmissima aetatum omnium, finiens in quinquagesimo anno. Quinta aetas senioris, id est, grauitas, quae est declinatio a iuuentute in senectutem, nondum senectus sed iam nondum iuuentus, quia senioris aetas est [...]. Quae aetas quinquagesimo anno incipiens septuagesimo

for his fourth age, *senectus* (ending at seventy or eighty), was probably based on Ps. 89:10 ("The days of our years in them are threescore and ten years. But if in the strong they be fourscore years"). Another influence on the age limits mentioned by both Byrhtferth and Isidore is the classical theory of the hebdomads, which divided human life into periods of seven years.[89] The threshold for old age will be discussed further below.

Lastly, Byrhtferth also made use of the four ages of man in two of his saints' lives: *Vita s. Oswaldi* (997–1002) and *Vita s. Ecgwini* (1016–1020). In his life of Oswald of Worcester (d. 992), archbishop of York and founder of Ramsey Abbey, for example, Byrhtferth describes how Oswald's uncle, Oda, "pueritie et adolescentie tempus transcendisset et tertium spatium iam aetatis sue adpropinquaret" [had passed the time of childhood and adolescence, and the third stage of his maturity was approaching].[90] In his *Vita s. Ecgwini*, Byrhtferth divided his account of Ecgwine, bishop of Worcester (d. 717?) and founder of Evesham Abbey, into four parts:

> Constat istius uita breuiter edita et in bis binis partibus diuisa; que quattuor partes demonstrant quid in pueritia uel adolescentia siue in iuuentute atque in senectute gessit.[91]

> [The life of this man is briefly set out and divided into four parts, these four parts explain what he did in his childhood and youth and maturity and old age.]

At the end of the *Vita s. Ecgwini*, the four ages of man are put into an allegorical framework: Ecgwine attacks each of the four gates of the Devil's city in the four successive stages of his life; the four gates are

---

terminatur. Sexta aetas senectus, quae nullo annorum tempore finitur, sed post quinque illas aetates quantumcumque uitae est, senectuti deputatur" [The first age, infancy, is of a child being born to the light. It continues for seven years. The second, childhood, is an age which is pure, and not yet able to engender. It stretches to the fourteenth year. The third is adolescence, when one is mature enough to produce offspring. It lasts until one is twenty-eight. The fourth is manhood, the most stable of all ages, ending at the fiftieth year. The fifth age is that of the elder, senior, that is of dignity, gravitas. It is the decline from manhood into old age. It is not yet old age, but it is no longer manhood, being the age of the elder ... This stage begins at the fiftieth year and ends at the seventieth. The sixth age is old age, bound by no period of years; whatever remains after the previous five stages of life is considered old age]. *Isidore of Seville's Etymologies*, trans. Throop.

[89] H. F. J. Horstmanshoff, 'De drempel van de ouderdom; medische en sociale zorg voor de oudere mens in de Grieks-Romeinse Oudheid', in *Verpleeghuiskunde. Een vak van doen en laten*, ed. J. F. Hoek et al. (Utrecht, 1996), 316.

[90] Byrhtferth, *Vita s. Oswaldi*, ed. and trans. M. Lapidge, *Byrhtferth of Ramsey: The Lives of St Oswald and St Ecgwine* (Oxford, 2009), I.4.

[91] Byrhtferth, *Vita s. Ecgwini*, ed. and trans. Lapidge, preface.

Definitions of Old Age

each manned by two evil leaders, whose wives represent eight deadly sins.[92]

A division of life in four phases appears to have been less common than a threefold division. In addition to the Old English confessional prayer in Vespasian D. xx,[93] this division only appears in the works of Bede and Byrhtferth, who were attracted to the scheme for its similitude to other sets of four found in natural philosophy. In each of the attestations described above, old age features as a single, final phase of life. In contrast to Cochelin's conclusions, it is typically the second of the three "main phases", *iuuentus*, which is subdivided into two phases, rather than the last.[94]

Five ages of man

Boll has remarked that, although a fivefold division of the life cycle seems a natural division, given the analogy with the five fingers, it is hardly ever attested in Antiquity.[95] The same holds true for early medieval English writings, which only feature two attestations.

The first features in the *Vita Bonifatii* by the Anglo-Saxon Willibald of Mainz (c.700–c.787). Similar to Byrhtferth of Ramsey in his *Vita s. Oswaldi*, Willibald explicitly used the ages of man to structure his hagiography of St Boniface, noting from the outset how Boniface flourished "in infantia et pueritia vel adolescentia et iuuentute aut etiam in senectute" [in infancy, childhood, adolescence and manhood and even in old age].[96] Walter Berschin has noted that Willibald, in using the five ages of man to structure his narrative, follows the example of other hagiographers, such as Hilary of Arles (c.403–49) in his *De vita S. Honorati*.[97]

The second attestation of the five ages of man is in Ælfric's homily for Septuagesima Sunday, which deals with the Parable of the Vineyard (Matt. 20:1–16). This parable relates how workers were called to a vineyard at five different hours. In Ælfric's interpretation, the various groups of workers mentioned in the parable signified people who became Christian at different moments in their lives:

> Eornostlice þonne sume beoð gelædde on cildhade to godum ðeawum and rihtum life. sume on cnihthade. sume on geðungenum wæstme.

---

[92] Byrhtferth, *Vita s. Ecgwini*, ed. and trans. Lapidge, IV.1–4.
[93] See above p. 30.
[94] Cf. Cochelin, 'Introduction: Pre-Thirteenth-Century Definitions', 11.
[95] Boll, 'Lebensalter', 176.
[96] Willibald, *Vita Bonifatii*, ed. R. Rau, *Bonifatii epistulae. Willibaldi vita Bonifatii* (Darmstadt, 1968), ch. 9. The word "uel" here probably means "and" rather than "or", since *pueritia* and *adolescentia* are rarely used interchangeably.
[97] W. Berschin, *Biographie und Epochenstil im lateinischen Mittelalter* (Stuttgart, 1991) III, 11.

sume on ylde. sume on forwerodre ealdnysse. þonne bið hit swylce hi beon on mislicum tidum to ðam wingearde gelaðode.

[Truly some are led in childhood to good deeds and a righteous life, some in youth, some in mature growth, some in old age, some in worn-out old age; then it is as though they had at diverse times been called to the vineyard.][98]

Ælfric was not the first to interpret the Parable of the Vineyard in this way. His rendition is a near word-for-word translation of the corresponding passage in a homily by Gregory the Great, who, in turn, probably based his interpretation on the Greek Church father Origen.[99] So far, this homily is the first Anglo-Saxon rendition of the ages of man in this overview to feature the subdivision of old age into two phases that Cochelin ascribed to virtually all life cycle definitions found from the sixth century to the year 1120.[100]

Six ages of man

The idea of the six ages of man stems from the analogy of the *sex aetates mundi* [six ages of the world] which was first proposed by St Augustine of Hippo. In various works, Augustine propagated the idea that the world passed through six ages which correspond to the human life cycle: *infantia* from Adam to Noah, *pueritia* from Noah to Abraham, *adolescentia* from Abraham to David, *iuuentus* from David until the Babylonian captivity, *senioris* from the Babylonian exile to the coming of Jesus Christ and, finally, *senectus* which would last until the end of time.[101] Although the six ages of the world was a popular *topos* in Anglo-Saxon writing,[102] only three authors connected the ages of the world with the ages of man, all of them writing in Latin: Bede, the author of the *Collectanea* and Alcuin. Further, three encyclopaedic notes on the six ages of man survive in eight Anglo-Saxon manuscripts.[103] In addition to the works of Augustine, Isidore of Seville's treatments of the sixfold division of life in his *Differentiae* and *Etymologiae* were highly influential.

Bede included a version of the division into six ages in both his *De temporibus* (c.703) and his *De temporum ratione* (c.725). Following

---

[98] *ÆCHom II*, hom. 5, lines 101–6. Cf. Burrow, *Ages of Man*, 61–3.
[99] Gatch, *Preaching and Theology*, 93–4; Godden, *Ælfric's Catholic Homilies: Introduction*, 383–4.
[100] Cf. Cochelin, 'Introduction: Pre-Thirteenth-Century Definitions', 11.
[101] Sears, *Ages of Man*, 54–61.
[102] H. L. C. Tristram, *Sex aetates mundi: Die Weltzeitalter bei den Angelsachsen und den Iren. Untersuchungen und Texte* (Heidelberg, 1985).
[103] For a study of encyclopaedic notes in Anglo-Saxon manuscripts, see K. Dekker, 'The Organisation and Structure of Old English Encyclopaedic Notes', *Filologia Germanica – Germanic Philology* 5 (2013), 95–130.

Definitions of Old Age

Augustine, Bede related the ages of the world to a division of the human life span into six parts.[104] In both texts, he distinguished between *infantia, pueritia, adolescentia, iuuenilis [aetas], senectus* and *aetas decrepita*. Thus, Bede divided old age into two parts: *senectus*, which he described as "graui" [serious], and *aetas decrepita*, a period of decrepitude "morte finienda" [ending in death].[105]

The ninth-century *Collectanea Pseudo-Bedae* features a different version of the theory of the six ages of man. Here, the six ages of man are treated separately from the ages of the world and, in contrast to Bede's and Augustine's versions, the text includes the number of years that each age will last:

> Sex aetates hominis sunt. Prima infantia: septem annos tenet; secunda pueritia: alios septem annos tenet; tertia adolescentia, quae quatuordecim annos tenet; quarta iuuentus, quae uiginti unum annum tenet; quinta senectus, quae uiginti octo annos tenet; sexta dicitur senium, ultima aetas uel decrepitus, quae nullum certum tenet numerum annorum.[106]

> [There are six ages of man. The first, infancy, lasts seven years; the second, boyhood, lasts another seven years; the third is adolescence, which lasts fourteen years; the fourth is youth, which lasts twenty-one years; the fifth is old age, which lasts twenty-eight years; the sixth is called senility, or decrepitude, the final age, which lasts no definite number of years.]

The years assigned to each stage of the life cycle are also found in the *Differentiae* by Isidore, who is the most probable source for this passage.[107]

The Anglo-Saxon scholar Alcuin of York (c.740–804) treated the six ages of man in some detail in his didactic text *Disputatio puerorum per interrogationes et responsiones*.[108] In the fifth chapter of this book, on the six ages of the world, he discusses the six ages of man, copying Isidore of Seville's *Etymologiae* almost verbatim:

---

[104] Bede, *De temporum ratione*, trans. Wallis, 158, n. 4.
[105] Bede, *De temporibus*, ed. C. W. Jones, *Opera didascalica*, CCSL 123 C (Turnhout, 1980), ch. 16; Bede, *De temporum ratione*, ed. Jones, trans. Wallis, ch. 60. Also discussed in Cochelin, 'Introduction: Pre-Thirteenth-Century Definitions', 24.
[106] *Collectanea*, ed. and trans. Bayless and Lapidge, no. 378. Bayless and Lapidge erroneously translate "uiginti unum" as "twenty years", rather than "twenty-one years". The multitudes of seven years show the influence of the classical theory of the hebdomads, for which see Horstmanshoff, 'De drempel van de ouderdom', 316.
[107] Isidore, *Differentiae*, II.19, see p. 35, n. 87 above. Cf. *Collectanea*, ed. and trans. Bayless and Lapidge, 273.
[108] Cf. Burrow, *Ages of Man*, 84; M. Lapidge, *Anglo-Latin Literature. Vol. 2: 900–1066* (London, 1993), 237, n. 10, notes that the text may not be Alcuin's.

INTER. Et si totidem sunt, quomodo nominantur; uel quae est earum ratio, aut quot annis continentur?
RESP. Prima earum infantia est pueri nascentis ad lucem, septem continens annos; nam infans dicitur homo primae aetatus, eo quod adhuc fari, id est, loqui nescit. Secunda pueritia est, pura et necdum ad generandum apta, tendens usque ad XIIII annum. Tertia adolescentia ad gignendum adulta, quae porrigitur usque ad XXVII annos. Quarta iuuentus firmissima aetatum omnium, finiens in quinquagesimo anno. Quinta aetas senior est grauitas, quae est declinatio a iuuentute in senectutem, nondum tamen senectus, sed iam nondum iuuentus; haec enim aetas a quinquagesimo anno incipiens, in septuagesimo terminatur. Sexta aetas senectus, quae nullo annorum tempore finitus, sed post quinque illas aetates quantumcumque uitae est, senectuti deputabitur.[109]

[Question: And if there are just as many (ages), how are they named? Or what is their calculation, how many years are included?
Answer: The first of them, infancy, is from the child's birth into the light, which contains seven years; a man in the first stage is called an infant, because he still does not know how to speak, that is, to talk. The second, childhood, is pure and not yet able to reproduce, extending until fourteen years. The third, adolescence, (when someone is) mature enough to reproduce, which extends until twenty-seven years. The fourth, manhood, the strongest of all ages, ends in the fiftieth year. The fifth age is that of the elder, *grauitas* (dignity), which is the decline from manhood into old age; it is not yet old age, but it is no longer manhood; this age begins in the fiftieth year and ends in the seventieth year. The sixth age, old age, which is not limited to any space of years, but whatever of life remains after these five ages, is considered old age.]

Like Isidore, Alcuin posits the stage *grauitas*, from the ages of fifty to seventy, as an intermediate stage between *iuuentus* and *senectus*, noting that it differs from both. Nevertheless, Alcuin's *grauitas* should probably be understood as representing the first stage of old age, called *senectus* by Bede, while Alcuin's *senectus* corresponds to Bede's *aetas decrepita*.

Alcuin also referred to the six ages of man in his commentary on John 4:6 ("Now Jacob's well was there. Jesus therefore, being wearied with his journey, sat thus on the well. It was about the sixth hour"): "Nam sexta aetas senectus est, quoniam prima est infantia, secunda pueritia, tertia adolescentia, quarta iuuentus, quinta grauitas" [Because the sixth hour is old age, just as the first is infancy, the second is child-

---

[109] Alcuin, *Disputatio puerorum per interrogationes et responsiones*, ed. L. E. Felsen, '"Disputatio puerorum": Analysis and Critical Edition', unpublished PhD dissertation, University of Oregon, 2003, V.3, lines 26–39. Cf. Isidore, *Etymologiae*, XI.ii, see pp. 35–6, n. 88 above. The only notable difference is that Isidore has the third age end at twenty-eight years of age, following the classical theory of the hebdomads, whereas Alcuin has it end at twenty-seven.

Definitions of Old Age

hood, the third is adolescence, the fourth youth and the fifth is *grauitas*].[110] According to Alcuin, the sixth hour here represents the sixth age of the world, *senectus*, in which Christ was born. Alcuin copied this passage from Augustine's theological treatise *De diversis quaestionibus octaginta tribus* [On eighty-three various questions].[111]

In addition to the work of the three authors mentioned above, three short encyclopaedic notes on the six ages of man have survived in eight Anglo-Saxon manuscripts. The first is the following note in a tenth-century manuscript:[112]

SEX AETATES HOMINIS SUNT
   s. aetas .vii. anni a .xiiii.   a. xxviii.   a .lix.
Prima infantia. ii. Pueritia iii Adolescentia. iiii iuuentus.
      .lxxvii.   a
Quinta senectus. vi. Senium. que nullo tempore finitur.[113]

[These are the six ages of man: The first infancy (until seven years); the second childhood (until fourteen); the third adolescence (until twenty-eight); the fourth manhood (until fifty-nine); the fifth senectus (until seventy-seven); the sixth decrepitude, which is not ended by any time span.]

The names of the ages and their age limits make clear that the source for this note is Isidore's *Differentiae*.[114] The same note is found in an eleventh-century manuscript.[115] The note was probably copied when both manuscripts were at St Augustine's, Canterbury, in the eleventh century, along with Bede's verse life of St Cuthbert, which is found in both manuscripts.[116]

---

[110] Alcuin, *Commentarii in s. Joannis evangelium*, ch. 7. PL 100, col. 792. Cf. Burrow, *Ages of Man*, 84–5.

[111] Augustine, *De diversis quaestionibus octaginta tribus*, ed. A. Mutzenbecher, CCSL 44 A (Turnhout, 1975), q. 64.

[112] London, British Library, Cotton Vitellius A. xix (s. x²/⁴ or x med., prob. Canterbury, St Augustine's), 114r. Ker, no. 217; Gneuss and Lapidge, no. 401.

[113] The edition of this note by D. J. Sheerin, 'John Leland and Milred of Worcester', *Manuscripta* 21 (1977), 179, erroneously gives "lxxxvii" [87] for "senectus"; The manuscript reading "lix" for "iuuentus" is probably a corruption for "xlix", cf. P. Sims-Williams, *Religion and Literature in Western England. 600–800* (Cambridge, 1990), 336, n. 33.

[114] See p. 35, n. 87 above.

[115] Rome, Vatican City, Biblioteca Apostolica Vaticana, Reg. lat. 204 (s. xi in., Canterbury, St Augustine's), 24v; cf. Sims-Williams, *Religion and Literature*, 337. For this manuscript, see Ker, no. 389; Gneuss and Lapidge, no. 913.

[116] Bede, *Bedas metrische Vita sancti Cuthberti*, ed. W. Jaager (Leipzig, 1935), 33. Vitellius A. xix and BAV, Reg. lat. 204, form a group with London, British Library, Harley 1117 (s. x/xi, prob. Canterbury CC) and Oxford, Bodleian Library, Bodley 109 (s. x/xi and xi¹, Canterbury, St Augustine's). Harley 1117 and Bodley 109 do not contain this note. For these two manuscripts, see Gneuss and Lapidge, nos. 427, 546. For Harley 1117, see also K. O'Brien O'Keeffe,

A second note on the six ages of man, also heavily reliant on the work of Isidore, is found in London, British Library, Cotton Tiberius C. i, 150r:[117]

> De .vi. Ętatibus hominis. In uno homine prima infantia .vii.+annos tenet. Secunda puericia alios vii annos tenet. Tercia adolescentia xiiii annos tenet. Quarta iuuentus .xxi annos habet. Quinta senectus .xxi. annos. Sexta dicitur senium ultima ętas uel decrepita. quę nullum certum numerum tenet annorum.[118]

> [Concerning the six ages of man. In (the life of) one person, the first, infancy, holds seven years. The second, childhood, holds another seven years. The third, adolescence, holds fourteen years. The fourth, manhood, has twenty-one years. The fifth, old age, twenty-one years. The sixth is called decrepitude, the last age or decrepitness, which holds no certain number of years.]

The names of the ages in this note are similar to the ones used by Isidore in his *Differentiae*, but the age for *senectus*, seventy, is the one used by Isidore in his *Etymologiae*.[119]

Another five manuscripts, dating from the ninth to twelfth centuries, contain a third, more elaborate note on the six ages of man, as part of a cluster of Latin encyclopaedic notes identified by Kees Dekker:[120]

> Prima ætas infantia .vii. annis. Secunda. pueritia . xiiii. tertia adulescentia .xxvii. annis. Quarta iuuentus . xlviii. uel .viiii. annis. Quinta senectus usque ad .lxx. uel .lxxx. annos. ab anno .lxxesimo, uel xxxesimo. Senium id est decrepitus et nimium senex dicitur. Infantia habet unam ebdomadam annorum. id est vii. annos pueritia alios .vii. adulescentia duas ebdomadas. id est anni .xxviii. Iuuentus iii. ebdomadas. id sunt anni .xlviiii. Senectus .iiii. ebdomadas. id sunt. anni . lxxvii. ebdomadas .xi. Senium nullo certo annorum numero finitur.[121]

Manuscripts Containing The Anglo-Saxon Chronicle, Works by Bede, and Other Texts (Tempe, 2003), 19–24.

[117] For this manuscript, see p. 30, n. 67 above.

[118] Tiberius C. i, 150r. I am indebted to Kees Dekker (Rijksuniversiteit Groningen) for sharing his transcription of this note with me.

[119] See pp. 35–6, ns. 87, 88 above.

[120] K. Dekker, 'Anglo-Saxon Encyclopaedic Notes: Tradition and Function', in *Foundations of Learning: The Transfer of Encyclopaedic Knowledge in the Early Middle Ages*, ed. R. H. Bremmer Jr and K. Dekker (Paris, 2007), 279–315. The manuscripts which include the note on the ages of man are: CCCC 183 (934x939, S England); CCCC 320 (s. x^2 or x ex., Canterbury, St Augustine's); London, British Library, Cotton Vespasian B. vi (805x814, Mercia); London, British Library, Royal 2 B. v (additions, s. x ex–xi[1], xi in., xi med. or xi[2]; the 'Royal Psalter'); Paris, Bibliothèque nationale de France, lat. 2825 (s. ix/x, NE France, prov. England s. x med.). Vespasian B. vi features this particular note, but does not contain the entire cluster of encyclopaedic notes. See Dekker, 'Anglo-Saxon Encyclopaedic Notes', 302. For these manuscripts, see Gneuss and Lapidge, nos. 56, 90, 385, 451, 882.

[121] Dekker, 'Anglo-Saxon Encyclopaedic Notes', 283, 314.

Definitions of Old Age

[The first age, infancy, (lasts to) seven years. The second, childhood, (to) fourteen years. The third, adolescence, (to) twenty-seven years. The fourth, youth, (to) forty-eight or -nine years. The fifth, old age, to seventy or eighty years. From the seventieth or eightieth year, senility, which is decrepit, and is said to be old age beyond measure. Infancy has one hebdomad of years – this is seven years – childhood another seven. Adolescence has two hebdomads – this is twenty-eight years. Youth has three hebdomads – these are forty-nine years. Old age has four hebdomads – these are seventy-seven years (or) eleven hebdomads. Senility is not ended by any certain number of years.]

Dekker suggests that Isidore of Seville's *Differentiae* is the probable source for this note.[122] I would argue, however, that this note is most probably a conflation of the various theories regarding the age limits of the six ages of man, since it combines the cut-off points for each age in Isidore's *Differentiae* (7, 14, 28, 49, 77) with those in Isidore's *Etymologiae* (7, 14, 28, 50, 70), those found in the work of Alcuin (7, 14, 27, 50, 70) and Ps. 89:10 (70 or 80 for *senectus*). In addition, this note adds forty-eight for *iuuentus*, a number which would later also be used by Byrhtferth. As such, this note appears to be a conglomeration of the various, competing divisions of the six ages of man that were available to an Anglo-Saxon scholar in the late Anglo-Saxon period.

Thus, the sixfold division of the human life cycle was known to a number of Anglo-Saxon scholars through the works of Augustine and Isidore. Whereas the theories of the three and four ages of man were on occasion adapted to the needs of the Anglo-Saxon writers and artists, the Anglo-Saxon texts dealing with the six ages of man are mostly copied, often verbatim, from well-known sources. All attestations listed above feature a subdivided old age, but there is no clear distinction into an active and healthy 'young' old age and an 'old' old age marked by decline, as proposed by Cochelin.[123] In fact, for Alcuin, at least, the penultimate stage of life was already characterised by "declinatio" [decline], rather than prolonged health and activity.

On balance, when it came to the human life cycle, Anglo-Saxon artists appear to have preferred a threefold division, whereas Anglo-Saxon writers, depending on their sources and the framework within which they wrote, worked with three, four, five or six phases. Although the theory of the seven ages of man was to become the most popular division of the life cycle from the twelfth century onwards, no Anglo-Saxon evidence of this particular scheme can be found. This absence of a sevenfold scheme of life confirms Burrow's statement that "[t]here

---

[122] Dekker, 'Anglo-Saxon Encyclopaedic Notes', 288–9.
[123] Cf. Cochelin, 'Introduction: Pre-Thirteenth-Century Definitions', 14.

is, so far as I know, no trace of the famous Seven Ages of Man in any pre-Conquest English writer".[124]

The threshold of old age

One of the most common misconceptions about old age in the past is that people were considered old around their forties.[125] This idea certainly does not hold true for the later Middle Ages: Shahar has convincingly shown that old age was commonly believed to start at sixty.[126] The Anglo-Saxons, however, appear to have favoured fifty years of age as the onset of old age.

Among the various divisions of human life discussed above, six Anglo-Saxon texts mention the ages of onset and end of the various stages of life. Table 2 lists and compares each of the age limits proposed by these texts.[127]

While these age limits undoubtedly belong to the world of monastic learning,[128] there are some indications that they may nonetheless have played a role in the daily life of Anglo-Saxons. The age limit of *infantia*, seven years of age, for example, certainly appears to have held some significance. According to Bede himself, he entered the monastery at Monkwearmouth at the age of seven.[129] Stephen of Ripon, in his *vita* of Wilfrid (c.634–709/10), bishop of Hexham, describes how Wilfrid asked a woman to bring her child, who had been miraculously resurrected, to his monastery at the age of seven, so that it could start its life as an oblate.[130] Wilfrid himself, according

---

[124] Burrow, *Ages of Man*, 39. H. C. Covey, 'Old Age Portrayed by the Ages-of-Life Models from the Middle Ages to the 16th Century', *The Gerontologist* 29 (1989), 697, mentions Alcuin as one of the proponents of the seven ages of man, but he provides no evidence, nor have I been able to find a reference to the seven ages in Alcuin's work. Cf. H. C. Covey, *Images of Older People in Western Art and Society* (New York, 1991), 34.

[125] Shahar, 'Who Were Old in the Middle Ages?', *Social History of Medicine* 6 (1993), 313, n. 1.

[126] Shahar, 'Old Age in the High and Late Middle Ages', 43–63.

[127] Bede did not add age limits to his discussion of the ages of man in his *De temporum ratione*, yet there is an indication that he was familiar with the age limit for *infantia* proposed by Isidore. Bede, *Vita s. Cuthberti*, ed. and trans. B. Colgrave, *Two Lives of Saint Cuthbert* (Cambridge, 1985), ch. 1: "Siquidem usque ad octauum aetatis annum qui post infantiam puericiae primus est, solis paruulorum ludis et lasciuiae mentem dare nouerat..." [For up to the eighth year of his age, which is the end of infancy and the beginning of boyhood, he could devote his mind to nothing but the games and wantonness of children].

[128] The recurrence of periods of seven years also suggests the influence of the classical theory of the hebdomads, for which see Horstmanshoff, 'De drempel van de ouderdom', 316.

[129] Bede, *HE*, V.24.

[130] Stephen of Ripon, *The Life of Bishop Wilfrid*, ed. and trans. B. Colgrave (Cambridge, 1927), ch. 18. On child oblation in general and this case in particular, see M. de

Table 2. Age limits in Anglo-Saxon texts

	Byrhtferth, Diagram	Collectanea Pseudo-Bedae	Alcuin, Disputatio	Note in Vitellius A. xix	Note in Tiberius C. i	Note in Vespasian B. vi
Divisions of human life (age in years)	pueritia (14)	infantia (7)	infantia (7)	infantia (7)	infantia (7)	infantia (7)
	adolescentia (28)	pueritia (14)	pueritia (14)	pueritia (14)	pueritia (14)	pueritia (14)
	iuuentus (48)	adolescentia (28)	adolescentia (27)	adolescentia (28)	adolescentia (28)	adolescentia (27/28)
	senectus (70/80)	iuuentus (49)	iuuentus (50)	iuuentus (49)	iuuentus (49)	iuuentus (48/49)
		senectus (77)	senectus (70)	senectus (77)	senectus (70)	senectus (70/77/80)
		senium (–)	senium (–)	senium (–)	senium (–)	senium (–)

to the same *vita*, had chosen to live as a monk at the age of fourteen, the age limit of *pueritia*, marking his entry into adult life.[131] While it is possible that Stephen of Ripon based the details of these, possibly fictional, episodes of his *vita* on the life cycle definitions mentioned above, these age limits for *infantia* and *pueritia* are also attested in other medieval traditions.[132]

Various Anglo-Saxon commentators on the life cycle placed the onset of old age at forty-eight, forty-nine or fifty years of age. Today, the last threshold is often associated with John 8:57 ("The Jews therefore said to him: You are not yet fifty years old. And have you seen Abraham?"). This text may have played a role for the Anglo-Saxons as well, although neither Bede, Alcuin nor Ælfric touches on the issue in his commentary on this biblical passage.[133] Gregory the Great, in his *Dialogi*, mentions the threshold of fifty years of age in relation to the law of the Levites, which ascribed those aged over fifty the task of instructing their brothers (Numbers 8:24–8).[134] Gregory's commentary, here in Wærferth's Old English translation, runs as follows:

> 'Be þon wæs þurh Moyses beboden, þæt þa diaconas sceoldon þegnian fram fif 7 twentigum wintra 7 ofer þæt, 7 þonne of þam fiftigoðan gære hi mihton beon hyrdas þara fata 7 madma þæs temples.'
>
> Petrus cwæð: 'Nu me betwyh læteð hwæthugu 7gytes þyssere forðlæddan cyðnysse. Ac þonne hwæþre ic bidde, þæt me þis geredelicor sy gerihted.'
>
> Gregorius him 7swarode: 'Cuþ þæt is, Petrus, þæt in geogoðhade þæs lichaman costung wealleþ, 7 þonne fram þam fiftigoðan geare colað seo hæte þæs lichaman. Witodlice þa halgan fatu syndon geleaffulra manna mod. Forþon þa gecorenan, þonne hi beoþ þa gyt in costunge heora lichaman, heom is neodþearf, þæt hi syn underþeodde 7 þeowian oðrum mannum 7 syn mid þegnungum 7 gewinnum geswencte. 7 þonne æfter þæt on þære smyltan ylde þæs modes, þonne seo hæte þære costunge onweg gewiteð, hi beoð þara fata hyrdas, forþon hi beoþ sawla lareowas.'[135]

Jong, *In Samuel's Image: Child Oblation in the Early Medieval West* (Leiden, 1996), 197.

[131] Stephen of Ripon, *Life of Wilfrid*, ed. and trans. Colgrave, ch. 2: "Postremo tamen quarto decimo anno in corde suo cogitabat paterna rura deserere, iura celestia quaerere" [At last, however, when fourteen years of age, he meditated in his heart leaving his father's fields to seek the Kingdom of Heaven].

[132] Cochelin, 'Introduction: Pre-Thirteenth-Century Definitions', 11–12. An example from fiction is Beowulf, who was entrusted to the court of King Hrethel when he was seven years old. *Beowulf*, lines 2428–30.

[133] Bede, *In s. Joannis evangelium expositio*, ch. 8. PL 92, col. 756b; Alcuin, *Commentaria in s. Joannis evangelium*, ch. 23. PL 100, col. 876. Ælfric discusses the passage in his homily for the fifth Sunday in Lent; *ÆCHom II*, hom. 13.

[134] Gregory, *Dialogues*, ed. A. de Vogüé (Paris, 1978–80), II.ii.3–4.

[135] *Bischof Wærferths von Worcester Übersetzung der Dialoge Gregors des Grossen über das Leben und die Wundertaten italienischer Väter und über die Unsterblichkeit der*

Definitions of Old Age

['Therefore, it was also commanded by Moses, that the Levites should serve from twenty-five winters and beyond and then, from their fiftieth year, they should be keepers of the vessels and of the treasures of the temple.'

Peter said: 'Now this allows me something of an understanding of this testimony that was brought forth. But then, still, I ask that it be explained to me more fully.'

Gregory answered: 'It is known, Peter, that the temptation of the body is hot in youth and then, from the fiftieth year, the heat of the body cools. Truly, the holy vessels are the souls of the faithful people. Therefore, for the chosen ones, when they are then still in the heat of their body, for them it is necessary, that they are subordinated and serve other men and are burdened with services and labours and then after that, in the calm old age of their mind, when the heat of temptation has gone away, they will be the keepers of vessels, because they will be teachers of souls.']

The idea, expressed by Gregory, that old age is characterised by the exhaustion of natural heat ultimately goes back to Aristotle.[136]

Fifty years of age also features as the threshold of old age in a medical text on the 'half-dead disease', which may have been part of Bald's *Leechbook*.[137] The half-dead disease is described as an affliction which involved the paralysis of one half of the entire body and has been identified as hemiplegia. According to the Anglo-Saxon text, hemiplegia only afflicted people over fifty (or forty) and should not be confused with a similar disease that could come upon people in their youth:

> Soðlice seo adl cymð on monnan æfter feowertigum oððe fiftigum wintra. Gif he bið cealdre gecyndo þonne cymð æfter feowertigum, elcor cymð æfter fiftigum wintra his gærgetales. Gif hit gingran men gelimpe þonne bið þæt eaðlæcnere 7 ne bið seo ylce adl þeah þe ungleawe læcas wenan þæt þæt seo ylce healfdeade adl si. Hu gelic adl on man becume on geogoðe on sumum lime swa swa seo healfdeade adl on yldo deð? Ne bið hit seo healfdeade adl ac hwilc æthwega yfel wæte bið gegoten on þæt lim þe hit on gesit ac bið eaðlæcnere ac seo soðe healfdeade adl cymð æfter fiftigum wintra.[138]

[Truly, this disease comes on a man after forty or fifty winters. If he is of a cold nature, then it comes after forty winters, otherwise, it comes after fifty winters of his life. If it should happen to a younger man, then it is easier to cure and it is not the same disease, even though ignorant

---

Seelen, ed. H. Hecht (Leipzig, 1900–7; rpt. Darmstadt, 1965), p. 102, lines 10–32, p. 103, lines 1–5.

[136] M. D. Grmek, *On Ageing and Old Age: Basic Problems and Historic Aspects of Gerontology and Geriatrics* (The Hague, 1958), 64–5. See also R. B. Onians, *The Origins of European Thought: About the Body, the Mind, the Soul, the World, Time and Fate* (Cambridge, 1951), 214–15, 219–21.

[137] M. L. Cameron, *Anglo-Saxon Medicine* (Cambridge, 1993), 16, n. 27.

[138] *Leechdoms, Wortcunning and Starcraft of Early England*, ed. T. O. Cockayne (London, 1864–6), II, 284–5. I have added capitalisation and punctuation.

physicians think that it is the same half-dead disease. How can a similar disease come on a man in youth in some limb, just as the half-dead disease does in old age? It is not the half-dead disease, but some kind of evil fluid poured on the limb, on which it remains, but it is easier of cure; and the true half-dead disease comes after fifty winters.]

The idea expressed in this text that fifty years signalled the onset of old age was taken from a Latin source, the *Pratica Petrocelli Salernitani* by Petrocellus.[139] The link between loss of heat and old age underlies the notion that people with a cold constitution would be affected sooner by this old person's disease.

A period of fifty years was also associated with old age in a more literary context, as examples from *Beowulf* and *Solomon and Saturn II* suggest. In *Beowulf*, Grendel's mother, Hrothgar and Beowulf are all said to have ruled their respective realms for fifty years.[140] Given the roundness of the number and its recurring use in the poem, 'fifty years' here is likely to be a symbolic marker of old age or simply 'a long period' of time, rather than a specific number of years.[141] Similarly, in the Old English poem *Solomon and Saturn II*, Saturn, a man bearing the name of the pagan god typically associated with old age,[142] complains to Solomon how a certain curiosity had vexed him for "L wintra" [fifty years].[143] Solomon explains Saturn's curiosity as being the murderous bird called "Vasa mortis", an answer that leaves Saturn's statement that he had been troubled by this bird for fifty years unexplained. Possibly, the reference to Saturn's fifty years foreshadows the following question that is dealt with in the poem: the riddle of old age.[144] As such, the period of fifty years is linked once again to old age.

In summary, various Anglo-Saxon texts, although mostly taking their cue from older, classical sources, placed the beginning of old age around the age of fifty. Whether these texts reflect social reality in any way is hard to establish, if not impossible.[145] While in Visigothic

---

[139] Cameron, *Anglo-Saxon Medicine*, 16; it is unknown when Petrocellus lived and wrote.
[140] *Beowulf*, lines 1498, 1769, 2209–10, 2732–3.
[141] Michael Swanton notes that the phrase 'fifty years' is sometimes used in *The Anglo-Saxon Chronicle* to mean a 'long time'. In annal 963 of manuscript E, for instance, one Ælfsige is said to have been abbot of Peterborough monastery for 'fifty years', even though he ruled from 1006/7 to 1042. *The Anglo-Saxon Chronicles*, ed. and trans. M. Swanton, rev. ed. (London, 2000), 24, 117.
[142] See H. Peters, 'Jupiter and Saturn: Medieval Ideals of "Elde"', in *Old Age in the Middle Ages*, ed. Classen, 375–91.
[143] *Solomon and Saturn II*, ed. and trans. D. Anlezark, *The Old English Dialogues of Solomon and Saturn* (Cambridge, 2009), line 70.
[144] Discussed in detail in chapter 3 below.
[145] Elaine Treharne's translation of the Old English *Life of St Nicholas* appears to provide a fifty-year old Anglo-Saxon who felt obliged to ask his readers not to judge him too harshly on account of his old age: "Eac, ic bidde eadmodlice

Definitions of Old Age

laws the age of fifty marked a category of elderly men for whom the wergild was lower than for men from other age categories,[146] no such age threshold is found in Anglo-Saxon law codes.

Conclusion

Table 3 summarises all the information discussed above schematically, following the example of the table in the overview of early medieval life cycle definitions by Cochelin.[147] The first column provides information about the text or artwork and the three following columns with bold outline represent the three main phases of an early medieval life cycle definition as posited by Cochelin: *pueritia*, *iuuentus* and *senectus*. Whenever an author subdivided any of these three main phases this is indicated by dividing the cell in that particular column.

On the whole, then, the 'universal' life cycle definition that Cochelin posited for the sixth century up until 1120 holds true: the life cycle was typically conceptualised as consisting of three main phases (*pueritia*, *iuuentus* and *senectus*), which could each be subdivided.[148] However, Cochelin's notion that an early medieval life cycle definition typically featured a "subdivided old age" does not hold up to scrutiny. In the majority of cases, Anglo-Saxon writers and artists preferred triadic and tetradic schemes of the life cycle, in which old age was presented as a single, long phase. Furthermore, whenever an author distinguished between two stages of old age, the first stage was never described as a 'green' old age without any deficiency. Rather, whether consisting of one or two stages, old age as a whole was identified as a period of physical decline, which set in around the age of fifty.

---

ealle þa wise rædderes þe to þissere rædinge ganggað, þæt heo me ne fordeman gif heom þær on aht mislicige, ac gemiltsigan hi, ic bidde, minre elde 7 minre gecynde. Gemunan heo eac hu ic eom nu fiftene gear on elde, tydderlic of gecynde" [Also I pray humbly to all the wise readers who come to this reading, that they may not prejudge me if anything seems amiss to them: but that they forgive me, I pray, because of my old age and my nature. They should remember moreover that I am now fifty years old and feeble of nature]. *Old English Life of St Nicholas with the Old English Life of St Giles*, ed. and trans. E. M. Treharne (Leeds, 1997), 83, lines 22–7; 101 (translation). However, Treharne's translation is problematic: "fiftene" should be translated as 'fifteen' and "tydderlic" is more likely to have meant 'tender'. We are rather dealing, therefore, with a youthful scribe, who apologises on account of his youth, rather than his old age. Semper, 'Byð se ealda man', 311, altered the Old English quotation to read "fiftig geare", in order to match Treharne's translation; the manuscript, CCCC 303 (s. xii), p. 172, however, clearly reads "fiftene geare".

[146] D. Herlihy, *Women, Family and Society in Medieval Europe: Historical Essays, 1978–1991* (Providence, 1995), 222–3.
[147] Cochelin, 'Introduction: Pre-Thirteenth-Century Definitions', 3–5.
[148] Cochelin, 'Introduction: Pre-Thirteenth-Century Definitions', 11.

Table 3. Definitions of the life cycle found in Anglo-Saxon England

Sources	*pueritia*	*iuuentus*		*senectus*
		Main phases (Cochelin)		
Bede, *In Lucam evangelium espocitio*	pueritia	adolescentia		senectus
Three Magi on Franks Casket	<youth>	<middle age>		<old age>
Three Magi in exemplar of Antwerp *Sedulius*	<youth>	<middle age>		<old age>
Confessional prayer, Book of Cerne	puerilis aetas	iuuentus		senectus
Collectanea Pseudo-Bedae	iuuenis	<middle age>		senex
Ælfric, ed. Assmann, hom. 4	cildhad	weaxende cnihthad		forwered yld
Ælfric, Pope, hom. 11	cild	geonge menn		ealdan
Wulfstan, *De temporibus Antichristi*	cild	medemre ylde mann		eald geðungen mann
Blickling Homily XIV	iugoþ	midfyrhtnes		yldo
Three Patriarchs in Harley Psalter	<youth>	<middle age>		<old age>
Three Magi in Bury St Edmunds Psalter	<youth>	<middle age>		<old age>
Three Magi on whale-bone carving	<youth>	<middle age>		<old age>
Bede, *De temporum ratione*	infantes	adolescentes	transgressores	senes
OE confessional prayer in Cotton Vespasian D. xx	cildhad	geogoð	strengð	yld
Byrhtferth, *Enchiridion*	pueritia	adolescentia	iuuentus	senectus
Byrhtferth, Diagram	pueritia / infantia	adolescentia	iuuentus	senectus
Byrhtferth, *Vita s. Ecgwini*	pueritia	adolescentia	iuuentus	senectus

	infantia	pueritia	adolescentia	iuuentus		senectus	
Willibald, *Vita Bonifatii*		cildhad	cnihthad	geðungen wæstm		yld	forwerod ealdnyss
Ælfric, ÆCHom II, hom. 5	infantia	pueritia	adolescentia	iuuenilis aetas		senectus	aetas decrepita
Bede, *De temporum ratione*	infantia	pueritia	adolescentia	iuuenilis aetas		senectus	aetas decrepita
Bede, *De temporibus*	infantia	pueritia	adolescentia	iuuentus		senectus	senium/decrepitas
Collectanea Pseudo-Bedae	infantia	pueritia	adolescentia	iuuentus		grauitas	senectus
Alcuin, *Disputatio puerorum*	infantia	pueritia	adolescentia	iuuentus		grauitas	senectus
Alcuin, *Commentarii in s. Joannis evangelium*	infantia	pueritia	adolescentia	iuuentus		senectus	senium
Encyclopaedic note in Vitellius A. xix and BAV, Reg. lat. 204	infantia	pueritia	adolescentia	iuuentus		senectus	senium
Encyclopaedic note in Tiberius C. i	infantia	pueritia	adolescentia	iuuentus		senectus	senium/decrepitas
Encyclopaedic note in CCCC 183, CCCC 320, Vespasian B. vi, Royal 2 B. v and BnF, lat. 2825							

2
Merits of Old Age

"Nothing fluctuates more than the contours of old age, that physiological, psychological and social complex", the historian George Minois wrote in his pioneering work *Histoire de la vieillesse: De l'Antiquité à la Renaissance*.[1] Studying the representation of old age across time, Minois posited a dominant image of senescence for each time period and noted that there was a consistent switching back and forth between respect for and ridicule of the elderly. More recent historical approaches have rejected this idea of a periodic pendulum shift between admiration and abhorrence. Instead, they have highlighted the persistence, continuity and durability of a dual image of old age: despised for its loss of physical prowess, but revered for its wisdom and experience.[2] This chapter, on the merits of age, and the next, on its drawbacks, review how various Anglo-Saxon poets and homilists dealt with these two opposing sides to old age.

The representation of old age is culturally defined; in gerontocratic communities, for instance, the elderly will usually be portrayed in a positive light, whereas societies that prefer the qualities of youth over age will generally devalue old age in their literature.[3] Literary texts have long since been studied as vehicles for the cultural construction of old age.[4] Thus, scholars of Modern English literature, such as Richard C. Fallis and Richard Freedman, have noted that old age is rarely depicted as something desirable, reflecting an overarching attitude of 'gerontophobia': the fear of old age.[5] These modern sentiments appear in stark contrast to what Burrow and Crawford proposed with respect

---

[1] Minois, *History of Old Age*, 1.
[2] Janssen, *Grijsaards in zwart-wit*, 14; R. Lazda-Cazers, 'Old Age in Wolfram von Eschenbach's *Parzival* and *Titurel*', in *Old Age in the Middle Ages*, ed. Classen, 201; Brandt, *Wirdt auch silbern mein Haar*, 243–4.
[3] J. Hendricks and C. A. Leedham, 'Making Sense: Interpreting Historical and Cross-Cultural Literature on Aging', in *Perceptions of Aging*, ed. von Dorotka Bagnell and Soper, 6–9.
[4] E.g., J. T. Freeman, *Aging: Its History and Literature* (New York, 1979); *De lastige ouderdom: De senex in de literatuur*, ed. J. H. Croon (Muiderberg, 1981); *Perceptions of Aging*, ed. von Dorotka Bagnell and Soper.
[5] R. C. Fallis, '"Grow Old with Me": Images of Older People in British and American Literature', in *Perceptions of Aging*, ed. von Dorotka Bagnell and Soper, 37; Freedman, 'Sufficiently Decayed: Gerontophobia', 49–61.

to the literary evidence of Anglo-Saxon attitudes towards senectitude. The former argued that the emphasis on the moral and spiritual superiority of the elderly was such that the Anglo-Saxons preferred old age above all other age categories. Burrow related this Anglo-Saxon predilection for agedness to the idea that "in a traditional society such as that of Anglo-Saxon England ... men must have relied more than they do today upon the wisdom of experience".[6] Crawford followed Burrow's lead and also linked the apparent appreciation of the elderly in texts to their position in society:

> According to the majority of the Old English literary evidence, old people were idealised and venerated in Anglo-Saxon society. There is minimal indication within the literary accounts that old people were in any way maltreated, or pushed to the limits of the social framework. According to the literary evidence, the later Anglo-Saxon period was the golden age for the elderly.[7]

In effect, both Burrow and Crawford propose an unambiguous appreciation for old age in Anglo-Saxon writings.

On closer inspection, however, their statements do not entirely hold up to scrutiny. For one, both Burrow and Crawford appear to have neglected the negative aspects of old age that will be the topic of the next chapter. In addition, even the analysis in this present chapter, which takes into account only the potentially positive aspects of old age – respect, spiritual superiority and wisdom –, does not allow an identification of the Anglo-Saxon period as a "golden age for the elderly". Although Anglo-Saxon writers often enumerated the positive qualities of old people, they did not do so without reservation; old age did not by definition result in respect, spiritual superiority and wisdom, nor was growing old always considered wholly desirable.

The literary evidence discussed in this chapter and the next consists primarily of pastoral texts and wisdom poetry. The first text type includes sermons and biblical commentary; these texts reveal how Anglo-Saxon scholars and priests discussed the theme of old age within the context of religious doctrine. While the ideas in these texts are mostly representative of the monastic milieu in which they were created and often took their cue from earlier patristic sources, they also spread, in the forms of homilies and sermons, from the pulpit to the people. As such, these texts provide an insight into the kind of notions with regard to old age that circulated among clerics and churchgoers in early medieval England. Wisdom poetry, the second genre under consideration, aims "primarily neither at narrative nor at

---

[6] Burrow, *Ages of Man*, 109.
[7] Crawford, *'Gomol is snoterost'*, 59.

self-expression, but deal[s] instead with the central concerns of human life – what it is; how it varies; how a man may hope to succeed in it, and after it".[8] Morton W. Bloomfield has noted that the wisdom mediated by this type of poetry is not personal but representative of a broader community:

> The speaker, or speakers in wisdom literature, is the poet speaking as prophet or teacher. He is mediating wisdom and is not speaking primarily of himself. His experiences are to be taken as representative experiences not personal experiences. ... They [wisdom poems] are not self-expression but the communication of inherited wisdom to society at large.[9]

In another publication, Bloomfield claimed that wisdom literature constitutes "the world-view of most traditional societies and the source of its practical morality. It is the framework in which the world is viewed."[10] The contents of wisdom poetry, in this way, may reflect "the core-clichés" of the society in which it was produced; these clichés represent what Anglo-Saxons would take for granted and thus provide an insight into their views on the world around them.[11] As such, both genres considered in this chapter and the next can be used to reconstruct the cultural conceptualisation of the merits and drawbacks of age in early medieval England.

Before providing a detailed analysis of how the literary evidence reveals Anglo-Saxon attitudes towards the potential advantages of age, this chapter first considers the communal roles fulfilled by old people, since their place in society, as Burrow and Crawford have rightly argued, inevitably influenced the attitudes towards them.

---

[8] Shippey, *PoW*, 1. The term covers a large variety of Old English texts, including instructional poems, such as *Precepts*; dialogues, such as *Solomon and Saturn II*; moral reflective poems, such as *The Wanderer*; and collections of proverbial material, such as *Maxims II*. This list can further be extended by adding catalogue poems and parts of longer poems, such as Hrothgar's 'sermon' in *Beowulf* and Cynewulf's epilogue to *Elene*. See also T. A. Shippey, 'The Wanderer and The Seafarer as Wisdom Poetry', in *A Companion to Old English Literature*, ed. H. Aertsen and R. H. Bremmer Jr (Amsterdam, 1994), 145–58; E. Tuttle Hansen, *The Solomon Complex: Reading Wisdom in Old English Poetry* (Toronto, 1988), 5–11; C. Larrington, *A Store of Common Sense: Gnomic Theme and Style in Old Icelandic and Old English Wisdom Poetry* (Oxford, 1993), 1–3.

[9] M. W. Bloomfield, 'Understanding Old English Poetry', *Annuale mediaevale* 9 (1968), 5–25, rpt. in *Essays and Explorations: Studies in Ideas, Language and Literature* (Cambridge, MA, 1970), 59–82, at 78–9.

[10] M. W. Bloomfield and C. W. Dunn, *The Role of the Poet in Early Societies* (Cambridge, 1989), 106. For a similar approach to gnomic material in Old English poetry, see P. Cavill, *Maxims in Old English Poetry* (Cambridge, 1999), 185.

[11] Bloomfield and Dunn, *Role of the Poet*, 24.

Storehouses of knowledge: The communal role of the elderly

"When an old man dies, a library burns down", an African motto holds.[12] Anthropologists have discovered that elderly people function in various tribal societies as 'storehouses of knowledge' concerning matters of history, ritual and identity.[13] A similar role was played in early medieval societies by 'the wise man', who is "the vehicle of wisdom and preserves and disseminates it".[14] There is some evidence to suggest that in Anglo-Saxon England, as in the tribal societies studied by anthropologists, this role was commonly associated with the elderly.

Indeed, older Anglo-Saxons were expected to teach and thus disseminate knowledge. In his canon law collection *Canons of Edgar* (1005–1008), Archbishop Wulfstan (d. 1023), for example, explicitly tasked the older members of communities to educate the young: "we lærað þæt ælc wurðige oðerne, and hyran þa gingran georne heora yldrum, and lufian and læran þa yldran georne heora gingran" [we instruct that each should honour the other, and that the younger should listen to their elders eagerly, and the elders should eagerly teach their youngers].[15] Similarly, Ælfric of Eynsham (c.950–c.1010) wrote in his *Grammar* that it befits the elderly to teach the young, as it is through learning that the faith is kept.[16] The Old English translation of *The Dicts of Cato* likewise encouraged old people to pass on their knowledge: "Ðonne þu eald sie 7 manegra ealdra cwydas 7 lara geaxod hæbbe, gedo hi ðonne ðam giongan to witanne" [When you are old and have heard the sayings and learning of many elders, make them known to the young ones].[17]

This didactic role ascribed to the elderly by these monastic texts was also put into practice: various aged individuals appear in the historical record as teachers. A prime example is Alcuin of York (c.740–804), one of the leading scholars at the court of Charlemagne, who remained a

---

[12] Minois, *History of Old Age*, 9.
[13] J. Sokolovsky, 'Status of Older People: Tribal Societies', in *Encyclopedia of Aging*, ed. D. J. Ekerdt (New York, 2002), 1341–6.
[14] Bloomfield and Dunn, *Role of the Poet*, 110.
[15] Wulfstan, *Canons of Edgar*, ed. R. Fowler, EETS os 266 (London, 1972), 2. Wulfstan wrote similar admonitions in 'De regula canonicorum' and 'Her ongynð be cristendome', Wulfstan, *Homilies*, ed. Bethurum, hom. 10a, lines 43–5, hom. 10c, lines 176–8. Wulfstan's source is ch. 145 of Amalarius' *De regula canonicorum*, Wulfstan, *Canons*, ed. Fowler, 23, n. 2. A similar rule is found in ch. 80 of *The Old English Version of the Enlarged Rule of Chrodegang*, ed. and trans. B. Langefeld (Frankfurt am Main, 2003), 327, lines 29–31.
[16] Ælfric, *Ælfrics Grammatik und Glossar*, ed. J. Zupitza (Berlin, 1880), p. 2, lines 24–5, p. 3, lines 1–2.
[17] R. S. Cox, 'The Old English Dicts of Cato', *Anglia* 90 (1972), 6, no. 9.

teacher until the end of his life.[18] Despite suffering from the physical drawbacks of old age, a fact he often lamented in his correspondence,[19] Alcuin remained a motivated teacher. His unrelenting desire to teach is evinced by one of his letters to Charlemagne:

> I shall not be slow to sow the seeds of wisdom among your servants in these parts, as far as my poor talent allows. ... In the morning, at the height of my powers, I sowed the seed in Britain, now in the evening, when my blood is growing cold, I still am sowing in France, hoping both will grow, by the grace of God.[20]

Like Alcuin, Theodore of Tarsus (602–690) continued to teach in a foreign environment in the evening of his life. Theodore was aged sixty-six when he came to England and established the famous school of Canterbury that he would lead for another twenty-two years.[21] According to Bede's account in his *Historia ecclesiastica*, Theodore had been chosen as archbishop precisely because of his years of experience, being both "probus moribus et aetate uenerandus" [of upright character and of venerable age].[22] Bede himself, who died in his sixties, remained engrossed in teaching even on his deathbed, as recorded by his student Cuthbert:

> ... his breathing became very much worse, and a slight swelling had appeared in his feet; but all the same he taught us the whole of that day, and dictated cheerfully, and among other things said several times: 'Learn your lesson quickly now; for I know not how long I may be with you, nor whether after a short time my Maker may not take me from you.'[23]

Even if there would have been younger tutors as well, the presence and fame of these vigorous elderly scholars may have lent credence to the stereotypical figure of the wise old man that can be traced in Anglo-Saxon wisdom poetry (to be considered below).

---

[18] D. Dales, *Alcuin: His Life and Legacy* (Cambridge, 2012), 127–38.

[19] Alcuin frequently complained of his old age in his letters, see Alcuin, *His Life and Letters*, trans. S. Allott (York, 1974), letter nos. 6, 8, 67, 68, 69, 91, 104, 116, 133.

[20] Alcuin, *Life and Letters*, trans. Allot, letter no. 8.

[21] M. Lapidge, 'The Career of Archbishop Theodore', in *Archbishop Theodore: Commemorative Studies on his Life and Influence*, ed. M. Lapidge (Cambridge, 1995), 26–9.

[22] According to Bede, *HE*, IV.1, the bishopric had first been offered to Hadrian of Canterbury (d. 710), who refused and "ostendere posse se dixit alium, cuius magis ad suscipiendum episcopatum et eruditio conueniret et aetas" [said that he could point to another much better fitted both by age and learning to undertake the office of bishop].

[23] *Cuthbert's Letter on the Death of Bede*, trans. B. Colgrave, in Bede, *The Ecclesiastical History of the English People, The Greater Chronicle, Bede's Letter to Egbert*, ed. J. McClure and R. Collins (Oxford, 1994), 301.

Merits of Old Age

In addition to their role as teachers, old people were also invoked as reliable witnesses in historiographical and hagiographical works. In his preface to his *Historia ecclesiastica*, for instance, Bede explicitly stated that his sources included the testimony of elderly men.[24] Throughout his historical narrative, he assigned particularly wonderful stories to the reports of old and venerable witnesses, such as the "ueracissimus et uenerandae canitiei presbyter" [a priest most truthful and of venerable age] who had heard from Ecgberht's own lips how that saint had been miraculously cured from pestilence through prayer.[25] Similarly, Ælfric's story of the death of King Edmund of East Anglia (d. 869) in the *Passion of St Edmund* ultimately relied on the testimony of an elderly eye-witness, mediated by another aged individual and a third source, Abbo of Fleury (c.945–1004). Abbo had heard the story from Dunstan (909–988) three years before Dunstan's death; Dunstan, in turn, had overheard the tale during a conversation between King Æthelstan (r. 924–939) and an elderly eye-witness, Edmund's own sword-bearer, "þa þa Dunstan iung man wæs, and se swurdbora wæs forealdod man" [when Dunstan was a young man and the sword-bearer was a very old man].[26] The complex origin of Ælfric's account of Edmund's death shows how the report of an event that took place in 869 was preserved over a period of over a hundred years by two elderly men: King Æthelstan's informant at least fifty-five years after the event and Dunstan aged over seventy, who told it to Abbo. As Semper has rightly noted, the old age of these witnesses seems to operate as "an index to their trustworthiness".[27]

In a similar vein, old people were called upon to give testimony in court cases, precisely because of their senectitude and the fact that they remembered things long past. An exemplary case took place in the aftermath of the Norman Conquest, during the Trial of Penenden Heath, a dispute over the restoration of pre-Conquest rights of the Church of Canterbury. King William I (d. 1087), according to one

---

[24] Bede, *HE*, preface, "seniorum traditione" [report of elderly men], translated in the Old English version as "ealdra manna gesægenum", *The Old English Version of Bede's Ecclesiastical History of the English People*, ed. T. A. Miller, EETS os 95, 96, 110 and 111 (London, 1890–8), 2, l. 22.

[25] Bede, *HE*, III.27. Other stories for which Bede used the testimony of senior brothers of his monastery include Bede, *HE*, III.19 and IV.7.

[26] *ÆLS*, no. 32, lines 3–7.

[27] Semper, 'Byð se ealda man', 304. The use of elderly witnesses is by no means unique to the Anglo-Saxons: Gregory the Great similarly credits some of his stories in the *Dialogi* to the testimony of old men. For example, Gregory's remarkable story about Bonifacius, bishop of Ferenti, saving a vegetable garden by praying for all the caterpillars to leave, is ascribed to the testimony of "senex quidam clericus" [a certain old cleric]. Gregory, *Dialogues*, ed. de Vogüé, I.ix.15. For more elderly witnesses, see *ibid.*, I.vii.1, I.ix.16, I.x.16–17, III.xii.2, III.xxi.1, III.xxxii.3.

record of the case, proceeded to gather nobles and elders from all across the land, in order to "diligenter ab antiquis Anglorum juris perquisita veritas" [ascertain carefully from old Englishmen the truth of the law].[28] To this end, William also arranged for the elderly bishop of Chichester to be brought to Penenden Heath: "Egelricus episcopus Cicestrensis, vir antiquissimus legum ac consuetudinum Anglorum eruditus qui regis jussione in quadriga illuc advectus est" [Bishop Æthelric of Chichester (d. 1076), a very old man and learned in the laws and customs of the English who had been fetched there at the king's command in a chariot].[29] Another venerable old cleric to be called to the stand in the 1070s was Abbot Ælfwine of Ramsey (d. 1079/1080). In a dispute between Bishop Herfast of Thetford (d. 1085) and the abbot of Bury St Edmunds over the latter's claim of exemption from episcopal jurisdiction, Ælfwine "tunc pleno dierum, ac sene" [then in the fullness of his days and an old man] provided testimony that went back to the time of King Cnut (d. 1035), over thirty-five years prior.[30] Thus, being called upon to provide their accounts of past events and regulations, these elderly witnesses instantiated the role of 'storehouses of knowledge' as defined by anthropologists.

Aside from authoritative teachers and reliable witnesses, the elderly were also associated with the role of councillor to the king, as part of his *witan*. Kazutomo Karasawa, for example, has noted that the *witan* often consisted "of old men with accumulated experience".[31] The basis for this observation is the use of the term "ieldstan witum" [oldest councillors] in the preface to the laws of King Ine of Wessex (d. ?726) and the portrayal in *Beowulf* of Hrothgar's councillors as elderly men.[32] Although the term "ieldstan" in law codes can also be interpreted as 'chief, most important', the councillors of Hrothgar are undeniably old, described as they are as "blondenfeaxe, gomele ymb godne" [Grey-haired, the old ones around the good one (Hrothgar)] (lines 1594b–1595a) and, in the case of Hrothgar's favourite advisor Æschere, as "frodan fyrnwitan" [old and wise councillor] (line 2123a). Karasawa's evidence can be supplemented by the real-life examples of elderly councillors, such as the above-mentioned Dunstan, Æthelwold, bishop of Winchester (904/909–984), and the noble councillor Oslac (fl. 963–975), who is described in *The Anglo-Saxon Chronicle* as "gamol-

---

[28] *English Lawsuits from William I to Richard I. Volume I: William I to Stephen*, ed. and trans. R. C. van Caenegem (London, 1990), 14. The text is that of a late copy of a late eleventh- or early twelfth-century report.
[29] *English Lawsuits*, ed. Van Caenegem, 14.
[30] *English Lawsuits*, ed. Van Caenegem, 27–8.
[31] K. Karasawa, 'Wise Old *Ceorl(as)* in *Beowulf* and Its Original Meaning', *English Studies* 97 (2016), 233.
[32] Karasawa, 'Wise Old *Ceorl(as)*', 233.

feax hæleð / wis 7 wordsnotor" [a grey-haired warrior, wise and loquacious].³³

The examples listed above show how elderly men could function in Anglo-Saxon society as 'vehicles of wisdom' or 'storehouses of knowledge' as teachers, witnesses and councillors.³⁴ Given the presence of venerable and sagacious individuals such as these, it is of little wonder that Anglo-Saxon writers on the whole wrote respectfully of elderly individuals and praised the old for their spiritual superiority and wisdom, even if they did not do so without at least some restraint.

"Honour the old man and fear your God": Respect and care for the elderly

Thane has noted that, according to popular belief, the 'past' was a time of great respect for the elderly. Because old people would be relatively scarce, they would be "culturally more valued and respected" than their present-day counterparts. This exceptional measure of respect towards the elderly would also have led to families taking good care of their aged relatives. Thane has rightly argued against this legendary time when elderly people were still unequivocally respected, claiming that "it is difficult to find in historical or anthropological studies of any place or time unambiguous respect for old age as such".³⁵ The literary evidence from Anglo-Saxon England supports Thane's claim: although various texts propagated the respect and care due to older individuals, old age did not automatically imply respect, nor were all old people cared for in equal measure.

"Arwurðe ealdne man 7 ondræd þe ðinne God" (Honour the old man and fear your God), the Old English version of the Heptateuch translates Lev. 19:32.³⁶ In a similar vein, several Old English texts demanded respect for the elderly. One of those texts was the translation of the *Theodulfi Capitula*, an instructional work for parish priests compiled by Theodulf, bishop of Orléans (c.760–821) which dictated that a good Christian should not only stay clear of pride and strife, but should also respect old people.³⁷ Similarly, monastic rules

---

³³ *The Death of Edgar*, ed. E. v. K. Dobbie, *The Anglo-Saxon Minor Poems*, ASPR 6 (New York, 1942), lines 26b–27a.
³⁴ Notably, as will be demonstrated in chapter 7, the roles of teacher, authoritative witness and councillor were not reserved for elderly males; old women were no different in this respect.
³⁵ Thane, *Old Age in English History*, 7.
³⁶ *The Old English Version of the Heptateuch*, ed. S. J. Crawford, EETS os 160 (London, 1922), 297.
³⁷ *Theodulfi Capitula in England. Die altenglischen Übersetzungen, zusammen mit dem lateinischen Text*, ed. H. Sauer (Munich, 1978), 331, lines 91–5.

advocated a respectful demeanour towards the elderly. The terms of address prescribed by the Old English translation of the Rule of St Benedict are certainly indicative of polite conduct towards the aged: the young had to call their elders "arwesa" [respected], while the old, in turn, were to call their juniors "leof" [dear].[38] In like manner, the Rule of Chrodegang evinces that priority seats for the elderly have a history that stretches back to the early Middle Ages, when young priests were expected to rise and offer their aged brothers their seat:

> And swa hwær swa ænig preost oðerne gemete, abuge se gingra, and bidde þæs yldran bletsunge. And gif se gingra sitte, and se yldra þær forðgange, arise se gingra, and beode þam yldran þæt setl, and ne geþristlæce he mid him to sittene, buton hine hate se yldra.[39]

> [And wherever a priest may meet another, the younger one shall bow and ask the older one for his blessing. And if the younger one is sitting and the older one passes by, the younger one shall get up and offer the old one his seat, and he shall not dare to sit beside him unless the older one orders him to do so.]

Thus, generally speaking, the old could expect a respectful treatment among the Anglo-Saxon clergy.

Not only were the elderly to be respected, they also needed to be taken care of in their old age. To this effect, Anglo-Saxon homilists appealed to the biblical commandment to honour one's parents.[40] Another biblical text that was used to propagate the care for elderly parents was Tob. 10:4. Here, the parents of Tobias express their regret over sending away their child, since he was supposed to be "lumen oculorum nostrorum baculum senectutis nostrae solacium vitae nostrae spem posteritatis nostrae" [the light of our eyes, the staff of our old age, the comfort of our life, the hope of our posterity]. Alcuin used the phrase "baculus senectutis" [the staff of old age] in a letter to the young prince Ecgfrith of Mercia (d. 796), explicitly admonishing the latter to take care of his elderly parents.[41] The author of the *vita* of St Cuthman also used phrases from Tob. 10:4 in his description of how this eighth-century Anglo-Saxon saint took care of his aged mother. According to the hagiographer, Cuthman became "baculus

---

[38] *Die angelsächsischen Prosabearbeitungen der Benediktinerregel*, ed. A. Schröer (Kassel, 1885), 115, lines 15–19.

[39] *Rule of Chrodegang*, ed. and trans. Langefeld, 175, lines 13–16; cf. *Prosabearbeitungen der Benediktinerregel*, ed. Schröer, 117, lines 1–13.

[40] Exod. 20:12, Deut. 5:16 and Eph. 6:1–3; e.g., ÆCHom II, hom. 19, lines 189–90, hom. 25, l. 89; Bazire and Cross, hom. 7, l. 176; cf. Shahar, *Growing Old*, 88–97.

[41] Alcuin, *Epistolae*, PL 100, col. 215a.

senectutis" [the staff of her old age] and "lumen oculorum" [the light of her eyes].[42]

Care for the elderly was not only the responsibility of the next of kin, however, since monastic rules also advocated the care of the old and sick as one of the prime duties of monasteries.[43] Indeed, even when physically disabled, a monk could reach an advanced age, as the striking example of Eilmer (b. c.985–d. after 1066), monk at Glastonbury, demonstrates. In his youth, Eilmer had been inspired by the tale of Daedalus to fashion himself a pair of wings; he jumped from a tower and broke both his legs, causing him to be lame for the rest of his life. Nevertheless, he grew old enough to remember seeing Halley's comet in 989 when, over 76 years later, the comet flew by again in the spring of 1066.[44] By and large, then, needy elderly could find care among their kinsfolk or at religious institutions.

However, the obligation of care did not extend to all elderly in equal measure, nor did old age per se guarantee a position of respect. The Rule of Chrodegang, for instance, made a notable distinction between ordinary elderly and those elderly who, despite their old age, were able to do some good for their brothers and the monastery:

> And hæbbe gymene seocra manna and mid ylde gehefogodra and þara mæst þe geornlice ymbe mynstres neode wæron þa hwile þe hi for ylde oððe for unhæle mihton.[45]
>
> [And care should be taken of all sick people and of those afflicted by old age, and especially those who diligently worked for the common good of their minster whilst they were able to do so in their old age and sickness.]

In the eyes of this rule, not all elderly were equal and the provisions for them depended, in part, on their actions rather than their old age alone. Likewise, respect did not depend solely on age. In fact, monastic rules repeatedly emphasised that the elderly were not per se superior to the young, referencing the biblical stories of Samuel and Daniel: "forði Samuel and Daniel cildgeonge forealdædum mæssepreostum demdon" [because the infants Samuel and Daniel judged the aged mass priests].[46] As a consequence, the old and young were to be treated

---

[42] *Vita s. Cuthmanni*, ed. Blair, 'Saint Cuthman', ch. 3–5. The source of the text is the *Acta Sanctorum* but the work has been related to the mid-eleventh-century revival of Anglo-Latin hagiography.
[43] E.g., *Rule of Chrodegang*, ed. and trans. Langefeld, 179, lines 26–8.
[44] William of Malmesbury, *Gesta regum Anglorum*, ed. and trans. R. A. B. Mynors, R. M. Thomson, and M. Winterbottom (Oxford, 1998–9), ch. 225.
[45] *Rule of Chrodegang*, ed. and trans. Langefeld, 179, lines 26–8.
[46] *Prosabearbeitungen der Benediktinerregel*, ed. Schröer, p. 12, lines 7–10, p. 13, lines 3–7, p. 114, lines 5–16, p. 115, lines 5–19. On Samuel and Daniel, see Burrow, *Ages of Man*, 96.

on equal terms and the elderly were to be given no privileges. This principle of equality suggests that old age alone was no guarantee for respect. Instead, the degree to which an old person was respected or cared for depended on circumstances other than age, such as reputation, character and ability. Even for the Anglo-Saxon elderly, respect was something to be earned rather than to be expected.

"Venerable old age is not that of long time": The spiritual superiority of the elderly

According to Burrow, the Anglo-Saxons particularly associated old people with spiritual superiority. At the basis of Burrow's claim lies the *puer senex* motif: "a medieval literary motif which telescoped old age and childhood in a single figure".[47] Various Anglo-Saxon authors ascribed to saints in childhood the qualities of old age, such as wisdom, a desire for religious instruction and abstaining from childish pastimes. Burrow argued that the transcendence of these saints from one age category to the other implied a "consistent bias" towards the age categories involved. In his analysis, Anglo-Saxon authors show a clear preference for transcendence in the upward-sort (i.e. the youth with qualities associated with old age), which would indicate that old age was regarded as the 'transcendence ideal' and, consequently, the most highly regarded age of man.[48] While Burrow's analysis of Anglo-Saxon saints' lives in this respect is not wholly accurate,[49] his main conclusion that old age was associated with those spiritual qualities that were typically lacking in youth holds some truth. Nevertheless, Anglo-Saxon writers did not attribute spiritual superiority to all old people alike.

In fact, at least one reference to a *puer senex* posits the virtuous qualities of a young saint against aged men who, apparently, lacked the virtues appropriate to their tally of years. When the young St Oswald was ordained a deacon at Winchester, according to Eadmer of Canterbury, he was selected to be an example for the elderly canons, who were stuck in their wicked ways:

> ... decanus factus, adolescens praeponitur senibus, quatinus canities sensus illius et immaculata uita illius maculatam senum uitam emacularet, ac pueriles sensus illorum studio disciplinae caelestis euacuaret. Sed illi, magis antiqua prauae senectutis itinera tenere uolentes.

---

[47] T. C. Carp, '*Puer senex* in Roman and Medieval Thought', *Latomus* 39 (1980), 736–9.
[48] Burrow, *Ages of Man*, 105–7.
[49] See the full discussion of the *puer senex* motif in chapter 4.

[… and he was made deacon, and though an adolescent, he was placed in charge of men older than himself so that his maturity and his pure life might purify the impure lives of the old men, and he might rid those men of immature thoughts with the study of heavenly teachings. But those men preferred to stick to the well-trodden paths of their corrupt old age.][50]

Oswald's "canities sensus" and "immaculate uita" recall the definition of venerable old age in Wisd. 4:8–9: "senectus enim venerabilis est non diuturna neque numero annorum conputata cani sunt autem sensus hominibus et aetas senectutis vita inmaculata" [For venerable old age is not that of long time, nor counted by the number of years: but the understanding of a man is grey hairs and a spotless life is old age].[51] Put differently, the qualities normally associated with age were not restricted to individuals who had lived a long time; *vice versa*, not all aged individuals were by definition devout people, as illustrated by the aged canons of Winchester.

The observation that not all old people were pious is found in various pastoral texts. One such explicit distinction between those who lived virtuously in old age and those who did not was made by Bede, in his commentary on the phrase *bona senectute* 'in good old age' in Tob. 14:15:

> For he [God] finds such as these in good old age when he rejoices that by his grace they have devoted themselves to good works for so long. By contrast, he sees in a bad old age, and so will pass by, those who though living longer are still childish in their judgement, not to be venerated for the lustre of their good deeds like one is for gray hair, but are doubled up under the weight of their vices. Of such as these Isaiah says "A boy shall die after a hundred years, a sinner of a hundred years shall be cursed" [Isa. 65:20]. Those who have lived childishly for many years and have never sought to put off a spirit of levity will justly be subject to condemnation for their sins.[52]

Bede here referred to the *puer centum annorum* 'child of a hundred years': a figure derived from Isa. 65:20 and the antithesis of the *puer senex*, telescoping the negative qualities of youth into an old man. Ælfric, too, appealed to the *puer centum annorum* noting, in his Homily 'De doctrina apostolica', that old people should not persist in youthful foolishness:

---

[50] Eadmer of Canterbury, *Vita s. Oswaldi*, in *Lives and Miracles of Saints Oda, Dunstan, and Oswald*, ed. and trans. A. J. Turner and B. J. Muir (Oxford, 2006), ch. 5.
[51] Cf. Burrow, *Ages of Man*, 101.
[52] Bede, *A Biblical Miscellany*, trans. W. Trent Foley and A. G. Holder (Liverpool, 1999), 78.

> Eft cwæð sum witega, *Puer centum annorum maledictus erit* : Hundteontigwintre cild byð awyrged. Ðæt is on andgite, Se mann ðe hæfð ylde on gearum, and hæfð cildes þeawas on dysige, þæt se byð awyrged. Ælc treow blewð ær þan þe hit wæstmas bere, and ælc corn bið ærest gærs. Swa eac ælc godes cinnes mann sceal hine sylfne to godnysse awendan, and wisdom lufian, and forlætan idelnysse.⁵³

> [Again, a certain prophet said: *Puer centum annorum maledictus erit*: a hundred-year-old child is cursed. That is in the sense: the man who has old age in years, and has the customs of a child in foolishness, let him be cursed. Every tree blooms before it bears fruit, and every grain is first grass. Likewise every man of good pedigree must turn to goodness and love wisdom and forsake frivolity.]

Ælfric's admonition to show behaviour appropriate to one's age reflects his awareness, along with Bede, that whereas some children rise above the rest of their generation through the display of behaviour generally associated with older individuals, some old people persevere in the follies of youth. In other words, virtuous behaviour was expected of the elderly, but this was by no means a foregone state of affairs.

In fact, some homilists worried about elderly individuals who rejected religious life altogether. Such a *senex sine religione* 'old man without religion' was one of the twelve abuses listed in the seventh-century Hiberno-Latin text *De duodecim abusiuis* [On the twelve abuses], along with, among others, the young man without obedience, the lord without strength and the wise man without good works.⁵⁴ This text was vastly popular and influential in medieval England and its ideas concerning the old man without religion were picked up by Ælfric and at least one other Anglo-Saxon homilist.⁵⁵ The former produced a vernacular version of the text and, for the *senex sine religione*, he followed his Latin source closely, though excluding the original's list of physical symptoms of age:⁵⁶

> Se ealda mann þe byð butan eawfæstnysse byð þam treowe gelic, þe leaf byrð and blostman, and nænne wæstm ne byrð, and byð unwurð his hlaforde. Hwæt byð æfre swa stuntlic swa þæt se ealda nelle his mod to Gode awendan mid goodum ingehyde, þonne his lima him cyðað þæt he ne byð cucu lange? Iungum mannum mæg twynian hwæðer hi moton lybban and se ealda mæg witan gewis him þone dead. Ðam

---

⁵³ Ælfric, *Homilies*, ed. Pope, hom. 19, lines 19–25.
⁵⁴ Ælfric, *Two Ælfric Texts: The Twelve Abuses and The Vices and Virtues*, ed. and trans. M. Clayton (Cambridge, 2013), 34–48.
⁵⁵ For the popularity of *De duodecim abusiuis* in England, see Ælfric, *Two Ælfric Texts*, ed. and trans. Clayton, 52–6.
⁵⁶ On the relation between Ælfric and his Latin source, see Ælfric, *Two Ælfric Texts*, ed. and trans. Clayton, 58. For the list of physical symptoms, which may have inspired other Anglo-Saxon authors, see below pp. 99–104.

Merits of Old Age

ealdan is to warnigenne wið þa yfelan geþohtas, for þan ðe seo heorte ne ealdað, ne eac seo tunge, ac þas twegen dælas deriað oft þam ealdum. Wite forþi se ealda hwæt his ylde gedafenige and þa þing forseo þe his sawle deriað.[57]

[The old man who is without religion is like the tree which bears leaves and blossoms and does not bear any fruit and is worthless to its lord. What is ever so foolish as that the old man should not wish to turn his spirit to God with a good intention, when his limbs show him that he will not be alive for long? It can be a matter of uncertainty for young people whether they may live but the old man can know that death is certain for him. The old man must guard against evil thoughts, because the heart does not grow old or the tongue either, but these two parts often harm the old. Let the old man know therefore what may be appropriate for his old age and let him abandon those things which harm his soul.]

In brief, an old person's irreligious behaviour is all the worse, since they should be aware that death is inevitable. On the verge of the afterlife, the elderly would be foolish not to devote themselves to good works. The warning against "se ealda mann ... butan eawfæstnysse" was issued by Ælfric in two further homiletic tracts.[58] As part of a list of abuses, without further explanation, it was also used by the eleventh-century composer of an Old English Rogationtide homily.[59] The appearance of the *senex sine religione* in these Anglo-Saxon sermons and tracts clearly contradicts Burrow's claim that Anglo-Saxon homilists unequivocally regarded the elderly as spiritually superior. Instead, Ælfric appears to have been worried that some old people, even on the brink of death, had not yet fully committed themselves to the Christian faith.

More specifically, Ælfric expressed his concern over the unrelenting sexual appetite of both elderly women and men, both in his letter to Sigefyrth and his homily for the second Sunday before Lent:

Hit byð swyþe sceandlic, þæt eald wif sceole
ceorles brucan, þonne heo forwerod byð
and teames ætealdod, ungehealtsumlice,
forðan ðe gesceafta ne beoð for nanum oðran þinge astealde
butan for bearnteame anum, swa swa us secgað halige bec.[60]

[It is very shameful that an old woman should have sex with a man, when she is worn out with age and too old for childbearing, unchastely,

---

[57] Ælfric, *Two Ælfric Texts*, ed. and trans. Clayton, 114–15, lines 23–31.
[58] Ælfric, *Two Ælfric Texts*, ed. and trans. Clayton, 156, lines 113–21; *ÆLS*, no. 13, lines 116–20.
[59] Bazire and Cross, hom. 7, lines 171–3. This homily is a compilation of various homiletic texts by Ælfric.
[60] Assmann, hom. 2, lines 157–61.

because sexual relations are not meant for any other thing but procreation only, just as holy books tell us.]

Hit is swiðe ungedafenlic and scandlic þæt forwerode menn and untymende gifta wilnian, ðonne gifta ne sind gesette for nanum ðinge, buton for bearnteame.⁶¹

[It is very improper and shameful that old and unfruitful people should desire marriage, since marriage is not meant for anything but procreation.]

As Semper has correctly noted: "[e]vidently advanced age does not necessarily result in godly living, since such exhortations to change remain necessary".⁶²

The concerns over impious elderly prompted some homilists to extend invitations to old people to convert and repent; others, by contrast, viewed such late acts of reconciliation with some apprehension. The first approach to elderly converts is exemplified by the homilies of Bede and Ælfric on Christ's Parable of the Three Vigils (Luke 12:36–8). The gist of these homilies is that it is never too late to turn to Christ, even for those who have already reached old age.⁶³ In like manner, Wulfstan reassured his audience that "[n]e sceamige ænegum cristenum men for his ylde" [no Christian man should be ashamed of his old age] and that, although it was preferable to be baptised as a child, old people could and should still be baptised.⁶⁴ By contrast, the anonymous author of a Rogationtide homily warned against those who delayed their religious responsibilities until old age. One should not be so bold, this Anglo-Saxon homilist said, following the *Liber exhortationis* of Paulinus of Aquileia (d. 802/804),⁶⁵ as to persist in the

---

⁶¹ *ÆCHom II*, hom. 6, lines 128–31. The exact source for these remarks about abstinence after child-bearing age has not been identified, although Ælfric himself cites Augustine as his source. Godden, *Ælfric's Catholic Homilies: Introduction*, 392. Possibly Ælfric based his ideas on Augustine's *De civitate Dei* XVI.28, where Augustine notes that an old man and an old woman are unable to bring forth children together, but that this would be possible if either partner was young, see Augustine, *The City of God against the Pagans*, ed. and trans. R. W. Dyson (Cambridge, 1998), XVI.28. This passage of Augustine was well known in Anglo-Saxon England. Bede, *On Genesis*, trans. C. B. Kendall (Liverpool, 2008), 294–5, cited it in his commentary on Gen. 18:11, discussing the birth of Isaac, son of the elderly Abraham and Sarah; the same passage is also found in a miscellany from St Gall, dated to c.800, which was probably copied from an Anglo-Saxon exemplar. For the latter, see R. H. Bremmer Jr, 'Leiden, Universiteitsbibliotheek, Vossianus Latinus Q. 69 (Part 2): Schoolbook or Proto-Encyclopaedic Miscellany?', in *Practice in Learning: The Transfer of Encyclopaedic Knowledge in the Early Middle Ages*, ed. R. H. Bremmer Jr and K. Dekker (Paris, 2010), 47.
⁶² Semper, 'Byð se ealda man', 301.
⁶³ For a discussion of these homilies, see chapter 1.
⁶⁴ Wulfstan, *Homilies*, ed. Bethurum, hom. 8c, lines 144–6.
⁶⁵ Bazire and Cross, p. 125.

Merits of Old Age

lusts and sins of youth and only plan to do truthful repentance once old age is reached: "Hwæt mæg beon mare dysignes þonne æni mann þis on his mode geþence?" [What can be a bigger folly than any man who thinks this in his heart?].[66] More damning still was the author of *Instructions for Christians*, a collection of versified instructional sayings. He held that those who turned to God in old age could never truly be good Christians:

> Næfre ic ne gehyrde   þæt wurde laford god
> eft on ylde,   se ðe ær ne was
> Gode oððe monnum   on iugoð þeowa,
> ne huru on ylde   æfre gewurðan
> wel geþeignod,   þonne wolde ær
> on his tale mette   tale wel þeignan.[67]

[I have never heard that he who had not been a servant to God or men in youth became a good lord afterwards in old age, nor indeed shall he ever become well served in old age lest he wished before to serve very well according to his measure.]

In other words, according to some, redemption was beyond reach for those who only desired it in old age.

To sum up, while good, pious behaviour was certainly expected of the elderly, especially given their proximity to death, there is no reason to assume that old people were always held up as religious role models. While Anglo-Saxon homilists certainly praised the spiritually superior elderly and the *puer senex*, they also voiced their concerns over their antitheses: the *senex sine religione* and the *puer centum annorum*. In the end, what mattered was not someone's age, but their religious devotion, as St Brendan reassured the young St Machutus after the latter had expressed doubts as to whether he was worthy of the position of priest, given his youth: "Nelle þu þe tweogean forþon þe seo geonglicu eld nænigum ne deraþ gif he fulfremed biþ on his mode. Ne seo ealdlicu eld nænigum ne frameþ gif he biþ on his mode gewemmed" [Do not doubt since a young age harms no one if he is virtuous in his heart. Nor does old age benefit anyone if he is corrupt in his heart].[68]

---

[66] Bazire and Cross, hom. 10, lines 27–35.
[67] J. L. Rosier, '*Instructions for Christians*: A Poem in Old English', *Anglia* 82 (1964), 15, lines 235–40; 21 (translation).
[68] *The Old English Life of Machutus*, ed. D. Yerkes (Toronto, 1984), 13, lines 8–12.

"Often there is cunning in a sooty bag": The old, wise man in Old English wisdom poetry

Like respect and spiritual superiority, wisdom was by no means the sole prerogative of the elderly. Nevertheless, the connection between senescence and sagacity was such that those who showed sagacity before their years would be called 'old in wisdom'. For example, an Old English note on various Old Testament figures listed Sem, the third son of Noah, as "heora geongost… þeh hwæðere on wisdome yldost" [he was their youngest though the oldest in wisdom].[69] The idea that people could be 'old in wisdom' without being old in years also underlies Ælfric's explanation of the word *eald-wita* 'priest, lit. old-knower' in his letter to Wulfsige: "Presbiter is mæssepreost oððe ealdwita. Na þæt ælc eald sy, ac þæt he eald sy on wisdome" [A presbyter is the priest or the *ealdwita*. Not that each of them is old, but he is 'old' in wisdom].[70] In a similar passage in a letter to Wulfstan, Ælfric claimed that the priests were called *eald-wita* because of "þam wurðscype" [the worthiness, dignity] and "þæm wisdome" [the wisdom] which came with their position, regardless of their actual age in years.[71] The idea of being 'old in wisdom' suggests that, while the elderly may not have had a monopoly when it came to sagacity, old age and wisdom were certainly connected in the Anglo-Saxon cultural record.[72]

---

[69] Found in London, British Library, Cotton Tiberius A. iii (s. xi med., Canterbury Christ Church); Ker, no. 186; Gneuss and Lapidge, no. 363. A. S. Napier, 'Altenglische Kleinigkeiten', *Anglia* 11 (1889), 2–3, lines 53–5.
[70] Ælfric, *Die Hirtenbriefe Ælfrics in altenglischer und lateinischer Fassung*, ed. B. Fehr (Hamburg, 1914), 11, lines 40–1.
[71] Ælfric, *Die Hirtenbriefe*, ed. Fehre, 108–11, lines 109–10. Ælfric follows Isidore's definition of Greek πρεσβύτερος 'elder, priest' in the latter's *Etymologiae*, VI.xii.20: "*Presbyter* grecum nomen est, quod latine senior dicitur, non pro aetate […] sed propter honorem et dignitatem ut sit senex in moribus et sapientia" [*Presbyter* is the name in Greek, which is called elder, *senior* in Latin, not for age but because of honor and dignity as if he is old in customs and wisdom]. Latin quotation provided by *DOE*, s.v. *eald-wita*.
[72] In the poem *Beowulf*, Beowulf, too, is a young man who displays intelligence in spite of his young years, as noted by Hrothgar:

> 'ne hyrde ic snotorlicor
> on swa geongum feore   guman þingian.
> Þu eart mægenes strang   ond on mode frod
> wis wordcwida.' (*Beowulf*, lines 1842b–5a)

['I have not heard a man so young in life speak more wisely. You are strong in might and old and wise in mind, wise in speeches.']

In other words, Beowulf, like a true *puer senex*, shows wisdom beyond his years, proving that young men may be wise and old in their minds. Cf. Burrow, *Ages of Man*, 131–2.

It is of little surprise, then, to find that old people played an important role in Old English wisdom poetry. In fact, one of the recurring clichés in this type of poetry, identified by T. A. Shippey, is the "image of the Ancient Sage, the fiction of an old, wise man talking".[73] That is to say, old men appear in Old English wisdom poems as disseminators of knowledge, as both narrators and teachers, mirroring the social role of old people as 'storehouses of knowledge', as mentioned above.

Various wisdom poems, such as *Vainglory*, *The Riming Poem*, *The Seafarer* and *The Wanderer*,[74] are narrated from the point of view of an elderly narrator. Each of these poems has traditionally been regarded as an 'elegy', a song of lament, but since they all share characteristics with other wisdom poems, such as the lack of a narrative and the use of gnomic generalisations, it has become common practice to treat them as part of that broader group of 'wisdom poetry'.[75] In all four poems, knowledge is imparted to the audience by means of an elderly speaker's monologue. These speakers are typically elevated to positions of authority through references to their lived experiences. In *Vainglory*, to begin with, the poet invokes a "frod wita on fyrn-dagum" [old and wise sage in days gone by].[76] This old, wise man next starts a religious meditation on the difference between the children of God and the children of the devil in poetic form.[77] *The Riming Poem*, too, is a dramatic, reflective monologue by an elderly speaker.[78] Having lived for a long time – "lif wæs min longe leodum in gemonge" [my life was long in the company of people] – the now aged narrator looks back at the successes and delights of his youth, meditating on the transience of life.[79] Two further reflections on the temporal nature of earthly happiness, *The Seafarer* and *The Wanderer*, also feature wise and experienced speakers, advanced in age.[80] The speaker in *The Wanderer*, in particular,

---

[73] Shippey, '*The Wanderer*', 145.
[74] All are found in Exeter, Cathedral Library, 3501 (s. x²; the 'Exeter Book'). Ker, no. 116; Gneuss and Lapidge, no. 257.
[75] Shippey, '*The Wanderer*', 145–58.
[76] *Vainglory*, ed. Shippey, PoW, line 1.
[77] The meditation is based on 1 John 3; J. McKinnell, 'A Farewell to Old English Elegy: The Case of *Vainglory*', *Parergon* 9 (1991), 67. McKinnell identifies the old speaker as Bede, on the basis of the poet's use of Bede's *In Epistolas Septem Catholicas*. However, following conventions of similar poems in the Old English corpus, the poet does not name his speaker but, rather, presents him as a nameless sage, old and wise.
[78] R. P. M. Lehmann, 'The Old English *Riming Poem*: Interpretation, Text and Translation', *JEGP* 69 (1970), 439.
[79] *The Riming Poem*, ed. Klinck, OEE, line 41.
[80] The narrator in *The Seafarer* is not explicitly called 'old', but does seem acutely aware of the emotional and social drawbacks of old age: *The Seafarer*, ed. Klinck, OEE, lines 9–13. Another indication that both poems feature an elderly speaker is the recurrent imagery of winter in these poems: *The Wanderer*, ed. Klinck, OEE, lines 47, 77, 102–5; *The Seafarer*, ed. Klinck, OEE, lines 8–9, 17, 31–3. Winter

is explicitly described as "frod in ferðe" [old and wise in mind] (line 90a) and he himself notes how "ne mæg weorþan wis wer, ær he age / wintra dæl in woruldrice" [a man cannot become wise before he has had a share of winters in the worldly kingdom] (lines 64–65a). Thus, each of the speakers in these sapiental poems possesses the wisdom of experience, allowing them to convey their messages with authority. Although Corey J. Zwikstra has noted that the '*frod* wisdom' shared by each of these speakers is presented as unambiguously positive,[81] it is worth noting that in *The Riming Poem*, *The Seafarer* and *The Wanderer*, at least, the speakers appear to have gained their wisdom through adversity – a notion I will return to in the next chapter.

Furthermore, elderly men are cast in the role of teacher in two Old English instructional poems identified by Elaine Tuttle Hansen.[82] In both poems, an old, wise man is set against a young figure lacking in experience.[83] The first of these poems is the long speech by Hrothgar addressing the young Beowulf in *Beowulf*, lines 1700–84, a section commonly known as Hrothgar's 'sermon'. Tuttle Hansen interprets this passage as a "'set piece' of wisdom literature", which depends on the characteristics of this type of writing.[84] Following the conventions of the other poems discussed so far, Hrothgar's sermon features an admonitory address with gnomic content, delivered by an aged speaker. Hrothgar's advanced age is stressed throughout the poem, as is his wisdom;[85] even in this sermon, Hrothgar three times reminds the young Beowulf that he speaks from lived experience: he introduces himself as "eald eþelweard" [old guardian of the homeland] (line 1702a), notes "ic þis gid be þe awræc wintrum frod" [I recite this tale to you, old and wise in winters] (lines 1722–4) and, finally, declares that he has ruled the Danish kingdom for fifty years.[86] Hrothgar's message to Beowulf, to be wary of pride and that nothing is eternal, is conventional and stated in the manner that also characterises other wisdom poems:

---

is traditionally linked to old age and the imagery, therefore, may symbolise the narrator's advanced age, cf. Bede, *De temporum ratione*, ed. Jones, trans. Wallis, ch. 35; Byrhtferth, *Enchiridion*, ed. and trans. Baker and Lapidge, I.1, lines 117–23.

[81] C. J. Zwikstra, '*Wintrum frod*: *frod* and the Aging Mind in Old English Poetry', *SiP* 108 (2011), 146.

[82] Tuttle Hansen, *Solomon Complex*, 46.

[83] Semper, '*Byð se ealda man*', 298.

[84] E. Tuttle Hansen, 'Hrothgar's "Sermon" in *Beowulf* as Parental Wisdom', *ASE* 10 (1981), 61.

[85] E.g., *Beowulf*, lines 1306, 1307, 1318, 1397; for a further discussion of the *Beowulf* poet's use of epithets for Hrothgar, see chapter 6.

[86] *Beowulf*, line 1769b.

'Bebeorh þe ðone bealonið,   Beowulf leofa,
secg bet[e]sta,   ond þe þæt selre geceos,
ece rædas;   oferhyda ne gym,
mære cempa.   Nu is þines mægnes blæd
ane hwile;   eft sona bið
þæt þec adl oððe ecg   eafoþes getwæfeð
oððe fyres feng,   oððe flodes wylm,
oððe gripe meces,   oððe gares fliht,
oððe atol yldo;   oððe eagena bearhtm
forsiteð ond forsworceð;   semninga bið
þæt ðec, dryhtguma,   dead oferswyðeð.' (lines 1758–68)

['Guard yourself against pernicious enmity, dear Beowulf, best of men, and choose for yourself the better thing, eternal benefits. Do not care for arrogance, famous champion. Now for one moment is the glory of your strength; yet immediately it will be that either sickness or edge will deprive you of strength, or the fangs of fire, or the surging of the flood, or the attack of the sword, or the flight of the spear, or terrible old age; or the brightness of eyes will diminish and grow dark; at last death will overpower you, warrior.']

Hrothgar's reference to "atol yldo" [terrible old age] once more emphasises his own senectitude and reinforces his authority as a 'vehicle of wisdom', much like the aged speakers in *Vainglory*, *The Riming Poem*, *The Seafarer* and *The Wanderer*.

The second instructional poem in Old English to feature an old man as a teacher is *Precepts*, once more found in the Exeter Book.[87] *Precepts* employs as its framing device an elderly father who teaches his son in the form of ten instalments of advice. No fewer than eight times, the poet emphasises that the father is old and that his authority derives from his lived experience: "frod fæder" [old and wise father] (line 1a), "maga cystum eald" [old/experienced in the customs of kinsmen] (2b), "fæder ... frod" [old and wise father] (15b), "frod guma" [old and wise man] (53a), "eald fæder" [old father] (59b), "se gomola" [the old one] (65b), "eald uðwita" [old sage] (66a) and "eald" [the old one] (77).[88] Throughout his teachings, the old man admonishes his son to respect his teachers:

Wes þu þinum yldrum   arfæst symle,
fægerwyrde,   ond þe in ferðe læt
þine lareowas   leofe in mode. (lines 11–13)

[You must always be respectful to your elders, fair-worded, and you must allow your teachers to be in your heart, dear in spirit.]

---

[87] E. Tuttle Hansen, '*Precepts*: An Old English Instruction', *Speculum* 56 (1981), 1–16.
[88] All references to *Precepts*, ed. Shippey, *PoW*.

Similarly, the son is told to choose an advisor who is "spella ond lara ræd-hycgende" [resourceful in stories and learning] (lines 25b–26a) and, finally, to "gemyne / frode fæder lare ond þec a wið firenum geheald" [remember the wise teachings of your father and always keep yourself from sins] (lines 93b–94). Michael D. C. Drout places *Precepts* in a monastic context and suggests that the poem does not depict a generic father/son interaction, but rather an "image of 'spiritual fatherhood'".[89] This proposed monastic context makes sense in the light of the didactic duties assigned to older monks in monastic rules. In fact, one of those rules even made the pseudo-paternal role of elderly monks explicit:

> Þa yldran mid godum bysnum and mid gelomlicre mingunge læron þa gingran, and lufion swa heora bearn, and þa gyngran wurðion þa yldran swilce heora fæderas, and mid ealre glædnysse hyrsumion heora hæsum.[90]

> [The older ones shall teach the younger ones through good examples and frequent admonitions, and love them as if they were their own children, and the younger ones shall honour the older ones as if they were their own fathers, and obey their instructions with complete willingness.]

As such, the old and wise father in *Precepts* may reflect the typical role and status of senior monks in Anglo-Saxon monasteries specifically, although the cultural association between old age and wisdom likely stretched beyond the confines of the monastery.

Illustrative of the widely held link between sagacity and senectitude are two Old English proverbs. A specific branch of wisdom literature, proverbs, according to Paul Cavill, "reflect the world view of the ordinary Anglo-Saxon, they are the common store of everyday knowledge which the Anglo-Saxon would take for granted".[91] The first of these two proverbs that link age to wisdom is part of *Maxims II*, a collection of versified articulations of general truths: "[G]omol snoterost, / fyrngearum frod, se þe ær feala gebideð" [the old man [is] the wisest, old in years gone by, he who has endured many things before].[92] The second proverb that assigns wisdom to the elderly is one of the *Durham Proverbs*, a collection of forty-six Old English proverbs,

---

[89] M. D. C. Drout, 'Possible Instructional Effects of the Exeter Book "Wisdom Poems": A Benedictine Reform Context', in *Form and Content of Instruction in Anglo-Saxon England in the Light of Contemporary Manuscript Evidence: Papers Presented at the International Conference, Udine, 6–8 April 2006*, ed. P. Lendinara, L. Lazzari and M. A. D'Aronco (Turnhout, 2007), 460.

[90] *Rule of Chrodegang*, ed. and trans. Langefeld, 327, lines 29–31.

[91] Cavill, *Maxims in Old English Poetry*, 185.

[92] Found in London, British Library, Cotton Tiberius B. i (s. xi med., Abingdon); Ker, no. 191; Gneuss and Lapidge, no. 370. *Maxims II*, ed. Shippey, *PoW*, lines 10–13.

some metrical, accompanied by Latin versions.[93] Number 7 of this collection reads:

> *Sepe in [u]ile sacculo fulget aurum.*
> Oft on sotigum bylige searowa licgað.[94]

While the Latin proverb can be translated as 'Often gold shines in a cheap purse' and hence expresses the general sense 'do not judge by appearances', the Old English proverb is best translated as 'Often there is cunning in a sooty bag'. The sooty bag, in this case, is someone who sits by the fire all day, hence: an inactive person. Extant Old Norse analogues of this proverb suggest that the sooty bag in question is likely an elderly individual.[95] As such, both proverbs encapsulate the idea that, typically, an old person would be wise. Still, the characterisation of the elderly in *Maxims II* as having endured much and the old person in the *Durham Proverbs* as a sooty bag implies that while they may have increased their knowledge, they had to suffer to attain it and have also grown physically inactive and unsightly. This other side of the coin will be explored in the following chapter.

Overall, it is safe to assume that Anglo-Saxons did, indeed, generally equate old age with wisdom, even if not all wise men were old, nor all old men wise.[96] The elderly certainly appear in Old English wisdom poetry in the stereotypical roles of wise man and teacher; references to their lived experience, accumulated in their long lives, rendered their advice and knowledge authoritative. The connection between senectitude and sagacity was also expressed in proverbs, suggesting that this was not mere poetic fancy but a widely held cultural notion. On the whole, Anglo-Saxons in search of wisdom, it would seem, expected to find it in a sooty bag: an old man by the fire.

Conclusion: Longing for longevity?

Given its general, albeit not wholly unambiguous, associations with respect, spiritual superiority and wisdom, the prospect of growing old may have sounded alluring to some Anglo-Saxons. Indeed, Brihtwold, archbishop of Canterbury (d. 731), wished a long life upon his friend

---

[93] Found in Durham, Cathedral Library, B. III. 32 (s. xi¹–xi med., Canterbury); Ker, no. 107; Gneuss and Lapidge, no. 244.
[94] O. S. Arngart, 'The Durham Proverbs', *Speculum* 56 (1982), no. 7.
[95] For a full discussion of this proverb and an exact precursor of its Latin equivalent in the ninth-century *Collectanea Pseudo-Bedae*, see T. Porck, 'Treasures in a Sooty Bag? A Note on *Durham Proverb 7*', *NQ* ns 62 (2015), 203–6.
[96] For examples of old men lacking wisdom, see the discussion of the *senex sine religione* and the *puer centum annorum* above.

Forthhere, bishop of Sherborne (d. 737): "May Jesus Christ our Lord preserve your Reverence unharmed to an advanced age."[97] St Leoba (d. 782) did something similar when she wished Boniface (672x5?–754) to remain "ever the happier in life as the older in years".[98] In a like manner, longevity was one of the blessings for a new bride in a nuptial benediction in the *Durham Ritual*:

> *sit in ea iugum dilectionis et pacis fidelis et casta nubat in christo imitatrisque sanctorum permaneat feminarum sit amabilis ut rachel uiro sapiens ut rebecca longeua et fidelis ut sarra* sie in ðær iwocc lvfes 7 sibbes gitriwa 7 hygdego gimvngia in criste ðu sie giliced æc halgawara ðerhwvnia vifmonna sie lufsvm svæ rah' vere snottor svæ rebec' longlif' 7 gileaffvll svæ sar'.[99]

[May in it (i.e. matrimony) be the yoke of love and peace, may you, faithful and chaste, marry in Christ and also remain an imitator of holy women, may you be as lovely to your husband as Rachel, as wise as Rebecca, as long-lived and faithful as Sarah.]

Ælfric, too, observed that people longed for longevity. However, he objected strongly against this desire, retorting:

> Gehwær is on urum life. ateorung 7 werignys 7 brosnung þæs lichaman: 7 þeahhwæþere wilnað gehwa þæt he lange lybbe. Hwæt is lange lybban buton lange swincan? Feawum mannum gelimpð on þyssum dagum þæt he gesundful lybbe hundeahtatig geara: 7 swa hwæt swa he ofer þam leofað hit bið him geswinc 7 sarnys. swa swa se witega cwæð: "Yfele sind ure dagas" 7 þæs þe wyrsan þe we hi lufiað.[100]

[Everywhere in our life is faintness and weariness, and decay of the body, and yet every one desires that he might live long. What is to live long but to suffer long? It happens to few men in these days to live over eighty years in health, and whatever he lives beyond that age, it is toil to him and pain, as the prophet said: "Evil are our days" (Eph. 5:6), and the worse that we love them.]

---

[97] *English Historical Documents. Volume 1: c.500–1042*, ed. and trans. D. Whitelock (London, 1955), 731. This letter is dated 709–731.

[98] *English Historical Documents*, ed. Whitelock, 735. This letter is dated soon after 732. In his *Propositiones ad acuendos iuvenes* [Problems to sharpen the young] (c.800), Alcuin has a father wish his son a long life, in a rather cryptic manner: "A son greeted his father: 'Hello father'; to which his father replied: 'Hello son. May you live long, as much as you have lived. If you triple that number of years and add one of my years you will have 100 years.' How old was the boy at that time?" (The answer: sixteen and a half years). Alcuin, *Propositiones ad acuendos iuvenes*, trans. J. Hadley and D. Singmaster, 'Problems to Sharpen the Young', *The Mathematical Gazette* 76 (1992), no. 44.

[99] *Rituale ecclesiae Dunelmensis: The Durham Collectar*, ed. U. L. Lindelöf (Durham, 1927), 109.

[100] *ÆCHom I*, hom. 32, lines 213–19. Ælfric appears to be following Augustine here, see Godden, *Ælfric's Catholic Homilies: Introduction*, 274.

Merits of Old Age

Why do people want to grow old, Ælfric asks, if all they will get in return is toil and pain? Ælfric's remark is hard to reconcile with Burrow's claim that Anglo-Saxons preferred old age above all other age categories and Crawford's notion that the Anglo-Saxon period was 'a golden age for the elderly'. Not only were Anglo-Saxons well aware that the merits of age were not for everyone, they also observed that there were serious downsides to growing old. These disadvantages and their expression in the early medieval English literary record are the topic of the next chapter.

3

Drawbacks of Old Age

One might be eaten by a wolf, die of hunger, perish of thirst, be killed by the hand of an aggressive drunk or fall, featherless, from a tree. The first fifty or so lines of the Exeter Book poem *The Fortunes of Men* consist of a depressing list of the various ways in which a young person might die. From line 58 onwards, the poem takes a more joyous turn:

> Sum sceal on geoguþe   mid godes meahtum
> his earfoðsiþ   ealne forspildan,
> ond *on yldo eft*   eadig weorþan,
> wunian wyndagum   ond welan þicgan,
> maþmas ond meoduful   mægburge on.

These lines have been translated by Shippey as follows:

> Another, through the power of God, will in his youth obliterate all his harsh experience, and then be fortunate *in old age,* living happy days and enjoying prosperity, riches and the mead-cup in the home of his family.[1]

Translated thus, it seems as if the Anglo-Saxon poet posits youth, filled with dangers, against old age, a time characterised by joy and prosperity. S. A. J. Bradley, however, rendered "on yldo eft" in a different way: 'in his maturity',[2] apparently translating "yldo" not as 'old age' but with the more general sense 'age, stage of life' and "eft" as 'afterwards', hence 'in the stage of life afterwards, the next stage', that is: maturity or adulthood, the stage of life after youth.[3] This

---

[1] *The Fortunes of Men*, ed. and trans. Shippey, *PoW*, lines 58–63.
[2] Bradley's translation reads: "One, through God's powers, shall expend all his misfortune during his youth, and in his maturity he shall become prosperous again and live out days of happiness and indulge in his wealth, treasures and the mead-flagon, in his family's midst." *Anglo-Saxon Poetry*, ed. and trans. S. A. J. Bradley (London, 1982), 342–3.
[3] A similar construction occurs in *Beowulf*, lines 20–4: "Swa sceal geong guma gode gewyrcean, / fromum feohgiftum on fæder bearme, / þæt hine *on ylde eft* gewunigen / wilgesiþas, þonne wig cume" [In such a way must a young man with liberality bring about, with splendid costly gifts in his father's lap (during his youth), so that when he comes of age close companions will stand by him, when war comes]. It is worth noting that various translations interpret the phrase "on ylde eft" as meaning something other than 'in old age'. E.g., Beowulf: *A Dual-Language Edition,* ed. and trans. H. D. Chickering Jr (New

alternative translation, which has also been suggested by Sánchez-Martí,[4] is preferable for two reasons. Firstly, the remainder of *The Fortunes of Men* is a list of occupations a man might fulfil as an adult and does not seem to be concerned with life as an old man. Secondly and more importantly in the context of this chapter, there is little to no other literary evidence that Anglo-Saxons expected to celebrate "wyndagum" [days of joy] in their old age. Rather, old age was associated primarily with physical, social and emotional drawbacks that rendered joy impossible.

These downsides of growing old are the central topic of this chapter, which reviews their representation in poems and homilies that circulated in early medieval England. The frequency and potency with which these drawbacks occur in the literary record illustrate that the claim that the Anglo-Saxon period was somehow a 'golden age for the elderly' is one-sided at best. In representations of old age in poetry and homiletic literature, the physical and emotional repercussions take central stage; growing old was associated with loss of physical aptitude, with loneliness and sadness. As a consequence, the old man became a symbol of the transience of worldly pleasures and old age was framed as a prefiguration of the torments of Hell.

"My poor weak body deteriorates": *Anglo-Saxon experiences of old age*

Declining health is part and parcel of the biological process of growing old and the physical ramifications of age were as inescapable for Anglo-Saxons as they are for us. Indeed, bio-archaeological research into the skeletal remains in Anglo-Saxon graves has found that elderly Anglo-Saxons were prone to suffer from multiple diseases, including osteoarthritis, chronic dental diseases and the development of malignant cancer tumours.[5] Medical texts of the time also exemplify that the elderly were susceptible to certain ailments. In the ninth-century *Leechbook* of Bald, for instance, the aged feature as typical sufferers of poor eyesight, indigestion and the "healfdeade adl" [half-dead

---

York, 1977), 49, and *The* Beowulf *Manuscript: Complete Texts and The Fight at Finnsburg*, ed. and trans. R. D. Fulk, DOML 3 (Cambridge, MA, 2010), 87, give "in his later years" and "later in life", respectively; *Beowulf*, ed. and trans. M. Swanton (Manchester, 1978), 35, and Beowulf *and Its Analogues*, ed. and trans. G. N. Garmonsway and J. Simpson (London, 1980), 3, both interpret the phrase as referring to the time when the young man "comes of age", i.e. reaches adulthood.

[4] Sánchez-Martí, 'Age Matters', 223–4.
[5] C. Lee, 'Disease', in *The Oxford Handbook of Anglo-Saxon Archaeology*, ed. H. Hamerow, D. A. Hinton and S. Crawford (Oxford, 2011), 704–23.

disease].⁶ The last ailment is described as an affliction which involved the paralysis of one half of the entire body and mainly affected the elderly: "Gif he bið cealdre gecyndo þonne cymð æfter feowertigum, elcor cymð æfter fiftigum wintra his gærgetales" [If he is of a cold nature, then it (the disease) comes after forty winters, otherwise, it comes after fifty winters of his life].⁷ In their treatments of the correspondences between the four ages and the four bodily humours, Bede and Byrhtferth, too, linked old age to physical ailments, specifically those associated with phlegm. The former noted that the elderly were typically "tardos, somnolentos, obliuiosos" [slow, sleepy and forgetful];⁸ the latter described them as "ceald and snoflig" [cold and rheumy].⁹

As sufferers of bad health, the aged were also exempt from certain regulations or were forced to give up their responsibilities. The Old English Rule of Chrodegang, for example, held that the elderly were to be spared from corporeal punishment; if a brother was too old to be physically chastised, he should be punished instead with public reproof, separation from his fellow priests and continuous fasting.¹⁰ On occasion, the elderly were even excused from fasting, as is demonstrated in a homily by Archbishop Wulfstan (d. 1023). During Lent, he wrote, everyone was required to hold the fast, except those who were unable to do so on account of their youth, ill health or old age.¹¹ On a practical level, aged individuals sometimes saw no other way than to discontinue their occupations. Bede reported in his *Historia abbatum* how the elderly Abbot Ceolfrith of Monkwearmouth-Jarrow (c.642–716) resigned from his abbacy, because he no longer considered himself up to the task:

> uidit se iam senior et plenus dierum non ultra posse subditis, ob impedimentum supremae aetatis, debitam spiritalis exercitii, uel docendo uel uiuendo, praefigere formam.
>
> [Now he (Ceolfrith) saw that, being old and full of days, he could no longer prove to be an appropriate model of spiritual exercise for those under him either by teaching or by example because he was so aged and infirm.]¹²

---

⁶ *Leechdoms*, ed. Cockayne, II, 197, 284.
⁷ *Leechdoms*, ed. Cockayne, II, 284.
⁸ Bede, *De temporum ratione*, ed. Jones, trans. Wallis, ch. 35.
⁹ Byrhtferth, *Enchiridion*, ed. Baker and Lapidge, I.1, lines 131–3.
¹⁰ *Rule of Chrodegang*, ed. and trans. Langefeld, 273, lines 35–43.
¹¹ Napier, hom. 50, p. 284, lines 28–9, p. 285, lines 1–14.
¹² Bede, *Historia abbatum*, ed. and trans. C. W. Grocock and I. N. Wood, *Abbots of Wearmouth and Jarrow* (Oxford, 2013), ch. 16; cf. *Vita Ceolfrithi*, ed. and trans. Grocock and Wood, *Abbots*, ch. 21: 'Namque ubi longo iam senior defessus uidit se ultra non posse exemplum pristini uigoris suis praemonstrare dis-

In the same year, Ceolfrith went on a pilgrimage to Rome, where he died at the age of seventy-four. A reasoning similar to Ceolfrith's can be presumed to have underlain the decision of King Ine of Wessex (d. ?726), who abdicated after a reign of thirty-seven years and left his kingdom to "younger men".[13]

Epigraphical evidence reveals some of the personal struggles of older individuals. Alcuin's correspondence, to cite a striking example, is rife with references to his ill health. While his bodily state did not force him to lay down his responsibilities, he did on occasion use his poor condition as an excuse for his absence from Charlemagne's court, preferring to stay at St Martin's in Tours instead:

> I beg humbly, meekly, devotedly that I may be allowed to say my prayers daily at St Martin's. For being so infirm of body, I cannot travel or do any other work. All my physical powers have lost their strength and will surely grow weaker day by day, nor, I fear, will they return in this world. I hoped and wished in days past to see your Majesty's face once more, but as my poor weak body deteriorates I know well that that is quite impossible. So I implore your infinite goodness that in goodwill and kindness you should not be vexed with my infirmity, but in compassion allow the weary to have rest.[14]

Similarly, the letters of Boniface (672x5?–754) bear witness to the physical decrepitude which this Anglo-Saxon missionary must have experienced in his later years. In one of his letters, he mentions his failing eyesight when he requests a book "in clear letter written in full", being no longer able to read "writing which is small and filled with abbreviations".[15] These specimens of first-hand experiences of age show that growing old could be an arduous road, paved with physical complications.

Another personal account of the ills of old age has come down to us in the form of a Latin prayer with a partial Old English gloss by an anonymous eleventh-century scribe. He added his prayer on a folio and a half that had intentionally been left open by the original scribe of the Lambeth Psalter.[16] The added prayer, written in the first person,

---

cipulis, inuenit utile consilium ut, relicto iuuenioribus regimine monasteriali, ipse apostolorum limina peregrinaturus adiret' [Now when he (Ceolfrith) saw that he could no longer set an example of his vigour of old to his pupils, being already exhausted through extreme old age, he decided that a suitable plan would be to leave the rule of the monastery to younger men, while he himself would set off on a pilgrimage to the abodes of the apostles (Rome)].

[13] Bede, *HE*, V.7. Elderly kings are discussed in chapter 6.
[14] Alcuin, *Life and Letters*, trans. Allott, letter no. 68.
[15] *The Letters of Saint Boniface*, trans. E. Emerton (New York, 1940), letter no. 51.
[16] London, Lambeth Palace Library, 427 (s. xi¹, Winchester?; the 'Lambeth Psalter'); Ker, no. 280; Gneuss and Lapidge, no. 517. The space was left blank between Psalms 108 and 109. P. O'Neill, 'Latin Learning at Winchester in the Early

addresses God and recalls sins committed in youth. The speaker seeks redemption now that he has grown old:

> Iam pertrahit me deuictum senectus ad occasum, floret uertex, hebet uisus, crescit dolor capitis, ruunt dentes, [t]remunt membra, decident tote uires.[17]
>
> [Now old age drags me, subdued, to my end, the crown of my head is blooming (i.e. growing white), my vision is fading, headache is increasing, my teeth are falling out, my limbs are trembling, my powers are completely diminishing.]

Unlike similar lists of symptoms of age found in Anglo-Saxon homilies,[18] this list has no known source and may, therefore, reflect the scribe's own experience.[19] The prayer continues with the speaker's fear of death and his prayers to God to redeem him, slacken the bonds of his sins, heal his wounds and forgive him for his sins. Finally, the speaker begs God not to deliver him unto Satan and ends with a description of Judgement Day. Evidently, this prayer was composed by an old man seeking forgiveness for his sins, afraid of his impending death which was announced by the decrepit state of his aging body.

The examples above illustrate that for many elderly Anglo-Saxons old age manifested itself as a source of physical woe and mental distress. It should come as no surprise, then, that these repercussions of age also feature widely in the literary record. These texts reflect not only what aged Anglo-Saxons actually suffered, but also what drawbacks were typically associated with growing old and how these were interpreted.

Eleventh Century: The Evidence of the Lambeth Psalter', *ASE* 20 (1991), 146, 162, has pointed out that, since Psalm 109 marks the first of a series of psalms intended for the daily use at Vespers in the Roman and Benedictine office, some space was always left open before this psalm, for an illustration or the addition of personal prayers.

[17] M. Förster, 'Die altenglischen Beigaben des Lambeth-Psalters', *Archiv* 132 (1914), 328–9. The partial Old English gloss reads "heafod, deorcaþ gesihð, wecsð sar heafdes, feallaþ teþ, cwaciaþ lima, hreosað ealle" [head, vision darkens, headache grows, teeth fall, limbs tremble, they all decay].

[18] To be discussed below.

[19] C. D. Wright, *The Irish Tradition in Old English Literature* (Cambridge, 1993), 98, n. 209, compares the list in the Lambeth Psalter to the *Vita Tertia* of St Patrick: "oculi non bene uident, aures non bene audiunt, lingua non bene loquitur, dentium numerus imminutus est, similiter et cetera membra" [the eyes do not see well, the ears do not hear well, the tongue does not speak well, the number of teeth is diminishing and the other limbs (fare?) likewise]. The two lists are, however, so divergent that even an indirect link between the two texts is unlikely.

atol yldo: *The terrors of old age and the transience of the world in Anglo-Saxon poetry*

On the whole, Anglo-Saxon poets appear to propagate a bleak image of old age. Typically, growing old was grouped with other negative aspects of life, such as evil, death and darkness, as in the group of versified gnomic statements known as *Maxims II*:

> God sceal wið yfele,   geogoð sceal wið yldo,
> lif sceal wið deaþe,   leoht sceal wið þystrum,
> fyrd wið fyrde,   feond wið oðrum.[20]

> [Good must be against evil, youth against old age, life against death, light against darkness, army against army, one enemy against the other.]

In another set of proverbs, found in the Royal Psalter,[21] aging is similarly linked to processes of degeneration rather than progress:

> *Ardor refriescit,   nitor quualescit;*
> *Amor abolescit,   lux obtenebrescit;*
> hat acolað,   hwit asolað,
> leof alaþað,   leoht aþeostrað.
> *Senescunt omnia   que aeterna non sunt.*
> æghwæt ealdað   þæs þe ece ne byð.[22]

> [What is hot grows cool, what is white becomes dirty, what is dear becomes hateful, what is light becomes dark. Everything which is not eternal grows old.]

Here, old age is framed as a negative outcome, akin to cold, filth, hate and darkness. Both these proverbial treatments of age are exemplary of the underlying negative attitude towards aging in Anglo-Saxon poetry.

In terms of the physical drawbacks of age, poets rarely provided detailed descriptions of old bodies. Rather, without much specification, old age was listed among other causes for physical impairment. A typical example is Hrothgar's 'sermon' in *Beowulf*, cited in the previous chapter, where "atol yldo" [terrible old age] is grouped with disease, fire and attacks by swords or spears.[23] Similarly, old age forms part of a cluster with illness and 'edge-hate' in *The Seafarer*:

---

[20] *Maxims II*, ed. and trans. Shippey, *PoW*, lines 50–2.
[21] London, British Library, Royal 2 B. v (s. xi med.; the 'Royal Psalter'); Ker, no. 249; Gneuss and Lapidge, no. 451.
[22] *Der altenglische Regius-Psalter. Eine Interlinearversion in Hs. Royal 2. B. 5 des brit. Mus.*, ed. F. Roeder (Halle, 1904), xii.
[23] *Beowulf*, line 1766a.

simle þreora sum   þinga gehwylce
ær his tidege   to tweon weorþeð;
adl oþþe yldo   oþþe ecghete
fægum fromweardum   feorh oðþringeð.[24]

[always one of three turns into doubt everything before its due: illness, old age or edge-hate tears away life from the ones fated to die.]

The collocation of *ādl* 'sickness' and *yldo* 'old age' is also found in two other poems. *Maxims I*, for example, notes that God is affected neither by "adl ne yldo" [sickness or old age].[25] Neither do "yldo ne adle" hurt the soul, as is implicated by *Riddle 43* in the Exeter Book.[26] Thus, while the connection with disease was often made, Old English poetry rarely features any explicit description of physical symptoms of old age, apart from the frequent use of the poetic word *hār* 'grey' to denote the hair colour of the elderly.[27]

In fact, poets appear more interested in the social and emotional repercussions of growing old. *The Seafarer*, once again, reminds its audience that old age also involves the loss of friends:

yldo him on fareð,   onsyn blacað,
gomelfeax gnornað,   wat his iuwine,
æþelinga bearn   eorþan forgiefene.[28]

[old age comes upon him, his face grows pale, grey-haired he mourns, he knows that his friends of old, children of earls, have been given to the earth.]

The treatment of old age in the poetic adaptation of *Genesis B*, as one of the consequences of Adam and Eve's choice to eat from the tree of knowledge,[29] likewise focuses on the social implications rather than its physical symptoms: old age is said to rob people of "ellendæda, dreamas and drihtscipes" [valorous deeds, joys and rulership].[30] These emotional and social consequences are also epitomised by a number

---

[24] *The Seafarer*, ed. Klinck, *OEE*, lines 68–71.
[25] *Maxims I*, ed. and trans. Shippey, *PoW*, lines 8–12; cf. *Beowulf*, line 1736a.
[26] *Riddle 43*, ed. G. P. Krapp and E. v. K. Dobbie, *The Exeter Book*, ASPR 3 (New York, 1936), line 4a.
[27] For a discussion of Old English *hār* and its derivatives, see C. P. Biggam, *Grey in Old English: An Interdisciplinary Semantic Study* (London, 1998), 100–271.
[28] *The Seafarer*, ed. Klinck, *OEE*, lines 91–3.
[29] Old age is also named as one of the consequences of Adam and Eve's disobedience in the *Old English Martyrology*, ed. and trans. Rauer, no. 53: "Ac þa hi þæt ne geheoldan, ða underðeoddon hi selfe ond eall ðæt mænnisce cynn to sare ond eldo ond to deaðe" [But when they did not obey it, they then subjected themselves and all of humankind to pain and old age and to death].
[30] *Genesis B*, ed. A. N. Doane, *The Saxon Genesis: An Edition of the West Saxon Genesis B and the Old Saxon Vatican Genesis* (Madison, 1991), lines 484–5.

Drawbacks of Old Age

of grieving, elderly characters in *Beowulf*. Hrothgar, for instance, is described by Beowulf as an old, desolate man, who, 'bound by age', sadly sings of his lost youth:

> 'gomela Scilding,
> felafricgende feorran rehte;
> hwilum hildedeor hearpan wynne,
> gome(n)wudu grette, hwilum gyd awræc
> soð ond sarlic, hwilum syllic spell
> rehte æfter rihte rumheort cyning;
> hwilum eft ongan eldo gebunden,
> gomel guðwiga gioguðe cwiðan,
> hildestrengo; hreðer (in)ne weoll
> þonne he wintrum frod worn gemunde.'[31]

'The old Scylding, the well-informed one, narrated things far back in time; sometimes the brave one greeted the pleasure of the harp, the wood of entertainment, sometimes he recited a song, true and sad, sometimes the great-hearted king narrated a wonderful story according to what is right; sometimes again, the old warrior, bound by old age, began to speak of his youth, his battle-strength; his heart surged inside, when he, old and wise in winters, remembered many things.'

Binding old age, it would seem, has broken the old king both physically and emotionally. Aside from Hrothgar, four other characters in *Beowulf* are described as both old and grieving, either for losses in the past or looming defeats in the future.[32] Thus, old age occurs in poetry not only as a cause for physical inaptitude, it also takes away joy, companionship and social standing.

The physical, as well as emotional and social, drawbacks of senescence also feature in two Latin poems by Alcuin, which have hitherto been ignored in the few studies on old age in Anglo-Saxon England: *De rerum humanarum vicissitudine et clade Lindisfarnensis monasterii* [On the mutability of human affairs and the destruction of the monastery of Lindisfarne] and *O mea cella* [O my cell]. In both poems, Alcuin explicitly linked the effects of old age to the idea of transience of worldly joys. In doing so, he introduced a theme into Anglo-Saxon poetry that can also be traced in the Old English elegiac wisdom poems *The*

---

[31] *Beowulf*, lines 2105b–2114.
[32] The four other characters are the old Heathobard warrior who, "geomor-mod" [sad-minded] (line 2044a), incites his younger colleague to take up arms once again; an old father, "geomorlic" [sad] (2444a) and singing a "sarigne sang" [a sorrowful song] (2447a), who has lost his son to the gallows; the Swedish king Ongentheow, "frod, felageomor" [old and wise and very sad] (2950a); and Beowulf himself, who is described twice with the phrase "gomol on gehðo" [the old man in grief] (2793a, 3095a). For a more detailed consideration of these characters in *Beowulf*, see chapters 5 and 6.

Wanderer, *The Seafarer* and *The Riming Poem*, as well as in the epilogue to *Elene* by Cynewulf: the decline in human old age as an analogue to the deterioration of the world in general.[33]

Alcuin's most extensive poetic treatment of this theme is found in the *De rerum humanarum vicissitudine*, a poem of lament and consolation addressed to the monks of Lindisfarne. The poem is dated shortly after the Viking raid on Lindisfarne in 793, which Alcuin places in the context of other disastrous historical happenings, including the death of Alexander the Great, the fall of Rome and the Islamic conquest of Spain. He next draws an analogy between the passing of empires and the decline in human old age:

> Thus was the order of this world subject to change and so it will be,
> let no one have trust in the permanence of joy.
> He who once hunted in the fields for the stag
> lies in bed, now that weary old age is at hand.
> He who once reclined joyously on his purple couch
> can scarcely cover his chill limbs with an old rag.
> The long day closes in black darkness eyes
> which used to count each solitary wandering mote.
> Hands which once brandished swords and mighty weapons
> now tremble and can barely convey their food to their mouths.
> Voices, clearer than trumpets, suddenly stick in the throat
> summoning up a subdued whisper for attentive listeners.[34]

In these lines, Alcuin paints a pessimistic picture of old age, characterised by a loss of strength and status, as well as sensory impairment. It is worth noting that Alcuin himself experienced the detrimental effects of old age first-hand, as his correspondence reveals,[35] and would have been in his late fifties when he wrote these lines. This particular passage, therefore, may have been inspired by his own familiarity with the decline resulting from age.

Nevertheless, his lament is more than a personal reflection, since he uses this image of old age to make a more general point:

> Let my poem be brief. All youth fades away,
> all physical beauty perishes and falls,
> only the empty skin clings with difficulty to the bones,
> and when a man grows old he does not even recognise his own limbs.

---

[33] This theme is not unique to early medieval England. See, e.g., Shahar, *Growing Old*, 45–7; G. R. Coffman, 'Old Age from Horace to Chaucer. Some Literary Affinities and Adventures of an Idea', *Speculum* 9 (1934), 249–77; S. M. Anderson, 'Old Age', in *A Handbook of Medieval Culture*, ed. A. Classen (Berlin, 2015), 1291–8.

[34] Alcuin, *De rerum humanarum vicissitudine et clade Lindisfarnensis monasterii*, trans. P. Godman, *Poetry of the Carolingian Renaissance* (London, 1985), lines 99–110.

[35] Alcuin, *Life and Letters*, trans. Allott, letter nos. 6, 8, 67, 68, 69, 91, 104, 116, 133.

> What he was, another will be, nor will he continue to be what he is,
> he will act as a thief from himself at different times.
> And so the day to come will change minds and bodies
> and may it mark better progress in good deeds!
> Therefore let us always love instead the things of the higher world,
> and what will remain in heaven rather than what will perish on earth.
> Here time changes and you see nothing that is not mutable;
> there one day will always be what it will be.[36]

In other words, the decline in human old age is similar to what happens to all worldly things. Loss and decline are inevitable in this life and eternity and fixedness can only be found in Heaven.

The notion of declining old age and a subsequent admonition to focus on the permanence of celestial joys is also found in Alcuin's elegiac poem *O mea cella*, which was most likely written after the poem on Lindisfarne, when Alcuin himself would have been in his sixties.[37] In *O mea cella*, Alcuin describes a beautiful place that he can no longer visit as it has deteriorated and has passed into the hands of other people. According to Carole Newlands, the poem is best read as "the lament of an exile, severed from homeland through political calamities".[38] From this personal lament, Alcuin moves into a general observation about the fleeting nature of worldly joys and the inevitable decline of a man in old age:

> All temporal beauty changes in this sudden way,
> all things alter in different fashions.
> Nothing remains eternal, nothing is truly immutable;
> the shadows of night cover the holy day.
> Cold winter suddenly shakes down the beautiful flowers
> and a dreary breeze churns up the peaceful sea.
> In the fields where the holy youths chased the stag
> the old man now leans wearily on his staff.[39]

Alcuin probably based this contrast between the active youth and the decrepit old man on the similar image in the poem about Lindisfarne.[40]

---

[36] Alcuin, *De rerum humanarum vicissitudine*, trans. Godman, lines 111–22.

[37] While P. Godman, 'Alcuin's Poetic Style and the Authenticity of *O mea cella*', *Studi Medievali* 20 (1979), 568–9, relates the poem to Alcuin's departure from Aachen to Tours and argues that Alcuin laments the decline of the palace school in his absence, C. Newlands, 'Alcuin's Poem of Exile: *O mea cella*', *Mediaevalia* 11 (1985), 27, argues that it was written on the occasion of Alcuin's departure from York and his vow never to return, following the murder of Æthelred, king of Northumbria, in April 796.

[38] Alcuin may have based his poem on Vergil's *Eclogue*, a poem similarly concerning political turmoil and exile, see Newlands, 'Alcuin's Poem', 30–3.

[39] Alcuin, *O mea cella*, ed. and trans. Godman, *Poetry of the Carolingian Renaissance*, lines 23–30.

[40] Cf. Alcuin, *De rerum humanarum vicissitudine*, trans. Godman, lines 101–2.

Like the latter poem, *O mea cella* continues with advice to focus on the permanence and eternity offered by God, rather than on the transient beauty of the world:

> Why do we wretches love you, fugitive world?
> You always fly headlong from us.
> May you flee away, and let us always love Christ,
> let love of God always possess our hearts.[41]

The pattern Alcuin established in *O mea cella*, moving from a personal lament to general reflection on worldly transience with a subsequent admonition to seek divine permanence, can also be found in various Old English poems: *The Wanderer*, *The Seafarer*, *The Riming Poem* and the epilogue to Cynewulf's *Elene*.[42]

The influence of Alcuin's poetry on the three Old English elegiac wisdom poems *The Wanderer*, *The Seafarer* and *The Riming Poem* is suggested by a number of shared characteristics. Michael Lapidge and Anne L. Klinck, for instance, both note that all three Old English poems echo the mood of Alcuin's poetry with their personal, reflective tone with respect to the transience of worldly joys.[43] More particularly, all three poems use the device of an aged narrator whose personal lament over the consequences of old age is linked to a more general regret over impermanence.[44] Like Alcuin's narrator in *O mea cella*, the aged persona in *The Wanderer*, first of all, is cut off from his former life, mourns the loss of his friends and now suffers exile in his old age.[45] This reflection on his private losses leads to a more universal treatment of transience, culminating in a series of exclamations starting with "hwær cwom" [where are], the Old English reflex of the well-known *ubi sunt* motif.[46] The monologue in *The Seafarer* also moves from personal to general, when the speaker, after recounting some of his private hardships, remarks: "Ic gelyfe no / þæt him eorðwelan ece stondað" [I do not believe that earthly treasures last

---

[41] Alcuin, *O mea cella*, trans. Godman, lines 31–4.
[42] Newlands, 'Alcuin's Poem', 34, has noted the similarity to *The Wanderer* and *The Seafarer*, tentatively suggesting that 'Alcuin introduced to Anglo-Latin literature the pattern that the Old English lyrics, whether consciously or not, would later follow'. The similarity between Alcuin's poetry and Cynewulf's *Elene* has hitherto gone unmentioned.
[43] Klinck, *OEE*, 232–3.
[44] Cf. G. V. Smithers, 'The Meaning of *The Seafarer* and *The Wanderer*', *Medium Ævum* 28 (1959), 10–11.
[45] M. Lapidge, *Anglo-Latin Literature. Vol. 1: 600–899* (London, 1996), 22; cf. Klinck, *OEE*, 233, who notes that the persona adopted in Alcuin's poem *De rerum humanarum vicissitudine* and the Old English elegies are "quite different"; she does not discuss Alcuin's *O mea cella*.
[46] *The Wanderer*, ed. Klinck, *OEE*, lines 92–3.

Drawbacks of Old Age

forever].[47] Additionally, Alcuin's link between the fall of kingdoms in biblical and classical history and the decline in human old age in his poem on Lindisfarne is echoed by the passage in *The Seafarer* that laments the passing of gold-giving kings, who have been replaced by weaker individuals:

> næron nu cyningas ne caseras
> ne goldgiefan swylce iu wæron,
> þonne hi mæst mid him mærþa gefremedon,
> ond on dryhtlicestum dome lifdon.
> Gedroren is þeos duguð eal; dreamas sind gewitene.
> Wuniað þa wacran ond þas woruld healdaþ,
> brucað þurh bisgo. Blæd is gehnæged;
> eorþan indryhto ealdað ond searað;
> swa nu monna gehwylc geond middangeard:
> yldo him on fareð, onsyn blacað,
> gomelfeax gnornað; wat his iuwine,
> æþelinga bearn eorþan forgiefene.[48]

[There are no kings, emperors and gold-givers as there were before, when they performed the most of glories among themselves and lived in the noblest glory. This entire noble band has fallen; joys have departed. Weaker ones remain and hold the earth, use it with toil. Glory is brought low. The very noble ones of the earth grow old and wither, as now does each person throughout the middle earth. Old age comes on him, his face grows pale, the grey-haired he mourns, knows that his friends of old, children of earls, have been given to the earth.]

Lastly, *The Riming Poem* also begins by relating the personal experience of an aged speaker, looking back at his youth. He, too, has suffered the mutability of pleasure first-hand and describes the difference between the pleasantries of his youth, such as joy and social standing, and their absence in old age in terms of day and night:

> Nu min hreþer is hreoh, heofsiþum sceoh,
> nydbysgum neah. Gewiteð nihtes in fleah
> se ær in dæge was dyre.[49]

[Now my heart is distressed, fearful of unhappy journeys, close to inescapable troubles. That which had been dear during the day, departs in flight during the night.]

As in the other poems, the narrator's experience of aging is subsequently linked to the fate of the world at large: "Swa nu world wendeþ,

---

[47] *The Seafarer*, ed. Klinck, OEE, lines 66b–67.
[48] *The Seafarer*, ed. Klinck, OEE, lines 82–93. Cf. Alcuin, *De rerum humanarum vicissitudine*, ed. and trans. Godman, lines 31–110.
[49] *The Riming Poem*, ed. Klinck, OEE, lines 43–45a.

wyrd sendeþ / ond hetes henteð, hæleþe scyndeð" [Thus now the world turns, sends disastrous events and seizes with hate, puts men to shame].[50] A final characteristic that these three Old English poems share with Alcuin's poetry is that each ends with an enjoinder to focus on the eternal joys, found in Heaven.[51] In sum, there are notable similarities between the three Old English elegiac poems and Alcuin's Latin poetry; precise parallels and a direct influence cannot be established, but the vernacular poets did share with Alcuin the conceit of relating old age to the more general idea of transience.

Another Anglo-Saxon poet who may have been inspired by Alcuin to draw an analogy between the decline in old age and worldly mutability is Cynewulf, author of the Old English poems *Fates of the Apostles*, *Christ II*, *Juliana* and *Elene*. Cynewulf's authorship of these poems is attested by the presence of closing epilogues that spell out his name in runes.[52] While Cynewulf is one of few vernacular poets known by name, his exact identity remains a mystery. Attempts to link the poet Cynewulf to historical figures, such as Cynewulf, bishop of Lindisfarne (d. c.783), Cynulf, priest of Dunwich (fl. 803) and Abbot Cenwulf of Peterborough (d. 1006), cannot be substantiated, since the name Cynewulf was simply very common: the ninth-century Lindisfarne *Liber Vitae* alone lists no fewer than twenty-one people named Cynewulf.[53] The works attributed to the poet Cynewulf are dated between c.750 and the end of the tenth century, though an early tenth-century date is most probable.[54]

Various scholars have suggested that Cynewulf himself may have been of an advanced age when he wrote some of his poetry. Rosemary Woolf, for example, has argued that Cynewulf wrote *Juliana* when he was an old man, because it was a work of "uninspired competence"; similarly, Eduard Sievers and Claes Schaar saw *Fates of the Apostles* as Cynewulf's latest poem, considering it "the work of an aged poet, still competent but uninspired".[55] The only overt indication that Cynewulf may have been an elderly poet is found in his epilogue to *Elene*, a poem about how St Helen found the True Cross. In this epilogue, written in

---

[50] *The Riming Poem*, ed. Klinck, *OEE*, lines 59–60.
[51] *The Wanderer*, ed. Klinck, *OEE*, lines 112–15; *The Seafarer*, ed. Klinck, *OEE*, lines 117–24; *The Riming Poem*, ed. Klinck, *OEE*, lines 80–7.
[52] Generally, *Guthlac B* is also considered part of the Cynewulfian corpus on the basis of style, though it lacks the epilogue, since the poem is incomplete. See: R. D. Fulk, 'Cynewulf: Canon, Dialect, and Date', in *The Cynewulf Reader*, ed. R. E. Bjork (New York, 2001), 3–22.
[53] E. R. Anderson, *Cynewulf: Structure, Style, and Theme in His Poetry* (London, 1983), 16.
[54] P. W. Conner, 'On Dating Cynewulf', in *Cynewulf Reader*, ed. Bjork, 47.
[55] Cited in Anderson, *Cynewulf*, 22. Arguably, assigning supposedly 'uninspired' poetry to an aged poet borders on ageism.

the first person, Cynewulf explicitly described himself as an old man: "ic frod ond fus þurh þæt fæcne hus" [I, old and wise, and ready for death because of this deceitful house].[56] Moreover, Cynewulf notes that God gave him the gift of poetry as a comfort in his old age:

> ... me lare onlag   þurh leohtne had
> gamelum to geoce,   gife unscynde
> mægencyning amæt   ond on gemynd begeat,
> torht ontynde,   tidum gerymde,
> bancofan onband,   breostlocan onwand,
> leoðucræft onleac.[57]

[... the mighty King gloriously bestowed on me His teaching as a comfort in my old age, meted out the noble gift and begot it in my mind, disclosed the brightness, extended it at times, unbound my bone-coffer, loosened my breast-hoard, unlocked the craft of poetry.]

While some scholars have taken this description of Cynewulf's own old age at face value, Earl R. Anderson points out that Cynewulf's revelation need not be autobiographical. Instead, he argues that Cynewulf may have used an 'aged author' motif.[58] Cynewulf's identification as an old man, in this case, would be a stylistic device, rather than a reflection of personal senescence. Similarly, Dolores W. Frese has argued that Cynewulf's use of the word *frod* to describe himself need not refer to the author's personal old age per se. Rather, this word connects Cynewulf to several characters in *Elene*, such as Sachius, Symon and Judas, who are described with the same word. Moreover, the poet's supposed acquisition of his poetic abilities in later life is paralleled by the 'mature conversions to Christianity' of Constantine, Helen (Elene), Symon and Judas.[59]

Indeed, Cynewulf's presentation of himself as an old man is certainly conventional and shows some similarities to the old wise man in wisdom poetry. As in these other poems, Cynewulf explicitly links his old age to wisdom: he calls himself "frod" [old and wise] and his craft,

---

[56] Cynewulf, *Elene*, ed. P. O. A. Gradon (New York, 1966), line 1236. The phrase 'fæcne hus' [deceitful house] is a metaphor for the elderly body. Anderson, *Cynewulf*, 17, argues that Cynewulf's use of this image is probably inspired by Eccles. 12:1–4, where the young are advised to remember their Creator and the body of an old man is compared to a household in decline. However, there is no need to presuppose a biblical source for this image; the metaphor of 'house' for body is well-attested, e.g., in the Old English kenning *bānhūs* 'bone-house, body'.

[57] Cynewulf, *Elene*, ed. Gradon, lines 1245–1250a.

[58] Anderson, *Cynewulf*, 18. See also: H. Soper, '*Eald æfensceop*: Poetic Composition and the Authority of the Aged in Old English Verse', *Quaestio Insularis* 17 (2016), 74–98.

[59] D. W. Frese, 'The Art of Cynewulf's Runic Signatures', in *Cynewulf Reader*, ed. Bjork, 333–4.

the ability to write poetry, has been granted to him at an advanced age, "gamelum to geoce" [as a comfort in (my) old age].[60] Moreover, Cynewulf continues his epilogue with his runic signature that features a now familiar image of an old man, in this case a former warrior, grieving over his diminishing prowess and the fleeting nature of youth and joys. As in Alcuin's poems discussed above, these physical and social drawbacks of old age are linked to the decline of the world as a whole:

> A wæs sæcg oð ðæt
> cnyssed cearwelmum, .ᚳ. drusende,
> þeah he in medohealle   maðmas þege,
> æplede gold .ᚣ. gnornode
> .ᚾ. gefera,   nearusorge dreah,
> enge rune,   þær him .ᛗ. fore
> milpaðas mæt,   modig þrægde
> wirum gewlenced. ᚹ. is geswiðrad,
> gomen æfter gearum,   geogoð is gecyrred,
> ald onmedla. .ᚢ. wæs geara
> geogoðhades glæm.   Nu synt geardagas
> æfter fyrstmearce   forð gewitene,
> lifwynne geliden,   swa .ᛚ. toglideð,
> flodas gefysde. .ᚠ. æghwam bið
> læne under lyfte;   landes frætwe
> gewitaþ under wolcnum   winde geliccost,
> þonne he for hæleðum   hlud astigeð,
> wæðeð be wolcnum,   wedende færeð
> ond eft semninga   swige gewyrðeð,
> in nedcleofan   nearwe geheaðrod,
> þream forþrycced;   swa þeos world
> eall gewiteð.[61]

[Until that time, the warrior had always been overwhelmed by sorrows, a failing TORCH,[62] though he received treasures in the mead-hall, appled gold, he grieved for his BOW, the companion in NEED, he endured crushing distress, a cruel mystery, where before a HORSE carried him over army-paths,[63] ran bravely adorned with wire-ornaments. JOY is diminished, pleasure after the years, youth has changed, the magnificence of old. Once was OURS the splendour of youth.[64] Now the days of

---

[60] Cynewulf, *Elene*, ed. Gradon, lines 1236a, 1246a.
[61] Cynewulf, *Elene*, ed. Gradon, lines 1256–77.
[62] For the 'failing torch' as a symbol of a warrior's life, see T. D. Hill, 'The Failing Torch: The Old English *Elene*, 1256–1259', *NQ* ns 52 (2005), 155–60.
[63] For the interpretation of "milpaþas" as 'army roads', see A. Breeze, '*Exodus*, *Elene*, and the *Rune Poem*: milpæþ "Army Road, Highway"', *NQ* ns 38 (1991), 436–8.
[64] In translating the ᚢ-rune as 'ours' I follow the majority of translators, see, e.g., Cynewulf, *Elene*, ed. Gradon, 73, n. 1265b. R. W. V. Elliott, 'Cynewulf's Runes in

yore have, after a period of time, passed away, bereft of the enjoyment of life, just as the WATER glides away, floods sent forth. WEALTH is for everyone transitory under the sky, treasures of the land, departs under the clouds, most like the wind. When it loudly proceeds in the presence of heroes, hunts under the clouds, goes, raving, and afterwards it becomes quiet of assemblies, restrained in a narrow prison, oppressed by throes. Thus, this world will depart completely.]

Cynewulf then launches into a description of Judgement Day, after which those who have been cleansed of their sins are allowed to "sybbe brucan / eces ead-welan" [to enjoy peace, eternal happiness].[65] Like Alcuin, then, Cynewulf relates the decline in human old age to the fleeting nature of earthly beauties and, similarly, draws a contrast with the eternity found in Heaven.

While the influence of Alcuin on the epilogue of Cynewulf's *Elene* has been suggested before, especially regarding the description of Judgement Day in lines 1277ff,[66] the parallels between Cynewulf's and Alcuin's poetic treatment of old age have hitherto remained unmentioned. Both poets, it should be noted, like the anonymous authors of the Old English elegies, used grieving, old speakers reflecting on their former joys as focal points for their discussions on the transience of earthly pleasures. Moreover, all poets use this idea to encourage their audience to put their minds to the eternal joys in Heaven instead. As we shall see below, this notion was used to much the same effect in later Anglo-Saxon homilies.

In the poems discussed above, the image of the aging speaker, suffering both physically and emotionally, was used as a demonstration of the transience of the world at large. Conversely, the author of *Solomon and Saturn II* reversed this idea and used the detrimental effect of time on Nature as a metaphor for the detrimental effects old age would have on Man. *Solomon and Saturn II* is an enigmatic debate poem between the pagan Saturn and the wise King Solomon, dating back to the early tenth century. The poem contains several riddles, of which one is the following 'Old Age' riddle, posed by Saturn:

'Ac hwæt is ðæt wundor   ðe geond ðas worold færeð,
styrnenga gæð,   staðolas beateð,
aweceð wopdropan,   winneð oft hider?
Ne mæg hit steorra ne stan   ne se steapa gimm,

Christ II and *Elene*', in *Cynewulf Reader*, ed. Bjork, 284–5, argues, however, that the rune here must be interpreted as 'aurochs, bison', the original sense of the rune as preserved in the Old English *Runic Poem*. As the name of the animal does not make sense in this context, Elliott then suggests it is to be translated as 'manly strength', as in 'Manly strength was once the splendour of youth'.
[65] Cynewulf, *Elene*, ed. Gradon, lines 1315–1316a.
[66] Cynewulf, *Elene*, ed. Gradon, 22.

wæter ne wildeor   wihte beswican,
ac him on hand gæð   heardes ond hnesces,
micles ond mætes;   him to mose sceall
gegangan geara gehwelce   grundbuendra,
lyft fleogendra,   laguswemmendra,
ðria ðreoteno   ðusendgerimes.'[67]

['But what is that strange thing that travels throughout this world, sternly goes, beats the foundations, arouses tears, often forces its way here? Neither star nor stone nor the broad gem, water nor wild beast can deceive it, but into its hand go hard and soft, the great and small. Each and every year the count of three times thirteen thousand of the ground-dwellers, of the air-flying, of the sea-swimming, must go to it as food.']

The answer to this riddle – old age or devouring time – is given by Solomon, who first notes how Nature is ravished by old age and then concludes that the same fate awaits mankind:

'Yldo beoð on eorðan   æghwæs cræftig;
mid hiðendre   hildewræsne,
rumre racenteage,   reced wide,
langre linan,   lisseð eall ðæt heo wile.
Beam heo abreoteð   and bebriceð telgum,
astyreð standendne   stefn on siðe,
afilleð hine on foldan;   friteð æfter ðam
wildne fugol.   Heo oferwigeð wulf,
hio oferbideð stanas,   heo oferstigeð style,
hio abiteð iren mid ome,   deð usic swa.'[68]

['Old age is, of all things, powerful on earth. With plundering shackles, capacious fetters, she reaches widely, with her long rope, she subdues all she will. She destroys the tree and shatters its branches, uproots the upright trunk on her way, and fells it to the earth; after that she feeds on the wildfowl. She defeats the wolf, she outlasts stones, she surpasses steel, she bites iron with rust, does the same to us.']

In other words, just as old age will destroy everything on earth, it will be devastating to Mankind. The author's use of feminine pronouns to refer to old age prompted Semper to argue that 'the personification of old age as an invincible *female* emphasises how unnatural this process appears to fighting men; she is a foe they cannot defeat, neither man

---

[67] *Solomon and Saturn II*, ed. and trans. Anlezark, lines 104–13. For a close Latin analogue to this riddle in the *Collectanea Pseudo-Bedae*, see T. D. Hill, 'Saturn's Time Riddle: An Insular Latin Analogue for *Solomon and Saturn II* Lines 282–291', *RES* ns 39 (1988), 273–6.

[68] *Solomon and Saturn II*, ed. and trans. Anlezark, lines 114–23.

Drawbacks of Old Age

nor monster'.[69] Given the clear monastic context of the text,[70] however, Semper's reference to 'fighting men' appears out of place and the feminine pronouns are more likely to reflect the grammatical gender of the noun *yldo* rather than expressing the unnaturalness of old age to men, martial or monastic.[71] If anything, old age is presented here as a natural force that leaves nothing in its wake.

In sum, Anglo-Saxon poets approached the drawbacks of old age with apprehension. They typically grouped growing old with other processes of decline and, as such, the old person became a metaphor for secular impermanence. Just as wealth, joy, friends and status do not last forever, so, too, youth is not eternal and old age is unavoidable.

The symptoms of old age: Anglo-Saxon geriatrics from the pulpit

Patristic and biblical texts were not wholly unsympathetic towards the sufferings of the elderly and could provide solace for some aged Anglo-Saxon readers. For instance, Alcuin wrote to Charlemagne how he found consolation for his physical weakness by reading the letters of St Jerome: "In my broken state of health I am comforted by what Jerome said in his letter to Nepotianus: 'Almost all the physical powers change in the old, wisdom alone increasing while the others decrease.'"[72] In another letter, Alcuin reminded his pupil Eanbald that physical weakness could help the soul and quoted the apostle Paul: "Let your bodily weakness make your spirit strong, and say with the apostle, 'When I am weak, then am I strong' [2 Cor. 12:10]. Physical affliction should help the soul."[73] Boniface used the same quotation from Paul's letter to the Corinthians, along with other biblical quotations, when he wrote to the aged Abbess Bugga in an attempt to console her in her old age, convincing her that God "desires to adorn the beauty of [her] soul with labour and sorrow".[74]

Whereas these epigraphical examples illustrate that the writings of Church fathers and biblical quotations could be used to console the

---

[69] Semper, '*Byð se ealda man*', 294.
[70] *Old English Dialogues*, ed. and trans. Anlezark, 49–57.
[71] A notable analogue to this female personification of old age is found in the Scandinavian *Gylfaginning* [The Tricking of Gylfi], part of Snorri Sturluson's *Prose Edda*. In a test of strength, the god Thor loses a wrestling match with an old crone called Elli, presented as the wetnurse of the giant Utgarda-Loki. As it turns out, this old woman is a personification of 'old age' and, as the giant later explains, "there never has been anyone, and there never will be anyone, if they get so old that they experience old age, that old age will not bring them all down". Snorri Sturluson, *Edda*, ed. and trans. A. Faulkes (London, 1987), 45.
[72] Alcuin, *Life and Letters*, trans. Allott, letter no. 8.
[73] Alcuin, *Life and Letters*, trans. Allott, letter no. 6.
[74] *Letters of Boniface*, trans. Emerton, letter no. 77.

elderly in times of physical distress, Anglo-Saxon preachers rarely if ever sought to soften the blow when they spoke of the drawbacks of old age. Rather, evocative descriptions of the physical and emotional repercussions of senescence pointed out the futility of loving secular life. Furthermore, homilists used the symptoms of old age to remind the audience of the inevitability of death and even argued that they constituted a prefiguration of the horrors of Hell. The following paragraphs outline the manner in which these Anglo-Saxon homilists used their Latin sources, often of an Irish origin, to create various images of the drawbacks of growing old in order to make their message hit home.

A recurring device in homilies is a list of symptoms of old age that serve to remind the audience that death is at hand and that one's attentions should be turned to Heaven. This theme can be traced as far back, at least, as the letter of St Jerome to the widow Furia, dated to AD 394. Jerome admonished Furia to remind her aged father that he would soon die and that he needed to focus on attaining the heavenly afterlife:

> Jam incanuit caput, tremunt genua, dentes cadunt: et fronte ob senium rugis arata, vicina est mors in foribus; designatur rogus prope. Velimus, nolimus, senescimus. Paret sibi viaticum, quod longo itineri necessarium est.[75]

> [Now his head grows grey, his knees tremble, his teeth fall out and his forehead is ploughed with wrinkles because of old age, death is near at the gates; a funeral pyre is almost prepared. Whether we want to or not, we grow old. Let him make a provision for himself, which is necessary for the long journey.]

Similar, and occasionally more evocative, descriptions of the aging body, often in combination with admonitions to focus on the eternal rather than the temporary, are found in at least five Anglo-Saxon homilies. Each homily was based on a Latin source and, on occasion, the vernacular preacher added symptoms of his own.

A first Latin text, used by both the Blickling homilist and Ælfric, is Pseudo-Basil's *Admonitio ad filium spiritualem* [Admonition to a Spiritual Son]. This late fifth-century text reflects, among other things, on the virtue of contempt for all earthly possessions. The eighth chapter, "De saeculi amore fugiendo" [Concerning fleeing the love of this world], in particular, warns its reader for loving worldly beauty: just as hay will wither in the summer's heat, so, too, will the loveliness of the body fade with time, along with other pleasures of the world.[76] Following a description

---

[75] Jerome, *Epistolae*, PL 22, col. 557.
[76] Pseudo-Basil, *De admonitio ad filium spiritualem*, ed. P. Lehmann (Munich, 1955), trans. J. F. LePree, 'Pseudo-Basil's *De admonitio ad filium spiritualem*: A New English Translation', *HA* 13 (2010), ch. 8.

Drawbacks of Old Age

of a body decayed through age and death, Pseudo-Basil adds a series of *ubi sunt* passages, such as "ubi est suavitas luxuriae et conviviorum opulentia?" [Where is the sweetness of luxury and opulence of banquets?],[77] underlining once more the fleeting nature of earthly delights.

Laura R. McCord has suggested that the eighth chapter of the *Admonitio* was the probable source for a similar series of Old English *ubi sunt* passages in Blickling Homily V.[78] While she formulated her claim hesitantly, her suggestion can be confirmed by the fact that the descriptions of the aging body that precede the *ubi sunt* passages in both texts also share some characteristics. First, both texts compare the human body to withering plants:

Nonne sicut fenum, cum a fervor aestatis percussum fuerit, arescit et paulatim pristinum decorum amittit? Similis est etiam humanae naturae species.[79]	We witon þæt Crist sylfa cwæþ þurh his sylfes muþ, 'þonne ge geseoþ growende 7 blowende ealle eorþan wæstmas, 7 þa swetan stencas gestincað þara wudu-wyrta, þa sona eft adrugiaþ 7 forþgewitaþ for þæs sumores hæton'. Swa þonne gelice bið þære menniscan gecynde þæs lichoman…[80]
[Surely it is like hay when it has been struck by the heat of summer: it dries up and little by little it loses its pristine state. The appearance of human nature is also like this.]	[We know that Christ himself said, through his own mouth: 'When you see all the earth's fruits growing and blooming, and smell the sweet odours of the plants, then immediately afterwards they shall dry up and wither away because of the summer's heat.' So it (the fruit) is like the nature of a man's body …]

The Blickling homilist, here, appears to have conflated two statements from the New Testament – 1 Pet. 1:24 and James 1:11[81] – in order to

---

[77] Pseudo-Basil, *Admonitio*, ed. Lehmann, trans. LePree, ch. 8.
[78] L. R. McCord, 'A Probable Source for the *ubi sunt* Passage in Blickling Homily V', *Neuphilologische Mitteilungen* 82 (1981), 360–1; see also C. Di Sciacca, *Finding the Right Words: Isidore's Synonyma in Anglo-Saxon England* (Toronto, 2008), 130–3.
[79] Pseudo-Basil, *Admonitio*, ed. Lehmann, trans. LePree, ch. 8.
[80] *Blickling Homilies*, hom. 5, pp. 58–9.
[81] Cf. M. McC. Gatch, 'The Unknowable Audience of the Blickling Homilies', *ASE* 18 (1989), 107.

formulate a biblical quotation to match the Latin original's image of drying hay. Next, both texts discuss the decaying body in old age:

Succedente enim senectute omnis decor pristinus iuventutis floridae deperit et quos in amorem sui antea concitabat, postmodum in odium eorum efficitur, et quando mors venerit, tunc penitus omnis pulchritudo delebitur. Et tunc recognosces, quia vanum est, quod antea inaniter diligebas.[82]	... þonne se geogoþhad ærest bloweþ 7 fægerost bið, he þonne raþe se wlite eft gewiteþ 7 to ylde gecyrreþ, 7 he þonne siþþon mid sare geswenced bið, mid mislicum ecum 7 tyddernessum. 7 eal se lichoma geunlustaþ þa geogoðlustas to fremmenne þa þe he ær hatheortlice luf ode, 7 him swete wæron to aræfnenne.[83]
[With the advent of old age, every pure beauty of florid youth is destroyed and what you loved before, you now find hateful, and when death comes, then all beauty will be totally destroyed and then you will recognise that what you loved vainly before was merely an illusion.]	[... when youth first blooms and is fairest, then quickly beauty fades and turns to old age, and afterwards he is troubled by pain and by various ailments and infirmities. And the whole body loathes to perform those youthful lusts that he loved so earnestly before, and which were sweet to him to perform.]

While the *Admonitio* makes the point that the observer no longer loves the body once its beauty has faded, the Blickling homilist observes that it is the old body itself that no longer loves its former pastimes. Furthermore, the Blickling homilist adds that an elderly person is typically troubled by pain and infirmities. Subsequently, both texts turn to what happens to the body after death:

Cum videris totum corpus in tumore et foetore esse conversum, none intuens maximo horror concutieris, nonne claudes nares tuas non sustinens foetorem durissimum?[84]	Hie him þonne eft swiþe bitere þencaþ, æfter þon þe se dead him tocymeþ Godes dom to abeodenne. Se lichoma þonne on þone heardestan stenc 7 on þone fulostan bið gecyrred, 7 his eagan þonne beoþ betynde, 7 his muþ 7 his næsþyrlo beoþ belocene, 7 he þonne se deada byð uneaþe ælcon men on neaweste to hæbbenne.[85]

---

[82] Pseudo-Basil, *Admonitio*, ed. Lehmann, trans. LePree, ch. 8.
[83] *Blickling Homilies*, hom. 5, pp. 58–9.
[84] Pseudo-Basil, *Admonitio*, ed. Lehmann, trans. LePree, ch. 8.
[85] *Blickling Homilies*, hom. 5, pp. 58–9.

[When you have seen an entire body swelling and smelling, surely contemplating it will have struck you with great horror. Surely you will hold your nose, not able to bear the most oppressive smell?]

[Then, again, they shall appear very bitter to him, after that death shall come to him to announce God's Judgement. The body then, shall be turned to the strongest and foulest stench, and his eyes shall then be sealed up, and his mouth and his nostrils shall be closed, and then with difficulty will the dead be kept in proximity to any living person.]

In both texts, the stench of the decayed corpse appalls those around it, but the Blickling homilist's description of the dead body with its sealed eyes, mouth and nostrils is more evocative. Summing up, both texts show a similar progression of ideas: withered plants are like the human body, the beauty of the aging body fades, the stinking corpse is oppressive. Along with the similarities between the *ubi sunt* passages that follow this series of ideas, the use of the *Admonitio* as a source of inspiration for the author of Blickling Homily V is beyond question, albeit that the homilist has varied significantly from the used source,[86] expanding the burdens of old age and creating a more haunting image of the sealed-up corpse.

The *Admonitio* was also used by Ælfric, who made a vernacular adaptation of the entire text.[87] A comparison between chapter 8 of the source text and Ælfric's reworking of it makes clear that Ælfric adds to the aging body some aspects that the *Admonitio* attributes to the dead body, namely the swelling and smelling:

> Swa byð þæs mannes wlite þe wyrðeð eall fornumen mid onsigendre ylde and se deað geendað þone ærran wlite þonne ongitt þin sawl þæt þu sylf lufodest idel. Foroft se mann gewyrðeð on ende toswollen and to stence awended mid unwynsumnysse þæt him sylfum byð egle and andsæte se stenc and his lustfullnysse him ne belifð nan þing and his wistfullnys him wyrðeð to biternysse.[88]

---

[86] S. Pelle, 'Sources and Analogues for Blickling Homily V and Vercelli Homily XI', *NQ* ns 59 (2012), 8–11, has noted the Blickling homilist's freedom with another Latin source, suggesting that he possibly drew from memory. The same case could be made for the author's use of the *Admonitio*.

[87] For this text, see M. A. Locherbie-Cameron, 'From Caesarea to Eynsham: A Consideration of the Proposed Route(s) of the *Admonition to a Spiritual Son* to Anglo-Saxon England', *HA* 3 (2000).

[88] Ælfric, *The Anglo-Saxon Version of the Hexameron of St Basil*, ed. and trans. H. W. Norman (London, 1848), 50–1 (translation slightly adapted).

[In like way is the beauty of man, which becomes thoroughly destroyed by approaching old age, and death puts an end to its former beauty, when your soul understands that you have yourself loved vanity. Very often in the end a man becomes swollen, and is perverted to a bad odour with unpleasantness, so that he is loathsome to himself, and his odour is abominable, and of his lustfulness nothing remains to him, and his good cheer becomes a bitterness to him.]

As such, Ælfric transforms the idea of the disgust over another person's decayed corpse into a poignant picture of a self-loathing old man, appalled by his own swollen and odorous state. In the subsequent adaptation of this chapter, Ælfric follows his source in adding various instances of the *ubi sunt* motif. In this way, the intended goal of the chapter remains intact: to remind readers that eternal spiritual life is superior to physical life, which is temporary.

Yet another description of the aging body, again by Ælfric in one of his *Catholic Homilies*, was based on the first homily of Gregory the Great's *Homiliae in Evangelia*.[89] Both texts discuss the idea that the world is weighed down by evils and will not last forever, just as a man's strength and health will deteriorate as a result of age. Ælfric once more elaborates on his source's list of symptoms of age:

Sicut enim in juventute viget corpus, forte et incolume manet pectus, torosa cervix, plena sunt brachia; in annis autem senilibus statura curvatur, cervix exsiccata deponitur, frequentibus suspiriis pectus urgetur, virtus deficit, loquentis verba anhelitus intercidit; nam etsi languor desit, plerumque sensibus ipsa sua salus aegritudo est.[90]	On geogoðe bið se lichama þeonde on strangum breoste: on fullum leomum 7 halum: witodlice on ealdlicum gearum bið ðæs mannes wæstm gebiged. his swura aslacod. his neb bið gerifod. & his leomu ealle gewæhte. His breost bið mid siccetungum geþread. & betwux wordum his orþung ateorað. Ðeah ðe him adl on ne sitte þeah forwel oft his hæl him bið adl.[91]

---

[89] Godden, *Ælfric's Catholic Homilies: Introduction*, 339.
[90] Gregory, *Homiliae in evangelia*, ed. Étaix, trans. Hurst, hom. 1, 18.
[91] *ÆCHom I*, hom. 40, lines 110–20.

[In youth the body is vigorous, the chest remains strong and healthy, the neck is straight, the arms muscular; in later years, the body is bent, the neck scrawny and withered, the chest oppressed by difficult breathing, strength is failing, and speech is interrupted by wheezing. Weakness may not yet be present, but often in the case of the senses their healthy state is itself a malady.]	[In youth the body is thriving with a strong chest and full and healthy limbs: truly, in later years a man's stature is bowed, his neck slackened, his face is wrinkled, and his limbs are all afflicted. His breast is tormented with sighs, and his breath fails between words. Although disease does not sit on him, nevertheless his health is often a disease for him.]

Specifically, Ælfric shortens the characteristics of the youthful body, but adds to the symptoms of age a wrinkled face and defines the original's "virtus deficit" [strength is failing] by referring to afflicted limbs, the antithesis of the full and healthy ones he has referred to earlier. Thus, when it came to describing the aging body, Ælfric did not shy away from taking some liberties to embellish the lists of symptoms of age he found in his sources, in both his reworking of Pseudo-Basil's *Admonitio* and Gregory's homily.

Similar, longer lists of symptoms of age circulated as a *topos* in early medieval Hiberno-Latin texts and gradually made their way into later Anglo-Saxon homilies. Charles D. Wright has called attention to two such lists, found in a seventh-century treatise on the twelve abuses, *De duodecim abusiuis*, and a ninth-century florilegium, *Catechesis Celtica*.[92] The former text provides the list of symptoms in its description of the *senex sine religione*, 'the old man without religion', noting that these symptoms ought to remind elderly men that their death was at hand:

> Dum oculi caligant, auris grauiter audit, capilli fluunt, facies in pallorem mutatur, dentes lassi numero minuuntur, cutis arescit, flatus non suauiter olet, pectus suffocatur, tussis cachinnat, genuat trepidant, talos et pedes tumor inflat, etiam homo interior qui non senescit his omnibus aggravatur, et haec omnia ruituram iam iamque domum corporis cito pronuntiant. Quid ergo superest, nisi ut, dum huius vitae defectus appropiat, nihil aliud cogitare quam quomodo futurae habitus prospere comprehendatur quisque senex appetat? Iuuenibus enim incertus huius vitae terminus instat, senibus uero cunctis maturus ex hac luce rexitus breviter concordat.[93]

---

[92] Wright, *Irish Tradition*, 96–102.
[93] Pseudo-Cyprian, *De duodecim abusiuis*, ed. S. Hellmann, *Texte under Untersuchungen zur Geschichte der altchristlichen Literatur*, Reihe 3, Band 4, Heft 1 (Leipzig, 1909), 34–5, trans. P. Throop, *Vincent of Beauvais, The Moral Instruction*

[When eyes cloud over, ears hear with difficulty, hair falls out, the face turns to pallid, teeth, having fallen out, diminish in number, the skin dries out, the breath does not smell sweet, the chest is suffocating, the cough grates, the knees tremble, the swelling inflates the ankles and feet, indeed the interior person (which does not grow old) is weighed down by all these things. All these conditions announce that the bodily home is quickly going to collapse. What remains except that, while the cessation of this life is approaching, any old person should seek to think about nothing else than how their future situation may successfully be grasped? For young people the end of this life exists as an uncertainty, but for all old people it is a sure thing that the exit from this life is soon at hand.]

The *Catechesis Celtica* provides a similar list of symptoms in its description of the five likenesses of Hell,[94] which includes old age:

Senectus assimilator quando V sensus in ecitem exeunt. Nam oculi caliginant, aures sordescunt, gustus non bene discernit, odoratus uitiatur, tactus rigescit; sed et dentes denudantur, lingua balbutiat, pectus licoribus grauatur, pedes tremore et tumore tumescunt, manus ad opus debilitantur, canities floret, et corpus omne infirmatur, sed sensus diminuitur.[95]

[Old age is likened to hell, when the five senses pass away at the end of life. For the eyes grow blurry, the ears grow deaf, the sense of taste distinguishes poorly, the sense of smell is corrupted, the sense of touch becomes numb; and also the teeth are revealed, the tongue stutters, the chest grows heavy with fluid, the feet swell with tumors and shaking, the hands are crippled for work, the grey hair grows, and the whole body is weakened, and perception is diminished.]

Wright has pointed out that the correspondences between the two lists, in combination with the divergence in wording, suggest that they were both independently translated from a vernacular list of symptoms of old age.[96] He further hints at the fact that enumerations of body parts are a frequent feature in Hiberno-Latin prayers, of which the list of symptoms of age may be a logical expansion.[97] *De duodecim abusiuis* and the *Catechesis* have been linked to two Old English homilies:

---

of a Prince, and Pseudo-Cyprian, *The Twelve Abuses of the World* (Charlotte, 2011), 117. The text was copied almost verbatim in the *Collectanea Pseudo-Bedae*, another ninth-century, insular florilegium of riddles and encyclopaedic material, albeit without the note about the uncertainty of death for young men; see *Collectanea*, ed. and trans. Bayless and Lapidge, no. 119.

[94] These are to be distinguished from the Five Horrors of Hell, cf. D. F. Johnson, 'The Five Horrors of Hell: An Insular Homiletic Motif', *English Studies* 74 (1993), 414–31.
[95] Cit. with translation in Wright, *Irish Tradition*, 96–7.
[96] Wright, *Irish Tradition*, 98–9.
[97] Wright, *Irish Tradition*, 99; similar lists are also found in the *Book of Cerne* and related Old English prayers, see Porck, 'Two Notes', 493–8.

Drawbacks of Old Age

Vercelli Homily IX and Pseudo-Wulfstan's 'Be rihtan Cristendome' (Napier XXX).

The late tenth-century Vercelli Homily IX, to begin with, describes five prefigurations of Hell which are the same as those listed in the *Catechesis*: pain, old age, death, the grave and torment. The list of symptoms of old age in Old English is similar to the Latin text but also features some notable differences:

> Þonne is þære æfteran helle onlicnes genemned oferyldo, for þan him amolsniaþ þa eagan for þære oferyldo þa þe wæron gleawe on gesyhþe, 7 þa earan adimmiaþ þa þe ær meahton gehyran fægere sangas, and sio tunge awlispaþ þe ær hæfde gerade spræce, 7 þa fet aslapaþ þe ær wæron ful swifte 7 hræde to gange, 7 þa handa aþindaþ þe ær hæfdon ful hwate fingras, 7 þæt feax afealleþ þe ær wæs on fullere wæstme, 7 þa teþ ageolewiaþ þa þe ær wæron hwite on hywe, 7 þæt oroþ afulaþ þe wæs ær swete on stence.[98]

> [Then is the second prefiguration of Hell named 'extreme old age', because his eyes weaken because of extreme old age, those that had been keen of sight, and his ears become dim, which had been able to hear beautiful songs, and his tongue lisps, that had possessed skilful speech, and his feet sleep, that had been very swift and quick in movement, and his hands become swollen, that had had fully active fingers, and his hair falls out, that had been very abundant, and his teeth become yellow, those that had been white in appearance, and his breath, which had been sweet of smell, becomes foul.]

First of all, references to the three general senses of *gustus* 'taste', *odoratus* 'smell', and *tactus* 'touch', as well as to the tormented *pectus* 'chest', all present in the *Catechesis*, are missing in Vercelli Homily IX. Conversely, the Vercelli homilist has expanded the list of symptoms by adding references to the former excellence of eyes, ears, tongue, feet, hair and teeth. A remark about ill-smelling breath, which is not featured in the *Catechesis*, has also been added. Moreover, the Old English text has teeth growing yellow and hair falling out, whereas the *Catechesis* has teeth falling out and hair growing grey. It is worth pointing out, however, that the list in *De duodecim abusiuis*, which shares its origin with that in the *Catechesis*, does feature a reference to breath and also has hair falling out. As such, some of the differences between Vercelli Homily IX and the *Catechesis* need not necessarily be attributed to the Anglo-Saxon homilist; in all probability, the discrepancy stems from the homilist's use of an unknown variant of the list of symptoms of age

---

[98] *Vercelli Homilies*, hom. 9, lines 84–97. This is the text as it is preserved in Vercelli, Biblioteca Capitolare, CXVII (s. x^2; the 'Vercelli Book'); Scragg has also edited a related, later reworking of this homily in Oxford, Bodleian Library, Hatton 115, fols. 140–7 (s. xi^2) that has a near-identical list but skips the reference to weakened eyes. *Vercelli Homilies*, pp. 167, 169, lines 71–8.

that stems from the same Hiberno-Latin tradition as the *Catechesis* and *De duodecim abusiuis*.[99] Whatever its direct source, the Vercelli homilist shared the Hiberno-Latin view that old age was a prefiguration of Hell, a clear indication that, in this respect at least, old age was not preferred over other age categories.

Another list of symptoms of old age, analogous to the one in Vercelli Homily IX, is the most likely source for the eleventh-century homily 'Be rihtan Cristendome' (Napier XXX), formerly attributed to Archbishop Wulfstan.[100] Donald G. Scragg has pointed out that Napier XXX is a 'cut-and-paste' homily, derived from a homiliary related to the Vercelli Book but now lost, as it contains parallels to various Vercelli homilies.[101] The list of symptoms of age is certainly similar to that in Vercelli Homily IX:

> Him amolsniað and adimmiað þa eagan, þe ær wæron beorhte and gleawe on gesihðe. And seo tunge awistlað, þe ær hæfde getinge spræce and gerade. And ða earan aslawiað, þa þe ær wæron ful swifte and hræde to gehyrenne fægere dreamas and sangas. And þa handa awindað, þa ðe ær hæfdon ful hwæte fingras. And þæt feax afealleð, þe ær wæs fæger on hiwe and on fulre wæstme. And þa teð ageolwiað, þa ðe wæron ær hwite on hiwe. And þæt oreð stincð and afulað, þe ær wæs swete on stence.[102]

> [His eyes weaken and become dim, that had been bright and keen of sight. And his tongue hisses, which had possessed fluent and skilful speech. And his ears become sluggish, which had been very swift and quick to hear beautiful stories and songs. And his hands bend, that had possessed fully active fingers. And his hair falls out, that had been fair in colour and in full abundance. And his teeth turn yellow, that had been white in appearance. And his breath, which had been sweet of smell, stinks and turns foul.]

Scragg has noted that the compiler of Napier XXX expanded his source by using pairs of near synonyms, such as "amolsniað and adimmiað" [weaken and become dim] for Vercelli Homily IX's "amolsniaþ" [weaken].[103] To this difference might be added that the compiler arranged

---

[99] J. E. Cross, *The Literate Anglo-Saxon – On Sources and Disseminations* (London, 1972), 5, rightly calls attention to the fact that the exact variant of a Latin text that an Anglo-Saxon author used may be lost. On Vercelli Homily IX and the *Catechesis*, specifically, he states "I, for one, would not presume to say more at present than that they are two examples of the theme. I could not indicate any relationship between one and the other without other evidence." (31); cf. Wright, *Irish Tradition*, 99–100.

[100] On this homily and its relation to Wulfstan's work, see L. Whitbread, '"Wulfstan" Homilies XXIX, XXX and Some Related Texts', *Anglia* 81 (1963), 347–64; D. G. Scragg, 'Napier's "Wulfstan" Homily XXX: Its Sources, Its Relationship to the Vercelli Book and Its Style', *ASE* 6 (1977), 197–211.

[101] Scragg, 'Napier's "Wulfstan" Homily', 198–205; *Vercelli Homilies*, p. lxxv.

[102] Napier, hom. 30, p. 147, lines 23–31, p. 148, lines 1–7.

[103] Scragg, 'Napier's "Wulfstan" Homily', 207.

Drawbacks of Old Age

the symptoms in a different order: eyes-tongue-ears as opposed to the more frequently attested eyes-ears-tongue.[104] Furthermore, the description of the ears appears to have been conflated with the description of the feet in Vercelli Homily IX that is missing in Napier XXX altogether. This conflation has caused the rather awkward remark in Napier XXX "ða earan aslawiað, þa þe ær wæron ful swifte" [the ears grow sluggish, those which had been very swift] in Napier XXX, which is closely resembled by Vercelli Homily IX's "þa fet aslapaþ þe ær wæron ful swifte" [the feet sleep, which had been very swift].[105] The list of symptoms in Napier XXX, then, appears to have been rather clumsily copied from a list of symptoms that was similar to that found in Vercelli Homily IX.

A more profound contrast between Napier XXX and Vercelli Homily IX is the context in which both feature the lists of symptoms. Whereas Vercelli Homily IX frames old age as one of the prefigurations of Hell, as does the *Catechesis Celtica*, Napier XXX places the list of symptoms in a context similar to that of the *De duodecim abusiuis*, as bodily signs that must warn an old person of impending death. In fact, the lines preceding the list in Napier XXX, for which Scragg was unable to find a source,[106] show some similarities to the lines that follow the symptoms of age in *De duodecim abusiuis*:

Iuuenibus enim incertus huius vitae terminus instat, senibus uero cunctis maturus ex hac luce rexitus breviter concordat.[107]	Þa geongan men hopiad, þæt hi moton lange on þissere worulde libban, ac se hopa hi bepæcð and beswicð, þonne him leofost wære, þæt hi lybban moston. Se ealda man him mæg gewislice witod witan, þæt him se deað genealæcð for ðære oferylde, þe him on sihð.[108]

---

[104] The order eyes-ears-tongue is attested in the *Catechesis* and the *Vita Tertia* of St Patrick (see above, p. 80, n. 19). Cf. *ÆCHom II*, hom. 1, lines 184–91: "Þonne beoð geopenode blindra manna eagan. and deaffra manna earan gehyrað. þonne hleapð se healta swa swa heort. and dumbra manna tungan beoð swiðe getinge" [Then the eyes of the blind people will be opened, and the ears of the deaf people will listen, then the lame will leap as a deer and the tongue of the dumb people will be very eloquent].

[105] Napier, hom. 30, p. 148, lines 1–2; *Vercelli Homilies*, hom. 9, line 93. On closer inspection, the reading in the Vercelli Book is closer to that in Napier XXX: "þa earan aslapað þe ær wæron ful swifte to gehyrenne", which Scragg emended to "þa fet aslapaþ þe ær wæron ful swifte" on the basis of the text in Hatton 115 (see p. 101, n. 98 above). It is worth noting that the form "aslawiað" [become sluggish] is more apt for formerly swift feet than is "aslapaþ" [become weak] and that, in Anglo-Saxon manuscripts, the "wynn" (ƿ) and the þ are easily confused. Napier XXX, then, may retain the correct reading for this word, as opposed to Vercelli Homily IX.

[106] Cf. Scragg, 'Napier's "Wulfstan" Homily', 198.

[107] Pseudo-Cyprian, *De duodecim abusiuis*, ed. Hellmann, 34–5, trans. Throop, 117.

[108] Napier, hom. 30, p. 147, lines 23–9.

[For young people the end of this life exists as an uncertainty, but for all old people it is a sure thing that the exit from this life is soon at hand.]	[Young people hope that they are able to live long in this world, but the hope that they are allowed to live, deceives and betrays them, when it would be most valuable to them. The old man can certainly know that death is approaching him because of old age, which then descends upon him.]

Napier XXX and *De duodecim abusiuis* share the notion that the aging body announces imminent death for the elderly, whereas young people are uncertain about their future. Possibly, the compiler of Napier XXX had read *De duodecim abusiuis* and wanted to use the text for his message that death is inexorable, but then preferred the list of symptoms he found in the now lost homiliary that was similar to the Vercelli Book.

The symptoms of old age, so much has become clear, appear as a recurring *topos* in Old English homilies. The often detailed descriptions of the aged body were freely adapted from (Hiberno-)Latin sources and even occasionally expanded rather than shortened, resulting in evocative depictions of an elderly person devoid of joy and sensory aptitude. Such images were employed for two distinct purposes: the Blickling homilist, Ælfric and the author of Napier XXX utilised the representation of the decaying body to remind their audiences that physical life would come to an end and was, therefore, inferior to spiritual life; the Vercelli homilist, by contrast, framed the drawbacks of age as one of the prefigurations of Hell. In all, the decrepit, aging body was a welcome device that Anglo-Saxon homilists could use to turn their audience's hopes and minds towards the afterlife; an afterlife, as we shall see below, where old age was either absent or present, depending on whether the hereafter would be Heaven or Hell.

Hellish old age and heavenly youth: Age in the afterlife

In her article on old age in Anglo-Saxon literature, Semper postulates that "Christianity does not simply promise Anglo-Saxons a life without end after death; it promises them an eternal life without old age".[109] She bases her claim on a single description of the resurrection of aged bodies at Judgement Day in the Old English translation of Augustine's *Soliloquies*:

---

[109] Semper, 'Byð se ealda man', 314.

Drawbacks of Old Age

Ge, furþum manna lichaman forealdiað, swa swa oðre gescæaftas ealdiat. Ac swa swa hy ær wurðlicor lybbað þonne treowu oðþe oðre nytenu, swa hy eac weorðfulicor arisað on domes dæge, swa þæt nefre syððam þa lichaman ne geendiað ne ne forealdiað.[110]

[Yes, even the bodies of men grow old, just as other creatures grow old. But just as they formerly lived more honourably than the trees and other animals, so they also arise more honourably on Judgement Day, so that the body will never afterwards come to an end nor grow old.]

In other words, when the dead are resurrected at Judgement Day they will no longer be old nor will they grow old in the future. Similar representations of a restored youth of aged bodies at the time of their resurrection exist, such as Ælfric's notion that "we sceolon arisan of deaðe on þære ylde þe crist wæs þa ða he þrowade: þæt is ymbe þreo 7 þrittig geara; Ðeah cyld forðfare oððe forwerod mann" [we shall arise from death at the age that Christ was when he suffered, that is about thirty-three years, whether departed as a child or as a worn-out man].[111] In another homily, Ælfric again noted that, upon resurrection, the dead will be as old as Christ was when he died.[112] Thus, whether death occurred in infancy or at an advanced age, everyone would be in their early thirties on the Day of Judgement.

Semper's assertion that old age was absent from the afterlife is further confirmed by various descriptions of Heaven in poetry and homilies.[113] Such literary representations of Paradise often enumerate the celestial joys in combination with the absence of certain horrors that typically include old age. Bede, for instance, writes in his eschatological poem *De die iudicii* [Concerning Judgement Day] that in the heavenly afterlife one will enjoy the greatest of joys and no longer suffer "fessa senectus" [wearied old age].[114] Bede's poem was extremely popular and also survives in the late tenth-century vernacular version *Judgement Day II*, which translates "fessa senectus" as "geswenced yld" [wearied old age].[115] The anonymous poet of *The Phoenix*, likewise, presents Heaven as a place without "yrmþu ne yldo" [misery or

---

[110] *King Alfred's Version of St Augustine's Soliloquies*, ed. T. A. Carnicelli (Cambridge, MA, 1969), 53, lines 22–6.

[111] *ÆCHom I*, hom. 16, lines 126–8. Ælfric here follows Julian of Toledo's *Prognosticon futuri saeculi*, see Godden, *Ælfric's Catholic Homilies: Introduction*, 133.

[112] Ælfric, *Homilies*, ed. Pope, hom. 11, lines 302–7.

[113] Semper, 'Byð se ealda man', 301–2.

[114] Bede, *De die iudicii*, ed. and trans. G. D. Caie, *The Old English Poem Judgement Day II* (Cambridge, 2000), line 129.

[115] *Judgement Day II*, ed. and trans. Caie, line 257b. On the popularity of Bede's poem, see *ibid.*, 35.

old age], as does Aldhelm in his *Carmen de virginitate*.[116] A recurring compositional device to describe the afterlife was the formula '*þær is* x *butan* y', where both x and y are antonyms.[117] A typical but expanded example is found in the poem *Christ III*:

> Ðær is leofra lufu,   lif butan endedeaðe,
> glæd gumena weorud,   gioguð butan ylde,
> heofonduguða þrym,   hælu butan sare,
> ryhtfremmendum   ræst butan gewinne,
> domeadigra   dæg butan þeostrum,
> beorht blædes full,   blis butan sorgum,
> frið freondum bitweon   orð butan æfestum,
> gesælgum on swegle,   sib butan niþe
> halgum on gemonge.[118]

[There is the love of loved ones, life without death, a joyous troop of men, youth without old age, glory of heavenly hosts, health without pain, rest without toil for the well-doers, a day of the renowned ones without darkness, bright, full of glory, bliss without sorrows, continuous peace between friends without envy, for the blissful in harmony, peace without envy among the saints.]

Thomas D. Hill has identified these lines in *Christ III* as belonging to the *topos* of 'The Seven Joys of Heaven', a numerical apothegm that stems from a Hiberno-Latin tradition.[119] Variants of this *topos* also regularly occur in Old English homiletic texts: in at least eleven homilies "geogoþ butan ylde" [youth without old age] is consistently listed as one of the assets of Heaven, along with light (without darkness), happiness (without sorrow) and health (without sickness).[120]

In only two cases is old age listed as a property of Heaven, albeit not without reservation. First, Vercelli Homily IX specifies that in Heaven

---

[116] *The Phoenix*, ed. N. F. Blake (Exeter, 1990), line 614a; Aldhelm, *Carmen de virginitate*, trans. J. L. Rosier, in Aldhelm, *The Poetic Works*, trans. M. Lapidge and J. L. Rosier (Cambridge, 1958), 153.

[117] H. L. C. Tristram, 'Stock Descriptions of Heaven and Hell in Old English Prose and Poetry', *Neuphilologische Mitteilungen* 79 (1978), 102–5.

[118] *Christ III*, ed. Krapp and Dobbie, *Exeter Book*, lines 1652–60a.

[119] T. D. Hill, 'The Seven Joys of Heaven in *Christ III* and Old English Homiletic Texts', *NQ* ns 16 (1969), 165. Early Hiberno-Latin analogues, including the eighth-century *Liber de Numeris*, the *Catechesis Celtica* and the *Collectanea Pseudo-Bedae*, are reproduced in Johnson, 'Horrors of Hell', 429.

[120] *Ancient Laws and Institutes of England*, ed. B. Thorpe (London, 1840) II, p. 400; *Blickling Homilies*, hom. 5, pp. 64–5; *Blickling Homilies*, hom. 8, pp. 102–3; Assmann, hom. 14, line 73; Napier, hom. 29, p. 142, line 27; M. Förster, 'A New Version of the Apocalypse of Thomas in Old English', *Anglia* 73 (1955), 18; Bazire and Cross, hom. 1, line 160; Bazire and Cross, hom. 4, line 93; *Vercelli Homilies*, hom. 19, lines 173–4; *Vercelli Homilies*, hom. 21, lines 243–4; 'Geherað nu mæn ða leofestan hu us godes bec', Dictionary of Old English Corpus transcript from Oxford, Bodleian Library, Junius 85/86.

one might experience old age, but that it will be "yld butan sare" [old age without pain].[121] This heavenly property is not attested elsewhere and Wright has hypothesised that it is probably a conflation of two more frequently used joys of Heaven: "geogoþ butan ylde" [youth without old age] and "hælo butan sare" [health without pain].[122] The second homily to deviate from the apparent norm is an anonymous homily,[123] edited by Susan Irvine as 'The Transience of Earthly Delights'. The homily describes Heaven as follows:

> þær is ece eadignesse: þær eald ne graneð, ne child ne scræmeð. Ne bið þær þurst, ne hungor, ne wop, ne teoðe gegrind, ne morþer, ne man, ne þær nan ne swæltæð, for þam ðe þær ne byð nan acenned; ne þer ne byð sar, ne seoregæ, ne nan longing, ne unlustes gewin.[124]

> [there is eternal happiness: there the old man does not groan and the child does not scream. There will be no thirst, no hunger, no weeping, no grinding of teeth, no murder, no crime, there no one will die, because no one is born there; there will be no pain, no sorrow, no longing, no strife of evil.]

Irvine was unable to make out the source for this passage. I suggest that it was probably derived from the Latin poem *De mundi transitu* [On the World's Impermanence] by the Irish missionary and author Columbanus (543–615). His description of Heaven in this poem on the fleeting nature of worldly pleasures corresponds in various places with that in 'The Transience of Earthly Delights':

> *Ubi senex non gemat,*
> *Neque infans uagitat,*
> Ubi laudis Domini
> Nulla uox retinetur,
> *Ubi non esuritur,*
> *Ubi numquam sititur,*
> Ubi cibo superno
> Plebs caelestis pascitur,
> *Ubi nemo moritur*
> *Quia nemo nascitur.* (correspondences in italics)[125]

> [where the old does not groan nor the infant cry, where no voice is restrained to praise the Lord, where there is no hunger, where there is never thirst, where on celestial food the heavenly folk are fed, where no one dies because no one is born.]

---

[121] *Vercelli Homilies*, hom. 9, lines 174–5.
[122] Wright, *Irish Tradition*, 105. Cf. *Vercelli Homilies*, p. 188, ns. 173–5.
[123] In Oxford, Bodleian Library, Bodley 343 [s. xii²]; Ker, no. 310.
[124] *Old English Homilies from MS Bodley 343*, ed. S. Irvine, EETS os 302 (Oxford, 1993), hom. 7, lines 86–90.
[125] Columbanus, *De mundi transitu*, ed. G. S. M. Walker, *Sancti Columbani opera* (Dublin, 1957), lines 95–104.

Thus, yet again, an Anglo-Saxon homilist turned to a Hiberno-Latin text for inspiration concerning the impact of old age.[126] As elsewhere, old age is here presented as a state that does not unproblematically fall into the category of the joys of Heaven.

Being generally absent from Heaven, old age in contrast does occur as one of the horrors of Hell in at least two other homilies. Contrary to the recurrent mention of old age in instances of the Seven Joys of Heaven, the parallel-reverse motif of the Five Horrors of Hell, identified by David F. Johnson, does not normally feature old age.[127] However, a unique, abbreviated version of this motif found in the homily 'Be heofonwarum 7 be helwarum' [On the inhabitants of Heaven and the inhabitants of Hell] reads: "Ðar syndon þa ytemestan þystro butan leohte, þar byþ yld butan geoguðe" [there is the utmost darkness without light, there is old age without youth].[128] The latter property of Hell is an obvious reversal of the frequently attested Joy of Heaven "geoguð butan yldo" [youth without old age]. Lastly, and unrelated to the Five Horrors of Hell, old age is enumerated in a Rogationtide homily as one of nine characteristics of Hell: "þær bið þeostru beþrycced and hungor and þurst and heto and yldo and unhælo and wanung and granung and toða grisbitung" [there will be oppressive darkness, hunger, thirst, heat, old age, ill health, deprivation, groaning and gnashing of teeth].[129]

To sum up the above, when Anglo-Saxons considered the afterlife, they imagined Heaven consistently as a place without old age, while their idea of hellish torment did on occasion include growing old. Thus, the restoration of bodies to their prime at Judgement Day, as claimed in Augustine's *Soliloquies* and the work of Ælfric, only lasted for those who would go to Heaven; for the souls assigned to the Abyss, their regained physical prime would turn out to be short lived.

Conclusion

Anglo-Saxon writers had much to say about the drawbacks of old age. Poets focused primarily on the emotional and social repercussions of growing old, linking human senescence to secular transience. The elderly narrators of various sapiential poems had gained their wisdom through adversity and thus embodied their own overarching message:

---

[126] The Bodley homilist also used Columbanus' *De mundi transitu* in various other passages, as I will show in a future publication.

[127] Johnson, 'Horrors of Hell', 414–31.

[128] Quoted in Johnson, 'Horrors of Hell', 427, who also gives an Old Norse analogue.

[129] Bazire and Cross, hom. 4, lines 47–8.

Drawbacks of Old Age

the fleeting nature of worldly joys. The most evocative depictions of the aging body, however, are to be found in pastoral texts. Rather than comforting those who suffered from the disadvantages of age, homilists referred to physical decrepitude in order to remind their audience of their impending death or to strike the fear of Hell into their hearts. Indeed, one of the alluring aspects of Heaven for an Anglo-Saxon was the absence of old age.

I started chapter 2 by juxtaposing the *gerontophobia*, 'fear of old age', established for Modern English literature, and Burrow's claim, followed by Crawford, that the Anglo-Saxons preferred old age above all other age categories.[130] Everything in chapter 3 suggests that the literary records of early medieval England are not wholly different from that of later ages and, arguably, it is more apt to ascribe to the Anglo-Saxons an apprehension for old age, rather than an appreciation. With that in mind, let me return to the start of this chapter and the interpretation of "on yldo eft" in *The Fortunes of Men* to indicate a period of "wyndagum" [days of joy]. Given the above, the translation 'in the next stage of life, i.e. maturity' is more likely than 'in old age': clearly, Anglo-Saxon writers did not associate the last stage of life with 'happy days'. Rather, in the perception of the Anglo-Saxons, the elderly typically spent their days in *gēomor*, *sār* and *gehðo*: sadness, pain and grief.

---

[130] Freedman, 'Sufficiently Decayed: Gerontophobia', 49–61. Cf. Burrow, *Ages of Man*, 109; Crawford, '*Gomol is snoterost*', 59.

4
frode fyrnwitan: Old Saints in Anglo-Saxon Hagiography

                    'Cuð is gehwilcum menn
þæt þis lif is geswinc-ful   and on swate wunað.
þis lif bið alefed   on langsumum sarum
and on hætum ofþefod   and on hungre gewæht
mid mettum ge-fylled   and modig on welum
mid hafen-leaste aworpen   and ahafen þurh iugoðe,
mid ylde gebiged   and to-bryt mid seocnysse
mid unrotnysse fornumen   and geangsumod þurh cara.'[1]

['It is known to every man that this life is full of hardship and it dwells in sweat. This life is given over to long-lasting pains and dried up by heat, weakened by hunger, filled with food, made proud by wealth, degraded by poverty, raised up by youth, bowed down by old age, broken down with sickness, overwhelmed with sadness and afflicted by sorrows.']

With these words, St Cecilia in Ælfric's rendition of her *vita* sums up how everyone will suffer from pain, heat, hunger, poverty, sorrow and old age. Since these factors affect everyone in this life, Cecilia maintains, everyone should want to be a Christian and attain Heaven, where such things are absent.

Naturally, old age did not affect everyone in equal measure and much depended on a person's way of life, occupation and social standing. After the discussion of the general merits and drawbacks of old age in chapters 2 and 3, the present chapter and the three following take into account some of these more specific parameters. These four chapters show how old age affected the lives and representations of four specific groups: saints, warriors, kings and women, respectively. How were older members of these groups portrayed in the cultural record, and what does this reveal about the expected roles of the elderly in Anglo-Saxon England? Since the representation of a person's old age is also influenced by the conventions and traditions of the particular text type in which their lives were recorded, due attention will also be given to the nature of the source material used in each chapter.

---

[1] *ÆLS*, no. 34, lines 141b–148.

Anglo-Saxon hagiography

The lives and deeds of saints were chronicled in hagiography. This genre enjoyed great popularity in the Anglo-Saxon period; around a hundred saints' lives survive in Old English and still more in Latin.[2] The term 'hagiography' covers a broad range of texts: from lengthy stand-alone *vitae* of native, Anglo-Saxon saints, written by eye-witnesses, such as Stephen of Ripon's *Vita s. Wilfrithi* (710–720), to vernacular adaptations of Latin texts about universal saints such as those collected in Ælfric's *Lives of Saints* (992–1002), through to the assembled, abbreviated lives in *legendae*, exemplified by the ninth-century *Old English Martyrology*.[3] While hagiographical texts thus differ in language and length, each has the same purpose: to present their subject as a recognizable member of the community of saints.[4] In order to do so, hagiographers tended to model their stories on earlier *vitae*, using conventional phrases and *topoi*. As a result, many saints' lives come across as "badly composed series of stereotypes".[5] Yet, abiding by hagiographical conventions was not caused by a lack of creativity on account of the hagiographer; it was born of necessity. The more saints had in common with other saints, the more likely it was that their sanctity would be accepted.[6]

Given their conventionality, even those saints' lives rooted in historical reality often reveal less about the historical individuals they portray than about the mentality of the hagiographer and his or her audience.[7] As the sociologist Pierre Delooz has noted:

> The reputation of sanctity is the collective mental representation of someone as a saint, whether based on a knowledge of facts that have *really* happened, or whether based on facts that have been at least in part *constructed* if not entirely imagined. But in truth, all saints, more or less, appear to be constructed in the sense that being necessarily saints in consequence of a reputation created by others and a role that others

---

[2] C. Watson, 'Old English Hagiography: Recent and Future Research', *Literature Compass* 1 (2004), 1.

[3] Helpful introductions to the text type include E. G. Whatley, 'An Introduction to the Study of Old English Prose Hagiography: Sources and Resources', in *Holy Men and Holy Women: Old English Prose Saints' Lives and Their Contexts*, ed. P. E. Szarmach (New York, 1996), 3–32; T. D. Hill, '*Imago Dei*: Genre, Symbolism, and Anglo-Saxon Hagiography', in *Holy Men*, ed. Szarmach, 35–50.

[4] Hill, '*Imago Dei*', 40; C. Cubitt, 'Universal and Local Saints in Anglo-Saxon England', in *Local Saints and Local Churches in the Early Medieval West*, ed. A. Thacker and R. Sharpe (Oxford, 2002), 429.

[5] Hill, '*Imago Dei*', 43.

[6] J. W. Earl, 'Typology and Iconographic Styles in Early Medieval Hagiography', *Studies in the Literary Imagination* 8 (1975), 17–21.

[7] Hill, '*Imago Dei*', 36.

expect of them, they are remodeled to correspond to collective mental representations.[8]

Put differently, a study of how saints behave in a given situation does not constitute a reconstruction of historical reality: it provides an insight into how the hagiographer and his audience would expect the saints to have reacted to their circumstances. The saints' behaviour was idealised, and hagiography, above all, provided its audience with role models, rather than accurately reporting the words and actions of historical individuals.

The representation of old age in hagiography has generally been neglected in existing scholarship. A remarkable example of the disinterest in the elderly saint is the wide-ranging, prosopographical study by Donald Weinstein and Rudolph M. Bell. They studied the lives of 864 European saints who lived between 1000 and 1700 and gathered statistical information for over forty social variables, ranging from area of birth to status of parental family, through to occupational category, gender, family dynamics and a saint's reputation. While some attention is given to different stages of the life cycle, the three categories used (children, adolescents and adults) did not, apparently, warrant any comments on the old age of some of these saints.[9] Perhaps more strikingly, Burrow, who mainly used hagiographical sources for his claim that the Anglo-Saxons preferred old age above all other age categories, never once referred to saints in their old age. Instead, he focused on young saints who showed behaviour beyond their years, the *puer senex* motif.[10]

There are, to my knowledge, two notable exceptions to the rule. The only study to focus exclusively on people in their later years in hagiographical sources is the analysis of forty-three twelfth- and thirteenth-century French texts by Cochelin.[11] She concludes that hagiography is one of the richest sources for the study of the perception of old age, since the texts feature numerous examples of the potential consequences of growing old, including frailty, the necessity of retirement and intergenerational conflicts. With respect to Anglo-Saxon saints, a valuable contribution has been made by Semper's overview of old age in Anglo-Saxon literature. Even though she uses only part

---

[8] Quoted and translated in D. Weinstein and R. M. Bell, *Saints and Society: The Two Worlds of Western Christendom, 1000–1700* (Chicago, 1982), 9.
[9] Weinstein and Bell, *Saints and Society*.
[10] Burrow, *Ages of Man*, 96–109.
[11] I. Cochelin, '*In senectute bona*: pour une typologie de la vieillesse dans l'hagiographie monastique des XIIe et XIIIe siècles', in *Les âges de la vie au Moyen âge: actes du colloque du Département d'études médiévales de l'Université de Paris-Sorbonne et de l'Université Friedrich-Wilhelm de Bonn*, ed. H. Dubois and M. Zink (Paris, 1992), 119–38.

of the hagiographical material available, Semper rightly observes that hagiographers included old age in their narratives for various purposes: to emphasise the humanity of saints, to provide didactic examples of endurance, and to accentuate the saint's dedication to his religious duties.[12]

Barring Semper's observations, the aged saint in Anglo-Saxon hagiography is still very much uncharted territory; this chapter presents a first foray into establishing and defining the *topos* of senescence in the hagiographical texts that circulated in early medieval England.[13] I will take a synchronic approach and focus on how the topic of a saint's old age was treated across the entire range of hagiographical texts produced in Anglo-Saxon England, in both Latin and Old English.[14] Altogether, the examples gathered here reflect the consequences of old age that Anglo-Saxon hagiographers and their audiences anticipated, as well as what they would have considered the ideal response to the challenges posed by growing old.

---

[12] Semper, '*Byð se ealda man*', 305–9.

[13] The analysis is based on all Old English saints' lives and the Latin saints' lives devoted to Anglo-Saxon saints that were available in modern editions. Helpful handlists of Anglo-Saxon saints and hagiographical texts include Whatley, 'Introduction', 3–32; D. G. Scragg, 'The Corpus of Vernacular Homilies and Prose Saints' Lives before Ælfric', in *Old English Prose: Basic Readings*, ed. P. E. Szarmach (New York, 2000), 73–150; J. Roberts, 'The English Saints Remembered in the Old English Anonymous Homilies', in *Old English Prose*, ed. Szarmach, 433–61; J. Blair, 'A Handlist of Anglo-Saxon Saints', in *Local Saints*, ed. Thacker and Sharpe, 495–566. Important editions of Anglo-Saxon hagiography published after these overviews include *The Cult of St Swithun*, ed. and trans. M. Lapidge (Oxford, 2003); Byrhtferth, *Lives*, ed. and trans. Lapidge; *The Early Lives of St Dunstan*, ed. and trans. M. Winterbottom and M. Lapidge (Oxford, 2012); *Old English Martyrology*, ed. and trans. Rauer; and *Abbots*, ed. and trans. Grocock and Wood.

[14] Watson, 'Old English Hagiography', 5, notes that discussing the genre in its entirety, rather than depending on authorial boundaries, is valuable, since different materials occur side-by-side in manuscripts. Although a consideration of how Anglo-Saxon authors adapted their source material can be highly revealing, a diachronic approach falls outside the scope of the present study. For research on the sources of Anglo-Saxon hagiography, see, e.g., *Sources of Anglo-Saxon Literary Culture: A Trial Version*, ed. F. M. Biggs, T. D. Hill and P. E. Szarmach (Binghamton, 1990) and *Fontes Anglo-Saxonici*. One interesting adaptation of Latin source material with respect to old age concerns Ælfric's vernacular adaptation of the smith who had a vision of St Swithun. In his Old English text, Ælfric transformed the sickly smith of his Latin source into an "ealdan smiðe" [old smith]. Ælfric, *Life of St Swithun*, ed. and trans. Lapidge, *Cult*, ch. 2, line 17. The adaptation may be an attempt to lend credence to the story of the smith, given that the appeal to reliable, elderly witnesses was commonplace in hagiographical and historiographical sources alike, see chapter 2.

The presence of old saints in Anglo-Saxon hagiography

In his *Vita s. Ecgwini*, an account of the life of Ecgwine (d. 717?), bishop of Worcester, Byrhtferth of Ramsey begins by stating that saintlihood could be revealed during all stages of life:

> ... uirorum ... – qui perplurimi a pueritia agoniste precipui effecti sunt, aliique in adolescentia emerito opere compti, plerique in iuuentute sumnis miraculis gloriosi, nonnulli in senectute et in cignea canitie sunt infulis supernis decorati (sicut millena congerie liquido probari et experiri possumus).
>
> [... these great men – of whom very many were made outstanding contestants from their childhood, others were adorned with veteran accomplishments while still in youth, several were distinguished by great miracles while in manhood, some during their old age and in swan-white senescence were honoured with heavenly insignia (as I could clearly demonstrate and establish with a thousandfold muster of examples).][15]

Despite Byrhtferth's insistence that he could muster a thousand examples of saints of all ages, elderly saints appear only marginally in the hagiography of early medieval England, as is illustrated by three influential hagiographical collections. In the two versions of *De laude virginitatis* [In praise of virginity] of Aldhelm (d. 709), for instance, old saints make up less than 10 per cent of the saintly virgins listed: in the prose version, only five of fifty-six virgins are identifiably old in the text and the figures are even worse for the poetic version, which features just three such virgins out of fifty-four.[16] The *Old English Martyrology* seems equally devoid of old saints: out of its 238 entries, only eleven are devoted to saints who are either called 'old' or are reported to have reached an age over fifty.[17] In Ælfric's *Lives of Saints*, made up of thirty-nine *vitae*, only Maurus, Luke the Apostle, Eleazar and Martin of Tours are described in this way.[18] The relatively low

---

[15] Byrhtferth, *Vita s. Ecgwini*, ed. and trans. Lapidge, I.6.

[16] Aldhelm, *De laude virginitatis*, trans. M. Lapidge, in Aldhelm, *The Prose Works*, trans. M. Lapidge and M. W. Herren (Cambridge, 1979), 80 (John the Apostle), 81–2 (Luke the Apostle), 87 (Felix), 87–8 (Paul the Hermit), 89 (John the Hermit); Aldhelm, *Carmen de virginitate*, trans. Rosier, 114 (Luke the Apostle), 120 (Paul the Hermit), 120–1 (Hilarion).

[17] *Old English Martyrology*, ed. and trans. Rauer, nos. 16 (Paul the Hermit), 22 (Anthony the Hermit), 85 (Calepodius), 120 (Tranquillinus), 136 (Simeon Stylites), 194 (Zachary), 196 (Ceolfrith), 207 (Luke the Apostle), 211 (Hilarion), 221 (Winnoc), 226 (Hild).

[18] *ÆLS*, no. 6, lines 367–71, no. 15, line 158, no. 25, lines 32–3, no. 31, lines 1371–2. In addition, two minor characters are called old: Eubolus in the *vita* of St Basil and Victor in the *vita* of St Maurice, *ibid.*, no. 3, line 50, no. 28, lines 95–110. This

number of aged saints in these hagiographical collections may be the result of the hagiographers' preference for martyrs, who, by definition, rarely grew old.

The statistics are slightly deceptive, however, as is often the case, since both the prose and poetic versions of *De laude virginitatis* and the *Old English Martyrology* often simply omit information about the age of saints. For instance, the prose *De laude virginitatis* refers to the fact that both John the Apostle and John the Hermit reached an old age, but mention of their senectitude is absent from the poetic version;[19] *vice versa*, Hilarion is called an old man in the poetic version, but no reference to his age is found in the prose version.[20] Similarly, the *Old English Martyrology* has entries for Benedict Biscop and Martin of Tours without mentioning their advanced ages.[21] A possible explanation for the lack of information regarding a saint's old age, in the cases of *De laude virginitatis* and the *Old English Martyrology*, is the relative brevity of the descriptions devoted to each saint. These brief entries only include those elements that the author deemed essential for the saints' sanctity, such as their virginity, martyrdom or extreme asceticism.

Nevertheless, even in longer saints' lives, hagiographers seldom comment on a saint's senescence. Only ten saints are identifiably old in the hundred or so Old English prose saints' lives listed by E. G. Whatley (see below).[22] Old saints occur only slightly more frequently in Anglo-Latin hagiography devoted to native, Anglo-Saxon saints (see below).[23] It is worth noting that the majority of the latter category of old saints are high-ranking members of the clergy, which means that the model of an elderly saint may reflect, in particular, the expectations an Anglo-Saxon hagiographer and his audience had of prominent clergymen.

---

overview excludes the elderly saints Zosimus and Mary of Egypt who feature in the *vita* of Mary of Egypt which is included in Skeat's edition of Ælfric's *Lives of Saints* but was not written by Ælfric himself, see *The Old English Life of St Mary of Egypt*, ed. and trans. H. Magennis (Exeter, 2002), 17–19.

[19] Aldhelm, *De laude virginitatis*, trans. Lapidge, 80, 89; Aldhelm, *Carmen de virginitate*, trans. Rosier, 113, 121.
[20] Aldhelm, *De laude virginitatis*, trans. Lapidge, 88–9; Aldhelm, *Carmen de virginitate*, trans. Rosier, 121. On the differences between the prose and poetic versions of *De virginitate*, see Aldhelm, *Poetic Works*, trans. Lapidge and Rosier, 99.
[21] *Old English Martyrology*, ed. and trans. Rauer, nos. 23, 136.
[22] Whatley, 'Introduction', 5–7, who, however, does not include the entries in the *Old English Martyrology*, for which see p. 114, n. 17 above.
[23] Anglo-Latin hagiography devoted to universal saints has not been considered, since the majority of these lives are still unavailable in modern editions. Some post-Conquest *vitae* have been included in the analysis, as these may preserve earlier traditions.

List 2. Saints whose old age is referred to in Old English prose saints' lives[24]

1. Eleazar (d. c.168), chief scribe and martyr[25]
2. Eventius (2nd century), martyr[26]
3. John the Apostle (d. late 1st century), evangelist[27]
4. Luke the Apostle (1st century), evangelist[28]
5. Martin of Tours (c.316–397), monk bishop[29]
6. Mary of Egypt (5th century?), penitent[30]
7. Maurus (6th century), monk[31]
8. Philip the Apostle (1st century)[32]
9. Sixtus II (d. 258), pope and martyr[33]
10. Zosimus (5th century), monk who met Mary of Egypt[34]

List 3. Native saints whose old age is referred to in Anglo-Latin hagiography[35]

1. Æthelwold (904/9–984), abbot of Abingdon and bishop of Winchester[36]
2. Aldhelm (d. 709/10), abbot of Malmesbury, bishop of Sherborne, and scholar[37]
3. Benedict Biscop (c.628–689), abbot of Wearmouth and scholar[38]

---

[24] Life dates and titles of all saints, except for Eventius and Zosimus, retrieved from *The Oxford Dictionary of Saints*, ed. D. H. Farmer, 5th rev. ed. (Oxford, 2011).
[25] *ÆLS*, no. 25. Eleazar is described as "har-wencge and eald" [grey-bearded and old] (lines 32–3).
[26] *ÆCHom II*, hom. 18. Eventius had been baptised 70 years before his martyrdom.
[27] *ÆCHom I*, hom. 4. John died at the age of 99.
[28] *ÆLS*, no. 15. Luke died at the age of 84.
[29] *ÆCHom II*, hom. 34; *ÆLS*, no. 31; *Vercelli Homilies*, hom. 18.
[30] *Life of Mary of Egypt*, ed. and trans. Magennis. Mary's age at death can be reconstructed as 67 and she is described as having long white hair.
[31] *ÆLS*, no. 15. Maurus died at the age of 72.
[32] *ÆCHom II*, hom. 17. Philip died at the age of 87.
[33] *ÆCHom I*, hom. 29. Sixtus II calls himself "ealde" [old] and is respected for his "ylde" [old age] (lines 37, 55).
[34] *Life of Mary of Egypt*, ed. and trans. Magennis. Zosimus first meets Mary of Egypt at the age of 53 and then continues to serve a monastery for a hundred more years.
[35] Life dates and titles for all saints retrieved from the *ODNB*.
[36] Wulfstan of Winchester, *The Life of St Æthelwold*, ed. and trans. M. Lapidge and M. Winterbottom (Oxford, 1991); Ælfric, *Vita s. Æthelwoldi*, in the same edition, is an abbreviated version of Wulfstan's *vita*.
[37] Faricius, *Vita s. Aldhelmi*, ed. M. Winterbottom, 'An Edition of Faricius, *Vita s. Aldhelmi*', *Journal of Medieval Latin* 15 (2005), 93–147; William of Malmesbury, *Gesta pontificum Anglorum*, ed. and trans. M. Winterbottom (Oxford, 2007), V.
[38] Bede, *Homilia in natale s. Benedicti*, ed. and trans. Grocock and Wood, *Abbots*; Bede, *Historia abbatum*, ed. and trans. Grocock and Wood, *Abbots*.

Old Saints

4. Boniface (672x5?–754), archbishop of Mainz, missionary and martyr[39]
5. Ceolfrith (642–716), abbot of Wearmouth and Jarrow[40]
6. Dunstan (d. 988), archbishop of Canterbury[41]
7. Ecgwine (d. 717?), bishop of Worcester[42]
8. Edward the Confessor (1003x5–1066), king of England[43]
9. Leoba (d. 782), abbess of Tauberbischofsheim[44]
10. Oswald (d. 992), archbishop of York[45]
11. Swithun (d. 863), bishop of Winchester[46]
12. Wilfrid (c.634–709/10), bishop of Hexham[47]
13. Willibald (c.700–787?), bishop of Eichstätt[48]
14. Willibrord (657/8–739), missionary, bishop of the Frisians and abbot of Echternach[49]
15. Wulfstan (c.1008–1095), bishop of Worcester[50]

The relatively low number of saints in the two lists confirms Catherine Cubitt's observation that "saints' *vitae* are generally uninterested in the process of aging and present a static view in which the saint moves from a holy childhood … to death without emphasis on aging".[51] Indeed, even when hagiographers do mention a saint's senescence,

---

[39] Willibald, *Vita Bonifatii*, trans. C. H. Talbot, *The Anglo-Saxon Missionaries in Germany* (London, 1954).
[40] *Vita Ceolfrithi*, ed. and trans. Grocock and Wood, *Abbots*; Bede, *Historia abbatum*, ed. and trans. Grocock and Wood, *Abbots*.
[41] *Vita s. Dunstani*, ed. and trans. Winterbottom and Lapidge, *Early Lives*. William of Malmesbury, *Vita Dunstani*, ed. and trans. M. Winterbottom and R. M. Thomson, in William of Malmesbury, *Saints' Lives. Lives of ss. Wulfstan, Dunstan, Patrick, Benignus and Indract* (Oxford, 2002).
[42] Byrhtferth, *Vita s. Ecgwini*, ed. and trans. Lapidge.
[43] *The Life of King Edward Who Rests at Westminster: Attributed to a Monk of Saint-Bertin*, ed. and trans. F. Barlow, 2nd ed. (Oxford, 1992).
[44] Rudolf, *Vita s. Leoba*, trans. Talbot, *Missionaries*.
[45] Byrhtferth, *Vita s. Oswaldi*, ed. and trans. Lapidge.
[46] Lantfred of Winchester, *Translatio et miracula s. Swithuni*, ed. and trans. Lapidge, *Cult*; Wulfstan of Winchester, *Narratio metrica de s. Swithuno*, ed. and trans. Lapidge, *Cult*. While little is known about Swithun's life, in both of these works he appears in various visions as a white-haired old man; this is not the case in Ælfric, *Life of St Swithun*, ed. and trans. Lapidge.
[47] Stephen of Ripon, *Life of Wilfrid*, ed. and trans. Colgrave.
[48] Huneberc, *Hodoeporicon*, trans. Talbot, *Missionaries*.
[49] Alcuin, *Vita Willibrordi*, trans. Talbot, *Missionaries*.
[50] William of Malmesbury, *Vita s. Wulfstani*, ed. and trans. Winterbottom and Thomson. This post-Conquest *vita* is a Latin reworking of the now lost Old English life of Wulfstan written by the Worcester monk Coleman (d. 1113).
[51] C. Cubitt, 'Memory and Narrative in the Cult of Early Anglo-Saxon Saints', in *The Uses of the Past in the Early Middle Ages*, ed. Y. Hen and M. Innes (Cambridge, 2000), 65–6.

they rarely elaborate. In his *vitae* of Maurus and Philip the Apostle, for instance, Ælfric merely mentions the age at which both saints died – seventy-two and eighty-seven, respectively – but refrains from any further comment.[52] More remarkably, despite the Anglo-Saxon nun Huneberc's announcement in her *Hodoeporicon* of Willibald to "speak of his early manhood, the time of his maturity and of his old age, even till he became decrepit", she does not discuss the saint's old age in the remainder of the text, focusing instead on Willibald's pilgrimage to the Holy Land and ending her narrative shortly after his election to the bishopric of Eichstätt at the age of forty-one.[53] Cubitt's observation on the Anglo-Saxon hagiographers' lack of interest in senescence is further reinforced by scholarly attempts to present a structural typology of a 'standard' medieval saint's life. These hagiographical moulds do not include old age as one of the typically recurring stages, along with birth, childhood, education, piety, martyrdom or death, translation of relics and post-mortem miracles.[54] In sum, a saint's senescence was not a standard part of a *vita*; whenever hagiographers commented on the topic at length, they may have made a conscious choice to do so.

Despite the relative rarity of descriptions of a saint's old age, an analysis of the lives of the elderly Anglo-Saxon saints in the two lists above reveals that hagiographical portrayals of saints in their later years are as stereotypical and conventional as other structural elements normally found in the lives of saints. Recurring motifs include senescent saints' roles as spiritual guides; their decrepitude; their necessitated successions; their unrelenting discipline despite their age; miracles that compensate for the drawbacks of age; and their joy over their long-anticipated deaths and release from their decrepit bodies. Before illustrating each of these elements in the Anglo-Saxon *vitae* of old saints, I first discuss another *topos* that has been considered important for the representation of old age in hagiography: the young saint who behaves like an old man.

The old child: The puer senex *motif in Anglo-Saxon hagiography*

Saints typically reveal their sanctity from a young age onwards. They disregard the frivolous activities of their peers and instead show a greater interest in spiritual matters. Occasionally, such saintly children

---

[52] *ÆLS*, no. 6, line 361; *ÆCHom II*, hom. 17, line 54.
[53] Huneberc, *Hodoeporicon*, trans. Talbot, *Missionaries*, 154.
[54] E.g., R. Boyer, 'An Attempt To Define the Typology of Medieval Hagiography', in *Hagiography and Medieval Literature: A Symposium*, ed. H. Bekker-Nielsen *et al.* (Odense, 1981), 27–36; R. S. Farrar, 'Structure and Function in Representative Old English Saints' Lives', *Neophilologus* 57 (1973), 83–93.

are said to have an 'old heart' or an 'old mind'. This *puer senex* motif is a "hagiographical cliché" that has its roots in Late Antiquity. The motif probably found its way to Anglo-Saxon England through the writings of Gregory the Great (c.540–d. 604),[55] as is suggested by a passage in Bede's *Historia abbatum* (c.716). Here, Bede describes the youth of Benedict Biscop by citing the phrasing that Gregory had used for Benedict's famous namesake Benedict of Nursia (c.480–550):

> Qui ut beati papae Gregorii uerbis, quibus cognominis eius abbatis uitam glorificat, utar: 'Fuit uir uitae uenerabilis, gratia Benedictus et nomine, ab ipso pueritiae suae tempore cor gerens senile, aetatem quippe moribus transiens, nulli animum uoluptati dedit.'

> [If I may use the words of the blessed Pope Gregory with which he praises the life of the abbot of that name, 'He was a man of admirable character, "called Blessed" by name and by grace. He had the heart of an old man, even from the time of his childhood, transcending his age in his behaviour, and gave his soul over to no lustful passion.'][56]

Burrow based much of his claim that the Anglo-Saxons preferred old age above all other categories on portrayals such as that of Benedict Biscop. In his analysis of Anglo-Saxon saints' lives, he noted that Anglo-Saxon hagiographers showed a clear preference for youthful saints transcending their age and behaving like an elderly person. Therefore, Burrow argued, old age was the 'transcendence ideal' and, hence, the most highly regarded age of man.[57]

At first sight, Burrow's observations appear sound. Apart from Benedict Biscop, several other saints are described as exhibiting the qualities of old age in their childhood, such as Willibrord (657/8–739) in the *vita* by Alcuin:

> In fact this highly gifted boy [Willibrord] made such progress as the days went by that development of his intelligence and character so outstripped his tender years that his small and delicate frame harboured the wisdom of ripe old age.[58]

Similarly, Ælfric describes both St Alexander and St Agnes as "iunglic on gearum, and aldlic on mode" [young in years and old in mind].[59] Occasionally, the saint himself would partake in the trivial

---

[55] Burrow, *Ages of Man*, 101.
[56] Bede, *Historia abbatum*, ed. and trans. Grocock and Wood, *Abbots*, ch. 1. Translation adapted to render literally the Latin phrase "cor gerens senile". For the corresponding passage in Gregory's *Dialogi*, see Gregory, *Dialogues*, ed. de Vogüé, II. prol.
[57] Burrow, *Ages of Man*, 105–7.
[58] Alcuin, *Vita Willibrordi*, trans. Talbot, *Missionaries*, 5.
[59] Ælfric, *Homilies*, ed. Pope, hom. 23, line 7; *ÆLS*, no. 7, line 9: "cild-lic on gearum and eald-lic on mode" [childlike in years and 'oldlike' in mind].

activities of children but was rebuked for doing so by one of his peers who showed behaviour beyond his years, as was the case for Cuthbert (c.635–687), bishop of Lindisfarne. Bede reports how a three-year-old boy, "senili constantia" [with the gravity of an old man], told Cuthbert to stop playing the childish game that had him twist his arms and legs into unnatural shapes and to devote himself to spiritual matters instead.[60] In all these cases, the intrinsic qualities associated with old age – wisdom and gravity – enabled the child to stand out from the rest of his generation. In this respect, Burrow was right to assume that old age was considered morally and spiritually superior to youth.[61]

A closer look at the *vitae* of other saints that Burrow included in his analysis, however, suggests that old age was not the only age category towards which saints could miraculously ascend. A clear example is the case of the Virgin Mary, whom Burrow included in his analysis as a *puella senex* [old girl]. In the Old English translation of the *Gospel of Pseudo-Matthew*, the way Mary transcended her youth is phrased as follows: "heo wæs on gange and on worde and on eallum gebærum gelic wynsuman men, þe hæfde XXX wintra" [she walked and spoke and behaved just like a comely person of thirty years old].[62] In this case, it would clearly be better to speak of a *puella matura* [mature girl] rather than a *puella senex*. In yet another of Burrow's examples, Æthelwold is described as overcoming the tender years of his childhood by his "uirtutum maturitate" [maturity in virtue].[63] In other words, the hagiographer compared Æthelwold's qualities to those of maturity or adulthood, rather than old age. In other cases of saints transcending their youth, including some that Burrow cited as confirming his hypothesis, the hagiographer did not specify whether these youthful saints were endowed with qualities of old age or adulthood, but simply stated that they differed from others of the same age.[64] Thus, the *puer senex* motif does not consistently identify old age as the only transcendence ideal: some saints were described with the qualities of adulthood, while the portrayals of

---

[60] Bede, *Vita s. Cuthberti*, ed. and trans. Colgrave, *Two Lives*, ch. 1. Arguably, a more accurate translation of "constantia" here would be 'self-control, perseverance'.
[61] Burrow, *Ages of Man*, 107–9.
[62] *The Apocryphal Gospels of Mary in Anglo-Saxon England*, ed. and trans. M. Clayton (Cambridge, 1998), 174–5; cf. Burrow, *Ages of Man*, 102.
[63] Wulfstan of Winchester, *Life of Æthelwold*, ed. and trans. Lapidge and Winterbottom, ch. 6; cf. Burrow, *Ages of Man*, 100.
[64] Boniface: Willibald, *Vita Bonifatii*, trans. Talbot, *Missionaries*, ch. 2; Guthlac: Felix, *Life of Saint Guthlac*, ed. and trans. B. Colgrave (Cambridge, 1956), ch. 12; Wilfrid: Stephen of Ripon, *Life of Wilfrid*, ed. and trans. Colgrave, ch. 2. These saints are also mentioned by Burrow, *Ages of Man*, 100. Another example is St Machutus: *Old English Life of Machutus*, ed. Yerkes, 5.

others leave unspecified to what age category the youthful saints had ascended.

Arguably, the only age category which is truly appraised by the Anglo-Saxon renditions of the *puer senex* motif is childhood. In many of the descriptions of the *puer senex* or *puer maturus*, the youngest generation is presented in a negative way. A clear example of the denunciation of childhood implied in the portrayals of saints transcending their age is found in Felix's *vita* of St Guthlac (c.674–714):

> Igitur transcensis infantiae suae temporibus, cum fari pueriliter temtabat, nullius molestiae parentibus nutricibusve seu coaetaneis parvulorum coetibus fuit. Non puerorum lascivias, non garrula matronarum deliramenta, non vanas vulgi fabulas, non ruricolarum bardigiosos vagitus, non falsidicas parasitorum fribulas, non variorum volucrum diversos crocitus, ut adsolet illa aetas, imitabatur.
>
> [And as the time of his infancy passed and he (Guthlac) tried to speak in his childish way, he was never troublesome to his parents or nurses or to the bands of children of his own age. He did not imitate the impudence of the children nor the nonsensical chatter of the matrons, nor the empty tales of the common people, nor the foolish shouts of the rustics, nor the lying trifling of flatterers, nor the different cries of the various kinds of birds as children of that age are wont to do.][65]

Felix presents childhood as an age of rashness and frivolity and Guthlac as behaving exceptionally by exhibiting prudence and gravity beyond his years. Compared with those of his peers, Guthlac's heart and mind are older, but not necessarily old.

Spiritual guides:
Senescent saints in their religious communities

The elderly in twelfth- and thirteenth-century hagiography often functioned as spiritual guides.[66] Old people commemorated in Anglo-Saxon hagiography were no different in this respect.[67] According to the *Old English Martyrology*, for example, the introduction of Simeon Stylites to the monastic life had been instigated by an old person, as was the case for the triplet saints Speusippus, Eleusippus and Meleusippus, who had all been taught about the Christian faith by their grandmother.[68] Elderly spiritual guides also featured in visions: when Dunstan was still a boy, he had a vision of "senem niueo uestitum candore" [an

---

[65] Felix, *Life of Guthlac*, ed. and trans. Colgrave, ch. 12.
[66] Cochelin, 'In senectute bona', 136.
[67] Semper, 'Byð se ealda man', 302.
[68] *Old English Martyrology*, ed. and trans. Rauer, nos. 23, 136.

old man, clad in snowy white], who pointed out to him where he would construct the buildings of the monastery at Glastonbury during his future abbacy.[69] Similarly, Æthelwulf, the author of *De abbatibus* (803–821), a poetic collection of monastic lives, reported dreaming of a venerable old man seated in a shining chair, who told him where to find his former teachers.[70]

When saints themselves grew old, they also served as spiritual guides to the younger members of their religious communities. Indeed, Benedict Biscop, Æthelwold and Dunstan, to name but a few, all spent their last years explaining monastic rules, leading church services and instructing the younger members of their communities.[71] Aldhelm did much the same, after he had been pressured into accepting the position of bishop of Sherborne despite his advanced age. He had been convinced by those around him that "quod quanto annis maturior, tanto esset uitiis defecatior, consiliis promptior" [the older he was, the more purged he was of vice, and the readier in counsel].[72] Ceolfrith, too, continued to prove a "spiritualis exercitii ... formam" [model of spiritual exercise] until, at the age of seventy-four, he felt no longer able to do so.[73] His departure for Rome was a cause for great distress among the younger monks at Monkwearmouth and Jarrow, indicating that the spiritual guidance of the old saint would be sorely missed. Not only do these examples testify to the spiritual superiority of these elderly saints, they also indicate that high-ranking clerical offices often fell to older members of the community.

A number of elderly saints are shown as being well aware of their exemplary role, especially when choosing torture and death over relinquishing their religious vows. The "har-wencge and eald" [greybearded and old] scribe Eleazar, an Old Testament martyr in Ælfric's homily on the Maccabees, is a case in point. When Eleazar had been forced to eat bacon and, upon refusal, had been offered the chance to eat imitation bacon instead, he declined the opportunity. He exclaimed that he did not wish to give a wrong example to the young:

---

[69] *Vita s. Dunstani*, ed. and trans. Winterbottom and Lapidge, *Early Lives*, ch. 3.4.

[70] Æthelwulf, *De abbatibus*, ed. and trans. A. Campbell (Oxford, 1967), ch. 22, line 734.

[71] Bede, *Homilia in natale s. Benedicti*, ed. and trans. Grocock and Wood, *Abbots*, ch. 13; Bede, *Historia abbatum*, ed. and trans. Grocock and Wood, *Abbots*, ch. 11; Wulfstan of Winchester, *Life of Æthelwold*, ed. and trans. Lapidge and Winterbottom, ch. 41; *Vita s. Dunstani*, ed. and trans. Winterbottom and Lapidge, *Early Lives*, ch. 38.2.

[72] William of Malmesbury, *Gesta pontificum*, ed. and trans. Winterbottom, V.ccxxxiii.5.

[73] Bede, *Historia abbatum*, ed. and trans. Grocock and Wood, *Abbots*, ch. 16; cf. *Vita Ceolfrithi*, ed. and trans. Grocock and Wood, *Abbots*, ch. 21.

Old Saints

Ða cwæð Eleazarus: 'Ic eom eald to hiwigenne
and wenað þa geongan þæt ic wille for-gægan
godes gesetnysse for ðisum sceortan life
and bið þonne min hiwung him to forwyrde
and ic sylf beo and-sæte þurh swylce gebysnunge.
Ðeah ðe ic beo ahred fram manna reðnysse
ic ne mæg þam ælmihtigan ahwar ætberstan
on life oþþe on deaðe; ac ic læte bysne
þam iungum cnihtum gif ic cenlice swelte
arwurðum deaðe for ðære halgan æ.'[74]

[Then said Eleazar: 'I am too old to pretend and the young ones will think that I want to forego God's decree in exchange for this short life and then my pretense will be their destruction and I will be hateful to myself because of such an example. Though I were saved from the cruelty of men, I cannot escape from the Almighty anywhere in life or in death, but I will set an example for the young boys if I bravely die an honourable death for the holy law.']

Eleazar's wish was fulfilled and he was killed on the spot. In Ælfric's *vita* of Lawrence, the saint's elderly teacher, the pope and martyr Sixtus II similarly chose death in front of his younger pupils over renouncing his faith.[75] In the Old English *Life of St Pantaleon*, the cruel Emperor Maximianus himself held up the aged martyr Anthimus of Nicomedia as an example to Pantaleon, when he threatened the young saint with torture:

And þa andswerade him Pantaleon 7 he cwæð, 'Gegearawa þu þine tintregan forðan ic eam gearo to þrowigenne for Cristes naman.' 7 þa cwæð se casere, 'Geher þu Pantaleon, hu manige tintregan se ealde Antimus þrowade.' And þa andswerade him Pantaleon 7 he cwæð, 'He þrowade swiðe manigfealdlice, 7 hi næs na þe raðer oferswiðed gif he þonne wæs eald 7 he manige tintregan þrowade for Cristes naman; me þænne gedafanað swa miccle swiðor to þrowigenne swa ic eam gingra, þæt ic geearnige þæt ic wære gewuldrad mid him.'[76]

[And then Pantaleon answered him and said: 'Prepare your tortures because I am prepared to suffer for Christ's name.' And then the emperor said: 'Have you heard, Pantaleon, how many torments the old Anthimus had to suffer?' And then Pantaleon answered him and said: 'He suffered very many and he was not quickly overpowered, even though he then was old and he suffered many torments for Christ's name; it seems appropriate for me that I suffer as much more as I am younger, so that I will be worthy to be honoured alongside him.']

---

[74] *ÆLS*, no. 25, lines 94–103.
[75] *ÆCHom I*, hom. 29, lines 3–74.
[76] P. Pulsiano, ed., 'The Old English Life of St Pantaleon', in *Via crucis: Essays on Early Medieval Sources and Ideas in Memory of J. E. Cross*, ed. T. N. Hall, T. D. Hill and C. D. Wright (Morgantown, 2002), lines 224–33.

Pantaleon's explicit retort to Maximianus' veiled threat is significant: not only does the young Pantaleon feel that Anthimus' actions are a model worth emulating, the latter's old age has made his actions all the more inspiring.

Summing up, aged saints, aware of their exemplary function, were typically shown leading the young onto the spiritual path of life. As noted above, the majority of these old saints were prominent members of the clergy. As such, their instructional zeal in their later years may be a reflection of monastic expectations, since canonical rules dictated that the elderly had to teach their younger brethren.[77] Old saints certainly rose to the occasion, even though, as the case of Ceolfrith illustrates, they were not immune to the physical decrepitude that came with the years.

The martyrdom of senescence:
Saints suffering the consequences of old age

Semper has observed that, for some aged saints, "extreme old age *without* physical decline is a marker of holiness".[78] The model for this *topos* was the influential *vita* of St Anthony the Hermit by Athanasius (c.296–373). Anthony had survived to the age of 105, but was still in good health, despite being exceedingly old, keeping to a moderate diet, never changing his clothes or even washing his feet:

> And yet his health remained entirely unimpaired. For instance, even his eyes were perfectly normal so that his sight was excellent; and he had not lost a single tooth, only they had worn down near the gums through the old man's great age. He also kept healthy hands and feet, and on the whole he appeared brighter and more active than did all those who use a diversified diet and baths and a variety of clothing.[79]

Anthony's prolonged health, despite his age and extreme living conditions, set a precedent that was followed in the hagiography devoted to various hermits and desert fathers. Anthony was celebrated in Anglo-Saxon England both in Aldhelm's *De laude virginitatis* and the *Old English Martyrology*, as were other saints, such as Paul the Hermit and Mary of Egypt, who similarly remained untouched, their long years and harsh lives in the desert notwithstanding.[80] Ælfric reported that

---

[77] For the monastic rules, see chapter 2; cf. Cochelin, 'In senectute bona', 134.
[78] Semper, 'Byð se ealda man', 305.
[79] Athanasius, *The Life of Saint Anthony*, trans. R. T. Meyer (London, 1950), ch. 93.
[80] Aldhelm, *De laude virginitatis*, trans. Lapidge, 87; *Old English Martyrology*, ed. and trans. Rauer, nos. 16, 22; *Life of Mary of Egypt*, ed. and trans. Magennis, lines 594–685.

John the Apostle likewise never experienced any bodily discomfort, even though he lived to the age of ninety-nine.[81] In each of these cases, the prolonged health of the saints was regarded as a blessing from God, a testimony to their sanctity.

Nevertheless, most senescent saints in Anglo-Saxon hagiography did eventually suffer from the various bodily restrictions of old age. For instance, when Bishop Wilfrid, "honorabili senior convectus" [bowed down by honourable age], undertook his final pilgrimage to Rome, he was struck by a seizure.[82] Boniface on his travels suffered from "limbs ... weary with old age", that forced him to rest at the court of the king of the Lombards.[83] Æthelwold, likewise, was troubled by infected limbs; Wulfstan of Winchester reports how the old archbishop had to be supported by two assistants in order to rise from his seat, because of his great age.[84] In addition, Æthelwold suffered from weak eyesight and spent hours training his eyes by concentrating on a manuscript page by the light of a candle.[85] These old saints, then, appear just as vulnerable to the physical repercussions of age as any other person.

A notable recurring ailment of old saints is their tendency to fall asleep. Æthelwold, to begin with, dozed off one evening while training his weak eyes and dropped his candle on his manuscript, which, miraculously, remained unscathed.[86] Dunstan, too, took occasional naps and even had a comfortable chair especially prepared for his "meridianum somnum more solito" [customary siesta].[87] Dunstan's chair and sleeping habits were recorded by William of Malmesbury (b. c.1090, d. in or after 1142) as part of an intriguing anecdote relating how the sleeping Dunstan started to levitate:

> ... cum ipse primum quodam leni motu percussus, mox cum ipso sedili ad tectum usque subuectus est, inaudito seculis omnibus miraculo, ut cum grauis carnis pondere uacuum per inane ferretur.

---

[81] *ÆCHom I*, hom. 4, lines 244–70.
[82] Stephen of Ripon, *Life of Wilfrid*, ed. and trans. Colgrave, ch. 53.
[83] Willibald, *Vita Bonifatii*, trans. Talbot, *Missionaries*, ch. 7.
[84] Wulfstan of Winchester, *Narratio metrica de s. Swithuno*, ed. and trans. Lapidge, *Cult*, ch. 4, line 859; cf. Wulfstan of Winchester, *Life of Æthelwold*, ed. and trans. Lapidge and Winterbottom, ch. 30. While Æthelwold's two assistants could be a historically accurate detail, it should be noted that St Anthony the Hermit was also supported by two assistants because of his great age, see Athanasius, *Life of Saint Anthony*, trans. Meyer, ch. 91.
[85] Wulfstan of Winchester, *Life of Æthelwold*, ed. and trans. Lapidge and Winterbottom, ch. 35.
[86] Wulfstan of Winchester, *Life of Æthelwold*, ed. and trans. Lapidge and Winterbottom, ch. 36.
[87] William of Malmesbury, *Vita Dunstani*, ed. and trans. Winterbottom and Thomson, II.22.

[… he was first shaken by a gentle movement, and then carried right up to the ceiling, chair and all: a miracle without precedent, that one weighed down by the burdensome flesh should be borne through empty space.][88]

The monks attending to Dunstan were struck with fear but their mood soon turned to relief when the bishop, still asleep, was let down as gently as he had been lifted up. When another, elderly saint, Wulfstan, fell asleep, he also scared the brethren around him, though not because he started to fly, but because they thought he had died:

> Circumsedentibus enim fratribus et multa ut fit mutuo sermone serenibus, cum repente obstipo capite sopori cessisset, singultantibus omnium lacrimis quasi festino eos obitu destituturus conclamatus est. Nec multo post discusso somno cum causam ploratus addidicisset, respondit his fere uerbis: 'Crede michi, quantum senile corpus durare poterit, non moriar, nec nisi longo senio dissoluetur haec compago. Postquam autem excessero, tunc uobis presentior ero, nec aliquis ex eis quos timetis uobis poterit nocere, si Deo uelitis fideliter seruire.'

> [The brothers were sitting around him conversing vigorously as usual, when Wulfstan's head suddenly drooped and he went off to sleep. Everyone started to sob, thinking that he was about to rob them of him by a swift demise, and giving him up for lost. But soon he shook off his slumber, and learning the reason for their grief replied in more or less the following words: 'Believe me, I shall not die as long as my aged body can last out; and my frame will only disintegrate after a prolonged old age. But after I am gone, I shall be the more present with you, and no one of those you fear will be able to do you harm, if you are ready to serve God in all loyalty.'][89]

Wulfstan's words proved prophetic and he died at the ripe age of eighty-six, severely ill and enfeebled. Thus, Dunstan, Æthelwold and Wulfstan all testify to Bede's observation, in his *De temporum ratione*, that old people were prone to sleepiness.[90]

The saints' decrepitude, coupled to their awareness of their impending death, often prompted them to retire from active life and to appoint suitable assistants or successors – a recurring theme in the lives of aged saints,[91] perhaps influenced by the biblical example of Elijah and Elisha. To cite a striking example, Benedict Biscop was impelled to

---

[88] William of Malmesbury, *Vita Dunstani*, ed. and trans. Winterbottom and Thomson, II.22. The editors note that William of Malmesbury probably used a now lost Old English life of Dunstan for this anecdote, as it does not occur in earlier Latin lives of Dunstan.
[89] William of Malmesbury, *Vita s. Wulfstani*, ed. and trans. Winterbottom and Thomson, III.21.
[90] Bede, *De temporum ratione*, ed. Jones, trans. Wallis, ch. 35.
[91] Cochelin, '*In senectute bona*', 125–7.

appoint a successor and went to great lengths to consult with the ailing abbot of Monkwearmouth, Sicgfrith (d. 698), as both were severely immobilised. Bede relates how the latter had to be carried into Benedict's room:

> ... Sigfridus in feretro deportaretur ad cubiculum ubi Benedictus et ipse suo iacebat in grabato, eisque uno in loco ministrorum manu compositis caput utriusque in eodem ceruicali locaretur, lacrimabili spectaculo, nec tantum habuere uirium ut propius posita ora ad osculandum se alterutrum coniungere possent, sed et hoc fraterno compleuerunt officio.
>
> [... Sicgfrith was carried on a litter to the room where Benedict himself lay on his bed. They were put together in the same place by their servants, with both their heads laid on the same pillow, a sight which brought tears to the eyes. They had so little strength that they could not move their faces, placed together, closer to one another to kiss one another, but only managed to do so with the dutiful assistance of the brothers.][92]

Following this touching scene, Benedict and Sicgfrith appoint Ceolfrith as their joint successor and next abbot of Monkwearmouth and Jarrow. The issue of succession is also given particular emphasis in Willibald's *Life of St Boniface*. No fewer than three times, the *vita* features an old man whose responsibilities needed to be taken over. Abbot Wimbert of Nursling, first of all, succumbed to old age and died, leaving the brethren at Nursling to implore Boniface to take up the role of abbot, which the saint refused on account of his youth.[93] Boniface appealed to the same excuse when he was later asked by Willibrord to become his assistant and "relieve him of the burden of the ministry in his declining years".[94] Eventually, when Boniface himself suffered from his senescence, the saint "now weak and decrepit, showed great foresight both as regards himself and his people by appointing a successor to his see".[95] As Cochelin has justly noted, the fact that these instances of retirement and succession of elderly saints are reported in a neutral or even positive manner reveals that the withdrawal of older members of the clergy was on the whole an accepted and natural phenomenon.[96]

To sum up so far, most saints suffer from all sorts of drawbacks of old age, often forcing them into retirement and necessitating the search for a successor. Bede even went so far as to describe Benedict

---

[92] Bede, *Historia abbatum*, ed. and trans. Grocock and Wood, *Abbots*, ch. 13.
[93] Willibald, *Vita Bonifatii*, trans. Talbot, *Missionaries*, ch. 5; similarly, in the anonymous *Vita s. Dunstani*, ed. and trans. Winterbottom and Lapidge, *Early Lives*, ch. 19.1, the aged Æthelgar, bishop of Crediton (934–953), dies and Dunstan is asked to take his place, but the saint refuses.
[94] Willibald, *Vita Bonifatii*, trans. Talbot, *Missionaries*, ch. 5.
[95] Willibald, *Vita Bonifatii*, trans. Talbot, *Missionaries*, ch. 8.
[96] Cochelin, 'In senectute bona', 126.

Biscop's senescence in terms of a martyrdom, noting that the saint was "longis uirtutum studiis exercitatus longo insuper annosae infirmitatis martyrio excoctus" [worn out by the lengthy exertions of his holy duty and debilitated by the prolonged martyrdom of the weakness of old age].[97] Such references to a saint's suffering may have been an attempt by hagiographers to humanise their subjects, as Semper has suggested,[98] but descriptions of how saints dealt with their old age could also have had the opposite effect. Indeed, as will be demonstrated below, a saintly senescence, like martyrdom, did not only entail physical suffering; it was also an opportunity for hagiographers to establish the holiness of their saints.

Forgetful of their age: Old saints overcoming their age

With respect to later medieval saints' lives, both Shahar and Cochelin have noted that the aging of the body becomes "an opportunity for spiritual elevation" of the saint.[99] Typically, the man of God refuses to temper his religious responsibilities when age or illness come knocking, displaying his unrelenting spirituality in the face of physical decline. An influential model for an old saint's inexorable religiousness was the *vita* of Martin of Tours (c.316–397) by Sulpicius Severus (c.363–c.425).[100] Three *vitae* of Martin survive in Old English and each shows the saint as someone who refuses to slacken his devotion despite being old and mortally ill. Ælfric's adaptation of Severus's work in his *Lives of Saints* is a case in point and has the saint address God in the following manner: "Ne ic ne beladige mine ateorigendlican ylde. Ic þine þenunga estful gefylde; under þinum tacnum ic campige swa lange swa þu sylf hætst" [I shall not be excused on account of my failing old age. I have devotedly fulfilled your service; under your insignia I fight as long as You yourself command].[101] When Martin's followers offer him softer bedding to ease his suffering in the hours before his death, Martin firmly declines, noting that he wishes to give them a fitting example.[102] The anonymous Latin life of Dunstan testifies to the influence of Severus' work, explicitly comparing the aged Dunstan's unrelenting religious activity to that of Martin: "oculis interim ac manibus more beati Martini in caelum semper intentis, inuictum numquam

---

[97] Bede, *Homilia in natale s. Benedicti*, ed. and trans. Grocock and Wood, *Abbots*, ch. 14.
[98] Semper, 'Byð se ealda man', 307.
[99] Shahar, *Growing Old*, 58; Cochelin, 'In senectute bona', 128–9.
[100] Sulpicius Severus, *Vita s. Martini*, ed. K. Smolak (Eisenstadt, 1997), epistle 3.
[101] *ÆLS*, no. 31, lines 1346–8; cf. *ÆCHom II*, hom. 34, lines 292–5; *Vercelli Homilies*, hom. 18, lines 263–7.
[102] *ÆLS*, no. 31, lines 1349–56; cf. *Vercelli Homilies*, hom. 18, lines 278–83.

ab oratione spiritum relaxans" [Like the blessed Martin, he always kept eyes and hands directed towards Heaven and he never relaxed his unconquered spirit from prayer].[103] The physical weakness of old saints thus allowed hagiographers to emphasise the saints' dedication to their religious calling.

In many Anglo-Saxon saints' lives, the saints' ability to continue their devout duties in spite of their physical decrepitude became a source of praise. Byrhtferth of Ramsey, for one, stated that Oswald was worthy of admiration, particularly because "usque in senectam et senium Deum studuit incessanter querere" [even into his old age and declining years he tried incessantly to seek God].[104] In his *vita* of Ecgwine, Byrhtferth likewise praised the saint's resilience by comparing the saint to an "emeritus miles" [veteran warrior].[105] More explicit approval came from William of Malmesbury, in his life of Wulfstan of Worcester:

Wlstanus humanorum excessuum confessione facta etiam disciplinam accepit (ita uocant monachi uirgarum flagra, quae tergo nudato cedentis infligit acrimonia). Quantus hic uir, qui aeuo inualidus, morbo infractus, conscientia etiam serenus, non abstinuerit flagellis corporis, ut discuteret si quid reliquum erat animae sordis!

[Wulfstan made confession of the shortcomings to which men are heir, and also received 'discipline', for that is what monks call the strokes of the rod inflicted harshly on the bared back. What a man! – who, though feeble with age, broken by illness, and quiet in conscience, yet did not flinch from corporal punishment to shake off any remaining stain on his soul!][106]

Cochelin points out that this unrelenting asceticism of elderly saints helped to establish their special, supernatural status, especially since monastic rules in general allowed some leniency in older monks' observance of their vows.[107]

Another recurring theme in the lives of elderly saints is that the saints, on occasion, miraculously overcame the bodily restrictions of their advanced age and accomplished unimaginable physical feats. Such was the case for Zosimus, who, inspired by seeing Mary of Egypt, "his ealdan ylde ofergetiligende and þæt geswinc his syðfætes

---

[103] *Vita s. Dunstani*, ed. and trans. Winterbottom and Lapidge, *Early Lives*, ch. 37.4. The anonymous hagiographer quotes Severus almost verbatim.
[104] Byrhtferth, *Vita s. Oswaldi*, ed. and trans. Lapidge, V.12.
[105] Byrhtferth, *Vita s. Ecgwini*, ed. and trans. Lapidge, I.6.
[106] William of Malmesbury, *Vita s. Wulfstani*, ed. and trans. Winterbottom and Thomson, III.21. Cf. William's similar praise of Aldhelm: William of Malmesbury, *Gesta pontificum*, ed. and trans. Winterbottom, V.ccxxvii.1–2.
[107] Cochelin, 'In senectute bona', 128–9.

ne understandende, mid hrædestan ryne þenigende arn" [overcoming his old age and taking no notice of the difficulty of his path, he ran exerting himself with a very rapid onward course].[108] Oswald, too, managed to exhort his decrepit body one more time, moments before giving up his spirit:

> ... cepit senilia membra solo prosternere sua, oblitus cigneam capitis sui canitiem, non recognoscens aetatis sue imbecillitatem; quem alma fides confortauit summe trinitatis et indiuidue unitatis. Tunc nobile caput pontificis cepit sobrie pedes tergere pauperum – non solum lintheo sed etiam capillis.
>
> [... he (Oswald) began to prostrate his aged limbs on the ground, forgetful of the swan-white hair of his head and not acknowledging the weakness of his advanced age; the kindly concern of the highest Trinity and undivided Unity comforted him. Then the noble figure of the bishop began circumspectly to wash the feet of the poor – not only with a linen towel, but also with his own hair.][109]

Likewise, on the brink of death and hardly able to speak, the old and weary Edward the Confessor woke from his sleep miraculously endowed with "tanta ... loquendi copia, ut cuiuis sanissimo nichil opus esset supra" [such resources of eloquence that even the healthiest man would have no need of more].[110] In a similar vein, *vitae* often featured aged, barren parents, whose infertility was overcome through divine power, allowing them to bring forth a saintly child. Typical examples include Æbba and Dynno, the aged parents of Leoba, and the mother of Machutus, who was sixty-six when she gave birth to the saint.[111] Old age thus provided a context in which miracles could occur.

Such miracles did not only involve the temporary revitalisation of the saintly body, but could also be manifested in the saint's surroundings. For instance, *The Old English Martyrology* reports how, when St Winnoc (d. 716/717), abbot of Wormhout, had grown too old to work outside, the mill that he used for grinding grain started to run "ðurh godcunde miht" [by divine power].[112] Equally miraculous is the arrival of a lion to help the aged Zosimus bury the lifeless body of Mary of Egypt. Zosimus implored the beast as follows:

---

[108] *Life of Mary of Egypt*, ed. and trans. Magennis, lines 227–9.
[109] Byrhtferth, *Vita s. Oswaldi*, ed. and trans. Lapidge, V.17. I altered the translation of "indiuidue unitatis" from "individual Unity" to "undivided Unity".
[110] *Life of King Edward*, ed. and trans. Barlow, II.11.
[111] Rudolf, *Vita s. Leoba*, trans. Talbot, *Missionaries*, 210–11; *Old English Life of Machutus*, ed. Yerkes, 3, lines 17–18. These aged couples have biblical precedents in Abraham and Sarah, Isaac and Rebecca, and Samson's parents, as well as the parents of the Virgin Mary and John the Baptist.
[112] *Old English Martyrology*, ed. and trans. Rauer, no. 221.

Old Saints

'Ic witodlice for yldum gewæht eom, þæt ic delfan ne mæg, ne naht gehyðes hæbbe þis weorc to begangenne, ne ic efstan ne mæg swa myccles siðfætes hider to bringanne. Ac þu nu mid þære godcundan hæse þis weorc mid þinum clifrum do, oþþæt wit þisne halgan lichaman on eorðan befæston.'[113]

['In truth I am weakened with old age, so that I cannot dig; nor have I anything suitable to carry out this task, nor am I able to rush away on so great a journey to bring anything here. But you do this task with your claws, in accordance with the divine command, until the two of us have committed this holy body to the earth.']

Wondrously, the lion obeys and Mary's corpse is interred into the ground. These examples show how the physical inaptitude of the old saint provided the occasion for God to conduct miracles to compensate for the saint's adversity.

The saint's physical enfeeblement could thus become a token of his venerability. Indeed, the white hair of saints, for some hagiographers, became a visual sign of holiness. Wulfstan of Winchester, for example, likened white-haired saints to angels. Specifically, he portrayed Dunstan as an unmoving pillar, "angelico uultu decorus" [beautiful as an angel], in his *vita* of Æthelwold and later, in his *Narratio metrica de s. Swithuno*, Dunstan appears as "canicie niueus Dunstan et angelicus" [Dunstan, angelic with snowy-white hair].[114] When Dunstan himself had a vision of an old priest, Wulfstan described the latter with similar angelic white hair.[115] For Wulfstan of Winchester, then, as well as for other Anglo-Saxon hagiographers, the physical deterioration of saints did not pose an obstacle for their sanctity. Quite the opposite, it created an opportunity for the hagiographer to mark them as worthy members of the saintly community.

Death as a release: The long-anticipated end of old saints

Ða Sanctus Hilarion wæs on hundeahtatigum wintrum þa he forðferde; ond þy dæge þe he geleorde, he cwæð to him sylfum: 'Gong ut, sawl, hwæt drædest ðu ðe? Gong ut, hwæt tweost ðu ðe nu? Hundseofontig geara þu þeowodest Gode, ond nu gyt þone deað þe ondrædest?' Ond æt ðissum worde he onsende his gast.[116]

---

[113] *Life of Mary of Egypt*, ed. and trans. Magennis, lines 932–7.
[114] Wulfstan of Winchester, *Life of Æthelwold*, ed. and trans. Lapidge and Winterbottom, ch. 14; Wulfstan of Winchester, *Narratio metrica de s. Swithuno*, ed. and trans. Lapidge, *Cult*, dedicatory letter, line 72.
[115] Wulfstan of Winchester, *Life of Æthelwold*, ed. and trans. Lapidge and Winterbottom, ch. 38.
[116] *Old English Martyrology*, ed. and trans. Rauer, no. 211.

[Then St Hilarion was eighty years old when he died, and on the day when he died, he said to himself: 'Leave, soul, why are you afraid? Leave, why do you hesitate? You have served God for seventy years, and you are still afraid of death?' And with these words he gave up the ghost.]

These dying words of the eighty-year-old St Hilarion are recorded in the entry for 21 October in the *Old English Martyrology*. Not only did the elderly saint readily accept death, he even urged his soul to leave his body. As such, Hilarion's death fits Michael Goodich's broad definition of a saintly death as "an example to that saint's followers of courageous acceptance and anticipation of life after death".[117]

Indeed, for various aged saints in Anglo-Saxon hagiography, death was a welcome release from the toil and labour of this world as well as from their decrepit bodies. Alcuin, for instance, described Willibrord's passing as follows: "He was then an old man coming to the end of his days and was about to receive from God a generous reward for his labours."[118] Boniface spoke of death in similar terms, according to the *vita* written by Willibald: "In a short time I shall lay aside the burden of my body and receive the price of eternal bliss."[119] The death of Dunstan, too, was described as merciful, putting an end to the saint's lifelong laborious struggles.[120] For these elderly saints, not immune to the physical decrepitude that came with the years, death not only meant a joyous passage to a higher reality, it also entailed a release from the corporeal vicissitudes of old age.[121]

The liberation from the elderly body upon death was visualised in some saints' lives through the rejuvenation of the saint on his deathbed. Wulfstan of Winchester, to give a striking example, related how Æthelwold's face turned to that of a seven-year-old after the saint had breathed his last.[122] Wilfrid, too, appears to have regained his youth after his death at the age of seventy-six. He appeared as a "hominem iuvenem stantem in albis et in manu sua crucem tenentem auream" [a young man in white who stood holding a golden cross in his hand] to a group of exiles who tried to burn down the monastery of Oundle where the saint lay dead, scaring the arsonists out of their wits.[123] Those attending to the corpse of Wulfstan of Worcester were equally

---

[117] M. Goodich, 'The Death of a Saint: A Hagiographical Topos', in *Hoping for Continuity. Childhood, Education and Death in Antiquity and the Middle Ages*, ed. K. Mustakallio *et al.* (Rome, 2005), 227.
[118] Alcuin, *Vita Willibrordi*, trans. Talbot, *Missionaries*, 18.
[119] Willibald, *Vita Bonifatii*, trans. *Missionaries*, Talbot, ch. 8.
[120] *Vita s. Dunstani*, ed. and trans. Winterbottom and Lapidge, *Early Lives*, ch. 38.1.
[121] Cf. Semper, 'Byð se ealda man', 309.
[122] Wulfstan of Winchester, *Life of Æthelwold*, ed. and trans. Lapidge and Winterbottom, ch. 41.
[123] Stephen of Ripon, *Life of Wilfrid*, ed. and trans. Colgrave, ch. 67.

Old Saints

shocked by the renewed youth of the deceased saint, particularly because the saint's protruding nose appeared to have been restored to its original size and colour:

> Lauerunt ergo corpus, quod iam spe resurrectionis perpetuae prefulgidum stupor et uenerationi uisentibus fuit: ita perspicuo nitore gemmeum, ita miranda puritate lacteum erat. Denique nasus, qui uiuenti citra modum protuberabat, ita pulchre defuncto subsedit et incanduit ut mirum uisentibus esset. Illud porro quod dicam non nullo presentibus fuit miraculo.
>
> [So they washed the corpse. It inspired amazement and reverence in those who saw it, gleaming as it already was in the hope of eternal resurrection; for it shone bright like a gem, and was white with a remarkable purity. His nose, excessively prominent while he lived, retreated and paled so beautifully in death that those who saw it marveled.][124]

Wulfstan's fingers, grown thin and bony from age and fasting, were similarly made anew and the saint himself appears to Bishop Robert of Hereford (d. 1095) with a youthful countenance.[125] This rejuvenation of saintly bodies after death can be related to the notion, described in the previous chapter, that the heavenly afterlife was a place of youth rather than age.[126]

Anglo-Saxon hagiographers, in sum, described the death of old saints not only as the long-awaited entry into the heavenly afterlife but also as a release from the physical repercussions of old age.

Conclusion

Despite the relative scarcity of descriptions of senescence in hagiography, there appears to have been a typical model for elderly saints. Characteristically, the aged saints embodied all the merits of old age and their wisdom, accumulated through the years or already shown at an early age, made them well respected. They often set a spiritual example for the youthful members of their community and their old age became a mark of venerability. Although some elderly saints defied the drawbacks of old age, most did eventually succumb to the bodily

---

[124] William of Malmesbury, *Vita s. Wulfstani*, ed. and trans. Winterbottom and Thomson, III.22.
[125] William of Malmesbury, *Vita s. Wulfstani*, ed. and trans. Winterbottom and Thomson, III.23.
[126] The archetype for the regeneration of the bodies of aged saints may have been the corpse of Martin of Tours shining brightly white: Sulpicius Severus, *Vita s. Martini*, ed. Smolak, epistle 3, though no reference is made there of a return to youth. Cf. Semper, 'Byð se ealda man', 309.

vicissitudes of age. Various old saints grew decrepit, fell asleep during meetings or were no longer able to walk unsupported and were thus forced to appoint assistants and look for worthy successors. Their aged bodies, in other words, became obstacles and, in one case, the saint's senescence was described as a martyrdom. As a consequence, saints welcomed death as a release from their aged bodies, a release that was, on occasion, instantaneously realised by the corporeal rejuvenation after the saint's passing.

Nevertheless, the physical duress of saints, while hampering their activities in some respects, also provided opportunity. Their unrelenting asceticism, in spite of their feebleness, became all the more remarkable, ascertaining once more the sanctity of the elderly individual. The physical weakness of the old saint also occasioned miracles that compensated for the saint's hardship. Thus, aged, barren couples were made fertile, and an old saint's duties were upheld in miraculous ways. In many ways, then, a description of the saint's old age contributed to, rather than detracted from the goal of the hagiographer: to show the sanctity of the individual and the divine power that worked through the saint.

In all, the old saint is represented in a positive way in Anglo-Saxon hagiography, enjoying the merits of old age and making the most of its drawbacks. Of course, the fact that old saints were praised need not entail a positive evaluation of elderly people in general. If anything, the aged saints set a standard that would have been hard to meet for mere mortals: to persevere, despite the physical frailty that came with the years. In this respect, as will be shown in the next chapter, an old saint was indeed, as Byrthferth of Ramsey remarked of Ecgwine, akin to the perfect "emeritus miles" [veteran warrior].[127]

---

[127] Byrhtferth, *Vita s. Ecgwini*, ed. and trans. Lapidge, I.6.

5

hare hilderincas: Old Warriors in Anglo-Saxon England

"Of what use is an old man in battle?", Alfred J. Wyatt asked long ago, as he argued against the standard interpretation of the phrase "unorne ceorl" in line 256 of *The Battle of Maldon* as 'an old churl'.[1] Rather than 'old', Dunnere, the character referred to, should be seen as being 'plain, humble', Wyatt maintained. Oliver Emerson confirmed Wyatt's translation and added that assigning the meaning 'old' to the word *unorne* is "a sad libel upon the valiant Dunnere".[2] While their semantic analysis of *unorne* is now generally accepted,[3] Wyatt and Emerson's reasoning strikes as odd, given that Dunnere belonged to the same group of warriors as the "eald geneat" [old companion] Byrhtwold, led by the "har hilderinc" [grey-haired warrior] Byrhtnoth.[4] Moreover, their comments seem to reflect a modern prejudice with respect to the aptness of elderly men for military activities.

Judging the past in modern terms is problematic; the Middle Ages in particular was a time when elderly men could make themselves useful on the battlefield. The history of the Crusades, for instance, provides numerous examples of active participants of an advanced age: Raymond of St Gilles (1041/1042–1105), Raynald of Châtillon (1125–1187) and the Holy Roman Emperor Frederick I Barbarossa (1122–1190) all died in the Holy Land, well into their sixties.[5] Perhaps the most impressive elderly warrior of the Middle Ages was Enrico Dandolo (1107–1205), the doge of Venice and leader of the Fourth Crusade (1202–1204). When the Crusade started, Dandolo was over ninety years old and blind. Despite his age and visual impairment, he participated actively in various battles. At the siege of Constantinople in 1203, to give a striking example, Dandolo sensed that his Venetian

---

[1] A. J. Wyatt, *An Anglo-Saxon Reader* (Cambridge, 1919), 282.
[2] O. Emerson, 'Notes on Old English', *Modern Language Review* 14 (1919), 207.
[3] E.g., *English and Norse Documents: Relating to the Reign of Ethelred the Unready*, ed. and trans. M. Ashdown (Cambridge, 1930), 87–8; *The Battle of Maldon*, ed. E. V. Gordon, with a supplement by D. G. Scragg (Manchester, 1976), 57, n. 256; M. A. L. Locherbie-Cameron, 'The Men Named in the Poem', in *Battle of Maldon*, ed. Scragg, 243–4. For a lexicological analysis of *unorne*, see Porck, 'Growing Old', 289–90.
[4] *Battle of Maldon*, lines 169a, 310a.
[5] Minois, *History of Old Age*, 193–4.

troops were hesitant to advance on the city walls and he gave orders to bring him ashore. He ran towards the enemy walls, carrying the Venetian banner; "as Dandolo had calculated, the Venetians were shamed by the old man's bravery; they could not abandon their venerable leader and rushed to join him".[6] Dandolo's charismatic leadership paid off: the people of Constantinople were surprised by the attack and suffered defeat. Dandolo participated in several other battles before he died in 1205, at the blessed age of 98. These examples suggest that elderly warriors, even those with severe physical disabilities, were a more common sight on the medieval battlefield than Wyatt and Emerson presumed.[7] Accordingly, Dunnere in *The Battle of Maldon* is not unimaginable as an old man and his aged comrades Byrhtwold and Byrhtnoth may not be as fantastical as the dragon fought by the grey-haired warrior Beowulf in the eponymous epic.

This chapter first establishes whether the presence of old warriors in *The Battle of Maldon* could be grounded in historical reality by surveying the evidence in archaeological, pictorial and documentary sources. Next, Old English heroic poetry is analysed in order to speculate about what roles were assigned to old men at arms, thus answering Wyatt's rhetorical question, "Of what use is an old man in battle?"

The (s)word from the grave: Archaeological evidence

Archaeological research into the grave furnishings of buried individuals in Anglo-Saxon cemeteries dating back to the fifth to eighth centuries has revealed that at least one in four men belonging to the oldest age group were inhumed with weapons. Crawford, for instance, has noted that 19 per cent of the oldest age group in her sample of 1600 excavated skeletons were buried with spears.[8] Taking into account all weapon types, Nick Stoodley calculated that weapons were found in 28 per cent of the graves of elderly individuals included in his study of 1230 undisturbed burials from Anglo-Saxon cemeteries.[9] An analysis of five further early Anglo-Saxon cemeteries from Hampshire

---

[6] J. Phillips, *The Fourth Crusade and the Sack of Constantinople* (London, 2004), 174–5.

[7] Another extraordinary elderly warrior that comes to mind is the English knight William Marshal (1146/1147–1219), who personally led the English army at the Battle of Lincoln (1217) at the age of seventy. S. Painter, *William Marshal: Knight-Errant, Baron and Regent of England* (Baltimore, 1933), 214–20.

[8] Crawford, *'Gomol is snoterost'*, 57.

[9] N. Stoodley, 'From the Cradle to the Grave: Age Organization and the Early Anglo-Saxon Burial Rite', *World Archaeology* 31 (2000), 462. Notably, Stoodley defines the oldest group as people aged over forty.

and Oxfordshire suggests that at least 33 per cent of elderly males were consigned to the grave with weapons, and in some instances all were.[10]

Archaeologists have furthermore observed some distinct features of the weapon burials of elderly men. In his discussion of Anglo-Saxon warrior graves, Heinrich Härke noted a positive correlation between the age of the interred and the size of spearheads; the older the individual buried, the longer the spearhead that accompanied him.[11] This correlation has been confirmed by later studies and even extended to include the length of the whole spear and that of the knife.[12] In addition to the presence of more sizable weapons, Stoodley has discovered that, on average, more elderly individuals were interred with three or more weapons than younger adults were.[13] Finally, two particular arms, axes and seaxes, have only been found in the graves of the oldest individuals.[14] Whereas no explanation has yet been offered for the connection between these two particular weapons and the elderly,[15] the presence of longer and more numerous weapons in the weapon burials of elderly individuals has been explained as reflecting a special, higher status of the deceased.[16]

Although the presence of weapons in a grave might appear to signal an active warrior function at time of death, Härke, in particular, has argued against this assumption. One of his main arguments is the age range of the burials containing weapons: "mature individuals too old to be effective fighters were accompanied by weapons, as were children too young to be warriors".[17] Rather than reflecting an active military career, "the Anglo-Saxon weapon burial rite was a 'symbolic act' ... the ritual expression of an ethnically, socially and perhaps ideologically based 'warrior status'".[18] Although it is not unthinkable that the inhumation with weapons may have had a symbolic background, Härke's underlying assumption that children and the elderly were

---

[10] R. Gowland, 'Ageing the Past: Examining Age Identity from Funerary Evidence', in *Social Archaeology of Funerary Remains*, ed. R. Gowland and C. Knüsel (Oxford, 2006), 151–2.
[11] H. Härke, 'Warrior Graves? The Background of the Anglo-Saxon Weapon Burial Rite', *Past and Present* 126 (1990), 22–43.
[12] H. Härke, 'Changing Symbols in a Changing Society: The Anglo-Saxon Weapon Burial Rite in the Seventh Century', in *The Age of Sutton Hoo: The Seventh Century in North-Western Europe*, ed. M. O. H. Carver (Woodbridge, 1992), 158; S. Crawford, *Childhood in Anglo-Saxon England* (Stroud, 1999), 72; Crawford, 'Gomol is snoterost', 58; Stoodley, 'From the Cradle', 467.
[13] N. Stoodley, 'Childhood to Old Age', in *Oxford Handbook*, ed. Hamerow, Hinton and Crawford, 649, 663; Stoodley, 'From the Cradle', 462.
[14] Stoodley, 'From the Cradle', 462.
[15] Härke, 'Changing Symbols', 156.
[16] Stoodley, 'From the Cradle', 467.
[17] Härke, 'Changing Symbols', 153.
[18] Härke, 'Warrior Graves?', 43.

unfit for warfare merely on account of their age is not supported by other evidence.

Härke's conclusion with respect to children has not gone unchallenged. In her study on Anglo-Saxon childhood, Crawford has convincingly argued that youngsters could in fact be martially active. Historical examples, in particular, such as the Anglo-Saxon saints Wilfrid, Guthlac and Cuthbert, who all started their fighting careers in their teens, support her argument.[19] Additionally, Crawford makes a more general point by referring to the use of child warriors in various present-day war situations: whereas prohibiting boys from fighting on the battlefield may fit modern Western ideals, this disposition is by no means a universal mentality.[20] Anglo-Saxon youths who were buried with weapons, then, may have actually used them, either in combat or on the training grounds.

Crawford's refutation of Härke can be extended to argue in favour of the likelihood of elderly warriors. While modern notions may rule out old people for warfare, medieval history, as noted above, offers numerous instances of active, grey-haired warriors. Moreover, archaeological finds of later periods also demonstrate the reality of elderly warriors: the bodies of three elderly men killed in battle were found at the site of the Battle of Towton (1461).[21] Pictorial and documentary evidence from Anglo-Saxon England, to be discussed below, confirms the possible presence of elderly warriors on the Anglo-Saxon battlefield. A proportion of the Anglo-Saxon elderly weapon burials, therefore, may indeed reflect active, military careers.

Picturing white beards in the vanguard: Pictorial evidence

Whereas archeological evidence has served to provide an insight into the early Anglo-Saxon period, detailed pictorial evidence of warfare is only available from the late tenth century onwards.[22] Detailed illustra-

---

[19] Crawford, *Childhood*, 159–61; cf. H. Ellis Davidson, 'The Training of Warriors', in *Weapons and Warfare in Anglo-Saxon England*, ed. S. Chadwick Hawkes (Oxford, 1989), 11–24.

[20] Crawford, *Childhood*, 158–9. Supporting Crawford's position that boys could and would fight among men in the Middle Ages, an Old Frisian law text, dating back to the thirteenth century but possibly reflecting even older traditions, describes an army as including "thrintera mare and ... twelfwintera maga" [three-year-old horses and twelve-year-old youths]. *Das Fivelgoer Recht*, ed. W. J. Buma and W. Ebel (Göttingen, 1972), XVI.2.

[21] R. Gilchrist, *Medieval Life: Archaeology and the Life Course* (Woodbridge, 2012), 62.

[22] Early stone carvings with battle scenes, such as the ninth-century Aberlemno Stone, depicting the Battle of Nechtansmere of 685 between Ecgfrith of Northumbria and the Picts, often lack the detail to identify the warriors as

tions of warfare appear in tenth- and eleventh-century Anglo-Saxon manuscripts of Prudentius' *Psychomachia*, the Old English Hexateuch and the Psalter, as well as the Bayeux Tapestry. In these visualisations of warfare, elderly warriors can be identified either by their likeness to other figures known to have been old, such as Abraham, or their long white beards.[23] As will be demonstrated below, these illustrations provide insight into how an Anglo-Saxon envisioned the battlefield and whether aged combatants, in his imagination or experience, were present or absent.

Prudentius' Psychomachia

The *Psychomachia* by the Roman poet Prudentius (348–413) is an allegory about a battle between the Vices and Virtues, personified as female warriors. In its preface, Prudentius starts by praising Abraham, then still named Abram, and emphasises his active role in the freeing of his nephew Lot, who had been captured by the Elamite army in the aftermath of the War of the Kings. Upon hearing this news, Abraham, aged over seventy-five according to the biblical account, prepares 318 of his servants and leads a successful rescue mission, which leads Prudentius to exclaim:

> quin ipse ferrum stringit et plenus Deo
> reges superbos mole praedarum graves
> pellit fugatos, sauciatos proterit,
> frangit catenas et rapinam liberat.
>
> [He himself (Abraham), too, draws the sword and, being filled with the spirit of God, drives off in flight those proud kings, weighed down with their booty, or cuts them down and tramples them under foot. He breaks the bonds and loosens the plunder.][24]

By describing Abraham as an active participant in the battle, Prudentius embellishes the account in Gen. 14, which glances over the fighting itself. In doing so, Prudentius created an image of Abraham as an elderly warrior. This was picked up and even elaborated upon by the illustrators of the Anglo-Saxon manuscripts of the text,[25] all of which

---

either old or young. See, e.g., N. Hooper, 'The Aberlemno Stone and Cavalry in Anglo-Saxon England', *Northern History* 29 (1993), 188–96.

[23] For long white beards as a characteristic of an old rather than a middle-aged man, see the depictions of the three ages of man discussed in chapter 1; Ohlgren, *Insular and Anglo-Saxon Illuminated Manuscripts* does not include 'old age' in its index of iconographic contents.

[24] Prudentius, *Psychomachia*, ed. and trans. H. J. Thomson (Cambridge, MA, 2015), preface, lines 26–9.

[25] The popularity of Prudentius' *Psychomachia* in Anglo-Saxon England is reflected in the use of the text by various Anglo-Saxon authors, including Alcuin, and the

Fig. 3. Abraham (on the far left) and his servants on their way to free Lot. CCCC 23, 2v.

depict the elderly Abraham as brandishing a spear and riding his horse into battle (see fig. 3).[26]

In nearly all manuscripts of the *Psychomachia*, Abraham is the only warrior to be depicted as elderly. However, one Anglo-Saxon artist added a second old man at arms in his illustration of lines 109–10 of the *Psychomachia*, "ecce modesta gravi stabat Patientia vultu / per medias inmota acies variosque tumultus" [Lo, mild Long-Suffering was standing with staid countenance, unmoved amid the battle and its confused uproar].[27] Here, the artist of CCCC 23 drew an armed, bearded figure (see fig. 4), similar to his rendition of Abraham a few folios earlier. While the depiction of the aged Abraham of the preface has parallels

---

number of Anglo-Saxon manuscripts containing the text: ten, of which four are illustrated. G. R. Wieland, 'The Anglo-Saxon Manuscripts of Prudentius's *Psychomachia*', *ASE* 16 (1987), 213–31. The four illustrated manuscripts are CCCC 23 (s. x^2 or x ex. or xi in. S England); London, British Library, Add. 24199 (s. x ex.); London, British Library, Cotton Cleopatra C. viii (s. x/xi, Canterbury, Christ Church); and the fragment Munich, Bayerische Staatsbibliothek, clm. 29336/1 (s. xi in.). For these manuscripts, see G. R. Wieland, 'The Origin and Development of the Anglo-Saxon *Psychomachia* Illustrations', *ASE* 26 (1997), 169–86. The cycles of illustrations in these manuscripts are reproduced in *Die illustrierten Prudentiushandschriften*, ed. R. Stettiner (Berlin, 1895–1905) II, pls. 31–66.

[26] CCCC 23, 1v, 3r; Add. 24199, 3r; Cotton Cleopatra C. viii, 1v, 2r. The artists of these manuscripts probably based themselves on various continental models, see Wieland, 'Origin and Development', 179–80. Abraham is not depicted in the Clm. 29336/1, which only survives as a fragment.

[27] Prudentius, *Psychomachia*, ed. and trans. Thomson.

Fig. 4. Elderly warrior to the left of Patientia, standing between the battle lines. CCCC 23, 8v.

in other, both Anglo-Saxon and continental, manuscripts, this inclusion of an elderly warrior on the frontline of one of the armies surrounding *Patientia* is not found in any other known manuscript depicting the scene.[28] The CCCC 23 artist, in this respect, was not following the established iconographical tradition associated with this text, and his inclusion of the old man in this scene may therefore reflect his conception of a typical line of battle as containing both young and old men.

The Old English Hexateuch

The story of Abraham's intervention to free Lot is also vividly depicted in the illustrated Old English Hexateuch,[29] a translation from the Latin Vulgate of the first six books of the Old Testament.[30] The illustrated

---

[28] *Prudentiushandschriften*, ed. Stettiner, provides plates of all manuscripts featuring this scene; CCCC 23 is unique in depicting one of the warriors in the likeness of the aged Abraham; all other manuscripts feature clean-shaven warriors.

[29] London, British Library, Cotton Claudius B. iv (s. xi$^{2/4}$, Canterbury, St Augustine's; the 'Old English Hexateuch'); Kerr, no. 142; Gneuss and Lapidge, no. 315.

[30] A large portion of this translation – Genesis up to 24:22, the second half of Numbers and Joshua – has been attributed to Ælfric, abbot of Eynsham. Ælfric's work was combined with that of anonymous translators to form the Hexateuch text, which survives in eight manuscripts. R. Barnhouse and B. C. Withers, 'Introduction: Aspects and Approaches', in *The Old English Hexateuch: Aspects and Approaches*, ed. R. Barnhouse and B. C. Withers (Kalamazoo, 2000), 1–13.

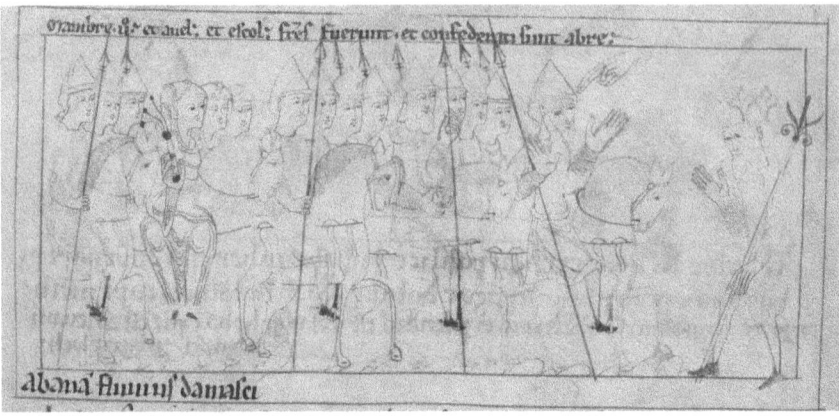

Fig. 5. Abraham (leading his army) meets the king of Sodom.
Old English Hexateuch, 25v.

manuscript of the Old English Hexateuch contains over four hundred coloured drawings, some of which have remained unfinished. The editors of the facsimile edition of the manuscript stress that the illustrations are original and made especially to conform to the text of this manuscript: "In other words, the artist was not copying the pictures of a remote and long-forgotten age; like other creative artists he was thinking in terms of his own life and times."[31] Jennifer Kiff has noted that this manuscript features detailed battle iconography, possibly to suit the tastes of the educated layman who had commissioned the manuscript.[32]

As in the Anglo-Saxon manuscripts of the *Psychomachia*, the elderly Abraham is shown armed and actively engaged in the freeing of Lot. Moreover, his band of 318 armed servants contains other elderly warriors with beards like Abraham's (fig. 5). Figures with a countenance similar to the aged Abraham also occur in many other battle scenes in this manuscript.[33] The depiction of the War of the Kings (Gen. 14:13), for example, features eight bearded individuals similar to Abraham, all actively engaged in battle (fig. 6). In the top, one of these figures is even pulled by his beard, enabling his opponent to strike him in the

---

[31] *The Old English Illustrated Hexateuch: British Museum Cotton Claudius B. iv*, ed. C. R. Dodwell and P. Clemoes, Early English Manuscripts in Facsimile 18 (Copenhagen, 1974), 71.
[32] J. Kiff, 'Images of War: Illustrations of Warfare in Early Eleventh-Century England', *Anglo-Norman Studies* VII (1984), 188.
[33] Old English Hexateuch, 25r, 75v, 95v, 103v, 119r, 123r, 124v, 125r, 127r, 127v, 151r, 152r, 152v, 153r, 153v, 154r, 154v.

Old Warriors

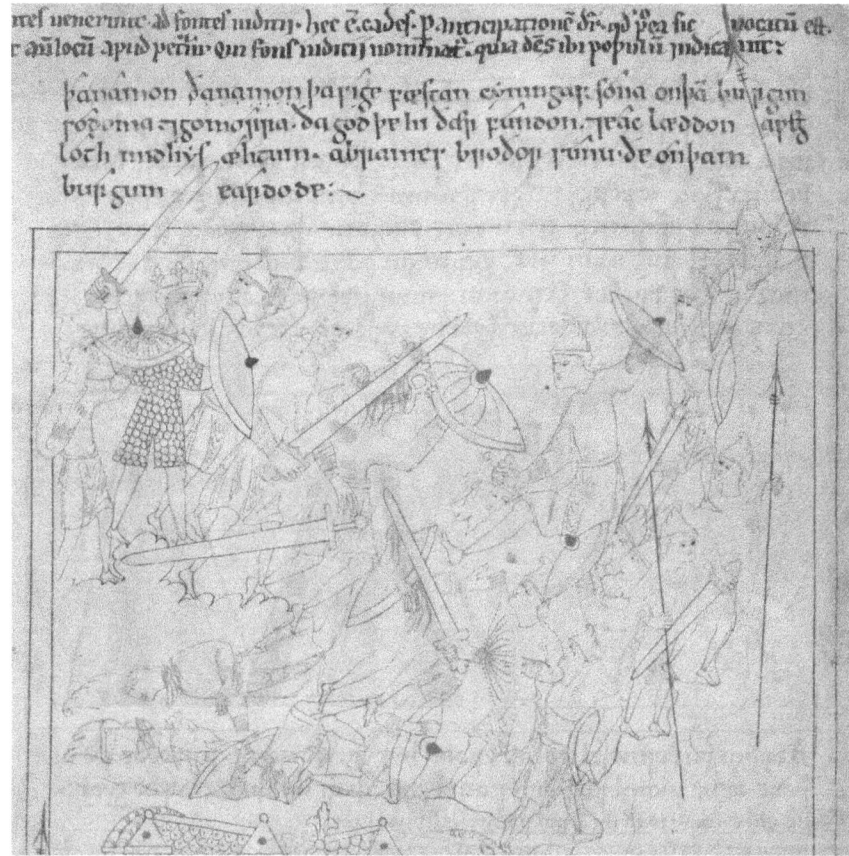

Fig. 6. War of the Kings. Old English Hexateuch, 24v.

face with a sword.[34] The presence of these elderly, bearded figures in the various battle scenes of this manuscript demonstrates that, for the Anglo-Saxon artist at least, elderly men were an integral part of the battlefield.[35]

---

[34] The scene is reminiscent of the early medieval maxim "Frontibus attritis barbas conscindere fas est" [when the heads are bald one must pull the beards], found in the eleventh-century Apocalypse of Saint-Sever. J. J. M. Timmers, *A Handbook of Romanesque Art* (New York, 1976), 82. I owe this reference to Mr G. Limburg (Oegstgeest).

[35] Another manuscript to feature a drawing of Abraham leading his army, which includes one other bearded figure (though his beard does not resemble Abraham's), is Oxford, Bodleian Library, Junius 11 (s. x^2 and xi^1, S England, Canterbury, Christ Church?; the 'Junius Manuscript'), 81; Ker, no. 334; Gneuss and Lapidge, no. 640. The image is reproduced in Ohlgren, *Insular and Anglo-Saxon Illuminated Manuscripts*, 571.

Fig. 7. Illustration of Psalm 7, showing an elderly man with a spear on the far left of the armed band. Harley Psalter, 4r.

The Harley Psalter

The Harley Psalter is one of the three medieval English psalters based on the Utrecht Psalter, along with the Eadwine Psalter and the Paris Psalter.[36] Like its Carolingian exemplar, the Harley Psalter features small groups of armed men engaged in or preparing for combat in some of its illustrations.

Within these armed groups, some bearded men carrying spears can be discerned.[37] The war band around a Christ-like figure brandishing a sword and a bow depicted in the illustration of Ps. 7:8, 13 ("And a congregation of people shall surround Thee ... He will brandish His sword; He hath bent His bow, and made it ready") is a clear example (fig. 7). The figure to the left of the war band has an extensive beard, to mark his advanced age. The interpretation of this figure as a senior is confirmed by the rendition of the same scene in the Paris Psalter, which not only shows the extended white beard but also a wrinkled face.[38]

---

[36] For a description of the Harley Psalter and related manuscripts, see p. 28, ns. 54–56 above.

[37] Harley Psalter, 2r, 4r, 6v, 13v, 15r, 59v, 60r.

[38] Paris Psalter, 12v. Interestingly, while the bearded man is present in the Utrecht Psalter (fol. 4r) that was the inspiration for the scene in the Harley Psalter, the

The presence in the Harley Psalter of men with extensive beards amidst bands of armed men, as well as the evidence from the CCCC 23 *Psychomachia* and the illustrated Old English Hexateuch, suggests that various Anglo-Saxon artists envisioned the battlefield as a place for warriors both young and old. In this respect, the designer of the Bayeux Tapestry, the principal visual representation of Anglo-Saxon warfare, was no different.

The Bayeux Tapestry

The Bayeux Tapestry is an embroidered cloth approximately 70 metres long, depicting the events leading up to and including the Battle of Hastings in 1066. Probably at the behest of Bishop Odo of Bayeux, the Tapestry was designed and made in the two decades following the Norman Conquest, possibly in St Augustine's, Canterbury.[39] Because of its monastic background, the realistic nature of the Bayeux Tapestry's depiction of warfare has been a matter of debate.[40] In particular, the English designer of the Tapestry failed to bring out the distinctions between the different armours and weapons used by the Normans and English, picturing them as identical instead. This ignorance of Norman attire has been attributed to the fact that the Bayeux Tapestry draws heavily on earlier iconographical depictions of warfare in manuscripts created in Canterbury, including the ones described above.[41] Brooks and Walker therefore conclude: "the Tapestry is a more dependable source of the armour and weapons of the English than of the Normans".[42]

While the depiction of helmets, byrnies and galloping horses reflect English iconographical traditions and may, hence, be somewhat removed from the reality of the battlefield,[43] the Tapestry gives nonetheless a faithful record of some of the events that took place

---

beard is absent in the Eadwine Psalter (fol. 12v). This difference between the Eadwine Psalter, on the one hand, and the Utrecht and Paris Psalters, on the other, reaffirms Noel's conclusion that the artists of the Paris Psalter did not only base their illustrations on Eadwine's Psalter, but must also have had access to the original Utrecht Psalter. Cf. Noel, 'Utrecht Psalter in England', 121–2.

[39] N. P. Brooks and H. E. Walker, 'The Authority and Interpretation of the Bayeux Tapestry', *Anglo-Norman Studies* 1 (1978), 1–18. Scolland, abbot of St Augustine's, Canterbury has been plausibly identified as the designer of the Tapestry by H. B. Clarke, 'The Identity of the Designer of the Bayeux Tapestry', *Anglo-Norman Studies* 35 (2013), 119–40.

[40] Brooks and Walker, 'Authority and Interpretation', 19.

[41] Kiff, 'Images of War', 190–4.

[42] Brooks and Walker, 'Authority and Interpretation', 20.

[43] Kiff, 'Images of War', 192–4. See also M. Lewis, 'The Bayeux Tapestry and Eleventh-Century Material Culture', in *King Harold II and the Bayeux Tapestry*, ed. G. R. Owen-Crocker (Woodbridge, 2005), 179–94.

during the Battle of Hastings. On panel 68,[44] for example, William the Conqueror lifts the visor of his helmet to dispel the rumour that he had died, as reported by other, written sources of the battle.[45] Similarly, the depiction of Harold's death by an arrow in the eye, on panel 71, is corroborated by other, near-contemporary sources, although these may have been based on the Bayeux Tapestry itself.[46] Clearly, then, the designer of the Bayeux Tapestry had been informed of some of the circumstances of the Battle of Hastings; his inclusion of elderly warriors on the side of the English, therefore, may have been grounded in reality.

The elderly warriors on the Bayeux Tapestry can be identified by their white beards and appear only in the English army. There are, it is true, a number of white-bearded figures among the Normans, yet these do not appear in the battle scenes: two white-bearded figures construct a boat on panel 36, another white-bearded man is the helmsman of the first ship on panel 40, while another is seated at Odo's dinner table on panel 48.[47] By contrast, warriors with white beards take up prominent positions in the English battle lines. Two clear examples are the white-bearded figures in the vanguard of the English shield walls on panels 61 and 62 of the Tapestry. The first elderly warrior, on panel 61, is distinguished from the remainder of the shield wall by his white beard, his longer spear and the colour of his shield (fig. 8a). These distinctive features and his position at the head of the shield wall symbolise the special status or high rank he must have had within this Anglo-Saxon war band. Much the same can be said for the bearded warrior in the second English shield wall on panel 62, facing the opposite direction. This warrior is second in line and carries the battle standard as he and his company await the onslaught of the approaching Norman cavalry (fig. 8b).

Five further elderly warriors belonged to King Harold Godwinson's personal bodyguard. Three of them are depicted on panel 70, under the inscription "ET CECIDERUNT QUI ERANT CUM HAROLDO" [and those who were with Harold have fallen] (fig. 8c). One has already

---

[44] All references to panel numbers of the Bayeux Tapestry are to D. M. Wilson, *The Bayeux Tapestry: The Complete Tapestry in Colour* (London, 1985).

[45] D. J. Bernstein, *The Mystery of the Bayeux Tapestry* (London, 1986), 141.

[46] H. H. Wood, *The Battle of Hastings: The Fall of Anglo-Saxon England* (London, 2008), 192–7.

[47] Perhaps these bearded individuals later occur as the archers in the lower margin of panels 68 and 69. The depiction of these archers, however, lacks sufficient detail to identify them definitively as either elderly or young, or, even, as either English or Norman. In the lower margin of panel 66, a detached head with a long beard lies amidst several corpses, but whether this body part belonged to an English or a Norman warrior is impossible to say, since the Tapestry comments "HIC CECIDERUNT SIMUL ANGLI ET FRANCI IN PRELIO" [Here the English and the French have fallen side by side in the battle].

Old Warriors

Fig. 8. a (top): Elderly warrior in the vanguard of the English shield wall. Bayeux Tapestry, panel 61. b (middle, left): Elderly warrior carrying the battle-standard in the English shield wall. Bayeux Tapestry, panel 62. c (middle, right), d (bottom, left), e (bottom, right): White-bearded bodyguards of Harold Godwinson. Bayeux Tapestry, panels 70–72.

fallen, literally, to the lower margin and lies dead, while the other two are in the process of being killed. The first has an arrow sticking out of his face, while the last is being struck down by a Norman sword. This last figure, in particular, demonstrates the resilience which these senior warriors apparently could show in battle; no fewer than five arrows stick out from his shield and one from the back of his head, but he still raises his two-handed battle axe in defence against the Norman invader. Surrounding the fallen King Harold on panels 71 and 72 are two other elderly warriors (figs. 8d and 8e). The first, on Harold's left, is identified by David Bernstein as "the bearer of the dragon standard, the old bearded man",[48] while the second, on Harold's right, is fending off two other Norman cavalrymen with his axe.

Along with the manuscript illuminations discussed above, the evidence from the Bayeux Tapestry clearly shows that there was a place for old men within the English army. In fact, their depiction in the tapestry at the vanguard of the shield wall and in the vicinity of the king indicates that these elderly warriors must have been held in high esteem among the English military ranks. As such, the Bayeux Tapestry confirms the special status attributed to elderly warriors through the early burial rite with more weapons and longer spears and knives, albeit that the archaeological evidence predates the tapestry by about four hundred years.

The stuff of legends: Documentary evidence

Relatively few documentary sources survive that reveal something of the precise composition and organisation of an Anglo-Saxon army.[49] Regulations dealing with age thresholds for joining the army or retiring from it, for example, have not survived from the Anglo-Saxon period. Such selection policies, however, may have existed around this time, as is suggested by two Icelandic sagas. The saga about the tenth-century elite warrior band called the Jomsvikings describes how they would not select "a member who was older than fifty or younger than

---

[48] Bernstein, *Mystery of the Bayeux Tapestry*, 145–6.
[49] In the early Anglo-Saxon period, an army probably consisted of a relatively small number of retainers, supplemented during expeditions by local forces that were levied for the occasion. With the exception of a brief period under King Alfred and his successors, a standing royal army never really replaced this system of a royal war band reinforced by *ad hoc* troops. In the late Anglo-Saxon period, these additional forces were levied according to the approximate value of landed estates and the army was organised territorially, containing smaller units led by local leaders. R. Abels, 'Army', in *A Blackwell Encyclopaedia of Anglo-Saxon England*, ed. M. Lapidge *et al.* (Oxford, 1999), 47–8.

eighteen".[50] Similarly, in the saga of Olaf Tryggvason, king of Norway from 995 to 1000, the crew of Olaf's boat is carefully selected, so that "no man was to be on Ormr inn langi older than sixty or younger than twenty, and they were to be chosen mainly for strength and valour".[51] These selection policies do not necessarily indicate that men aged over fifty or sixty were never part of an early medieval war band. Quite the reverse, the fact that these elite forces limited membership to men in their prime and excluded the elderly suggests that this practice was exceptional, rather than exemplary.

Anglo-Saxon armies certainly contained a mixture of experienced and inexperienced warriors. In a letter to Ecgberht, bishop of York, dated to 734, Bede makes a distinction between junior members of a household and experienced warriors.[52] A similar distinction was made some three hundred years later, in Byrhtferth of Ramsey's *Vita s. Oswaldi*, where Ealdorman Byrhtnoth addresses the "seniores et juniores" of his assembled levy.[53] In descriptions of war bands in Old English poetry, too, the *geoguþ* 'young, untried soldiers' are distinguished from the *duguþ* 'tried warriors'.[54] The difference between the two groups, however, does not appear to be based on age. Instead, a member of the *geoguþ* was promoted to the ranks of *duguþ* through the donation of land by the king after he had proved himself to his lord's satisfaction.[55] The 'youths' of the Anglo-Saxon war band, then, were young, untried warriors who lived with their lord, while the *duguþ* were experienced warriors, endowed with land of their own but not necessarily aged. Nicholas Hooper estimates that a warrior's career started in his early teens and that he might be expected to be endowed with land in his mid-twenties.[56] The distinction between *geoguþ* and *duguþ* in the Anglo-Saxon armies, therefore, cannot straightforwardly be translated as a difference between 'green' and 'grey'.

Ryan Lavelle sketches the prototypical career of an Anglo-Saxon warrior as starting in his teens and, if he survived, lasting for about two decades.[57] The careers of two elderly warriors recorded in

---

[50] *The Saga of the Jomsvikings*, trans. N. F. Blake (London, 1962), ch. 16.
[51] Snorri Sturluson, *Óláfs saga Tryggvasonar*, in *Heimskringla*, trans. A. Finlay and A. Faulkes (London, 2011), ch. 93.
[52] The letter is discussed in detail in R. Abels, *Lordship and Military Obligation in Anglo-Saxon England* (London, 1988), 28–35.
[53] Byrhtferth, *Vita s. Oswaldi*, ed. and trans. Lapidge, IV.13.
[54] See, for example, *Beowulf*, lines 160, 621 and 1674; *Andreas*, ed. G. P. Krapp, *The Vercelli Book*, ASPR 2 (London, 1931), lines 150, 1121.
[55] Abels, *Lordship*, 32. See also G. Halsall, *Warfare and Society in the Barbarian West, 450–900* (London, 2003), 58.
[56] N. Hooper, 'The Anglo-Saxons at War', in *Weapons and Warfare*, ed. Chadwick Hawkes, 196.
[57] R. Lavelle, *Alfred's Wars: Sources and Interpretations of Anglo-Saxon Warfare in the Viking Age* (Woodbridge, 2010), 15.

Anglo-Saxon history – Byrhtnoth, ealdorman of Essex (d. 991) and Siward, earl of Northumbria (d. 1055) –, however, reveal that an old man could maintain an elevated military status for a longer period of time. Both men were active warriors well into their later years and became cult figures after their death.

Byrhtnoth led the Anglo-Saxon forces in the Battle of Maldon against the Vikings in 991. By that time, he had already been ealdorman of Essex for thirty-five years, having been appointed in 956; he is estimated to have been in his sixties at the time of his death.[58] During his life, Byrhtnoth had been an influential landowner in Essex, possessing more than fifty holdings in various shires, and his death at Maldon was considered important enough to merit mention in all extant versions of *The Anglo-Saxon Chronicle*.[59] A near-contemporary description of the battle of Maldon in Byrhtferth of Ramsey's *Vita s. Oswaldi* explicitly mentions Byrhtnoth's military prowess, despite his old age:

> Percutiebat quoque a dextris, non reminiscens cigneam caniciem sui capitis, quoniam elemosine et sacre misse eum confortabant. Protegebat se a sinistris, debilitationem oblitus sui corporis, quem orationes et bone actiones eleuabant.
>
> [He (Byrhtnoth) struck blows from his right side, not paying heed to the swan-white hair of his head, since alms and holy masses gave him consolation. He protected himself on the left-hand side, forgetful of the weakness of his body, for prayers and good deeds uplifted him.][60]

This passage, as has been noted by Michael Lapidge, is romanticised and has clear biblical overtones. Nevertheless, Byrhtferth does confirm Byrhtnoth's old age and personal participation in the battle.[61]

After his death, Byrhtnoth achieved something of a legendary status. The compiler of the twelfth-century *Liber Eliensis* remarked that Byrhtnoth was "an outstanding and famous man whose righteous life and deeds English histories commend with no small praises".[62] The *Liber Eliensis* itself also celebrated Byrhtnoth's bravery at Maldon and described the honorary entombment in Ely, years after the battle, of his remains.[63] Byrhtnoth's deeds also appear to have been celebrated on a

---

[58] Abels, 'Byrhtnoth (d. 991)', *ODNB*.

[59] J. M. Bately, '*The Anglo-Saxon Chronicle*', in *Battle of Maldon*, ed. Scragg, 37–50.

[60] Byrhtferth, *Vita s. Oswaldi*, ed. and trans. Lapidge, V.5.

[61] M. Lapidge, 'The *Life of St Oswald*', in *Battle of Maldon*, ed. Scragg, 51–8.

[62] *Liber Eliensis*, trans. J. Fairweather (Woodbridge, 2005), II.62. This and other twelfth-century accounts of Byrhtnoth's death are reproduced in A. Kennedy, 'Byrhtnoth's Obits and Twelfth-Century Accounts of the Battle of Maldon', in *Battle of Maldon*, ed. Scragg, 59–78.

[63] The Ely monks were able to recognise Byrhtnoth's body by the round lump of wax that had been used to replace the ealdorman's head, after it had been stolen by the Vikings. *Liber Eliensis*, trans. Fairweather, II.62. A 1769 study

tapestry: following his death in 991, Byrhtnoth's wife Ælfflæd reportedly gave the monastery of Ely "a hanging woven upon and embroidered with the deeds of her husband, in memory of his probity".[64] This Anglo-Saxon precursor to the Bayeux Tapestry, however, has not survived.[65] Byrhtnoth's deeds at the Battle of Maldon were also commemorated in the Old English poem devoted to the battle, which will be discussed in more detail below.

Another elderly commander, comparable to Byrhtnoth, was Siward, earl of Northumbria, who first appears in a charter of King Cnut in 1033. He held the position of earl, first of southern Northumbria and later of all Northumbria and, possibly, Huntingdon, until his death twenty-two years later. Like Byrhtnoth, Siward actively participated in warfare well into his later years. During a series of battles against Scotland in 1054, Siward was at least old enough to hear of the death of his own son Osbeorn in battle. Henry of Huntingdon's twelfth-century *Historia Anglorum* reports that, upon hearing the news, Siward inquired whether his son had been stabbed in the back or in the front. When he was told his son had incurred a fatal breast wound, Siward said: "Gaudio plane, non enim alio me uel filium meum digner funere" [I am completely happy, for I consider no other death worthy for me or my son].[66] He then led his troops into Scotland himself and defeated the Scottish forces in retaliation, before dying as an old man in 1055. Huntingdon's chronicle describes how Siward had been struck by dysentery and, feeling death's approach, exclaimed:

> 'Quantus pudor me tot in bellis mori non potuisse, ut uaccarum morti cum dedecore reseruarer! Induite me saltem lorica mea inpenetrabili, precingite gladio. Sullimate galea. Scutum in leua. Securim auratam michi ponite in dextra, ut militum fortissimus modo militis moriar.'

> ['How shameful it is that I, who could not die in so many battles, should have been saved for the ignominious death of a cow! At least clothe me in my impenetrable breastplate, gird me with my sword, place my helmet on my head, my shield in my left hand, my gilded battle-axe in my right, that I, the bravest of soldiers, may die like a soldier.'][67]

---

of the skeletal remains in Byrhtnoth's tomb suggested that the man buried there had indeed been decapitated with a two-handed sword or battle axe. See E. Coatsworth, 'Byrhtnoth's Tomb', in *Battle of Maldon*, ed. Scragg, 279–88.

[64] *Liber Eliensis*, trans. Fairweather, II.62.

[65] M. Budny, 'The Byrhtnoth Tapestry or Embroidery', in *Battle of Maldon*, ed. Scragg, 262–78.

[66] Henry of Huntingdon, *Historia Anglorum*, ed. and trans. D. E. Greenway (Oxford, 1996), VI.22. E. Parker, 'Siward the Dragon-Slayer: Mythmaking in Anglo-Scandinavian England', *Neophilologus* 98 (2014), 484–5, notes that Siward's enquiry about the location of his son's wounds has a close parallel in a similar scene in the Icelandic *Egils saga*.

[67] Henry of Huntingdon, *Historia Anglorum*, ed. and trans. Greenway, VI.24.

C. E. Wright has identified two parallels to this story in Scandinavian literature: both Starkad, in Saxo Grammaticus' *Gesta Danorum*, and Egil Ulserk, in Snorri Sturluson's *Heimskringla*, are elderly warriors who express their wish to die in battle rather than anywhere else.[68] These old men, it appears, did not want to go down without a fight.

Given their analogues in Scandinavian literature, the stories of Siward's reaction to the death of his son and Siward's speech on his deathbed, both reported by Henry of Huntingdon close to a century after Siward's death, may not be historically accurate. Rather, they may have originated in Anglo-Saxon or Anglo-Scandinavian oral traditions surrounding Siward, or, as Wright put it, they are "the *disject membra* of a *Siwards saga* which must have been still current in Northumbria during the twelfth and thirteenth centuries".[69] The parallels with Icelandic saga material, as identified by Wright, may imply that these episodes belong to the same realm of fictionality as Siward's supposed descent from a polar bear and his slaying of a dragon, as reported by a Latin narrative in a thirteenth-century manuscript from Crowland Abbey.[70] Regardless of the questionable historicity of the episodes, Earl Siward, like Ealdorman Byrhtnoth, is a prime example of a vigorous elderly warrior, who reached a legendary status after his death. In this way, both he and Byrhtnoth prove that it was possible for an old man to maintain an active military career well beyond his physical prime.

A possible third elderly warrior to appear in the documentary record is Oslac (fl. 963–975). Little is known about Oslac, apart from the fact that he was elevated to the position of earl of southern Northumbria in 963 and exiled from England in 975, following the death of King Edgar the Peaceful (c.943–975). *The Anglo-Saxon Chronicle* entry for the year 975 in manuscripts A, B and C describes his expulsion as follows:

7 þa wearð eac adræfed,   deormod hæleð,
Oslac of earde   ofer yða gewealc,
ofer ganotes bæð,   gamolfeax hæleð,
wis 7 wordsnotor,   ofer wætera geðring,
ofer hwæles eðel,   hama bereafod.[71]

---

[68] C. E. Wright, *The Cultivation of Saga in Anglo-Saxon England* (Edinburgh, 1939), 128. In addition, Siward's request to be armed faintly echoes Paul's description of the 'Armour of Faith' in Eph. 6:14–17, which would certainly have been known to Henry of Huntingdon, who served as an archdeacon. I owe this suggestion to prof.dr.em. A. A. MacDonald (University of Groningen).

[69] Wright, *Cultivation*, 129. See also E. Mason, *The House of Godwine: The History of a Dynasty* (London, 2004), 88.

[70] Parker, 'Siward the Dragon-Slayer', 488.

[71] *The Anglo-Saxon Chronicle: A Collaborative Edition. Vol. 3: MS A*, ed. J. M. Bately (Cambridge, 1986), 77.

[and then Oslac, the courageous warrior, was driven from the land across the rolling of the waves, across the gannet's bath, the grey-haired warrior, wise and eloquent, across the tumult of waters, over the land of the whale, bereft of his home.]

Given the lack of any further information about Oslac, we need not take his poetic description as a "gamolfeax hæleð" [grey-haired warrior] at face value, since the use of "gamolfeax hæleð" might be nothing more than a poetic convention,[72] used to alliterate with the equally conventional kenning "ganotes bæð" [gannet's bath] for 'sea'. On the other hand, the word *gamolfeax* is exclusively used for people in old age and, given the examples of Byrhtnoth and Siward, an aged, grey-haired warrior need not seem unlikely.

To summarise so far, the archaeological, pictorial and documentary evidence provided above demonstrates that old men could still be active in a military capacity. Archaeologists have shown that older Anglo-Saxon individuals were still regularly buried with weapons, a possible indication that an active military career was not a prerogative of younger individuals. A similar conclusion can be drawn from the presence of bearded figures of an advanced age depicted among younger warriors in battle scenes in manuscripts of Prudentius' *Psychomachia*, the Old English Hexateuch and the Psalter, and in the Bayeux Tapestry. Lastly, Byrhtnoth, Siward and Oslac were living proof that elderly individuals did remain martially active, even at an advanced age. In short, those warriors who survived the first twenty to thirty years of their military careers could certainly continue to serve in the armed forces. Their presence in Old English heroic poetry, to be discussed next, then, was at least partially rooted in reality.

hare hilderincas: *Elderly warriors in Old English heroic poetry*

Whereas the historical presence of elderly warriors in Anglo-Saxon England, as established above, has rarely been commented on, their role in Old English heroic poetry has given rise to a number of passing remarks in secondary literature. Amos, for example, argued that the occurrence of the compound "har hilderinc" [grey-haired warrior] in various Old English poems suggests that "[i]n the heroic world of Old English poetry grey or white hair was no stigma".[73] Similarly, Carole

---

[72] The phrase "gamolfeax hæleð" occurs nowhere else in the Old English corpus, but is synonymous with the frequently occurring "har hilderinc" [grey-haired warrior], for which see the Appendix at the end of this chapter.
[73] Amos, 'Old English Words for Old', 102.

Biggam claimed that there is no suggestion that the old warriors in heroic poetry, such as Byrhtnoth in *The Battle of Maldon* and King Constantine in *The Battle of Brunanburh*, were considered redundant in a military context.[74] By contrast, Semper noted that "grey hair and success in battle are not usually found together" and that elderly men, unlikely to have been the most effective warriors, typically functioned as advisors instead.[75] All in all, there is no consensus about the status and role of elderly warriors in Old English heroic poetry; hence, a detailed discussion of their representation in this type of poetry is in order here.

Old English heroic poetry "comprises poems that deal with warriors endowed with often superhuman courage whose actions are motivated by a special set of values, the heroic ethos".[76] Central to this heroic ethos is the idea that the achievement of a lasting reputation is a warrior's paramount goal.[77] "Ure æghwylc sceal ende gebidan worolde lifes" [each of us must await the end of life in the world], Beowulf tells Hrothgar, "wyrce se þe mote domes ær deaþe; þæt bið drihtguman unlifgendum æfter selest" [he who can, should endeavour to win glory before death; that will be best for a warrior after his death].[78] Lasting glory and fame were especially won on the battlefield, usually by risking death in combat.[79]

Another important element of the heroic ethos was reciprocal loyalty. This ideal required the king or lord to bestow gifts upon his warriors, who, in turn, were expected to show unswerving loyalty in battle.[80] The act of lordly generosity is proverbially treated in *Maxims II*: "Cyning sceal on healle beagas dælan" [a king must in his hall distribute rings].[81] The loyalty of retainers ideally continued after the death of their leader; a famous passage in *The Anglo-Saxon Chronicle* relates how the retainers of King Cynewulf refused to be paid off by the rebel Cyneheard and, instead, vowed to avenge the death of their lord.[82] Similarly, Old English heroic poetry, especially *Beowulf* and *The*

---

[74] Biggam, *Grey in Old English*, 236.
[75] Semper, 'Byð se ealda man', 296–8.
[76] R. H. Bremmer Jr, 'Old English Heroic Literature', in *Readings in Medieval Literature. Interpreting Old and Middle English Literature*, ed. D. F. Johnson and E. M. Treharne (Oxford, 2006), 76.
[77] K. O'Brien O'Keeffe, 'Heroic Values and Christian Ethics', in *The Cambridge Companion to Old English Literature*, ed. M. Godden and M. Lapidge, 2nd ed. (Cambridge, 2013), 101–3.
[78] *Beowulf*, lines 1386–9.
[79] Bremmer, 'Old English Heroic Literature', 76.
[80] J. Bazelmans, *By Weapons Made Worthy: Lords, Retainers and Their Relationship in Beowulf* (Amsterdam, 1999), 149–88.
[81] *Maxims II*, ed. and trans. Shippey, *PoW*, lines 28–9.
[82] For an analysis of this event, see R. H. Bremmer Jr, 'The Germanic Context of Cynewulf and Cyneheard Revisited', *Neophilologus* 81 (1997), 445–65.

Battle of Maldon, abounds in acts of vengeance to repay the death of a lord.[83]

The heroic tradition in Old English poetry was part of the Germanic 'cultural baggage' of the Anglo-Saxons.[84] Heroic literature in other (Old) Germanic languages, such as Old Norse, Old Saxon and Old High German, reflect similar themes and values, even though much of the non-English material was written down at a later date.[85] Furthermore, several Old English heroic poems, such as *Waldere*, *Widsith*, *The Finnsburg Fragment* and *Beowulf*, refer to heroes who lived on the Germanic continent, rather than in Anglo-Saxon England; their stories, moreover, also feature in the literary traditions of other Germanic peoples.[86] As a consequence, the heroes of Old English heroic poetry are not unique to the Anglo-Saxons, but are part of a broader, pan-Germanic tradition.[87]

These heroic narratives may have had a didactic function. Their main purpose, as described by Edward Irving Jr, was "to provide models of behavior for semi-aristocratic warrior classes" who listened to these poems.[88] Indeed, Hilda Ellis Davidson has argued that heroic literature was part of the instruction of young warriors and had a practical function in their training.[89] However, young warriors were not the only ones catered to by these poems: the Germanic heroic tradition also has a variety of characters to whom elderly men might have related. Aged men taking up arms include, to name a few: Árni Audunarson (*Sturlunga saga*), Egil Ulserk (*Heimskringla*), Hagen (*Nibelungenlied*), Hathagat (Widukind's *Res gestae Saxonicae*), Heime (*Thidrekssaga*), Hildebrand (*Hildebrandlied*, *Thidrekssaga*), Hjálmgunnar (*Völsunga saga*), Innstein (*Hálfs saga*), Sigemund (*Völsunga saga*), Starkad (Saxo Grammaticus' *Gesta Danorum*), Volsung (*Völsunga saga*)

---

[83] O'Brien O'Keeffe, 'Heroic Values', 109–11.

[84] R. H. Bremmer Jr, 'Across Borders: Anglo-Saxon England and the Germanic World', in *The Cambridge History of Early Medieval English Literature*, ed. C. A. Lees (Cambridge, 2013), 206.

[85] C. Țăranu, 'The Elusive Nature of Germanic Heroic Poetry: A Rhizomatic Model', *Neighbours and Networks* 1 (2013), 44–66.

[86] Bremmer, 'Across Borders', 203–7.

[87] Naturally, the various traditions are geographically and temporally far apart and will also show much influence of their local and contemporaneous contexts, including those texts that deal with much earlier periods. See, e.g., T. Vidal, 'Houses and Domestic Life in the Viking Age and Medieval Period: Material Perspectives from Sagas and Archaeology', unpublished PhD dissertation, University of Nottingham, 2013, who shows contemporary influences on descriptions of the material world in thirteenth-century sagas set in the Viking Age (c.800–1100).

[88] E. B. Irving Jr, 'Heroic Role-Models: Beowulf and Others', in *Heroic Poetry in the Anglo-Saxon Period: Studies in Honor of Jess B. Bessinger, Jr*, ed. H. Damico and J. Leyerle (Kalamazoo, 1993), 347.

[89] Ellis Davidson, 'Training of Warriors', 22.

and Wate (*Kudrun*).⁹⁰ These old warriors may have functioned as role models for aged men and, thus, provide insight into how they were expected to act on the battlefield.

The remainder of this chapter focuses primarily on the old warriors found in Old English poetry that might be added to the impressive list of grey-haired heroes from Germanic legend. These elderly warriors, found in *Beowulf* and *The Battle of Maldon*, not only reaffirm the conclusion that their military careers could be prolonged until a very ripe age, but they also show what roles, ideally, old men were expected to fulfil on the battlefield.

The old advisor

As noted in previous chapters, old age was associated with wisdom and elderly people were expected to pass on their experience. In this respect, the elderly warriors of Germanic legend and Old English heroic poetry were little different. They functioned first of all as advisors, military experts who shared their experience with younger warriors.⁹¹ Their advice often took the form of a whetting speech, spurring the young into taking action. A typical but late example survives in the fifteenth-century Old West Frisian *Gesta Fresonum*, in which the aged Frisian warrior Popta rouses his younger companions:⁹²

> 'O myn liauwe broren, alle ws hoep ende traest wolla wy sette aen Goede. Ende stridet Godes stryd mit froliched ende bescermet wse land! Wynna wy't iefta verlese wy't iefte wirda wy foerslayn, altida foercrya wy bata ende wynningha, hwant dat ewighe lyand wert ws sonder twiuel iouwen!'⁹³

---

⁹⁰ List based on H. Naumann, *Germanisches Gefolgschaftswesen* (Leipzig, 1939), 54–75; W. Dinkelacker, 'Der alte Held. Belege aus mittelalterlicher Heldendichtung und ihr kulturhistorischer Quellenwert', in *Alterskulturen des Mittelalters und der frühen Neuzeit*, ed. E. Vavra (Vienna, 2008), 183–202; and my own observations. The elderly warrior appears to have been a common Germanic literary *topos* and invites further study, as most of these warriors show striking similarities; e.g., both Starkad and Egil Ulserk explicitly express their wish to die in battle rather than of old age, just like Siward of Northumbria.

⁹¹ Dinkelacker, 'Der alte Held', 189, 192, identifies this role for elderly warriors in both Hildebrand (in the Old High German *Hildebrandlied*) and Wate (in the Middle High German *Kudrun*).

⁹² Popta's legend is much older than the extant text and was known in the thirteenth century, see R. H. Bremmer Jr, *An Introduction to Old Frisian* (Amsterdam, 2011), 181–3. The legend of Popta, though not his speech, may have been inspired partially by traditions surrounding Henry of Bonn, who participated in the Crusade of 1147, see Y. Poortinga, *De Palmridder fan Lissabon* (Ljouwert, 1965).

⁹³ *Codex Aysma, die altfriesischen Texte*, ed. W. J. Buma, P. Gerbenzon and M. Tragter-Schubert (Assen, 1993), 524.

['O my dear brothers, let us place all our hope and trust in God. And fight God's fight with happiness and protect our land! Whether we win or lose or are defeated, we will always obtain profit and gain, because the eternal land will be given to us without any doubt!']

Popta uttered these daring words when a group of two hundred crusading Frisians was pitched against an overwhelming force of at least thirty thousand Saracens, near Lisbon. Miraculously, the Frisians came out victorious, aided by St Maurice and a group of knights who descended from Heaven and defeated the heathen forces. The audacious Popta survived the battle, only to be shot by an arrow when he unsuspectingly took off his armour to quench his thirst. Despite his rather unfortunate death, Popta was remembered for his inspiring speech and declared a martyr of the Christian faith. This late, Christianised legend of an aged Frisian warrior saint may be a remnant of the Germanic heroic tradition which features several comparable aged motivational speakers on the brink of battle.

An earlier prototypical example from the Germanic heroic tradition is Starkad in Saxo Grammaticus' *Gesta Danorum*. In a segment that has been identified as the *Lay of Ingeld*, a tenth-century Danish poem that survives only in Saxo's twelfth-century Latin rendering, the elderly Starkad incites the young Heathobard king Ingeld to avenge the Danish murder of his father Froda.[94] Starkad, an old veteran and eye-witness to Froda's murder, is disgusted by the presence at Ingeld's court of Froda's murderers as well as by the young king's lethargic and gluttonous behaviour. Outraged, Starkad breaks into song:

'And why, Ingel, submerged in sin,
do you hesitate to revenge your father?
You cannot view your noble parent's death
with equanimity?

Why, you sluggard, do you worship feasting,
softer than harlots lean back your belly?
Does vengeance for your slaughtered father
mean so little to you?'[95]

Starkad's song is lengthy and contains various admonitions to avenge Froda's death, as well as criticisms of Ingeld's demeanour and of his foreign wife. Eventually, Starkad's words do not fall on deaf ears; Ingeld's spirit is kindled towards revenge. Saxo comments: "The

---

[94] For this lay and Saxo's reworking of his vernacular source, see K. Friis-Jensen, *Saxo Grammaticus as Latin Poet: Studies in the Verse Passages of the Gesta Danorum* (Rome, 1987), 120–51.

[95] Saxo Grammaticus, *History of the Danes*, ed. H. Ellis Davidson, trans. P. Fisher (Cambridge, 1979), 188.

young man's integrity had been in exile but had certainly not breathed its last; brought to light with the old man's assistance".[96] In other words, Starkad has reminded the young Ingeld of his obligations and, as such, he exemplifies the advisory and inspirational role that an elderly warrior could fulfil.

The story of Ingeld was well known in Anglo-Saxon England.[97] Famously, Alcuin mentions Ingeld in a letter to the bishop of Leicester, dated to A.D. 797: "Quid Hinieldus cum Christo?" [What has Ingeld to do with Christ?], the Anglo-Saxon monk asks, complaining of the popularity of heroic stories in monasteries, as opposed to the Word of God.[98] Alcuin's letter certainly suggests that stories about Ingeld were circulating at this time in early medieval England. A reference to Ingeld is indeed found in *Widsith*, an Old English catalogue poem probably composed in the seventh century.[99] The poem lists various ancient and legendary rulers and tribes of whom the eponymous poet Widsith [lit. 'broad journey'] had heard or among whom he had lived. The poem also has a reference to Ingeld's attack on the Danes:

Hroþwulf ond Hroðgar   heoldon lengest
sibbe ætsomne   suhtorfædran,
siþþan hy forwræcon   wicinga cynn
ond Ingeldes   ord forbigdan,
forheowan æt Heorote   Heaðobeardna þrym.[100]

[Hrothulf and Hrothgar, nephew and uncle, held peace together for very long, after they drove off the kin of the men of the Wic (the Heathobards) and caused Ingeld's front line of battle to retreat, they killed the force of the Heathobards at Heorot.]

Widsith does not mention that Ingeld's attack against Hrothgar and Hrothulf was prompted by the rebuke of the elderly warrior Starkad, as described by Saxo Grammaticus. Yet the instigating role played by

---

[96] Saxo, *History of the Danes*, ed. Ellis Davidson, trans. Fisher, 194.
[97] For all references to Ingeld in Anglo-Saxon and other Germanic sources and a reconstruction of the tale of Ingeld, see K. Malone, 'The Tale of Ingeld', in *Studies in Heroic Legend and in Current Speech by Kemp Malone*, ed. S. Einarsson and N. E. Eliason (Copenhagen, 1959), 1–62.
[98] For an exhaustive study of the context of this phrase, see M. Garrison, '"Quid Hinieldus cum Christo?"', in *Latin Learning and English Lore: Studies in Anglo-Saxon Literature for Michael Lapidge*, ed. K. O'Brien O'Keeffe and A. Orchard (Toronto, 2005), I, 237–59.
[99] L. Neidorf, 'The Dating of Widsið and the Study of Germanic Antiquity', *Neophilologus* 97 (2013), 165–83; cf. E. Weiskott, 'The Meter of *Widsith* and the Distant Past', *Neophilologus* 99 (2015), 143–50, who argues against this early date, but his criticisms of Neidorf's original arguments are convincingly countered in L. Neidorf, 'On the Epistemology of Old English Scholarship', *Neophilologus* 99 (2015), 631–47.
[100] *Widsith*, ed. K. Malone (Copenhagen, 1962), lines 45–9.

the aged warrior Starkad was probably familiar to the audience of *Beowulf*, which also refers to Ingeld's fight with the Danes.

The matter of Ingeld features in Beowulf's report to his lord Hygelac, king of the Geats (*Beowulf*, lines 2014–66). Here, Beowulf describes the future marriage between the Danish princess Freawaru and the Heathobard prince Ingeld as part of the settlement of a feud between the two groups. Beowulf predicts that this attempt at 'peaceweaving' is doomed to fail, remarking: "Oft seldan hwær / æfter leodhryre lytle hwile / bongar bugeð, þeah seo bryd duge" [Very seldom anywhere, after the fall of a prince, does the deadly spear rest for a little while, even if the bride is good] (lines 2029b–31).[101] Beowulf supposes that an "eald æscwiga" [old spear-warrior] (line 2042a), likely a reference to Starkad,[102] will convince a younger comrade to resume the feud, pointing out that the Danes are carrying heirlooms that formerly belonged to the Heathobards:

þonne cwið æt beore   se ðe beah gesyhð,
eald æscwiga,   se ðe eall ge(man),
garcwealm gumena   – him bið grim (se)fa –,
onginneð geomormod   geong(um) cempan
þurh hreðra gehygd   higes cunnian,
wigbealu weccean. (lines 2041–2046a)

[Then he, who sees the ring, the old spear-warrior, who remembers everything, the spear-death of warriors, speaks at his beer – he has an angry spirit –, he begins, sad-minded, to tempt the spirit of the young warrior through thought of glories,[103] to stir up war.]

In this way, the old Heathobard warrior, like Saxo's Starkad, reminds his younger companion of the obligation to avenge his fallen lord.[104]

Two further examples of "the old and barbaric [who] whets the young and feckless to his venerable duty" are found in *The Battle of Maldon*.[105] A fragmentary poem of 325 lines, *The Battle of Maldon* commemorates the battle between Vikings and Anglo-Saxons that

---

[101] For the discussion of 'peaceweavers' in *Beowulf*, see G. R. Overing, 'The Women of *Beowulf*: A Context for Interpretation', in *The Beowulf Reader*, ed. P. S. Baker (New York, 2000), 219–60; A. Hall, 'Hygelac's Only Daughter: A Present, a Potentate and a Peaceweaver in *Beowulf*', *Studia Neophilologica* 78 (2006), 81–7.

[102] For the identification of Starkad with the old spear-warrior, see Malone, 'Tale of Ingeld', 10.

[103] I interpret "hreðra" as the gen. pl. of *hrēð* 'glory, triumph', rather than the gen. pl. of *hreðer* 'breast, heart', as the latter interpretation would render the phrase redundant. Cf. *Beowulf*, 232, 399.

[104] The implications of this passage are discussed in full by J. M. Hill, *The Anglo-Saxon Warrior Ethic: Reconstructing Lordship in Early English Literature* (Gainesville, 2000), 47–60.

[105] R. Frank, '*The Battle of Maldon* and Heroic Literature', in *Battle of Maldon*, ed. Scragg, 199.

took place in the year 991.[106] The poem features two aged warriors, Byrhtnoth and Byrhtwold, who both encourage the younger troops and embolden them to fight bravely. Byrhtnoth, ealdorman of Essex, is the leader of the English war band and also occurs in other, documentary sources. The *Maldon* poet calls attention to Byrhtnoth's old age by calling him "frod" [old and wise] (line 140a) and "har hilderinc" [a grey-haired warrior] (line 169a). Despite the fact that the English lose the battle as a result of a possible strategic error by Byrhtnoth, the elderly leader is presented in a positive light, never ceasing to inspire his entourage, even after the battle turns sour.[107] Before the fighting starts, Byrhtnoth reminds his younger retainers of the ideal of achieving glory before death: "bæd þæt hyssa gehwylc hogode to wige, / þe on Denon wolde dom gefeohtan" [he asked that each young warrior who wanted to win glory from the Danes would give thought to the battle] (lines 128–9). Even when Byrhtnoth himself is brought to his knees by fatal wounds, he continues to encourage his men:

> Þa gyt þæt word gecwæð
> har hilderinc,   hyssas bylde,
> bæd gangan forð   gode geferan.
> Ne mihte þa on fotum leng   fæste gestandan. (lines 168b–171)

[Still then he spoke that speech, the grey-haired warrior, encouraged the young warriors, asked his good companions to go forward. Then he was no longer able to stand firmly on his feet.]

The old warrior's words seem to have the desired effect; even though some of his retainers flee after his demise, most decide to stay and die alongside their leader. Some of them express their ideals of loyalty in the form of short speeches, while others let their swords and spears do the talking. Byrhtwold, an "eald geneat" [old companion] (line 310a), is the last one to be given a speech in the poem as it is extant.

Like his leader Byrhtnoth, Byrhtwold reminds the younger warriors of the loyalty that they owe their stricken lord:

> 'Hige sceal þe heardra,   heorte þe cenre,
> mod sceal þe mare,   þe ure mægen lytlað.
> Her lið ure ealdor   eall forheawen,
> god on greote.   A mæg gnornian
> se ðe nu fram þis wigplegan   wendan þenceð.' (lines 312–19)

---

[106] The poem, which lacks beginning and end, survives only in an eighteenth-century transcript, made from London, British Library, Cotton Otho A. xii, which was irreparably damaged in the Ashburnham House fire of 1731. With no extant manuscript, the poem is hard to date, but most scholars agree that the poem must have been composed shortly after the battle in 991. See *Battle of Maldon*, ed. Scragg, 32.

[107] G. Clark, 'The Hero of Maldon: *Vir pius et strenuus*', *Speculum* 54 (1979), 257–82; I. J. Kirby, 'In Defence of Byrhtnoth', *Florilegium* 11 (1992), 53–60.

['Spirit must be the harder, heart the bolder, courage must be the greater, as our strength diminishes. Here lies our leader entirely hewn apart, the good one in the dust. He will surely mourn forever, who now intends to turn from this battle-play.']

The first two lines of Byrhtwold's speech encapsulate the heroic ethos in the form of a maxim. As such, the lines can be regarded as a general, traditional expression of what defined heroic behaviour.[108] However, coming from the lips of an old man, these words may bear a particular significance for Byrhtwold's own situation as well, since as an old man he would no longer have been in prime physical condition. Nevertheless, Byrhtwold reminds himself, his own physical decline need not be a limitation; it can be compensated for by displaying greater courage. In fact, Byrhtwold's words show some similarity to the speech of the old warrior Starkad in Saxo's *Gesta Danorum* referred to above. In his rebuke of Ingeld, Starkad too notes how an old man's courage can compensate for the whitening of his hair, a reference to his own physical decline:

'Let weakling youth yield to old age
and reverence an elder's numerous years;
let none reproach his long span of seasons
when the man is courageous.

Although an ancient's hairs grow white,
his valour persists unaltered, nor
can sliding Time calumniate his virile heart.'[109]

The courage shown by elderly warriors like Starkad, Byrhtnoth and Byrhtwold not only demands respect from their younger companions but also serves as an inspiration; they remain role models, their grey hairs notwithstanding.

There is, of course, a long-standing tradition of depicting old warriors as counsellors and advisors to younger men, stretching back as far as Homer's Nestor. Nestor's wisdom and experience, acquired in years of warfare, made his advice valuable and he was respected and listened to by his younger companions. At the same time, Nestor's own fighting abilities had clearly diminished and he is not shown as actively involved in the fighting himself. As Hanna Roisman explains: "Nestor no longer needs to prove himself and he can accept with grace and honour the younger heroes' superiority in strength, agility, and the other virtues of youth. In fact, he must accept it if he is not to become a laughing stock."[110] The elderly warriors of the Germanic

---

[108] P. Cavill, 'Maxims in *The Battle of Maldon*', *Neophilologus* 82 (1988), 638–41.
[109] Saxo, *History of the Danes*, ed. Ellis Davidson, trans. Fisher, 187.
[110] H. M. Roisman, 'Nestor the Good Counsellor', *The Classical Quarterly* ns 51 (2005), 38.

heroic tradition often function in a way similar to Nestor – providing advice to younger warriors – yet, as is demonstrated below, their role is rarely that of the passive advisor; they still intend to do battle alongside their younger colleagues, often fighting on the forefront, rather than comfortably receding into the background.

The active old warrior

> 'ih wallota sumaro enti wintro   sehstic ur lante,
> dar man mih eo scerita   in folc sceotantero,
> so man mir at burc enigeru   banun ni gifasta;
> nu scal mih suasat chind   suertu hauwan,
> breton mit sinu billiu,   eddo ih imo ti banin werdan.'

> ['I have been wandering of summers and winters sixty, where I have always been assigned to the company of the spearmen, whereas at no city has death been inflicted on me; now must my own child strike me with the sword, smite me with his blade, or I become his killer.'][111]

The eighth-century Old High German *Hildebrandlied* describes how the elderly warrior Hildebrand, after fighting in the vanguard for thirty years, has to fight his own son Hadubrand. The latter does not recognise his father, whom he thinks long dead, and considers his aged opponent an "alter Hun, ummet spaher" [exceedingly crafty old Hun].[112] The fragmentary *Hildebrandlied* ends with the moment that father and son engage in one-on-one combat, striking at each other with their spears. Other versions of the same story in later texts, the *Thidrekssaga* and *Das jüngere Hildebrandlied*, suggest that the old father won the fight, tragically killing his own son.[113] Hildebrand, who is estimated to have been fifty-five to sixty years of age at the time of this fight,[114] is one of many elderly individuals who still take up arms in the Germanic heroic tradition.[115] In Old English heroic literature, too, the elderly warriors do not sit idly by; they fight in the vanguard, leading by example.

In terms of its structure, theme and poetic technique, the *Hildebrandlied* shows similarities with *The Battle of Maldon*.[116] The elderly warriors at the centre of both poems are also comparable. Like Hildebrand, Byrhtnoth is an experienced warrior who shows no signs

---

[111] *Hildebrandlied*, ed. and trans. H. Broszinski, 3rd ed. (Kassel, 2004), lines 50–4.
[112] *Hildebrandlied*, ed. and trans. Broszinski, line 39.
[113] J. Knight Bostock, *A Handbook of Old High German Literature*, 2nd rev. ed., ed. K. C. King and D. R. McLintock (Oxford, 1976), 67–72.
[114] Knight Bostock, *Handbook*, 49.
[115] For a list of elderly warriors of Germanic legend, see above.
[116] R. W. V. Elliott, 'Hildebrand and Byrhtnoth: A Study in Heroic Technique', *Comparative Literature* 14 (1962), 53–70.

of having grown passive in old age. Indeed, Byrhtnoth's behaviour on the battlefield is nothing short of heroic; having been wounded by a Viking spear, Byrhtnoth furiously removes the weapon from his body, stabs the Viking who wounded him and quickly kills another, roaring with laughter. Soon, he is pierced by another spear, which is pulled out by Wulfmær, "hyse unweaxen, / cniht on gecampe" [a young warrior not fully grown, a youth in battle] (lines 152b–153a). The poet's description of this scene confirms that, within an Anglo-Saxon army, the very young did fight side by side with the very old. Overall, the *Maldon* poet paints a picture of Byrhtnoth that is true to Byrhtnoth's own description of himself: "unforcuð eorl mid his werode / þe wile gealgean eþel þysne" [a dauntless earl with his band who wants to defend this homeland] (lines 51–2). Whereas Semper regards Byrhtnoth's portrayal as "hardly a reference which emphasises men's ability to function as successful warriors during their old age",[117] the examples highlighted above show that the poet at the very least describes an old man more than capable of holding his own on the battlefield.

Condemnations of Byrhtnoth's martial prowess are based on the aged warrior's decision to fight the Vikings on equal terms. At the start of the poem, the English defence is described as highly effective, since the Vikings could only reach the shore via a narrow and easily defendable causeway. Byrhtnoth's "ofermode" [excessive courage, pride] (line 89a) inspired the elderly leader of the English to grant the Vikings safe passage and an open fight. Whether this was a tactical blunder made by an "aging English earl",[118] "too foolish to be heroic",[119] or an act of courageous self-sacrifice has long since been a matter of debate.[120] Whatever the case may be, Byrhtnoth's decision is certainly not condemned by his own followers, most of whom decide to stay and die alongside their leader.[121] While the outcome of the battle is a definitive defeat, the poet does not describe Byrhtnoth as a failed warrior, succumbing to his own old age. It is quite the opposite; Byrhtnoth leads by example and dies a hero's death.

---

[117] Semper, 'Byð se ealda man', 296.
[118] T. D. Hill, 'History and Heroic Ethic in Maldon', *Neophilologus* 54 (1970), 291–6.
[119] J. R. R. Tolkien, 'Ofermod', in *Tree and Leaf, Including the Poem Mythopoeia. The Homecoming of Beorhtnoth* (London, 2001), 146.
[120] E.g., J. Halbrooks, 'Byrhtnoth's Great-Hearted Mirth, or Praise and Blame in *The Battle of Maldon*', *Philological Quarterly* 82 (2003), 235–55; H. Gneuss, 'The Battle of Maldon 89: Byrthnoð's *ofermod* Again', *SiP* 73 (1976), 117–37; S. Gwara, *Heroic Identity in the World of Beowulf* (Leiden, 2008), 311–50.
[121] Clark, 'Hero of Maldon', 278; Gwara, *Heroic Identity*, 342–9, argues that Byrhtnoth's decision did not necessarily cause the defeat, but that it was Godric's flight on Byrhtnoth's horse that led to the downfall of the English forces.

Like his leader, the old companion Byrhtwold also intends to fight actively alongside his comrades. The last lines of his speech show the old man's willingness to die alongside his lord:

'Ic eom frod feores: Fram ic ne wille,
ac ic me be healfe minum hlaforde,
be swa leofan men, licgan þence.'

['I am old and wise of life: I do not want to go from here, but by his side, by my own lord, by such a beloved man, I intend to lie.'] (lines 312–19)

Byrhtwold's explicit mention of his old age may be intended to spur on his younger companions, who may not want to be outdone by the older man. At the same time, Byrhtwold here consciously chooses to die on the battlefield rather than shirk away from the fight and die of old age, the only logical alternative. Like Byrhtnoth, Byrhtwold intends to lead by example, not only talking the talk, but also walking the walk.

Beowulf, too, is rife with old warriors, most of whom are described as unrelentingly active, despite their age. Aside from the main protagonists Hroþgar and Beowulf, both called "har hilderinc" [grey-haired warrior] (lines 1307a, 3136a), the poem refers to several other old, militant characters, such as Healfdene, father of Hrothgar, "gamol ond guðreouw" [old and fierce in battle] (line 58a) and Ongentheow, king of the Swedes, "eald and egesfull" [old and terrible] (line 2929a).[122] In addition, the *Beowulf* poet alludes, either implicitly or explicitly, to four other active, elderly warriors of Germanic legend: Volsung and Sigemund (lines 875, 884, 897), two aged kings who die in battle in the *Völsunga saga*;[123] Heime (line 1198), an aged warrior who is asked to return from his retirement in the *Thidrekssaga*;[124] and Saxo's Starkad (lines 2020–69; see above). Given these allusions and the fact that two of the main protagonists are old warrior kings, the role of an old man on the battlefield must have been very much on the mind of the *Beowulf* poet. The role of the elderly kings in *Beowulf* is an important topic that requires a full, in-depth analysis, which will be provided in the next chapter. Below, I focus on the poet's characterisation of Ongentheow as a vigorous old warrior and, briefly, on the difference between Hrothgar and Beowulf in relation to the role the poet propagates for elderly warriors.

---

[122] S. Gwara, 'A Metaphor in *Beowulf* 2487a: *guðhelm toglad*', *SiP* 93 (1996), 333–48.
[123] These references or allusions will be discussed in more detail in the following chapter.
[124] *Die Thidrekssaga oder Dietrich von Bern und die Niflungen*, ed. H. Ritter-Schaumburg, trans. F. H. von der Hagen (St Goar, 1989), ch. 393–8.

Old Warriors

The martial deeds of the elderly Swedish king Ongentheow are referred to on more than one occasion in the poem.[125] The most detailed account of Ongentheow is found in the messenger's speech following Beowulf's death (lines 2922–98). The messenger recounts how the old Ongentheow avenged himself on the Geats by killing their leader Hæthcyn. Ongentheow initially pursued the Geats, but was soon driven back by a superior force led by Hæthcyn's brother Hygelac. Ongentheow, described as "se goda ... frod fela-geomor" [the good one, old, wise and deeply sorrowful] (lines 2949a, 2950b), then retreated to Ravenswood where he was hunted down and ultimately slain by the brothers Eofor and Wulf. Ongentheow, however, did not go down without a fight; his last stand is nothing short of heroic and deserves quotation at length:

> Þær wearð Ongenðio   ecgum sweorda,
> blondenfexa   on bid wrecen,
> ...   Hyne yrringa
> Wulf Wonreding   wæpne geræhte,
> þæt him for swenge   swat ædrum sprong
> forð under fexe.   Næs he forht swa ðeh,
> gomela Scilfing,   ac forgeald hraðe
> wyrsan wrixle   wælhlem þone,
> syððan ðeodcyning   þyder oncirde.
> Ne meahte se snella   sunu Wonredes
> ealdum ceorle   ondslyht giofan,
> ac he him on heafde   helm ær gescer,
> þæt he blode fah   bugan sceolde,
> ...
> Let se hearda   Higelaces þegn
> bradne mece,   þa his broðor læg,
> ealdsweord eotonisc   entiscne helm
> brecan ofer bordweal;   ða gebeah cyning,
> folces hyrde,   wæs in feorh dropen. (lines 2961–2, 2964b–2974, 2977–81)

[There the grey-haired Ongentheow was brought to bay by the edges of swords ... Wulf, son of Wonred, struck him angrily with his weapon, so that because of the blow the blood burst forth from the veins beneath his hair. Nevertheless he was not afraid, the old Scylfing (i.e. Ongentheow), but he, the king of a people, quickly repaid the onslaught with a worse exchange after he had turned to that place. The quick son of Wonred could not give the old man a counter-blow, because he (Ongentheow) had cut through the helmet on his head, so that he (Wulf) had to sink down, covered with blood ... The brave thane of Hygelac (Eofor), when his brother lay dead, made his broad giant sword, the old sword, break

---

[125] *Beowulf*, lines 2472–89, 2922–98. In addition, Hygelac is called "bonan Ongenþeoes" [the slayer of Ongentheow] (line 1968a) and Onela, king of the Swedes, is called "Ongenðioes bearn" [the son of Ongentheow] (line 2387b).

the giant helmet over the shield; then the king bowed, the guardian of the people was mortally wounded.]

In this episode, as elsewhere in the poem, Ongentheow comes across as an admirable, courageous old king.[126] Ongentheow is not shown as being hindered by his old age and still demonstrates fighting prowess, proving a match for the younger warrior Wulf.

As will be discussed in detail in the next chapter, much of the main narrative of *Beowulf* revolves around the juxtaposition of two elderly warrior kings, Hrothgar and Beowulf. While both are called "har hilderinc" [grey-haired warrior] (lines 1307a, 3136a), it is clear that only Beowulf fulfils the role of an active elderly warrior, akin to Hildebrand, Byrhtnoth, Byrhtwold and Ongentheow. Even in old age, Beowulf displays great courage and leads his men into battle against a dragon. Hrothgar, by contrast, is depicted as a retired warrior, "eldo gebunden" [bound by age] (line 2111b), who is no longer able to protect his people. As I will argue, this juxtaposition of the active Beowulf and the passive Hrothgar leads to two distinct evaluations of both kings. The elderly warrior king Beowulf is praised as "wyruldcyning[a] / manna mildust ond mon(ðw)ærust, / leodum liðost ond lofgeornost" [of worldly kings the most generous of men, the most gentle, the most gracious among peoples and the most eager for fame] (lines 3180b–3182). By contrast, the poem's description of Hrothgar can be read as particularly negative. In this way, the *Beowulf* poet, like the poet of *The Battle of Maldon*, advocates an active role for elderly warriors. Indeed, like Byrhtnoth in *The Battle of Maldon*, both Ongentheow and Beowulf are shown as unrelentingly energetic in their later years.[127]

A final example of a vigorous, old warrior who leads his troops into battle is found in the Old English poem *Genesis A*, in a passage that describes Abraham's freeing of Lot.[128] As Barbara Raw has noted, the description of the War of the Kings and Abraham's mission to save Lot shares several characteristics with Old English heroic poetry:

> Both the vocabulary and the sentiments are those of poems like *Beowulf* and *The Battle of Maldon*. The king of Elam, like Scyld, exacts tribute

---

[126] L. M. Carruthers, 'Kingship and Heroism in *Beowulf*', in *Heroes and Heroines in Medieval English Literature: A Festschrift Presented to André Crépin on the Occasion of his Sixty-Fifth Birthday*, ed. L. M. Carruthers (Cambridge, 1994), 26.

[127] Gwara, *Heroic Identity*, 324, rightly identifies Byrhtnoth as Beowulf's Doppelgänger; similarly, Ongentheow has been termed Beowulf's "double" by L. Georgianna, 'King Hrethel's Sorrow and the Limits of Heroic Action in *Beowulf*', *Speculum* 62 (1987), 845.

[128] *Genesis A, B*, a close paraphrase of Gen. 1–22, with additional material on the creation and the fall of the angels, is one of the four poems in the Junius Manuscript.

from the people of Sodom and Gomorrah; the warriors are equipped with the yellow shields, javelins, and ring-patterned swords of Anglo-Saxon heroes; birds of prey tear the corpses; Abraham's friends, like Byrhtnoth's *comitatus*, promise to avenge his injury or fall among the slain, and Abraham himself, like Byrhtnoth, gives war as a pledge instead of gold.[129]

Andy Orchard similarly describes these passages in *Genesis A* as "a heroic set piece", illustrative of the way a "poet steeped in heroic tradition can interpret and elaborate a promising piece of scripture".[130] Abraham, aged over seventy-five according to the biblical account and described in the poem as "dæg-rime frod" [old and wise in the number of days],[131] is shown to fulfil the two roles of elderly warriors: speaking strategic and encouraging words as well as jumping into the fray himself:

>   Þa he his frumgaran,
> wishydig wer,   wordum sægde,
> þares afera,   – him wæs þearf micel –
> þæt hie on twa healfe
> grimme guðgemot   gystum eowdon,
> heardne handplegan.   cwæð þæt him se halga,
> ece drihten,   [ðe] eað mihte
> æt þam sperenide   spede lænan.
> …   abraham sealde
> wig to wedde   nalles wunden gold
> for his suhtrigan,   sloh and fylde
> feond on fitte.
> …   gewat him abraham ða
> on þa wigrode   wiðertrod seon
> laðra monna.[132]

[Then he, the wise-minded man, Terah's descendant, spoke with words to his princes – his need was great – that they would show the grim battle, the difficult encounter, to their enemies on two fronts; he said that the holy one, the eternal Lord, could the better grant success to them in the spear-hate. … Abraham gave war as a ransom, not at all wound gold, for his nephew, he slew and killed the enemy in the struggle. … Then Abraham set out on the war-road to see the retreat of the hated men.]

---

[129] B. C. Raw, *The Art and Background of Old English Poetry* (London, 1978), 82.
[130] A. Orchard, 'Conspicuous Heroism: Abraham, Prudentius, and the Old English Verse *Genesis*', in *Heroes and Heroines*, ed. Carruthers, 57; Orchard suggests the *Genesis* poem may have been influenced by Prudentius' *Psychomachia*.
[131] *Genesis A*, ed. A. N. Doane, *Genesis A: A New Edition, Revised* (Tempe, 2013), line 2174b.
[132] *Genesis A*, ed. Doane, lines 2052b–2059, 2069b–2072a, 2083b–2085a.

The Abraham in *Genesis A* is a "fyrd-rinc fruman" [the leader of warriors], "elne gewurðod, dome and sigore" [made worthy by courage, honour and victory]:[133] more like Beowulf and Byrhtnoth and less like the Abraham of the biblical account. In other words, Abraham is presented as an energetic, elderly warrior from the Germanic heroic tradition with which the *Genesis A* poet and his Anglo-Saxon audience would have been familiar.

The retired warrior

As established above, elderly warriors in the Germanic heroic tradition were ideally expected to continue participating actively in warfare, despite their physical decline. Those who failed to live up to this ideal became the object of scorn and mockery. Carol Clover, for instance, has commented on how Egil Skallagrímsson, having grown old and no longer able to fight, is mocked and teased by women as he crawls over the floor.[134] In Scandinavian sagas, Clover argues, old warriors, once they had lost their strength, moved to the category of 'powerless' people. As a result, their condition became linked to femaleness; retired warriors are described as being in the company of women and they also acquire attributes commonly associated with women, such as mourning excessively.[135]

In Old English heroic poetry, those old men who no longer participated actively in battle also appear to have been treated negatively. King Constantine II of Scotland (d. 952) in *The Battle of Brunanburh* provides a telling example.[136] Constantine, a "har hildering" [grey-haired warrior], is shamefully put to flight, while his opponents Æthelstan and Edmund achieve "ealdorlangne tir" [lifelong glory].[137] Having fled the battlefield, the elderly Constantine is denounced for not having acted like a hero on the battlefield, where his younger retainers, among them his own son, have died:

> Swilce þær eac se froda mid fleame com
> on his cyþþe norð, Costontinus,
> har hildering; hreman ne þorfte
> mecga gemanan; he wæs his mæga sceard,
> freonda befylled on folcstede,

---

[133] *Genesis A*, ed. Doane, lines 2104a, 2137b–2138a.
[134] C. J. Clover, 'Regardless of Sex: Men, Women and Power in Early Northern Europe', *Speculum* 68 (1993), 382–3.
[135] Clover, 'Regardless of Sex', 382–5.
[136] *The Battle of Brunanburh* is one of the poems in *The Anglo-Saxon Chronicle* and commemorates a victory in 937 by the West-Saxon King Æthelstan and his brother Edmund over the combined forces of Norsemen, Scots and Irish.
[137] *The Battle of Brunanburh*, ed. A. Campbell (London, 1938), lines 39, 3.

beslagen æt sæcce,   and his sunu forlet
on wælstowe   wundun forgrunden,
giungne æt guðe.   Gelpan ne þorfte
beorn blandenfeax   bilgeslehtes,
eald inwidda.[138]

[Likewise the old and wise man came through flight in his native North, Constantine, the grey-haired warrior; he did not need to boast of the meeting of swords; he was bereft of his kinsmen, of friends felled on the battle-field, killed at strife, and he left his son, young in battle, in the place of slaughter, destroyed by wounds. The grey-haired warrior did not need to boast of the sword-clash, the old wicked one.]

The poet's application of the term "inwidda" [wicked one, deceitful one] to Constantine, in particular, has strong negative overtones. The word is also used for the evil commander Holofernes in *Judith*, and compounds with the element *inwid-* are used for both Grendel and the dragon in *Beowulf*.[139] In his description of Constantine, the *Brunanburh* poet foregrounds Constantine's age by employing four different words for 'old': "frod", "har", "blandenfeax" and "eald". Constantine's age is further emphasised by contrasting it with the youth of his son, "giungne æt guðe" [young in battle]. Sparse though this description is, the juxtaposition between the young warrior who fell on the battle-field and the elderly warrior who fled the scene adds insult to injury. Constantine is not only unheroic because he took flight, but he has also failed in the responsibilities that his age required.

As we shall see in the next chapter, Hrothgar's lack of fighting spirit in the poem *Beowulf* also leads to a rather negative evaluation of him as an old warrior king who can no longer fulfil his responsibilities as a warlord. While Hrothgar is neither mocked nor scorned explicitly, critics have linked Hrothgar's condition, like that of Clover's old men in Scandinavian literature, to femaleness. To give an example, Howell Chickering Jr has described Hrothgar's tears at Beowulf's departure (lines 1870–80) as "weak, unmanly".[140] Similarly, Brian McFadden has pointed out that, after Grendel's defeat, Hrothgar returns to Heorot having spent the night in the company of women, in the "bryd-bure" [bride-chamber; women's chambers?] (line 921), illustrating that "Hrothgar's defeat in the hall has feminised the lord".[141] The feminine

---

[138] *The Battle of Brunanburh*, ed. Campbell, lines 37–46.
[139] D. Schürr, 'Hiltibrants Gottvertrauen', *Amsterdamer Beiträge zur älteren Germanistik* 68 (2011), 17–19.
[140] *Beowulf*, ed. and trans. Chickering, 348.
[141] B. McFadden, 'Sleeping after the Feast: Deathbeds, Marriage Beds, and the Power Structure of Heorot', *Neophilologus* 84 (2000), 633.

side of Hrothgar may not be unequivocally accepted,[142] but Hrothgar at least appears to constitute an interesting English parallel to what Clover has described for the Scandinavian sagas; an audience familiar with the tradition of linking defunct warriors to women may immediately have grasped what the poet tried to imply.

Thus, whereas some aged warriors, such as Byrhtnoth, Byrhtwold and Beowulf, found ways to make themselves useful on the battlefield, others were no longer able or willing to fulfil their heroic obligations. Constantine and Hrothgar were not excused by the Old English poets on account of their age, but rather appear to have been stigmatised.

Exclusion of elderly warriors from the battlefield

While most Old English heroic poems discussed so far advocate both an advisory and active role for elderly warriors, the Old English *Exodus* uniquely features an explicit admonition against enlisting old men.[143] One of the poem's defining characteristics is the manner in which the account of the Israelites' flight from Egypt has been adapted to the Anglo-Saxon tradition of heroic poetry: the Israelites are designated as a "wiglic werod" [a warlike host], led by Moses, the "herges wisa" [leader of the army].[144] The poem's description of the Israelite army is of particular interest, since it makes clear that the Israelites excluded from their ranks men who were unable to fight, either because of youth, injury or old age:

> þæt wæs wiglic werod. Wace ne gretton
> in þæt rincgetæl ræswan herges,
> þa þe for geoguðe gyt ne mihton
> under bordhreoðan breostnet wera
> wið flane feond folmum werigean,
> ne him bealubenne gebiden hæfdon
> ofer linde lærig, licwunde spor,
> gylpplegan gares. Gamele ne moston,
> hare heaðorincas, hilde onþeon,
> gif him modheapum mægen swiðrade.[145]

[that was a warlike host. The leaders of the army did not welcome the weak into that company of warriors, those who because of youth could not yet defend the coat of mail of men against a hostile enemy with

---

[142] E.g., B. C. L. Rothauser, 'Winter in Heorot: Looking at Anglo-Saxon Perceptions of Age and Kingship through the Character of Hrothgar', in *Old Age in the Middle Ages*, ed. Classen, 103–20.
[143] *Exodus*, one of the four poems of the Junius Manuscript, is a poetic adaptation of the Old Testament Exodus, though mainly focusing on chapters 12–15.
[144] *Exodus*, ed. P. J. Lucas (London, 1977), lines 233, 13.
[145] *Exodus*, ed. Lucas, lines 233–42.

hands under a shield, nor those who had experienced a serious wound over the rim of a shield, the mark of a wound, valorous combat of the spear. Nor were the aged, grey-haired warriors allowed to be successful in battle, if strength had diminished for them among the bold troops.]

The source of this passage remains uncertain. John Hermann has noted that "no source for this selection episode can be found in the biblical book of Exodus".[146] Several verses in Numbers 1 refer to able-bodied warriors among the tribes of Israel and these verses are frequently cited as analogous passages.[147] The verses in Numbers, however, only mention that people over the age of twenty-four are fit for war and do not speak of people being too old for military enlistment. Paul Remley has suggested that the episode in *Exodus* ultimately goes back to the Vulgate text of Exod. 12:37: "Profectique sunt filii Israhel ... sescenta ferme milia peditum uirorum absque paruulis" [And the children of Israel set forward ... being about six hundred thousand men on foot, beside children]. Remley argues that the Anglo-Saxon poet has expanded the phrase "absque paruulis" to mean "not counting the young, small, weak, deficient and infirm", making use of the semantic range of Latin *paruus*, of which *paruulus* is a diminutive.[148]

A hitherto overlooked parallel to the passage in *Exodus* appears in the selection policies of the Jomsvikings and Olaf Tryggvason in much later Icelandic sagas (see above). These regulations likewise stipulated that warriors should not be enlisted if they were too young or too old. Importantly, these Viking war bands are explicitly presented as elite forces and their selection policies are therefore not a reflection of general practice, but, rather, what gave them the edge over 'normal' war bands which, we must assume, did include young and old warriors. The passage in the Old English *Exodus* may express a similar idea. Their strict selection policy marks the Israelite host as an elite force.

While the Israelite host was particular in choosing their warriors, the Egyptian army was not. The Pharaoh's forces consisted of two thousand of the Pharaoh's own kinsmen, who, in turn, "ut alædde wæpnedcynnes wigan æghwilcne þara þe he on ðam fyrste findan mihte" [led out each male warrior that he could find in that period of time].[149] In other words, a chaotic mustering as opposed to the clear and balanced selection procedure of the Israelites.[150] In this Egyptian

---

[146] Cited in P. G. Remley, *Old English Biblical Verse: Studies in Genesis, Exodus and Daniel* (Cambridge, 1996), 183.
[147] *Exodus*, ed. E. B. Irving Jr (New Haven, 1953), 82; *Exodus*, ed. Lucas, 109; Remley, *Biblical Verse*, 183.
[148] Remley, *Biblical Verse*, 183–4.
[149] *Exodus*, ed. Lucas, lines 187b–189.
[150] N. Speirs, 'The Two Armies of the Old English *Exodus*: *twa þusendo*, Line 184b, and *cista*, Lines 229b and 230a', *NQ* ns 34 (1987), 145–6.

"chaotic herd", Nancy Speirs also identifies old warriors: "hare heorowulfas hilde gretton" [grey sword-wolves greeted the battle].[151] In her interpretation, the exclusion from the Israelites of elderly men who lacked strength is seen as positive, while the Egyptian "hare heorowulfas" carry a negative association: they are a sign of the Pharaoh's army's inferiority. Biggam, commenting on the same passage, however, argues that the "hare heorowulfas" here are not 'old', but that the word *har* 'grey' refers to the colour of the mailcoats worn by the warriors or suits the metaphor of the sword-*wolves*, since wolves are typically described as *har* in Old English poetry.[152]

Whether we interpret the Egyptian army as containing old men or not, the passage in *Exodus* regarding the Israelite army makes clear that, to this Anglo-Saxon poet at least, old men who had lost their strength were no longer suitable as warriors. However, the other Old English heroic poems discussed above suggest that even those elderly individuals who had grown weaker could still participate actively and at least encourage their younger companions. In that manner, they too were considered valuable additions to a military gathering.

Conclusion

> militat omnis amans, et habet sua castra Cupido;
> Attice, crede mihi, militat omnis amans.
> quae bello est habilis, Veneri quoque conuenit aetas.
> turpe senex miles, turpe senilis amor.[153]

> [Every lover serves as a soldier, and Cupid has his own camp. Believe me, Atticus, every lover serves as a soldier. The age which is apt for war, is also suitable for Love: disgraceful is the elderly soldier, disgraceful is an elderly lover.]

Love is a battlefield, the Roman poet Ovid writes, and it is no place for an old person. However, with the exception of the passage in *Exodus*, there is no evidence that his sentiment was shared by the Anglo-Saxons. Rather than being regarded as disgraceful, old warriors appear to have enjoyed a special status within the Anglo-Saxon war band. This status is reflected in the archaeological record, which shows that weapons found in the graves of the oldest individuals tended to be longer and more numerous than those found in other adult graves. Elderly warriors also feature in depictions of warfare in manuscripts of Prudentius' *Psychomachia*, the Old English Hexateuch and various

---

[151] *Exodus*, ed. Lucas, line 181; Speirs, 'Two Armies', 145.
[152] Biggam, *Grey in Old English*, 174–5.
[153] Ovid, *Amores*, ed. E. J. Kenney, 2nd ed. (Oxford, 1994), I.9, verses 1–4.

Old Warriors

Psalters. In the Bayeux Tapestry, they take up prominent positions, in the vanguard of the shield wall or in the vicinity of the king, highlighting their high-status positions. Finally, the cases of Siward and Byrhtnoth illustrate that real-life elderly warriors even achieved something of a legendary, heroic status after their death.

The question 'Of what use is an old man in battle?', posed by Wyatt, is answered by Old English heroic poetry, which features a two-fold role model for warriors in their later years: the old advisor, encouraging the troops, reminding them of their heroic duties, and the active warrior, who despite a decrease of strength, displays greater courage and leads by example.

Emerson, as mentioned in the introduction to this chapter, considered calling *Maldon*'s Dunnere an 'old warrior' libellous and offensive. This interpretation seems far removed from the sentiments of the Anglo-Saxon authors of heroic poetry, who, on the whole, have been shown in this chapter to value those elderly warriors who remained active. Outside heroic poetry, too, as noted in chapter 4, the phrase "emeritus miles" [veteran warrior] is used as a term of praise by Byrhtferth of Ramsey to describe the vigour of St Ecgwine in his later years.[154] What Anglo-Saxon poets thought disgraceful, then, was not an active old warrior. By contrast, they denounced the grey warrior who failed to maintain an active role on the battlefield, such as Constantine in *The Battle of Brunanburh*, and, to be discussed more fully in the next chapter, Hrothgar in *Beowulf*.

To a modern audience, elderly warriors may seem unlikely heroes. However, if the idea is accepted that heroic reputation can only be won under the least favourable odds, perhaps it is old age, and its physical repercussions, that enables rather than hampers the achievement of heroic status. In Anglo-Saxon England, old people could still be warriors and, indeed, even heroes.

---

[154] Byrthferth, *Vita s. Ecgwini*, ed. and trans. Lapidge, I.6.

Appendix: The "har hilderinc" in The Rewards of Piety

The phrase *hār hilderinc* 'grey-haired warrior' is one of the so-called formulae of Old English poetry, since it occurs in no fewer than four different poems. In *The Battle of Maldon* it is applied to ealdorman Byrhtnoth; in *Beowulf* it refers to both Hrothgar and, later, Beowulf; in *The Battle of Brunanburh* it denotes King Constantine of Scotland. Lastly, the phrase also occurs in a less canonical poem, *The Rewards of Piety*.[1]

In contrast to the other three, *The Rewards of Piety* is not a narrative poem, but a poem of religious instruction, outlining the proper way to live and earn a place in Heaven. One of the poem's striking characteristics is its direct address to the sinner, who is repeatedly referred to with second-person singular pronouns. Near the end of the poem, the poet uses the abbreviation "N" for Latin *nomen* 'name' to indicate that this is the point where the reciter of the poem can speak the name of the person addressed:

and þa unþeawas   ealle forlætan
þe þu on þis life ær   lufedest and feddest;
þænne gemiltsað þe, N,   *mundum qui regit.*[2]

[and abandon all the vices, which you previously practised and loved in this life; then the King of nations will show mercy on you, N.]

According to Graham Caie, the replacement of the sinner's name with the abbreviation N suggests that the poem may have been intended for the use of a priest during confession.[3] In accordance with Caie, Fred Robinson notes that the inclusion of the abbreviation N is a common feature of Anglo-Saxon texts of religious instruction; it suggests that, originally, the poem was once addressed to a particular, named, person and was then adapted to a more general audience.[4]

The person to whom this poem was originally addressed may have

---

[1] This poem was formerly known as two distinct poems – *An Exhortation to Christian Living* and *A Summons to Prayer* – until F. C. Robinson, 'The Rewards of Piety: Two Old English Poems in Their Manuscript Context', in *Hermeneutics and Medieval Culture*, ed. P. J. Gallacher and H. Damico (New York, 1989), 193–200, based on manuscript evidence, suggested that these poems must be two parts of the same poem, which he called *The Rewards of Piety*.
[2] *Rewards of Piety*, ed. and trans. F. C. Robinson, 'The Rewards of Piety: "Two" Old English Poems in Their Manuscript Context', in *The Editing of Old English*, ed. F. C. Robinson (Oxford, 1994), lines 80–2.
[3] G. D. Caie, 'Codicological Clues: Reading Old English Christian Poetry in Its Manuscript Context', in *The Christian Tradition in Anglo-Saxon England*, ed. P. Cavill (Cambridge, 2004), 9.
[4] Robinson, 'Rewards', in *Editing*, 194, n. 82.

been an old warrior. In line 57, the reader or listener is addressed with the term "har hilderinc" [grey-haired warrior]:

> And ondræd þu ðe   dihle wisan,
> nearwe geþancas,   þe on niht becumað,
> synlustas foroft   swiðe fremman
> earfoðlice,   þy þu earhlice scealt
> gyltas þine   swiðe bemurnan,
> *har hilderinc*;   hefie þe ðincaþ
> synna þine.[5]

> [And be fearful of furtive habits, dangerous thoughts that come in the night (and) very often cause desires to sin exceedingly, grievously, for which you must abjectly (and) exceedingly bewail your sins, *grey-haired warrior*, your sins (will?) seem oppressive to you.] (emphasis mine)

Elliott van Kirk Dobbie considered the poet's use of "har hilderinc" a mere "archaising conceit on the part of the poet, rather than [...] as a reference to a specific 'grey-haired warrior' to whom the poem is addressed".[6] In an early article, Robinson likewise argued against interpreting "har hilderinc" as referring to a specific, old man: "I suspect *hār hilderinc* had only the most general meaning such as Modern English 'old man', which in familiar address could be said to a twelve-year-old boy as well as to a mature adult".[7] In the light of the discussion of elderly warriors above, Robinson's argument for the phrase *hār hilderinc* to have been used for young people appears unfounded; the fact that *hār hilderinc* is used specifically for elderly warriors in *The Battle of Maldon*, *Beowulf* and *The Battle of Brunanburh* pleads against the use of the phrase as a familiar address suitable for both twelve-year-old boys and old men. Moreover, Old English *hār*, when applied to humans, is used exclusively for old people, as Biggam has demonstrated.[8] Not quite surprisingly, therefore, Robinson moderated his argument in a later article, noting that the vices described in the poem are, in fact, applicable to an older individual:

> The poet's implied interlocutor is portrayed as one who has accumulated wealth and property throughout his life (ll. 22–4, 34–7, 58–60, 63), as one who has long practiced vices (l. 79), as one who needs to be warned against drunkenness and fornication (ll. 43, 74), and as one for whom death may be imminent (ll. 2–3, 14–15, 19, 60–4, 72–3). All these are consistent with an older man.[9]

---

[5] *Rewards of Piety*, ed. and trans. Robinson, lines 52–8.
[6] *Anglo-Saxon Minor Poems*, ed. Dobbie, lxxii.
[7] Robinson, 'Rewards', in *Hermeneutics*, 199, n. 4.
[8] Biggam, *Grey in Old English*, 219–23.
[9] Robinson, 'Rewards', in *Editing*, 193–4, n. 57.

To Robinson's list may be added the poet's warning against "ungemet wilnung ... slæpes" [unlimited desire of sleep] (line 45), since sleepiness was also regarded as a characteristic of the elderly.[10] Thus, the original addressee certainly may have been an old man.

Whether that old man was also a warrior cannot be established on the basis of the present poem. Nothing in *The Rewards of Piety* seems to pertain specifically to the life of a warrior, although the lines describing how the sinner must protect himself from demons could be said to have military overtones:

> Nu þu ðe beorgan scealt,
> and wið feonda gehwæne　fæste healdan
> sauwle þine;　a hi winnað embe þæt
> dæges and nihtes　ongean drihtnes lif.
> þu miht hy gefleman,　gif þu filian wilt
> larum minum.[11]

[Now you must protect yourself and guard your soul firmly against every demon; they will always strive around that (soul) day and night, contrary to the lord's leave. You can put them (the demons) to flight if you will obey my teachings.]

In its initial form, then, *The Rewards of Piety* was probably written for an older man, whose warrior status is uncertain, but, in light of the above, definitely not implausible.

In any case, the poem is a reminder of the fact that the audience of a didactic poem may well have consisted of elderly people; even in early medieval England, one was never too old to learn or change one's ways. This line of thought is taken up in the next chapter, which considers *Beowulf* as a didactic text for elderly kings.

---

[10] E.g., Bede, *De temporum ratione*, ed. Jones, trans. Wallis, ch. 35.
[11] *Rewards of Piety*, ed. and trans. Robinson, lines 64–9.

6

ealde eðelweardas: *Beowulf* as a Mirror of Elderly Kings

'Remember too that it is no crime to undermine senility, which sags and tumbles to ruin under its own weight. Your father-in-law should be content to have borne office as long as he has. Only a dotard's power would come your way, and, if you missed it, would fall to someone else. Every attribute of the elderly is next door to decay.'[1]

With these words, Princess Ulvild tried to convince her husband Guthorm to rebel against her father, King Hadding. This legendary king of Denmark had grown old and his power had already started to crumble – overthrowing this aged ruler was justifiable, Ulvild held, on account of his years alone. This anecdote, recorded in Saxo Grammaticus' twelfth-century *Gesta Danorum*, is illustrative of the problems that faced early medieval kings once they had reached old age – problems that the poet of *Beowulf*, as will be shown in this chapter, was well aware of.

Mentioning no fewer than twenty-three different kings, the poet of *Beowulf* certainly shows a keen interest in kingship.[2] While some of these rulers appear only as part of a royal genealogy, others, such as Scyld Scefing, Heremod and Hygelac, are further developed and function as *exempla* of good or bad rulership. It is unsurprising, therefore, that Levin Schücking's suggestion that *Beowulf* must be read as a *Fürstenspiegel*, 'a mirror of princes', has met with widespread agreement.[3] George Garmonsway, for example, concluded:

> Taken as a whole, the story with its episodes and digressions does form a kind of eighth-century *Mirror for Magistrates* or *Book named the Governor*, wherein those in authority might have seen pictured their obligations and responsibilities, and from which they could have gleaned political wisdom had they so desired, and learned some useful lessons about

---

[1] Saxo, *History of the Danes*, ed. Ellis Davidson, trans. Fisher, 34–5.
[2] Carruthers, 'Kingship and Heroism', 20.
[3] L. L. Schücking, 'Das Königsideal im *Beowulf*', *MHRA Bulletin* 3 (1929), 143–54, translated as 'The Ideal of Kingship in *Beowulf*', in *An Anthology of* Beowulf *Criticism*, ed. L. E. Nicholson (Notre Dame, IN, 1963), 35–50. On the reception of Schücking in *Beowulf* scholarship, see E. G. Stanley, *In the Foreground:* Beowulf (Cambridge, 1994), 32–7.

current moral sanctions governing behavior in general, and heroic conduct in particular.[4]

In other words, the intended audience for *Beowulf* may have been a king or a prince who could draw inspiration from the poem.

Schücking further hypothesised that *Beowulf* was composed for the young son of a ruler, possibly the son of a Danelaw king, for whom the poem was intended as a means to learn the Anglo-Saxon language.[5] Whereas Schücking's suggestion of *Beowulf* as a Danelaw language acquisition project has mostly been rejected,[6] his suggestion that the poem's lessons were mainly intended for a young audience has gained wide acceptance.[7] Marjorie Daunt, for instance, identified the intended audience as "all the *geogoþ* ['youth'], from a well-educated young prince down to a simple retainer".[8] Similarly, Alexander Bruce argued that the lessons of *Beowulf* were intended for young, fledgling warriors, for whom the young heroes Beowulf and Wiglaf were role models.[9] Indeed, at certain points in the poem, the narrative voice explicitly provides advice for a young person:

> Swa sceal geong   guma gode gewyrcean,
> fromum feohgiftum   on fæder bearme,
> þæt hine on ylde   eft gewunigen
> wilgesiþas,   þonne wig cume,
> leode gelæsten;   lofdædum sceal
> in mægþa gehwære   man geþeon. (lines 20–5)

[In such a way must a young man with liberality bring about, with splendid costly gifts in his father's lap (during his youth), so that when he comes of age close companions will stand by him, when war comes, people will serve him; in each nation a man must prosper with praiseworthy deeds.]

---

[4] G. N. Garmonsway, 'Anglo-Saxon Heroic Attitudes', in *Franciplegius: Medieval and Linguistic Studies in Honor of Francis Peabody Magoun, Jr*, ed. J. B. Bessinger Jr and R. P. Creed (New York, 1965), 139.

[5] L. L. Schücking, 'Wann entstand der Beowulf? Glossen, Zweifel und Fragen', *BGdSL* 42 (1917), 406–8.

[6] D. Whitelock, *The Audience of* Beowulf (Oxford, 1951), 25–6, argued strongly against this idea: "I should be sorry to believe that the poem was from the beginning what it has since too often become, a work studied by young people to whom the language is unfamiliar."

[7] M. Swanton, *Crisis and Development in Germanic Society 700–800:* Beowulf *and the Burden of Kingship* (Göppingen, 1982), 11, for example, similarly envisions a "young prince" who might "learn the attitudes appropriate to his place in heroic society".

[8] M. Daunt, 'Minor Realism and Contrast in *Beowulf*', in *Mélanges de linguistique et de philologie. Fernand Mossé in memoriam* (Paris, 1959), 87.

[9] A. M. Bruce, 'An Education in the Mead-Hall', *HA* 5 (2001).

On occasion, then, the poem does cater for an unexperienced prince, but not all the poem's lessons and role models are appropriate to the tastes of a young person.

In fact, such is the role of elderly kings in the poem that it is more probable that the poet also wanted to accommodate a more mature audience. For instance, the two main royal protagonists, Hrothgar and Beowulf, are both very old men and could hardly have figured as role models for a young king-to-be. Rather, they, as well as other elderly kings in *Beowulf*, such as Hrethel and Ongentheow, demonstrate how a king could act in his old age. If the poem is a mirror for princes, most of the examples it provides relate to kings who, like Beowulf and Hrothgar, had been on the throne for a long time and, in their old age, were faced by threats to their authority.

In this chapter, I propose that *Beowulf* should be read within the historical context of the political problems that faced elderly kings in the early Middle Ages.[10] Within this context, a close reading of the depiction of elderly kingship in *Beowulf* will show that the poem, by juxtaposing the passive Hrothgar and the active Beowulf, offers two models of conduct for aged kings. As such, the poem comments on a contemporary political issue: the problematic position of kings grown old.[11]

Historical context: Elderly rulers in the early Middle Ages

In the early Middle Ages, elderly rulers faced serious political problems.[12] Paul Dutton has convincingly shown that the central power of the Carolingians started to crumble in the ninth century, during the later years of the reigns of Charlemagne (c.743–814), Louis the Pious (778–840) and Louis the German (806–876), all of whom lived relatively long lives (they died at the ages of 71, 62 and 70, respectively). Dutton

---

[10] Swanton, *Crisis and Development*, 28–9, has questioned the applicability of the poem's heroic attitude to the historical practicalities of early medieval kingship. However, P. Clemoes, *Interactions of Thought and Language in Old English Poetry* (Cambridge, 1995), 3–67, has shown that there are clear correlations between the actual practice of early Anglo-Saxon kingship and what is presented in the poem.

[11] For a similar approach of linking the poem to contemporary political issues (succession and lordlessness, respectively), see F. M. Biggs, 'The Politics of Succession in *Beowulf* and Anglo-Saxon England', *Speculum* 80 (2005), 709–41; E. G. Stanley, '*Beowulf*: Lordlessness in Ancient Times is the Theme, as Much as the Glory of Kings, if not More', *NQ* ns 52 (2005), 267–81.

[12] P. E. Dutton, *Charlemagne's Mustache and Other Cultural Clusters of a Dark Age* (New York, 2004), 151–68; P. E. Dutton, 'Beyond the Topos of Senescence: the Political Problems of Aged Carolingian Rulers', in *Aging and the Aged*, ed. Sheehan, 75–94.

argues that the old age of these Carolingian rulers lay at the heart of the problems at the end of their reigns:

> If they lived long lives, Carolingian rulers faced particular problems that arose from the very joining of agedness and title, which they could not have easily anticipated when younger. Since Carolingian kingship was largely personal, anything that affected a ruler personally affected his governance of the kingdom, and age and health were chief among these things. Efficient government depended more on the king's willingness, energy, and ability to respond to outbreaks of trouble than it did on any administrative agencies within the kingdom.[13]

In a time when kingship depended more on personal, martial prowess than on administrative structures,[14] an old ruler's dwindling health formed a serious obstacle.

Dutton has identified three main political problems of elderly rulers. First of all, a ruler's old age impaired his 'peripatetic function': elderly rulers typically stopped travelling around their kingdoms. Given that touring the realm was a means to establish and maintain authority, the influence of an old, sedentary king often lessened in outlying areas.[15] Charlemagne, for example, remained in Aachen for most of the last twenty years of his reign and, as a result, local abuses of justice went unchecked.[16] A somewhat gruesome anecdote concerning Frodo III of Denmark in Saxo's *Gesta Danorum* demonstrates the importance for kings to travel around their realm, even in old age. After Frodo III had been killed, his retainers tried to keep the king's death a secret by carrying the embalmed body of the king around in a royal carriage for three years:

> After drawing out his entrails, the nobles kept him embalmed for three years, since they feared the provinces would revolt if their sovereign's end became known. ... For this reason they would carry his lifeless body about, not, so it seemed, in a hearse, but a royal carriage, pretending that this was a service due from his soldiers to a feeble old monarch not in full possession of his strength.[17]

---

[13] Dutton, *Charlemagne's Mustache*, 161.
[14] For the martial nature of medieval kingship, see, e.g., Carruthers, 'Kingship and Heroism', 25–6; I. P. Stephenson, *The Late Anglo-Saxon Army* (Stroud, 2007), 21.
[15] Dutton, 'Beyond the Topos', 86.
[16] Dutton, *Charlemagne's Mustache*, 162. Another telling illustration of the dwindling might of a sedentary old king is found in the thirteenth-century *Egils saga*, which reports that when King Harald Fairhair (c.850–c.932) had grown old, tribute proved more difficult to collect than when he was younger. *Egil's Saga*, ed. S. Óskarsdóttir, trans. B. Scudder (London, 2004), ch. 71.
[17] Saxo, *History of the Danes*, ed. Ellis Davidson, trans. Fisher, 157–8. Another story by Saxo shows that a carriage was considered a suitable means of transportation for an old man: a peasant named Hather mockingly tells the elderly

Elderly Kings

The anecdote illustrates that kings, even if they had grown feeble, were nevertheless expected to visit outlying provinces to prevent outright rebellion. In other words, kings who were unable or unwilling to go to the corners of their dominion ran the risk of losing their position of power.

A second problem ascribed to elderly rulers by Dutton is their reluctance or inability to anticipate and respond actively to foreign invasions or internal revolts. Old rulers grew passive and rarely initiated military action. They only responded to incursions, rather than anticipating them; as such, "they played a dangerous game of catch-up they could never quite win".[18] Their hesitancy to go into battle may, in part, have been caused by their apprehension about personally leading their armies. "Ðonne se heretoga wacað, þonne bið eall se here swiðe gehindred" [when the army leader grows weak, the whole army is greatly hindered], an Old English proverb holds, suggesting that, in general, the physical repercussions of old age made an elderly king a liability on the battlefield.[19]

Thirdly, elderly kings often found it difficult to secure the succession of their sons, while, at the same time, keeping those same sons in check. Dutton notes that the sons of aged Carolingian rulers often rebelled against their fathers:

> Charlemagne was fifty when his son Pepin the Hunchback led a revolt against him in 792, Louis the Pious was fifty-two when his elder sons first rebelled in 830, Louis the German suffered the first of a series of rebellious machinations by his sons in 860 when he was fifty-four, and Charles the Bald's son Carloman revolted in 871 when his father was forty-eight.[20]

It is not hard to imagine that ambitious sons, who were often given some measure of control over specific regions of a kingdom, grew impatient and wanted to overthrow their fathers. Whereas having potentially rebellious sons thus was a problem for an old king, Dutton notes that the converse situation was equally undesirable; an aged king without offspring was subjected to the ambitions of suitors of another sort.[21]

---

warrior Starkad to sell his sword for a carriage, suggesting that infirm elders had better "be drawn by mules; turning wheels are more use to those who stagger on hopeless feet" (247–9).

[18] Dutton, *Charlemagne's Mustache*, 162.

[19] This proverb is found in annal 1003 in MS E of *The Anglo-Saxon Chronicle*. For this proverb and its Anglo-Saxon analogues, see T. D. Hill, '"When the Leader Is Brave...": An Old English Proverb and Its Vernacular Context', *Anglia* 119 (2001), 232–6.

[20] Dutton, 'Beyond the Topos', 87–8.

[21] Dutton, *Charlemagne's Mustache*, 90.

The political problems identified for elderly Carolingian rulers would have equally applied to elderly Anglo-Saxon kings. Establishing whether an Anglo-Saxon king reached old age, however, is difficult, since their dates of birth were often not recorded. Nevertheless, judging by the length of some of their reigns, a good number of Anglo-Saxon kings are likely to have lived long lives. Table 4 lists those Anglo-Saxon kings who remained in office for at least twenty-five years or of whom it can be established that they were aged over fifty upon their death.[22]

Of course, a long time on the throne does not necessarily imply that a king reached old age: Æthelred the Unready (966/968–1016), for instance, was consecrated at a very early age; despite a thirty-seven-year reign, he did not live beyond the age of fifty. Conversely, a king could be consecrated at a later age and, hence, may have been old despite a relatively shorter reign, as may be the case for Æthelwulf of Wessex (d. 858). Æthelwulf became king of the West Saxons after his father Ecgberht (d. 839) had been on the throne for thirty-seven years; he was reportedly past the age of fifty when he married the Frankish teenage princess Judith in 856, two years before his death.[23] Nevertheless, Æthelwulf's reign lasted only nineteen years. Table 4, therefore, may not be an exhaustive list of elderly rulers in Anglo-Saxon England.

Like their Carolingian counterparts, Anglo-Saxon rulers often found kingship difficult to combine with their old age. Some decided to retire, such as Æthelred of Mercia (d. ?716), who abdicated after thirty years on the throne and became abbot of Bardney,[24] and Ine of Wessex (d. ?726), who "left his kingdom to younger men" after a reign of thirty-seven years and went on a pilgrimage to Rome.[25] Others remained in office until their death, but had to deal with rebellious sons. Æthelwulf of Wessex, to give a striking example, was confronted by a plot of one of his sons to eject him from office. When the old king had gone to Rome in 855 and wanted to return to England with his new bride Judith the following year, his son Æthelbald (d. 860) had made plans to overthrow his father's regime. Bishop Asser, the biographer of Æthelwulf's youngest son Alfred, described the event as follows:

> When King Æthelwulf was returning from Rome, his son Æthelbald, with all his councillors – or rather co-conspirators – attempted to

---

[22] Overview based on *ODNB* and S. Keynes, 'Rulers of the English, c. 450–1066', in *Blackwell Encyclopaedia*, ed. Lapidge *et al.*, 500–20.

[23] For this marriage, see M. J. Enright, 'Charles the Bald and Æthelwulf of Wessex: The Alliance of 856 and Strategies of Royal Succession', *Journal of Medieval History* 5 (1979), 291–302.

[24] A. Williams, 'Æthelred (d. after 704)', *ODNB*.

[25] Bede, *HE*, V.7.

Table 4. Overview of long-reigning Anglo-Saxon kings, c.650–1066

	Year of birth	Start of reign	End of reign	Year of death	Age at death	Length of reign
Oswiu of Northumbria	611/612	642	670	670	58/59	28
Aldwulf of East Anglia	–	663/664	713	713	–	49/50
Æthelred of Mercia	–	674/675	704	?716	–	29/30
Ine of Wessex	–	688	726	??726	–	38
Wihtred of Kent	–	690	725	725	–	35
Ælfwald of East Anglia	–	713	749	749	–	36
Æthelbald of Mercia	–	716	757	757	–	41
Offa of Mercia	–	757	796	796	–	39
Cynewulf of Wessex	–	757	786	786	–	29
Coenwulf of Mercia	–	796	821	821	–	25
Ecgberht of Wessex	–	802	839	839	–	37
Alfred the Great	848/849	871	899	899	50/51	28
Edward the Elder	870s?	899	924	924	?50	25
Æthelred the Unready	966/968	978+1014	1013+1016	1016	48/50	35+2
Edward the Confessor	c.1004	1042	1066	1066	c.62	24

perpetrate a terrible crime: expelling the king from his own kingdom; but God did not allow it to happen, nor would the nobles of the whole of the Saxon land have any part in it.²⁶

Æthelbald's attempt proved unsuccessful and Æthelwulf appears to have forgiven his son, who became king after his father two years later. Oswiu of Northumbria (611/612–670), similarly, was dragged into a power struggle by his son Alchfrith (d. 664).²⁷ Conversely, Edward the Confessor (c.1004–1066) did not have any sons to succeed him; as a result, Edward spent the last years of his reign searching for a suitable heir and suffered the unwanted attention of several suitors, including Harold and Tostig Godwinson, as well as William of Normandy.²⁸ In many ways, then, the aged Anglo-Saxon rulers suffered from the same problems as their aged Carolingian counterparts.²⁹

Whereas most of the long-reigning Anglo-Saxon kings abdicated or died relatively peacefully while in office, at least one Anglo-Saxon king appears to have become the victim of an entourage dissatisfied with its aged ruler. According to Nicholas Brooks, Æthelbald of Mercia (d. 757) was killed by his own bodyguard because he, like the Carolingian rulers described by Dutton, had grown reluctant to initiate military action: "Indeed the insecurity generated within an overlord's retinue, as age made him less willing to lead profitable military expeditions, may help to explain Æthelbald's murder by his own retainers at Seckington (Warwickshire) in 757."³⁰ Arguably, the contemporary evidence for Æthelbald's murder is limited and it is possible that another conflict may have motivated the king's bodyguard.³¹ Nevertheless, the event does suggest that, after forty-two years, Æthelbald's retinue thought it was time for a change: the old king needed to be replaced.

In short, old age was a genuine threat to the authority of an early medieval king, on the European continent as well as in Anglo-Saxon England. Ideally, an aged ruler would remain as active as ever; in

---

²⁶ Asser, *Vita Ælfredi*, trans. S. Keynes and M. Lapidge, *Alfred the Great: Asser's Life of King Alfred and Other Contemporary Sources* (Harmondsworth, 1983), ch. 12.
²⁷ Alchfrith backed the Roman Christianity of Bishop Wilfrid rather than following his father's example in supporting the Irish Church, a conflict which was ultimately resolved at the Synod of Whitby in 664. D. J. Craig, 'Oswiu (611/12–670)', *ODNB*.
²⁸ F. Barlow, *Edward the Confessor* (London, 1970), 214–39.
²⁹ Of course, there were also exceptions. A case in point is Offa of Mercia (d. 796), who had his son Ecgfrith (d. 796) consecrated as a king in 787 and thus paved the way for a smooth transition of royal power after his death. For a discussion of Offa's reign, see the Appendix at the end of this chapter.
³⁰ N. Brooks, 'The Social and Political Background', in *Cambridge Companion*, ed. Godden and Lapidge, 8.
³¹ G. Williams, 'Military Obligations and Mercian Supremacy in the Eighth Century', in *Æthelbald and Offa: Two Eighth-Century Kings of Mercia*, ed. D. Hill and M. Worthington (Oxford, 2005), 107–8.

practice, however, a king's old age could impact negatively on his willingness and ability to live up to all of his royal responsibilities. As a consequence, an old king ran the risk of becoming a *rex inutilis*, 'a useless king'.[32]

The problems of aged kings also inspired Anglo-Saxon poets. *The Riming Poem*, for instance, is an Old English elegiac monologue of an old ruler who looks back at the successes of his youth and contrasts these to his state of misery in old age.[33] The first part of the poem describes how the narrator used to be a prosperous ruler, sharing treasures with his followers:

> Þegnum geþwære   þeoden wæs ic mære;
> horsce mec heredon,   hilde generedon,
> fægre feredon,   feondon biweredon.
> Swa mec hyhtgiefu heold,   hygedrygt befeold,
> staþolæhtum steald,   stepegongum weold,
> Swylce eorþe ol   ahte ic – ealdorstol,
> galdorwordum gol,   gomelsibbe ne ofeoll.[34]

[Mild to thanes, I was a famous ruler; the bold ones praised me, they defended me in battle, they acted fairly, protected me against enemies. Thus the joyful gift held me, the band of household retainers surrounded me, I possessed landed estates, I had control over journeys, whatever the earth brought forth I owned – the ancestral seat, I sang charms, I did not neglect the ancient peace.]

The mood of the poem changes suddenly after line 43 when the narrator reflects on his old age. As an old man, he suffers from enmity, sorrow and the loss of friends, like so many other elderly narrators in Old English wisdom poetry.[35] He further laments his fleeting courage, which he directly relates to old age: "bald ald þwiteð" [old age cuts off boldness] (line 63b).[36] In other words, while the ruler was able to control his realm in his youth, he is no longer able to exert his power now he has grown old: "dreamas swa her gedreosað, dryhtscype

---

[32] For this term and its application in the Middle Ages, see E. Peters, *The Shadow King: Rex Inutilis in Medieval Law and Literature, 751–1327* (New Haven, 1970).
[33] K. P. Wentersdorf, 'The Old English *Rhyming Poem*: A Ruler's Lament', *SiP* 82 (1985), 265–94.
[34] *The Riming Poem*, ed. Klinck, *OEE*, lines 18–24.
[35] See chapter 3 above.
[36] The two adjectives "bald" and "ald" function as abstract nouns and, despite the lack of an accusative marker on either of the two, it makes more sense to assume that the second element is the subject, given that this is also the case in the preceding lines 62b–63a: "flan man hwiteð / burg sorg biteð [a man fletches the arrow / sorrow frets the city]. *Riming Poem*, ed. Klinck, *OEE*, 155, n. 63.

gehreosað" [In this way joys decline here, lordly power falls].[37] Thus, the author of the *Riming Poem* was well aware of the political problems of elderly kings – in this respect, he was no different from the poet responsible for *Beowulf*.[38]

Old age in Beowulf

The theme of old age is central to *Beowulf*, at least in view of the high number of elderly characters in the poem, the implied senectitude of its monsters and the way the poem invites a comparison between its two aged protagonists, Hrothgar and Beowulf.

Aside from the two old kings at the centre of the poem, another eight characters are explicitly described as 'old'. Some of these elderly characters appear as family members or companions of other characters: Hrothgar's father Healfdene, "gamol ond guðreouw" [old and fierce in battle] (line 58a); Beowulf's father Ecgtheow, "gamol of geardum" [old among settlements] (line 265a); Hrothgar's "frodan fyrnwitan" [old and wise councillor] (line 2123a) Æschere; and Wiglaf's father Weohstan, who "of ealdre gewat" [died of old age] (line 2624b). Others are first brought to the fore in various speeches given by Beowulf: the "eald æscwiga" [old spear-warrior] (line 2042a) in Beowulf's report to Hygelac; the "gomelum ceorle" [old man] (line 2444b) who had lost his son, in Beowulf's speech before the fight with the dragon; and, in the same speech, the Swedish king Ongentheow, the "gomela Scylfing" [old Scylfing] (line 2487b), whose exploits against the Geats are also described elsewhere in the poem. This Ongentheow, "eald and egesfull" [old and terrible] (line 2929a), is said to have saved his wife, who, like him, was also old: "gomela(n) iomeowlan" [the old woman of a former day] (line 2931a). To this tally might be added two further characters who are old by implication: Scyld Scefing ruled for a long time (line 31) and King Hrethel of the Danes is compared to the

---

[37] *Riming Poem*, ed. Klinck, OEE, line 55.
[38] Another Old English text that touches upon the problem of elderly kings is found in the *Beowulf* manuscript. In the *Letter of Alexander to Aristotle*, ed. and trans. A. Orchard, *Pride and Prodigies: Studies in the Monsters of the* Beowulf-*Manuscript* (Cambridge, 1995), par. 24, King Porus expresses his joy upon hearing that Alexander the Great is an old man by exclaiming: "'Hu mæg he la ænige gewinne wið me spowan swa forealdod mon, for þon ic eom me self geong 7 hwæt?'" ['How can he have any success in battle against me, when he is such an extremely old man and I myself am young and fit?']. Porus' rhetorical question as to whether an old man can have success in battle is one of the many thematic parallels between the Old English *Letter* and *Beowulf*, though previously unnoted. Cf. A. Orchard, *A Critical Companion to* Beowulf (Cambridge, 2003), 25–39; K. Powell, 'Meditating on Men and Monsters: A Reconsideration of the Thematic Unity of the Beowulf Manuscript', *RES* ns 57 (2006), 1–15.

"gomelum ceorle" of line 2444b, as both had suffered a similar loss (lines 2438–44).[39]

Not only does the human society in *Beowulf* suffer from societal aging, the same can be said for the monsters in the poem. Grendel's mother is certainly old: she had roamed the monster mere for fifty years, "hund missera" [a hundred half-years] (line 1498b), when Beowulf came to kill her. The poet used the same period of fifty years on two other occasions: Hrothgar had similarly ruled the Danes for "hund missera" (line 1769b) when Grendel's attacks began, and Beowulf had held the throne of the Geats for the same number of years when the dragon started to stir.[40] Rather than an accurate, specific description of the time Grendel's mother, Hrothgar and Beowulf ruled their respective kingdoms, 'fifty years' appears to be a symbolic marker of a long time and, by extension, old age.[41] Like Grendel's mother, the dragon that attacks Beowulf's people must also have reached an old age: it is called "frod" [old and wise] (line 2277a) and "eald" [old] (lines 2271a, 2415a, 2760a) throughout the poem; its senectitude is also implied by the number of years it has held its barrow: "se ðeodsceaða þreohund wintra / heold on hrusan hordærna sum" [the people's enemy held a certain treasure-house in the earth for three hundred years] (lines 2278–9).[42] The old age of both Grendel's mother and the dragon make them suitable opponents for the equally aged kings Hrothgar and Beowulf. They may even be regarded as mirror images of the old kings themselves or as symbolic representations of the senescence that threatened both rulers.[43]

In *Beowulf* scholarship, Hrothgar and Beowulf as old men have mostly been studied as part of the contrast between 'youth and old age';[44]

---

[39] Hrethel and the old father may be one and the same person, see J. Thormann, 'Enjoyment of Violence and Desire for History in *Beowulf*', in *The Postmodern Beowulf: A Critical Casebook*, ed. E. A. Joy and M. K. Ramsey (Morgantown, 2006), 288–91.

[40] *Beowulf*, lines 2208–2210, 2732b–2733a; see also Orchard, *Critical Companion*, 64.

[41] Notably, fifty years of time was also a marker of old age used in Gregory's *Dialogi*, Bald's *Leechbook* and *Solomon and Saturn II*. These references are discussed in chapter 1 above. Cf. R. M. Liuzza, 'The Sense of Time in Anglo-Saxon England', *Bulletin of the John Rylands Library* 89:2 (2013), 132.

[42] Even without these explicit references to the dragon's senectitude, an Anglo-Saxon audience would associate the dragon with old age, as is suggested by the poem *Maxims II*, ed. and trans. Shippey, *PoW*, lines 26b–27a: "Draca sceal on hlæwe, / frod, frætwum wlanc" [A dragon must live in a barrow, old and proud of his treasures].

[43] Georgianna, 'King Hrethel's Sorrow', 848, n. 61, has called attention to the fact that Beowulf and the dragon are described in similar terms and resemble each other in being old, wise, guardians of a hoard and, at specific points in the narrative, swollen with rage.

[44] J. R. R. Tolkien, '*Beowulf*: The Monsters and the Critics', in *Interpretations of Beowulf: A Critical Anthology*, ed. R. D. Fulk (Bloomington and Indianapolis,

as the opposites of young Beowulf and young Wiglaf, respectively.[45] While this approach clearly demonstrates how the wisdom of the old men serves to inspire the young warriors, it has also led to a neglect of another contrast that looms large over the entire poem: the contrast between the passive old king Hrothgar and the active old king Beowulf. The importance of this second contrast was hesitantly suggested by Adrien Bonjour:

> Indeed, I am not sure whether we should not perhaps add to the significant contrast pointed out by critics in reference to the Danish part, between Hrothgar the hoary king, and young Beowulf, a contrast between Hrothgar, an embodiment and picture of a king, and Beowulf's own figure as a ruler in the Dragon part.[46]

To my knowledge, a full-fledged comparison between Hrothgar and Beowulf as elderly kings is still lacking in *Beowulf* scholarship.[47]

Nevertheless, it is hard to ignore how the poet sets up a comparison between the two aged rulers. For one, their situations show clear parallels: both have been on the throne for fifty years and both are faced by a monstrous threat. In addition, the poet uses twenty-one terms to describe old King Beowulf that he had previously reserved for Hrothgar. These terms range from the simple "se goda" [the good one], "se gomela" [the old one] and "se wisa" [the wise one] to more specific terms, such as "eald eðelweard" [old guardian of the country], "ætheling ærgod" [nobleman, old and hitherto excellent] and "har hilderinc" [grey-haired warrior] (see the list below). This similitude invites a comparison between the two people to whom these terms are applied.

Table 5. Epithets shared between Beowulf and Hrothgar[48]

King Beowulf	King Hrothgar
frod cyning (l. 2209)	frod cyning (l. 1306)
eald eðelweard (l. 2210)	eald eðelweard (l. 1702)

1991), 33, 35; E. B. Irving Jr, 'The Text of Fate', in *Interpretations of* Beowulf, ed. Fulk, 172.

[45] Cf. K. Sisam, *The Structure of* Beowulf (Oxford, 1965), 22–4, who argued that the contrast between youth and age, especially in the second part of the poem, lacks elaboration.

[46] A. Bonjour, *The Digressions in* Beowulf (Oxford, 1950), 52.

[47] E. B. Irving Jr, 'What To Do with Old Kings', in *Comparative Research on Oral Traditions: A Memorial for Milman Parry*, ed. J. M. Foley (Columbus, 1987), 259–68, and Rothauser, 'Winter in Heorot', 103–20, focus solely on Hrothgar as an old king, while J. C. Pope, 'Beowulf's Old Age', in *Philological Essays: Studies in Old and Middle English Language and Literature in Honour of Herbert Dean Meritt*, ed. J. L. Rosier (The Hague, 1970), 55–64, centres only on Beowulf as an old king.

[48] In each case, the form given in the list is the form of the first occurrence in the poem (l./ll. = line/s).

ðam godan (l. 2327)	se goda (l. 355)
se wisa (l. 2329)	þone wisan (l. 1318)
guðkyning (ll. 2335, 2563, 2677, 3036)	guðcyning (l. 199)
Wedera þioden (ll. 2336, 2656, 2786, 3037)	þeoden Scyldinga (ll. 1675, 1871)
æþeling ærgod (l. 2342)	æþeling ærgod (l. 130)
þæt wæs god cyning (l. 2390)	þæt wæs god cyning (l. 863)
goldwine Geata (ll. 2419, 2584)	goldwine gumena (ll. 1171, 1476, 1602)
ðone gomelan (ll. 2421, 2851)	se gomela (l. 1397)
Weder-Geata leod (l. 2551)	leod Scyldinga (l. 1653)
mærum þeodne (ll. 2572, 2721, 2788, 3141)	mære þeoden (ll. 129, 201, 345, 353, 1046, 1598, 1992)
ðiodcyning (ll. 2579, 2694, 3008)	ðeodkyning (l. 2144)
mæra maga Ecgðeowes (l. 2587)	mæra mago Healfdenes (ll. 1474, 2011)
freodryhtne (l. 2627)	freodrihten (l. 1169)
folces hyrde (l. 2644)	folces hyrde (l. 610)
hildfruman (ll. 2649, 2835)	harum hildfruman (l. 1678)
Wedra helm (l. 2705)	helm Scyldinga (ll. 371, 456, 1321)
winedryhten (l. 2722)	winedrihtne (l. 360)
rices hyrde (l. 3080)	rices hyrde (l. 2027)
har hilderinc (l. 3136)	har hilderinc (l. 1307)

Yet another method used by the poet to prompt his audience to connect old Beowulf to Hrothgar is the sudden 'flash forward' in lines 2207–11:

> syððan Beowulfe   br(a)de rice
> on hand gehwearf;   he geheold tela
> fiftig wintr(a)   – wæs ða frod cyning,
> eald eþel(w)eard –   oð ðæt (a)n ongan
> deorcum nihtum   draca rics[i]an. (lines 2207–11)

[Afterwards the broad kingdom passed into the hand of Beowulf; he held it well for fifty winters – he was then an old and wise king, old guardian of the country – until one, a dragon, began to hold sway in dark nights.]

This sudden transition to the time when Beowulf is an old king has not been satisfactorily explained.[49] The poet's choice initially to ignore

---

[49] It has been argued that this flash forward is an indication that the second part of the poem, the fight against the dragon, was an independent composition, added on to the story of Beowulf's exploits in Denmark as a sequel. However, there are few who still doubt that the poem as a whole has a unity and was composed by one and the same poet. Cf. W. P. Ker, *Epic and Romance: Essays on Medieval Literature*, 2nd rev. ed. (New York, 1957), 161–3; A. G. Brodeur, 'The Structure and the Unity of *Beowulf*', PMLA 68 (1953), 1183–95; *Beowulf*, lxxxviii–xci.

the first fifty years of Beowulf's reign may be attributed to his desire to set up a comparison between two elderly kings. The sudden transition immediately shifts the focus from the matter of the old king Hrothgar to how Beowulf acted as an old king; this effect would be lost if the poet had narrated the first fifty years of Beowulf's reign in a chronological fashion.

By juxtaposing Hrothgar and Beowulf, the poem presents its audience with two models of conduct for aged kings. The first represents a 'passive, diplomatic model', while the latter represents an 'active, heroic model'. After discussing Hrothgar and Beowulf in turn below, I argue that this mirror of elderly kings shows a preference for the latter of the two models.

Passive and peaceable: Old king Hrothgar

Hrothgar is introduced as a successful king who has earned glory in battle at the outset of his reign. After fifty years on the throne and having amassed a great following, Hrothgar decides to build a hall called Heorot, "medoærn micel ... / þon[n]e yldo bearn æfre gefrunon" [a bigger mead-hall than the children of men had ever heard of] (lines 69–70). The celebrations following the completion of Heorot anger the monster Grendel, who slaughters thirty of Hrothgar's men during the night. Hrothgar, faced by a conflict "to strang, / laþ and longsum" [too strong, hateful and long-lasting] (lines 133b–134a), proves helpless against Grendel and has to give up control of his hall to the monster after sundown. It is only twelve years later that the terror of Grendel and the subsequent revenge by Grendel's mother is laid low by the young Geat, Beowulf, who comes to the old king's aid.

As a king, Hrothgar unquestionably fulfils one of the main requirements of his position – the generous bestowal of treasure upon his followers. After Heorot has been finished, Hrothgar "beot ne aleh: beagas dælde, / sinc æt symle" [did not leave his promise unfulfilled: he distributed rings, treasure at the feast] (lines 80–81a). Hrothgar's generosity is also foregrounded after Beowulf has defeated Grendel and his mother; the old king rewards the young Geat with various treasures, including horses and weapons, and his own saddle.[50] Hrothgar's generosity is further underlined by the poet's frequent references to the Danish king as the "beaga brytta" [distributor of rings] (lines 352a, 1487a), "sinces brytta" [dispenser of treasure] (lines 607b, 1170a) and "goldwine gumena" [gold-friend of warriors] (lines 1171a, 1476a, 1602a).

---

[50] *Beowulf*, lines 1020–49, 1866–9.

Elderly Kings

The king as a provider of treasures is an essential element of the ideals of the Germanic *comitatus*, as described by the Roman historian Tacitus (c. AD 56–after 117). In his *Germania*, Tacitus noted how a Germanic leader had to provide for his retainers with feasting, rings and armour in return for future service.[51] These Germanic ideals also underlie much of Old English heroic literature.[52] In *Beowulf*, the importance of royal generosity is illustrated by the negative example of King Heremod,[53] who is presented as a bad leader due to his greed and refusal to share his riches:

> Ðeah þe hine mihtig God   mægenes wynnum,
> eafeþum stepte   ofer ealle men,
> forð gefremede,   hwæþere him on ferhþe greow
> breosthord blodreow,   nallas beagas geaf
> Denum æfter dome;   dreamleas gebad
> þæt he þæs gewinnes   weorc þrowade,
> leodbealo longsum. (lines 1716–1722a)

> [Although the mighty God raised him over all men with the joys of strength and powers, he would advance further, but in his mind grew a blood-thirsty spirit, he did not at all give rings to the Danes in pursuit of glory; joyless he lived to see that he suffered distress of the struggle, long-lasting harm to a people.]

Another instance in *Beowulf* of the importance of gift-giving for kings is cited above, at the beginning of this chapter: the advice to a young prince to distribute gifts in return for future assistance. Through his generous bestowal of treasures, then, Hrothgar upholds this ideal of kingship.

A second royal ideal that the *Beowulf* poet appeals to in his characterisation of Hrothgar is that of the wise king. This model, based on the Old Testament King Solomon and the writings of St Augustine of Hippo, among others, was used by several medieval commentators, including Bede.[54] The latter included in his *Historia ecclesiastica* a letter by Abbot Ceolfrith, which reads:

---

[51] Tacitus, *Germania*, ed. and trans. H. W. Benario (Warminster, 1999), ch. 13.
[52] Bazelmans, *By Weapons Made Worthy*, 149–88; K. O'Brien O'Keeffe, 'Values and Ethics', 101–2. The ideal of a generous king is, however, by no means solely Germanic: the ninth-century author Sedulius Scottus offered his audience of *De rectoribus christianis* [On Christian rulers], written for Lotharingian king Lothar II (d. 869), a similar model: "a peaceful king in the glory of his kingdom, when in the royal palace he bestows many benefits by displaying gifts and distributing grants", quoted in P. S. Baker, *Honour, Exchange and Violence in Beowulf* (Cambridge, 2013), 25.
[53] Baker, *Honour, Exchange*, 56–7.
[54] P. J. E. Kershaw, *Peaceful Kings: Peace, Power, and the Early Medieval Political Imagination* (Oxford, 2011), 174–261.

quia felicissimo mundus statu ageretur, si uel reges philosopharentur uel regnarent philosophi. ... quo plus in mundo quique ualent, eo amplius eius, qui super omnia est, Iudicis mandatis auscultare contendant, atque ad haec obseruanda secum eos quoque, qui sibi commissi sunt, exemplis simul et auctoritate instituant.

[the world would be in a happy state if kings were philosophers and philosophers were kings. ... the more powerful men grow in this world, the more they may strive to obey the commands of Our Judge who is over all things; and by their example and authority induce their subjects to observe these commands as well.]55

Ælfric of Eynsham, too, considered wisdom an essential characteristic of a good king. A clear illustration is found in his discussion of the concept of 'etymology' in his *Grammar*:

rex cyning is gecweden A REGENDO, þæt is fram recendome, forðan ðe se cyning sceal mid micelum wisdome his leode wissian and bewerian mid cræfte.56

[*rex* 'king' gets its name from *regendo*, that is from 'governance', because the king must instruct his people with great wisdom and protect them with might.]

Similar remarks about the king's requirement to instruct his people with great wisdom feature in other works by Ælfric.57 Thus, during the entire Anglo-Saxon period, from Bede to Ælfric, a king's sagacity was considered a prerequisite for successful leadership.

Throughout *Beowulf*, Hrothgar is unambiguously presented as embodying this ideal of the wise king. The poet repeatedly describes him as "snotor" [wise] (lines 190b, 1313b, 1384a, 1786b), "frod" [old and wise] (lines 279a, 1306b, 1724a, 1874a, 2114a) and "wis" [wise] (lines 1318a, 1400b, 1698b). Like King Solomon, Hrothgar is not only sagacious, but he also acts as a teacher for the young Beowulf in his so-called 'sermon' (lines 1700–84): "Ðu þe lær be þon, / gumcyste ongit; ic þis gid be þe / awræc wintrum frod" [Teach yourself by this, understand manly virtue. I recite this tale to you, old and wise in winters] (lines 1722b–1724a).58 Notably, Hrothgar's sermon, which R. E. Kaske classified as "the greatest expression" of the old king's

---

55 Bede, *HE*, V.21.
56 Ælfric, *Ælfrics Grammatik*, ed. Zupitza, 293, lines 7–9.
57 See M. Clayton, '*De Duodecim Abusiuis*, Lordship and Kingship in Anglo-Saxon England', in *Saints and Scholars. New Perspectives on Anglo-Saxon Literature and Culture in Honour of Hugh Magennis*, ed. S. McWilliams (Cambridge, 2012), 153–63.
58 See the discussion of this passage in chapter 2, pp. 70–1.

Elderly Kings

sapientia 'wisdom',[59] also features a warning for 'terrible old age', when he discusses the fleeting nature of bodily strength:

> 'Bebeorh þe ðone bealonið,   Beowulf leofa,
> secg bet[e]sta,   ond þe þæt selre geceos,
> ece rædas;   oferhyda ne gym,
> mære cempa.   Nu is þines mægnes blæd
> ane hwile;   eft sona bið
> þæt þec adl oððe ecg   eafoþes getwæfeð
> oððe fyres feng,   oððe flodes wylm,
> oððe gripe meces,   oððe gares fliht,
> oððe atol yldo;   oððe eagena bearhtm
> forsiteð ond forsworceð;   semninga bið
> þæt ðec, dryhtguma,   deað oferswyðeð.' (lines 1758–68)

['Guard yourself against pernicious enmity, dear Beowulf, best of men, and choose for yourself the better thing, eternal benefits. Do not care for arrogance, famous champion. Now for one moment is the glory of your strength; yet immediately it will be that either sickness or edge will deprive you of strength, or the fangs of fire, or the surging of the flood, or the attack of the sword, or the flight of the spear, or terrible old age; or the brightness of eyes will diminish and grow dark; at last death will overpower you, warrior.']

Hrothgar's mention of the detrimental effects of old age calls attention to the effects of his own senectitude. Part of Hrothgar's characterisation suggests that this warning was based on personal experience.

Using Kaske's terminology, Hrothgar has become "a model of kingly *sapientia* ['wisdom'] no longer supported by *fortitudo* ['physical might and courage']".[60] Hrothgar's lack of physical strength is made clear at the outset of the poem, when he is described as unable to cope with Grendel's terror: "Swa ða mælceare maga Healfdenes / singala seað, ne mihte snotor hæleð / wean onwendan" [Thus, then the kinsman of Healfdane continually brooded over the sorrow of the time, the wise hero was not able to change the misery] (lines 189–191a). The old king's bodily weakness is further symbolised by the poet referring, three times, to Hrothgar retreating wearily to his sleeping quarters.[61] This image of Hrothgar as an old man frequenting his bed is further emphasised by the slightly humorous scene when Beowulf, unaware of the fact that Hrothgar's favourite retainer Æschere has just been

---

[59] R. E. Kaske, '*Sapientia et fortitudo* as the Controlling Theme of Beowulf', in *Anthology of Beowulf Criticism*, ed. Nicholson, 280.
[60] Kaske, '*Sapientia et fortitudo*', 279.
[61] *Beowulf*, lines 662–5, 1232–7, 1789–92. Possibly, the Dane who needs to look for quarters elsewhere, mentioned in lines 138–42, can be identified as Hrothgar as well.

killed, asks the old king whether he has had a good night's sleep.[62] Thus, the *Beowulf* poet hammers home the message that Hrothgar has been forced to exchange the field of battle for his bed.

Another recurring element in the poet's portrayal of Hrothgar is passiveness. With the exception of a single jump onto a horse, the strolls to his bedchamber are Hrothgar's only physical actions in the poem. Generally, Hrothgar either sits on his throne or is simply absent. Irving has noted that Hrothgar's absence from scenes of action in the poem underscores his passiveness; it is a form of "zero grade narration", whereby "action and Hrothgar exclude each other".[63] Hrothgar's inaction is also addressed by Beowulf, in his speech following the death of Æschere. Beowulf tells the old king to stop worrying and avenge his friend's death:

> 'Ne sorga, snotor guma. Selre bið æghwæm
> þæt he his freond wrece þonne he fela murne.
> Ure æghwylc sceal ende gebidan
> worolde lifes; wyrce se þe mote
> domes ær deaþe; þæt bið drihtguman
> unlifgendum æfter selest.
> Aris, rices weard, uton raþe feran.' (lines 1384–90)

['Do not worry, wise man. It is better for anyone to avenge his friend than to mourn much. Each of us must await the end of life in the world; he who can, should endeavour to win glory before death; that will be best for a warrior after he is dead. Get up, guardian of the kingdom, let us go quickly.']

Inspired by the young warrior's words, Hrothgar leaps up, leads Beowulf and his men to the monster mere and then fades into the background again. Notably, this episode is the exact opposite of those discussed in the previous chapter, where the old warriors inspired their younger comrades rather than *vice versa*. As Irving has rightly observed, Hrothgar's paralysed anguish at his friend's death is "merely a symbolic intensification of his twelve years of immobilised suffering during Grendel's earlier raids".[64]

Hrothgar's passiveness appears to disqualify him as a protector of his people, a term that is nevertheless applied to him. Indeed, Hrothgar does not seem to deserve the epithets "leodgebyrgean" [protector of the people] (line 269a), "helm Scyldinga" [protector of the Scyldings] (lines 371b, 456b, 1321b) and "eald eðelweard" [old guardian of the country] (line 1702a), since he fails to protect his people himself. Scott

---

[62] *Beowulf*, lines 1306–20.
[63] Irving, 'What To Do', 264–5.
[64] Irving, 'What To Do', 262–3.

Elderly Kings

DeGregorio interprets this contrast as ironically serving "to underscore Hrothgar's inaction and, by implication, his fundamental inability to discharge the office of *hyrde* [shepherd, protector] so prominent in these epithets".[65] In other words, Hrothgar fails to live up to the titles bestowed on him by the poet.

Some scholars, however, have taken the designation of Hrothgar as a protector of his people at face value.[66] According to John Leyerle, for instance, Hrothgar's decision not to fight Grendel was motivated by the old king's fears over his succession.[67] Like the elderly Carolingian rulers described by Dutton, Hrothgar had reason to worry about his sons' succession, since their position was threatened by his nephew Hrothulf. While these worries are never made explicit, the poet does hint at a future conflict between the king and his nephew.[68] Leyerle suggests that Hrothgar considered the threat of Grendel the lesser of two evils, the other being a power struggle for the Danish throne following his own death while his sons were still young.[69] Leyerle's hypothesis about Hrothgar's concerns over a peaceful succession by his own sons, however, is not supported by textual evidence. Moreover, Hrothgar's supposed anguish over his sons' future is certainly contradicted by his apparent symbolic adoption of Beowulf as a son and possible heir, an act that is criticised by Queen Wealhtheow.[70]

Other scholars championing Hrothgar's case argue that, rather than getting physically involved himself, Hrothgar uses diplomatic measures to take care of his people; hence, he still deserves the epithet 'protector'.[71] One example of this diplomatic, peaceful approach is Hrothgar's intervention in the feud started by Beowulf's father Ecgtheow. Hrothgar had settled this feud with money and now expected Beowulf's loyalty in return:

'Fore fyhtum þu, wine min Beowulf,
ond for arstafum usic sohtest.
Gesloh þin fæder fæhðe mæste;

---

[65] S. DeGregorio, 'Theorizing Irony in *Beowulf*: The Case of Hrothgar', *Exemplaria* 11 (1999), 324.
[66] R. P. Tripp, 'The Exemplary Role of Hrothgar and Heorot', *Philological Quarterly* 56 (1977), 123; Rothauser, 'Winter in Heorot', 116–20. See also the authors listed in DeGregorio, 'Theorizing Irony', 315, n. 21.
[67] J. Leyerle, 'Beowulf: The Hero and the King', *Medium Ævum* 34 (1965), 92.
[68] For this conflict between uncle and nephew, see R. H. Bremmer Jr, 'The Importance of Kinship: Uncle and Nephew in *Beowulf*', *Amsterdamer Beiträge zur Älteren Germanistik* 15 (1980), 37–8; cf. W. Cooke, 'Hrothulf: A Richard III, or an Alfred the Great?', *SiP* 104 (2007), 175–98.
[69] Leyerle, 'Beowulf: The Hero', 92.
[70] For Hrothgar's problematic succession, see S. Hollis, 'Beowulf and the Succession', *Parergon* 1 (1983), 39–54; J. M. Hill, *The Cultural World in Beowulf* (Toronto, 1995), 85–107; Biggs, 'Politics of Succession'.
[71] Rothauser, 'Winter in Heorot', 116; Carruthers, 'Kingship and Heroism', 27.

> wearþ he Heaþolafe to handbonan
> mid Wilfingum; ....
> Siððan þa fæhðe feo þingode:
> sende ic Wylfingum ofer wæteres hrycg
> ealde madmas; he me aþas swor.' (lines 457–461a, 470–472)

> ['You, my friend Beowulf, sought us for fights and for favours. Your father brought about the greatest feud; he became a hand-slayer of Heatholaf among the Wylfings ... Afterwards I settled the feud with money: I sent ancient treasures to the Wylfings over the water's back; he swore oaths to me.']

Hrothgar places a claim on Beowulf's service on account of his past diplomatic dealings, as well as his present generosity. As such, Hrothgar can be credited with ultimately finding the solution to the monstrous incursions against his people, even though they had to suffer twelve years until this solution was brought about.

Another problem Hrothgar tries to solve diplomatically is the threat posed by the Heathobards. He does so by marrying his daughter Freawaru to the Heathobard prince Ingeld. Although this move seems an effective, peaceful solution to a long-standing feud, the poet describes the political strategy of using a woman as a *freoðuwebbe* 'peace-weaver' in mostly negative terms.[72] The inclusion of a long digression on a similar and tragic political marriage between the Danish princess Hildeburh and the Frisian king Finn (lines 1063–1159a) illustrates the poet's reservations with regard to this political strategy. Hildeburh and Finn's union ends in tragedy: the violent enmity between the Danes and Frisians resumes despite the marriage and Hildeburh loses her son, her brother Hnæf and also her husband, leaving her a "geomuru ides" [sad woman] (line 1075b). In his report to his uncle Hygelac, Beowulf prophesies a similar, tragic end to the marriage between Freawaru and Ingeld. The Heathobards, Beowulf predicts, will find it difficult to forget past injuries: "Oft seldan hwær / æfter leodhryre lytle hwile / bongar bugeð, þeah seo bryd duge" [Very seldom anywhere, after the fall of a prince, does the deadly spear rest for a little while, even if the bride is good] (lines 2029b–2031). Sources outside *Beowulf* reveal that Beowulf's prophecy came true; the feud between the Heathobards and Danes would flare up again and Hrothgar's measure, in the end, proved unsuccessful.[73]

To sum up, the model of kingship represented by Hrothgar is that of a generous and wise king. Like the elderly rulers analysed by Dutton, however, Hrothgar has become sedentary and the loss of his strength

---

[72] Overing, 'Women of *Beowulf*', 219–60.
[73] For this feud and the role played by the "eald æscwiga" [old spear-warrior] (line 2042a), see also the previous chapter.

has left him passive. Rather than taking action himself, Hrothgar seeks diplomatic solutions to the violent threats to his people. The question whether the poet presents this type of rulership as the ideal model of conduct for an aged king or as an ultimately insufficient example of elderly rulership will be considered after reviewing the portrayal of the old king who takes central stage in the second part of the poem, Beowulf.

Old, but not obsolete: Old king Beowulf

The description of Beowulf's kingship in the second part of the poem starts in line 2207, at the point when Beowulf has ruled the Geats for fifty years and faces his final struggle against a dragon. Details of Beowulf's time on the throne can be pieced together from various flashbacks and speeches. In lines 2354–90 the poet narrates how, following the death of Hygelac in Frisia, Queen Hygd had offered the kingdom to Beowulf, who declined in favour of Hygelac's son Heardred. Only after Heardred had died by the hands of the Swedes did Beowulf ascend the throne of the Geats, much to the approval of the poet: "þæt wæs god cyning" [that was a good king] (line 2390b). Later, upon his deathbed, Beowulf himself gives a brief and positive evaluation of his own reign:

>   'Ic ðas leode heold
> fiftig wintra;   næs se folccyning,
> ymbesittendra   ænig ðara
> þe mec guðwinum   gretan dorste,
> egesan ðeon.   Ic on earde bad
> mælgesceafta,   heold min tela,
> ne sohte searoniðas,   ne me swor fela
> aða on unriht.   Ic ðæs ealles mæg
> feorhbennum seoc   gefean habban.' (lines 2732b–2740)

['I ruled the people for fifty years; there was no folk-king, not any of the neighbours, who dared greet me with warriors, threaten with fear. On earth I waited for destinies, I held mine well, I did not look for treacherous quarrels; I did not swear many unlawful oaths. I, ill of mortal wounds, am able to have enjoyment of all that.']

Other details about Beowulf's rule are provided after his death by the speeches of Wiglaf (lines 2864–91, 3077–119) and the anonymous messenger (lines 2900–3027).

Like Hrothgar before him, Beowulf was known for his generosity, which is reflected in the poet's use of the epithets "goldwine Geata" [gold-friend of the Geats] (lines 2419a, 2584a), "hringa fengel" [lord of rings] (line 2345b) and "goldgyfan" [gold-giver] (line 2652a). Beowulf, as was expected from a Germanic king, had generously shared out treasures to his followers in return for future service, a fact referred to by his successor Wiglaf on various occasions.[74] Beowulf even displays his generosity on the brink of death, when he takes satisfaction from the fact that he has at least secured the dragon's treasure for his people: "Ic ðara frætwa Frean ealles ðanc / … / þæs ðe ic moste minum leodum / ær swylt-dæge swylc gestrynan" [For these treasures I (express) all gratitude to the Lord, for those which I was able to acquire for my people before my dying day] (lines 2794, 2797–8). It is little wonder, then, that his followers remember Beowulf as "manna mildust" [the most generous of men] (line 3181a).

Beowulf is also portrayed as a wise king, as borne out by the epithets "frod" [old and wise] (lines 2209b, 2513a, 2800a), "wis" [wise] (lines 2329a, 3094a) and "gewittig" [knowledgeable] (line 3094a). Even before Beowulf had reached old age, his wisdom had been noted by Hrothgar. The Danish king commented that Beowulf was wise beyond his years and that the young Geat, therefore, was fit for rulership: "Sæ-Geatas selran næbben / to geceosenne cyning ænigne" [the Sea-Geats do not have any better one to choose for a king] (lines 1850–1).[75] Beowulf certainly lived up to Hrothgar's expectations and ruled the Geats wisely for fifty years. Kaske finds evidence of Beowulf's wisdom in the old king's manner of responding to the dragon's attacks: Beowulf's "þeostrum geþoncum" [gloomy thoughts] (line 2332a) suggest "a proper and wise *tristitia*" and the old king prudently provides for an iron shield in preparation for his fight with the fiery dragon.[76]

Whereas Hrothgar and Beowulf thus appear similar in terms of generosity and wisdom, the main difference between the two kings is the manner in which they respond to the monstrous incursions against their people. Hrothgar shunned personal interference, but Beowulf decides to take matters into his own hands and attacks the dragon himself. Although there are no explicit references to Beowulf losing his former strength,[77] the old king eventually realises that his physical prowess will be no match for the dragon and that he is probably going to die: "Him wæs geomor sefa, / wæfre ond wælfus" [he had a sorrowful mind, he was restless and ready for death] (lines 2419b–2420a). Nevertheless, Beowulf decides to act:

---

[74] *Beowulf*, lines 2633–48, 2864–91.
[75] Burrow, *Ages of Man*, 132, has interpreted this youthful wisdom of Beowulf as an example of the hagiographical *puer senex* motif, the idea of a young man who is old of mind.
[76] Kaske, 'Sapientia et fortitudo', 296–7.
[77] Pope, 'Beowulf's Old Age', 56, suggests Beowulf is "still untouched by the ordinary infirmities of age".

Elderly Kings

Beowulf maðelode, beotwordum spræc
niehstan siðe: 'Ic geneðde fela
guða on geogoðe; gyt ic wylle,
frod folces weard fæhðe secan,
mærðu fremman, gif mec se mansceaða
of eorðsele ut geseceð.' (lines 2510-15)

[Beowulf spoke, he said with words of promise for the last time: 'I engaged in many battles in youth; I, old and wise guardian of the people, still want to seek battle, perform a glorious deed, if the man-harmer from the earth-hall seeks me out.']

He fights the dragon and, with the help of Wiglaf, manages to kill the beast, but he has to pay for this act with his life. Beowulf's decision to die in battle rather than shirk away from the fight aligns the old king with other elderly warriors of Germanic legend and Old English heroic poetry, described in the previous chapter.

Three elderly warriors from Germanic legend who, like Beowulf, were also kings, receive a brief mention in the poem: Healfdene, Sigemund and Volsung.[78] The first of these is mentioned in the genealogy of Danish kings: "heah Healfdene; heold þenden lifde / gamol ond guðreouw glæde Scyldingas" [high Healfdene; he ruled the bright Scyldings as long as he lived, old and fierce in battle] (lines 57-8). Healfdene also features in several Scandinavian sources, in which he is similarly denoted as 'high' and 'old'.[79] Sigemund (= Sigemundr) and his father Wæls (= Volsung) are mentioned in lines 875-915, a digression which compares the young Geat Beowulf to the dragon-slayer Sigemund. Both Sigemund and Volsung appear in the Icelandic *Völsunga saga*, where they are described as kings who meet their end in battle after having reached an advanced age, not unlike Beowulf.[80] Indeed, a speech attributed to Volsung prior to his fatal battle shows some parallels to Beowulf's speech cited above:

'while yet unborn ... I swore an oath that fear would make me run from neither fire nor iron. Up to this moment I have acted accordingly, and why should I not keep to it in old age? ... And my decision is that we do not run, and let us act our part as bravely as we can.'[81]

---

[78] For another possible parallel to Beowulf as an old and active king, Wermund, see the Appendix at the end of this chapter.
[79] Various accounts of Healfdene and his children are summarised in K. Malone, 'The Daughter of Healfdene', in *Studies in Heroic Legend*, ed. Einarsson and Eliason, 124-41; K. von See *et al.*, *Kommentar zu den Liedern der Edda. Bd. 3: Götterlieder* (Heidelberg, 2000), 950-8; *Beowulf*, liv.
[80] *The Saga of the Volsungs*, ed. and trans. R. G. Finch (London, 1965), ch. 5, 11.
[81] *Saga of the Volsungs*, ed. and trans. Finch, ch. 5.

Like Beowulf, Volsung reminisces about his active youth and, knowing he will probably die, he too makes the conscious decision to meet his fate head on. The resolve Beowulf shows in his old age, then, is in line with the behaviour of other elderly kings of Germanic legend.

Beowulf, as an old but battle-eager king, has one further parallel within the poem: the Swedish king Ongentheow, whose deeds are referred to on more than one occasion.[82] As has been noted in the previous chapter, Ongentheow comes across as an admirable, courageous old king, who is always shown in a positive light.[83] It has even been argued that "Ongentheow is portrayed not as an enemy, but as something like Beowulf's double, an 'old', 'wise' king who dies protecting his 'hoard', here defined with pathos as consisting of his wife and children."[84] In fact, Beowulf's decision to engage the dragon may, in part, have been inspired by the example of Ongentheow, to which Beowulf himself refers in his long speech prior to the fight (lines 2425–2515).

In this speech, Beowulf contemplates the advantages and disadvantages of inaction; he "explores possible responses to the challenge before him ... to resolve the Hamlet-like question of whether – and how – to act or not to act".[85] Beowulf first considers the case of King Hrethel, who was unable to avenge the killing of his eldest son Herebeald because this had been caused by his other son Haethcyn. Hrethel ultimately died of grief, caused by his inability to act.[86] Subsequently, Beowulf compares Hrethel's sorrow to that of a fictitious old father, who is similarly helpless to save his son from hanging from the gallows. Like Hrethel, the old father succumbs to melancholy and lethargy, caused by his failure to avenge the death of his son. Beowulf then brings to mind the Swedish and Geatish wars and ponders about the consequences of an active response to threats, touching upon Ongentheow among others. Ultimately, Beowulf decides to act, rather than fall prey to the sorrow caused by inaction.[87] Beowulf's decision, therefore, appears partly inspired by the active role played by his Swedish counterpart in the Swedish-Geatish war, Ongentheow.

---

[82] *Beowulf*, lines 2472–89, 2922–98. In addition, Hygelac is called "bonan Ongenþeoes" [the slayer of Ongentheow] (line 1968a) and Onela, king of the Swedes, is called "Ongenðioes bearn" [the son of Ongentheow] (line 2387b).
[83] Carruthers, 'Kingship and Heroism', 26.
[84] Georgianna, 'King Hrethel's Sorrow', 845.
[85] L. N. de Looze, 'Frame Narratives and Fictionalization: Beowulf as Narrator', *Texas Studies in Literature and Language* 26 (1984), 146.
[86] Georgianna, 'King Hrethel's Sorrow', 835–8.
[87] De Looze, 'Frame Narratives', 156. For a detailed discussion of Beowulf's speech prior to the dragon fight, see Georgianna, 'King Hrethel's Sorrow', 829–50.

Elderly Kings

Beowulf's fight against the dragon has profound implications; he dies and his final act, as the anonymous messenger and Wiglaf both prophesy afterwards, results in the demise of the Geats. The messenger announces that they can expect retaliation from various tribes – Franks, Frisians and Swedes – now that the news of the death of their king will spread.[88] Wiglaf, similarly, in what is often interpreted as a critical note,[89] predicts that the Geats will suffer as a result of Beowulf's actions: "Oft sceall eorl monig anes willan / wræc adreogan, swa us geworden is" [Often many a warrior must endure misery for the will of one, as it has happened for us] (lines 3077–8). This anguish concerning the Geatish future is also expressed by the Geatish woman who sings a dirge at Beowulf's funeral and repeatedly speaks of invasions and terror to come.[90] Despite their gloomy thoughts concerning their own future, the Geats all agree that Beowulf deserves a worthy funeral. The messenger, for example, is the first to suggest that the dragon's hoard, an unfathomable amount of treasure, be burned with Beowulf.[91] Wiglaf commands the Geats to do just this and, in addition, heeds Beowulf's final request to build a memorial tower on the coast.[92] The Geats ceremonially burn Beowulf's body along with the dragon's hoard and praise him as "wyruld-cyning[a] / manna mildust ond mon(ðw)ærust, / leodum liðost ond lofgeornost" [of worldly kings the most generous of men, the most gentle, the most gracious among peoples and the most eager for fame] (lines 3180b–3182).

In all, the mode of elderly kingship represented by Beowulf has some elements in common with that of Hrothgar. Both elderly kings are wise and generous, but Beowulf prefers heroic action over diplomatic passivity. As such, he fits the mould of a Germanic warrior king, who, above all, defends his tribe and tries to gain lasting glory, despite the consequences this may have for his personal well-being. His funeral is appropriate for a heroic king, beloved by his people.

Beowulf *as a mirror for elderly kings*

The *Beowulf* poet presents his audience with two elderly kings who, at the end of a long reign, are confronted by monsters. These monsters, the mysterious Grendel, his aged mother and the ancient dragon, may

---

[88] *Beowulf*, lines 2910–27.
[89] Leyerle, 'Beowulf: The Hero', 97–8; cf. Gwara, *Heroic Identity*, 50–1.
[90] *Beowulf*, lines 3152–5. These lines of the manuscript are heavily damaged and the reading "Geatisc meowle" is an emendation proposed by the editors of *Klaeber's Beowulf*. For a further discussion of this passage, see Porck, 'Growing Old', 266–7.
[91] *Beowulf*, lines 2999–3027.
[92] *Beowulf*, lines 2802–8, 3120–36.

well represent the threat posed by old age itself to the authority of elderly kings, a genuine political concern in the early Middle Ages. By juxtaposing Hrothgar and Beowulf, the poet invites a comparison between two models of conduct for such aged monarchs. While both models entail the generosity and wisdom required of any early medieval king, the manner in which these old rulers stand up to the monstrous challenges to their reign differs: Hrothgar shows restraint and turns to diplomatic means, whereas Beowulf acts with heroic resolve. In essence, then, the question regarding elderly kingship in *Beowulf* boils down to whether an old king must still act heroically in battle or whether a passive, diplomatic approach is more suitable behaviour for an aged ruler.[93]

If centuries of *Beowulf* scholarship have shown anything, it is that scholars have found enough material in the poem to argue both ways. While some regard Hrothgar as an empty shell, whose lacklustre performance against the Grendelkin does not weigh up to the heroic epithets bestowed on him, others view Hrothgar as an ideal king, whose wisdom, generosity and diplomacy ultimately save his people.[94] Similarly, many praise Beowulf as the ideal role model for a medieval king, but some have found fault with his decision to fight the dragon on his own.[95] Perhaps it was the poet's intention to evoke discussion on the topic as a whole, as Scott Gwara has argued with respect to Beowulf's decision to fight the dragon.[96] Nevertheless, I argue that the poet sets up Beowulf as the ideal model, whereas his characterisation of Hrothgar can hardly have inspired emulation.

One argument against reading Hrothgar as the ideal role model is that his policies are not always depicted as fully effective. For instance, Hrothgar's restraint against the terror of Grendel leads to twelve years of "hynðo on Heorote" [humiliation in Heorot] (lines 475, 593), something the poet repeats twice and is the cause of great grief for the king and his people. Moreover, Hrothgar's diplomatic solution to the feud between the Danes and Heathobards, as has been pointed out above, is ultimately futile. In fact, the audience is told at the beginning of the poem that the hall Heorot will burn as a result of this renewed Danish-Heathobard conflict.[97] DeGregorio concludes: "As it turns out, then, Hrothgar's wise act of policy not only fails; worse, it leads to

---

[93] Carruthers, 'Kingship and Heroism', 25.
[94] For an overview of the scholarly debate concerning Hrothgar, see DeGregorio, 'Theorizing Irony', 315–16, n. 22. Some scholars tread the middle ground: Irving, 'What To Do', 260, concludes that we cannot see Hrothgar consistently as either admirable or contemptible.
[95] For an overview of the scholarly debate concerning Beowulf, see Gwara, *Heroic Identity*, 8–12.
[96] Gwara, *Heroic Identity*, 26.
[97] *Beowulf*, lines 82–5.

Elderly Kings

the destruction of Heorot, the social pillar supporting the society of the Danes."[98] In addition, the image of Hrothgar's political wisdom, although referred to frequently, is somewhat undermined by the poet's further hinting at a future conflict between the king and his nephew Hrothulf.[99] The presence in Hrothgar's hall of the potentially treacherous Hrothulf, as well as the cowardous kin-slayer Unferth,[100] raises questions concerning the state of Hrothgar's court and, by extension, the wisdom of the aged ruler's political choices.[101]

Those who praise Hrothgar, regardless of his inactivity and defective political decisions, note that there is no textual evidence to support the image of Hrothgar as a failed king.[102] That is to say, the poet never explicitly denounces Hrothgar. This is a valid point. In fact, the poet even notes that the Danes do not condemn Hrothgar as a leader after the young Beowulf has defeated Grendel:

> Ðær wæs Beowulfes
> mærðo mæned; monig oft gecwæð
> þætte suð ne norð be sæm tweonum
> ofer eormengrund oþer nænig
> under swegles begong selra nære
> rondhæbbendra, rices wyrðra.
> Ne hie huru winedrihten wiht ne logon,
> glædne Hroðgar, ac þæt wæs god cyning. (lines 856b–863)

[There Beowulf's fame was remembered; many often said that neither south nor north, nor between the two seas, nor over the spacious earth nor anywhere under the expanse of the sky was a better shield-bearer, more worthy of a kingdom. However, they did not find fault in any way with the friendly lord, the gracious Hrothgar, but that was a good king.]

However, it is hard not to agree with John D. Niles that these "last two lines read as a classic example of praise that damns",[103] rather than a 'rehabilitation' for Hrothgar. The praise for the aged king certainly pales in comparison with the description of Beowulf as the worthiest warrior between the two seas, under the sky and over the earth. Moreover, while the authorial voice never condemns Hrothgar, the aged king himself makes at least two self-deprecatory remarks. When Hrothgar discusses the death of his older brother, he notes: "se wæs betera ðonne ic" [he was a better man than I] (line 469b) and he says

---

[98] DeGregorio, 'Theorizing Irony', 332–3.
[99] For this conflict between uncle and nephew, see Bremmer, 'Importance of Kinship', 37–8.
[100] *Beowulf*, lines 587–601a.
[101] DeGregorio, 'Theorizing Irony', 328–9.
[102] Rothauser, 'Winter in Heorot', 111; Tripp, 'Exemplary Role', 123.
[103] J. D. Niles, Beowulf: *The Poem and Its Tradition* (Cambridge, MA, 1983), 111.

the same of Beowulf when the latter returns home.[104] If Hrothgar is not convinced that he is the best possible king, the audience of *Beowulf* is unlikely to have disagreed with him.

Another aspect that makes Hrothgar into a less appealing role model is the poet's continuous description of Hrothgar as a sorrowful, almost bitter man. Time and time again, Hrothgar's frustration over his inability to stand up against the monster Grendel is brought to the fore:

> Mære þeoden,
> æþeling ærgod, unbliðe sæt,
> þolode ðryðswyð, þegnsorge dreah
> syðþan hie þæs laðan last sceawedon,
> wergan gastes; wæs þæt gewin to strang,
> lað ond longsum. (lines 129b–134a)

> [The famous king, the good old prince, sat sorrowfully, the strong one suffered, he experienced sorrow for thegns, since they beheld the tracks of the loathsome one, of the accursed spirit; that hardship was too strong, hateful and long-lasting.][105]

Even after Grendel has been defeated, Hrothgar's first reaction to another setback, the murder of his beloved thegn Æschere, translates into immobilised anguish and sorrow. Hrothgar is described as "on hreon mode" [of a troubled mind] (line 1307b) when he responds to Beowulf's question whether the old king has slept well: "Ne frin þu æfter sælum, sorh is geniwod / Denigea leodum!" [Don't you ask about pleasures; grief is renewed for the Danish people!] (lines 1322–1323a). As pointed out above, it is the young Beowulf who then has to remind the king that deeds are better than a long period of mourning, a complete reversal of the typical scene in the Germanic heroic tradition where an elderly warrior spurs on the young.[106]

After all monstrous threats to his reign have been defeated, Hrothgar is still characterised as a lamenting old man. When he and Beowulf share a last embrace upon the latter's departure, the old king starts to cry, realising that the two might never meet again.[107] Hrothgar's tears have been interpreted as a sign of weakness and even a lack of manliness.[108] Beowulf's departure is not the only time that the old king

---

[104] *Beowulf*, lines 1702b–1703a.
[105] For other instances of Hrothgar's anguish concerning Grendel, see *Beowulf*, lines 170–171a, 189–93, 473–8.
[106] See chapter 5.
[107] *Beowulf*, lines 1870–80.
[108] The various interpretations of Hrothgar's tears are discussed by Rothauser, 'Winter in Heorot', 118. For a brief discussion of Hrothgar's manliness, see chapter 5 above. Not everyone has considered the old king's tears as a sign of weakness: E. R. Anderson, *Understanding* Beowulf *as an Indo-European Epic: A*

Elderly Kings

is described as overwhelmed by emotions; in his report to Hygelac, Beowulf also paints a picture of Hrothgar as a sad man, bound by old age, whose eyes well up when he remembers his youth:

> 'gomela Scilding,
> felafricgende   feorran rehte;
> hwilum hildedeor   hearpan wynne,
> gome(n)wudu grette,   hwilum gyd awræc
> soð ond sarlic,   hwilum syllic spell
> rehte æfter rihte   rumheort cyning;
> hwilum eft ongan   eldo gebunden,
> gomel guðwiga   gioguðe cwiðan,
> hildestrengo;   hreðer (in)ne weoll
> þonne he wintrum frod   worn gemunde.' (lines 2105b–2114)

['The old Scylding, the well-informed one, narrated things far back in time; sometimes the brave one greeted the pleasure of the harp, the wood of entertainment, sometimes he recited a song, true and sad, sometimes the great-hearted king narrated a wonderful story according to what is right; sometimes again, the old warrior, bound by old age, began to speak of his youth, his battle-strength; his heart surged inside, when he, old and wise in winters, remembered many things.']

Hrothgar's continual grief does not make him an attractive role model. As had happened with King Hrethel and the old father mentioned in Beowulf's speech before the dragon fight, inaction has left Hrothgar sorrowful. As such, the moral of that speech, and of Beowulf's rejection of the modes of inaction represented by Hrethel and the old father, could well be applied to the poem as a whole; Hrothgar's passiveness leads to grief and, therefore, should ultimately be rejected.[109]

Some scholars have regarded Hrothgar's old age as a valid excuse for his lack of heroic deeds.[110] Britt Rothauser, specifically, claimed that "Hrothgar's expressions of grief and failure to protect his people do not suggest his failure as king, but are instead continued evidence of his advanced age" and, moreover, that the heroic ideal of kingship only applies to young kings.[111] This idea that martial heroism was a mode appropriate only to young and middle-aged men has been refuted in the previous chapter; old men were still expected to fight on

---

Study in Comparative Mythology (Lewiston, 2010), 243–7, for example, interprets Hrothgar's weeping as a public demonstration of charismatic affection.

[109] Carruthers, 'Kingship and Heroism', 28, has suggested that Beowulf's "insistence on defending his people single-handed against the dragon is at least partly inspired by a reaction against Hrothgar's lackluster performance against Grendel so many years before".

[110] Peters, *Shadow King*, 100, notes that old age was "one of the canonically recognised causes for certain ecclesiastical exemptions".

[111] Rothauser, 'Winter in Heorot', 109, 114.

the battlefield and the same would have been expected of old kings. In fact, references in *Beowulf* itself to elderly warrior-kings of Germanic legend, such as Healfdene, Sigemund, Volsung and Ongentheow, create an expectation for old kings to act heroically despite their years.[112] Arguably, the frequent references to Hrothgar as the 'son of Healfdene' ironically call attention to the contrast between the "gamol ond guðreouw" [old and battle-fierce] (line 58a) father and the equally old, but battle-shunning, son.

Hrothgar's lack of heroism is made all the more painfully clear by the manner of conduct shown by Beowulf in his old age. In what has been considered an act of self-sacrifice,[113] Beowulf decides to fight the dragon and, in doing so, steers clear from the sorrowful frustrations suffered by Hrothgar. Beowulf has no reason to feel humiliated and can take pride in the fact that he has ruled the Geats well and that he has at least gained them the dragon's treasure, a sharp contrast to Hrothgar's mournful songs and tears. The poet's final words concerning the two elderly kings also show Beowulf as the more glorious of the two. Whereas the last hundred lines of the poem are an elaborate description of the honours bestowed on Beowulf, one of the last comments of the poet on Hrothgar is short and blunt:

> þæt wæs an cyning,
> æghwæs orleahtre   oþ þæt hine yldo benam
> mægenes wynnum   se þe oft manegum scod. (lines 1885b–1887)

[That was a unique king (Hrothgar), blameless in all things, until old age, which has often harmed many, took from him the joys of strength.]

While most critics agree that Beowulf as an old king is presented in a positive light, there are those who criticise Beowulf's decision to fight the dragon on his own. Judith Garde, for instance, called Beowulf's final act "an unwise heroic undertaking that effectively destroys the nation".[114] Niles has summarised the criticism of Beowulf's death into the four following statements: Beowulf's decision to fight the dragon was taken rashly and without a thought; Beowulf acted out of pride and put too much trust in his own physical strength; Beowulf

---

[112] The assumption that the audience of *Beowulf* was familiar with the stories of Germanic legends referred to in the poem is generally accepted. L. Neidorf, 'Germanic Legend, Scribal Errors, and Cultural Change', in *The Dating of Beowulf: A Reassessment*, ed. L. Neidorf (Cambridge, 2015), 37–57, has argued that the Germanic legends circulated in Anglo-Saxon England mainly in the seventh and eighth centuries, the period when *Beowulf* was probably composed.

[113] Bonjour, *Digressions in Beowulf*, 52; Gwara, *Heroic Identity*, 298.

[114] J. Garde, 'Christian and Folkloric Tradition in *Beowulf*: Death and the Dragon Episode', *Literature & Theology* 11 (1997), 325.

left the Geats leaderless; and Beowulf's death ushers in the demise of the Geats, who will now fall prey to the attacks of neighbouring tribes.[115]

However, most of these charges can be shown to be ill-founded. For one, Beowulf's decision to fight the dragon was not taken on a whim, but was the result of an intellectual reconnaissance of the options available to him. Especially compared with his rash and reckless uncle Hygelac, Beowulf is a "model of restraint".[116] Secondly, Beowulf's decision to fight the dragon on his own can only partially be attributed to pride and his yearning for personal glory: before the end, Beowulf realises he will die fighting the dragon and still decides to sacrifice his life for the well-being of his people. Moreover, by facing the dragon alone, Beowulf also ensures that none of his retainers will perish on his behalf.[117] Slighting Beowulf for leaving the Geats leaderless is also ungrounded. Beowulf appointed Wiglaf as his successor before his death; the Geats, therefore, have a leader and one who has proven himself capable of heroic deeds. Finally, Beowulf can hardly be blamed for dying, since his old age had already brought him to death's door.[118] His decision not to die of old age may, in part, have been motivated by personal glory, but, in killing the dragon and gaining the treasure, he has also saved his people from a great threat. Moreover, he did not leave them entirely without means of survival. In securing the dragon's treasure for his people, as William Cooke has suggested, Beowulf actually enabled them to bind the best warriors to their cause, had they not decided to rid themselves of it.[119] If blame has to be put anywhere, the Geats themselves are responsible for their ill-advised plan to burn the treasure along with the old king who died in their defence, rather than putting it to better use.

In conclusion, the model of elderly kingship represented by Hrothgar is one of inaction, which proves ineffective and ultimately leads to humiliation and grief. By contrast, Beowulf's sacrificial act as an old king not only leads to personal glory for himself and safeguards him from years of personal humiliation, it also creates the opportunity for his people to survive and prosper. At the end of the day, the Geats themselves decided to waste their own chances; this cannot be blamed on their old king but rather on the decisions of those who came after

---

[115] Niles, *Beowulf*, 240. For more critical views of King Beowulf, see: Swanton, *Crisis and Development*, 140–2; Leyerle, 'Beowulf: The Hero', 97–102; Gwara, *Heroic Identity*, 48–53.
[116] De Looze, 'Frame Narratives', 147–8.
[117] Niles, *Beowulf*, 240–7.
[118] Niles, *Beowulf*, 245.
[119] W. Cooke, 'Who Cursed Whom, and When? The Cursing of the Hoard and Beowulf's Fate', *Medium Ævum* 76 (2007), 208.

him.[120] For any elderly king listening, then, the choice between the two models presented by the *Beowulf* poet is an easy one: "*gyt* ic wylle, frod folces weard, / fæhðe secan, mærðu fremman!" [I, old and wise guardian of the people, *still* want to seek battle, perform a glorious deed!].

---

[120] Some argue that Wiglaf was unsuitable for kingship since he was not Beowulf's son, see F. M. Biggs, '*Beowulf* and Some Fictions of the Geatish Succession', *ASE* 32 (2003), 71–5.

Appendix: An elderly patron for Beowulf?

In 1949, Dorothy Whitelock called any attempt to connect *Beowulf* to a specific royal court "idle speculation that would lead us nowhere".[1] Despite Whitelock's warning, the search for a patron has never really stopped; various scholars have placed the poem at the courts of Offa, Alfred, Æthelred the Unready and even Cnut, mostly on the basis of circumstantial evidence.[2] It is to this body of circumstantial evidence that a reading of *Beowulf* as a mirror for elderly kings can contribute. Young kings would find little to emulate in the examples of grey-haired Hrothgar and Beowulf; therefore, the poem certainly seems out of place in the courts of teenage kings such as Ælfweard (c.902–924) and Eadwig (c.940–959), who died at the ages of twenty-two and nineteen, respectively. If a potential patron for the poem is to be found, attention needs to be turned to those Anglo-Saxon kings whose reign, like that of Hrothgar and Beowulf, extended over a long period of time and for whom old age was a potential but real threat to their authority. Consequently, the long-reigning Anglo-Saxon kings listed at the beginning of this chapter could all be considered potential patrons of *Beowulf*. Their old age would make them interested in a poem that addresses the problems of elderly kingship. Of course, it would be at best a speculative argument which would need to be further substantiated with reference to other linguistic, historical and cultural considerations.

The search for a patron is part of the contentious and voluminous discussion about the dating of *Beowulf* and, as such, falls outside the scope of this book. Nevertheless, I want to offer one further speculation which fits with the metrical, linguistic, palaeographical and lexical arguments that date the composition of *Beowulf* to eighth-century Mercia.[3] Offa of Mercia (d. 796) was one of the longest reigning kings in Anglo-Saxon history and may have entertained a particular interest in elderly kingship, which makes him a probable candidate for the poem's patronage.

Offa would certainly have been familiar with the ill-fated careers of two other elderly kings: his predecessor Æthelbald of Mercia (d. 757)

---

[1] D. Whitelock, 'Anglo-Saxon Poetry and the Historian', *Transactions of the Royal Historical Society* 31 (1949), 87.

[2] Some of these attempts at finding a patron are summarised in Whitelock, 'Anglo-Saxon Poetry', 87; C. Chase, 'Opinions on the Date of Beowulf, 1815–1980', in *The Dating of* Beowulf, ed. C. Chase (Toronto, 1981), 3–8; S. Newton, *The Origins of* Beowulf *and the Pre-Viking Kingdom of East Anglia* (Cambridge, 1993), 18–53.

[3] The dating of *Beowulf* is a contentious issue in *Beowulf* scholarship, but the case for an early date for *Beowulf* is convincingly brought forward by all the papers in *Dating of* Beowulf, ed. Neidorf. For alternative views and a summary of the debate up to the year 2000, see R. M. Liuzza, 'On the Dating of *Beowulf*', in Beowulf *Reader*, ed. Baker, 281–302.

and his ancestor Wermund. The former had been killed – after ruling the Mercians for forty-two years – by his own bodyguard, who, as Brooks has suggested, were dissatisfied with the passive attitude of their elderly king.[4] Offa became king of the Mercians in the year of Æthelbald's death (757) and must have known how his aged predecessor fared. Furthermore, Offa was probably familiar with the story of his ancestor who faced a foreign invasion in his old age: Wermund, father to Offa's namesake Offa of Angeln. Saxo Grammaticus' *Gesta Danorum* describes how King Wermund, having grown old and blind, was attacked by the king of Saxony, who claimed that the aged king was no longer suited to rule his people. Although Wermund at first wished to fight in a duel himself, he was ultimately saved by his son Offa who took his father's place.[5] This anecdote of Wermund's problematic old age was also known in England and was recounted in the twelfth-century *Vitae Offarum duorum* [The Lives of Two Offas], a text chronicling the lives of Offa of Angeln and Offa of Mercia.[6] Since it is generally assumed that Offa of Mercia was interested in his Anglian namesake,[7] he must also have known the story of the aged Wermund. Given the difficulties that both his predecessor Æthelbald and his ancestor Wermund experienced in their old age, Offa likely anticipated that old age could be a real threat to someone who had occupied the throne as long as himself. Could he have commissioned a poem about elderly kings for guidance in this matter?

Scholars have advanced several other reasons that make Offa of Mercia a likely patron for *Beowulf*. Whitelock and Clemoes, for instance, have both argued for an eighth-century Mercian provenance of the poem on historical and cultural grounds,[8] while a similar date and place of origin have been proposed on the basis of linguistic similarities between *Beowulf* and other eighth-century Mercian texts.[9] The main argument for the involvement of Offa in the commission of *Beowulf*, however, is a digression which praises Offa's ancestor Offa of Angeln and also mentions Wermund (= Garmund). These lines describe how Offa of Angeln subdued his aggressive wife Fremu:[10]

---

[4] Brooks, 'Social and Political Background', 8.
[5] Saxo, *History of the Danes*, ed. Ellis Davidson, trans. Fisher, 106–7.
[6] *The Lives of Two Offas*, ed. and trans. M. Swanton (Crediton, 2010), 1–16.
[7] Offa of Angeln also features in a genealogy of Offa of Mercia and his exploits are mentioned in the poem *Widsith*, two texts which scholars have associated with Offa of Mercia. *Lives of Two Offas*, ed. Swanton, xlvi–lvii; M. Atherton, 'Mentions of Offa in *The Anglo-Saxon Chronicle*, *Beowulf* and *Widsith*', in *Æthelbald and Offa*, ed. Hill and Worthington, 65–74.
[8] Whitelock, *Audience of* Beowulf, 60–4; Clemoes, *Interactions*, xiii, 58–65.
[9] *Beowulf with the Finnesburg Fragment*, ed. C. L. Wrenn, 2nd rev. ed. (London, 1958), 15–9; R. D. Fulk, *History of Old English Meter* (Philadelphia, 1992), §§353–75.
[10] On the name Fremu rather than Modthryth for Offa's wife, see *Beowulf*, 222–6.

> hiold heahlufan   wið hæleþa brego,
> ealles moncynnes   mine gefræge
> þone selestan   bi sæm tweonum,
> eormencynnes;   forðam Offa wæs
> geofum ond guðum,   garcene man,
> wide geweorðod,   wisdome heold
> eðel sinne;   þonon Eomer woc
> hæleðum to helpe,   Hem[m]inges mæg,
> nefa Garmundes,   niða cræftig. (lines 1954–62)

[she held great esteem for the lord of heroes (Offa), the best of all mankind, of humankind, between the two seas, as I have heard; because Offa was, with gifts and battles, a spear-brave man, honoured widely, he held his homeland with wisdom; from him Eomer was born, as a help to the heroes, kinsman of Hemming, grandson of Garmund, strong in battles.]

This digression and the explicit praise for Offa of Angeln as the 'best of all mankind between the two seas' has been considered to be an attempt to compliment Offa's eighth-century Mercian namesake, in whose court, therefore, the poem may have been composed.[11]

Interestingly, the eighth-century Offa of Mercia himself exemplifies that old age did not necessarily have a negative impact on a king's willingness to take action and conduct military affairs. In fact, he was very proactive in his later years. In setting up his son Ecgfrith as the co-ruler of Mercia in 787, for example, Offa used dire measures, as the Anglo-Saxon scholar Alcuin reminded ealdorman Brorda in a letter: "You know very well how much blood his father [Offa] shed to secure the kingdom for his son [Ecgfrith]."[12] Later, in the 790s, Offa became entangled in a conflict with Charlemagne and, only two years before his death, he had the rebellious sub-king Æthelberht of East Anglia beheaded.[13] So, while the patron of *Beowulf* may never be identified beyond any doubt, I would not deem it unlikely that Offa's energetic old age was inspired by listening to a poem that encouraged active elderly kingship, not unlike *Beowulf*.

---

[11] E.g., J. M. Wallace-Hadrill, *Early Germanic Kingship in England and on the Continent* (Oxford, 1971), 120-1; Swanton, *Crisis and Development*, 153; Clemoes, *Interactions*, 58. Not everyone shares this view; see Newton, *Origins of Beowulf*, 64–71; cf. F. Leneghan, 'The Poetic Purpose of the Offa-Digression in *Beowulf*', *RES* ns 60 (2009), 538–60.

[12] The letter is dated after Offa's death, in 797. Quoted in S. Keynes, 'The Kingdom of the Mercians in the Eighth Century', in *Æthelbald and Offa*, ed. Hill and Worthington, 18. If Offa did commission *Beowulf*, his co-rulership with his son would explain the presence of lessons for young princes, noted in the introduction to this chapter, alongside the elderly role models in the poem.

[13] For a summary of Offa's career, see Keynes, 'Kingdom of the Mercians', 8–18.

7

gamole geomeowlan: Old Women in Anglo-Saxon England

> bryd ...
> gomela iomeowlan   golde berofene
> Onelan modor   ond Ohtheres (*Beowulf*, lines 2930b–2932)

[(Ongentheow's) wife, the old woman of a former day,[1] deprived of gold, mother of Onela and Ohthere]

With the possible exception of Grendel's monstrous mother, Ongentheow's wife is the only woman who is explicitly described as 'old' in Old English poetry. Typically, she remains nameless and is identified only by her relationship to three men: her husband Ongentheow and her two sons. This nebulousness is indicative of the relative lack of interest Anglo-Saxon poets appear to have shown in elderly women. Even in the unique case of the poem *Elene*, in which the main protagonist is the aged Helen (c.250–c.330), the poet Cynewulf appears indifferent to the old age of his main character. Though Helen is estimated to have been in her seventies when she made her pilgrimage to the Holy Land,[2] Cynewulf never once refers to her old age.[3] The paucity of older women in Old English poetry is enigmatic, especially given the widespread popularity of elderly female characters in classical and late medieval literature, such as Ovid's Dipsas and Geoffrey Chaucer's Wife of Bath.[4]

---

[1] For this translation of "iomeowlan", see *DOE*, s.v. *geomeowle*.
[2] J. W. Drijvers, *Helena Augusta: The Mother of Constantine the Great and the Legend of Her Finding of the True Cross* (Leiden, 1992), 55–72.
[3] Cynewulf, *Elene*, ed. Gradon. An interesting parallel to Cynewulf's blind spot for the old age of his protagonist is found in the anonymous prose *Life of St Mary of Egypt*. Although Mary's age can be reconstructed as being around seventy-six, this is never made explicit and the author only implicitly refers to her old age once, by mentioning her white hair. *Life of Mary of Egypt*, ed. and trans. Magennis, lines 217, 362, 372, 594–5; cf. C. A. Lees and G. R. Overing, *Double Agents: Women and Clerical Culture in Anglo-Saxon England* (Philadelphia, 2001), 209, n. 76. By contrast, the other male protagonist of this saint's life, Zosimus, a man aged around fifty-three, is frequently called old, see *Life of Mary of Egypt*, ed. and trans. Magennis, lines 226–7, 236, 299, 304, 352, 359, 703, 711, 834, 843, 852, 927, 932, etc.
[4] V. Rosivach, '*Anus*: Some Older Women in Latin Literature', *The Classical World* 88 (1994), 107–17; Classen, 'Old Age in the Middle Ages', 24–8; G. Mieszkowski, 'Old Age and Medieval Misogyny: The Old Woman', in *Old Age in the Middle Ages*, ed. Classen, 299–319.

Old Women

In pastoral texts from the Anglo-Saxon period, old women feature only marginally. For Ælfric, the most prolific homiletic author of the Anglo-Saxon period, only one issue with regard to old women was worth commenting on at some length – their unabashed sexual appetite despite their inability to bring forth children.[5] In his letter to Sigefyrth, for example, he classified the sexual needs of an elderly woman as shameful, since intercourse was only meant for procreation:

> Hit byð swyþe sceandlic, þæt eald wif sceole
> ceorles brucan, þonne heo forwerod byð
> and teames ætealdod, ungehealtsumlice,
> forðan ðe gesceafta ne beoð for nanum oðran þinge astealde
> butan for bearnteame anum, swa swa us secgað halige bec.[6]

> [It is very shameful that an old woman should have sex with a man, when she is worn out with age and too old for childbearing, unchastely, because sexual relations are not meant for any other thing but procreation only, just as holy books tell us.]

In his homily for the second Sunday before Lent, Ælfric repeated this notion: "[h]it is swiðe ungedafenlic and scandlic þæt forwerode menn and untymende gifta wilnian, ðonne gifta ne sind gesette for nanum ðinge, buton for bearnteame" [It is very improper and shameful that old and unfruitful people should desire marriage, since marriage is not meant for anything but procreation].[7] On the whole, the sporadic presence of explicit comments on old women in the Bible, such as Paul's encouragement for old women to teach young women how to be good wives (Titus 2:3–5),[8] do not appear to have prompted Anglo-Saxon homilists to devote much attention to elderly women in general.

Given this lack of poetic attestations of and explicit attitudes towards old women, it is little wonder that the topic has received hardly any scholarly attention in the field of Anglo-Saxon studies.[9] The present

---

[5] On this issue, see R. H. Bremmer Jr, 'Widows in Anglo-Saxon England', in *Between Poverty and the Pyre: Moments in the History of Widowhood*, ed. J. Bremmer and L. van den Bosch (London, 1995), 77.

[6] Assmann, hom. 2, lines 157–61.

[7] *ÆCHom II*, hom. 6, lines 128–31. See p. 66, n. 61 above.

[8] Ælfric mentions Paul's Epistle to Titus in his letter to Sigeweard, but, like Bede, Wulfstan and other Anglo-Saxon homilists, he refrained from commenting on this particular passage. See V. Heuchan, 'All Things to All Men: Representations of the Apostle Paul in Anglo-Saxon Literature', unpublished PhD dissertation, University of Toronto, 2010, 182, 255–8. On the knowledge of Paul's Epistle to Titus in Anglo-Saxon England, see also A. R. Rumble, 'Church Leadership and the Anglo-Saxons', in *Leaders of the Anglo-Saxon Church: From Bede to Stigand*, ed. A. R. Rumble (Woodbridge, 2012), 4–5.

[9] Various pivotal publications on Anglo-Saxon women do not pay explicit attention to old women, e.g., C. Fell, with C. Clark and E. Williams, *Women in Anglo-Saxon England and the Impact of 1066* (London, 1984); S. Hollis, *Anglo-Saxon*

chapter aims to fill this gap in the scholarship and focuses on the roles and functions that old women could fulfil in early medieval England. In view of the apparent underrepresentation of old women in Anglo-Saxon literature, this chapter first considers evidence drawn from the fields of archaeology and anthropology. It then provides an overview of how the lives and actions of aged women were recorded in the written documents of the Anglo-Saxon period, such as chronicles, letters and wills. Despite the fragmented and often anecdotal nature of this written source material, some light can be shed onto the status and possible communal roles of these Anglo-Saxon elderly women.

Grave goods and culture bearers: Perspectives from archaeology and anthropology

Some archaeologists have claimed that the transition to old age effected a decline in social status for women. For instance, early Anglo-Saxon graves of elderly women contain fewer precious metals and feminine-specific grave goods, such as girdle items, than the graves of younger women.[10] This negative trend has been interpreted as implying a reduced social value for women once they reached post-menopausal age, since "reproductive fertility defined the social value of women in the early medieval period".[11] Guy Halsall, who described similar trends in Merovingian Francia, concluded that the value of a woman "to her family was derived from her potential to have children, and thus her value as a marriage counter in alliances with other families".[12] Put differently, with the discontinuation of their roles as mothers and potential marriage partners, elderly women moved to the margins of their community.

However, these conclusions with regard to a reduction in social status once women reached old age have recently been challenged.[13] The archaeologist Rebecca Gowland, for instance, has pointed out that the number of burial furnishings for older women may reflect an alteration in gender signification and social role, rather than a reduction of social status. No longer taking on the role of bride or mother, old

---

Women and the Church: Sharing a Common Fate (Woodbridge, 1992); S. Foot, *Veiled Women: Female Religious Communities in England, 871–1066* (Aldershot, 2000). One exception is the chapter on early medieval dowager queens in P. Stafford, *Queens, Concubines and Dowagers: The King's Wife in the Early Middle Ages* (London, 1983), 143–90.

[10] Crawford, *'Gomol is snoterost'*, 58.
[11] Gilchrist, *Medieval Life*, 4.
[12] G. Halsall, 'Female Status and Power in Early Merovingian Central Austrasia: The Burial Evidence', *Early Medieval Europe* 5 (1996), 15.
[13] Stoodley, 'Childhood to Old Age', 663.

women may have given their own jewelry and other gender-specific items to their daughters at the time of their marriage or bequeathed them as heirlooms.[14] The fact that these items are no longer found in the graves of older women, then, may be a reflection of their different roles within their communities, rather than an expression of lower social value.[15]

Gowland's suggestion of a change rather than a decline in status for elderly women finds support in a study of old women in Carolingian Francia, as well as in a number of anthropological studies of modern societies. For Carolingian Francia, a society in many respects comparable and contemporary with that of Anglo-Saxon England, Valerie Garver has shown that old women could still play important roles: as grandmothers, landowning widows, abbesses and dowager queens.[16] Discussing more modern cultures, anthropologists have similarly shown that aging need not necessarily result in a reduced status for women, but may also involve empowerment and liberation from social constraints that govern the lives of younger women.[17] Setting aside their role of child bearer, old women in these non-industrial societies can function as 'culture bearer'; they become actively involved in the upbringing of their grandchildren, act as religious role models and function as conveyors of local or tribal history as well as other cultural knowledge, including herbal medicine and dream divination.[18]

As I argue below, the examples of old women which are traceable in the Anglo-Saxon cultural record provide no grounds for assuming that all elderly women held a particularly low status or were considered socially less valuable than younger women. Rather, like Garver's

---

[14] Gowland, 'Ageing the Past', 150–1; Cave and Oxenham, 'Sex and the Elderly', 214, make the same suggestion.

[15] Notably, Cave and Oxenham, 'Sex and the Elderly', 213, have pointed out that older women in early Anglo-Saxon cemeteries were less likely to receive a high status burial than elderly men. They attribute this differential treatment to the fact that more women reached old age than men.

[16] V. L. Garver, 'Old Age and Women in the Carolingian World', in *Old Age in the Middle Ages*, ed. Classen, 121–41.

[17] R. Gowland, 'Age, Ageism and Osteological Bias: The Evidence from Late Roman Britain', *Journal of Roman Archaeology* ss 65 (2007), 167; Gowland, 'Ageing the Past', 151.

[18] Anthropological scholarship on old women is a vast and growing field. Some studies highlight the role of old women as culture bearers, including S. J. Rasmussen, 'From Childbearers to Culture-Bearers: Transition to Postchildbearing among Tuareg Women', *Medical Anthropology: Cross-Cultural Studies in Health and Illness* 19 (2000), 91–116; J. Dickerson-Putman, 'Old Women at the Top: An Exploration of Age Stratification among Bena Bena Women', *Journal of Cross-Cultural Gerontology* 9 (1994), 193–205; J. W. Peterson, 'Age of Wisdom: Elderly Black Women in Family and Church', in *Cultural Context of Aging*, ed. Sokolovsky, 276–92; H. Bar-Itzhak, 'Old Jewish Moroccan Women Relate in an Israeli Context', in her *Israeli Folk Narratives: Settlement, Immigration, Ethnicity* (Detroit, 2005), 97–152.

Carolingian women, some of these elderly Anglo-Saxon women were still prominent political players; others, like the 'culture bearers' identified by anthropologists in non-industrial societies, played important cultural roles as grandmothers, religious role models, teachers, remembrancers and explainers of dreams.

Tracing old women in the Anglo-Saxon documentary record

To note that women in general are mostly absent from the Anglo-Saxon cultural record borders on tautology.[19] Yet the figures are staggering: *PASE* (*Prosopography of Anglo-Saxon England*), "a relational database which provides access to structured information relating to all the recorded inhabitants of Anglo-Saxon England from the late sixth to the late eleventh century",[20] lists just 973 individuals who are certainly female, as opposed to 17,196 individuals who are certainly male. These figures reflect the male bias of the period's written sources and the fact that in the Anglo-Saxon period most of the business considered worth recording, including secular and spiritual politics, was conducted by men.[21] For aged women, the situation appears even worse: only two of the 973 women listed by *PASE* are labelled as 'old'.[22] In part, this low figure is due to a methodological oversight of the creators of *PASE*: other women who are called old in the sources are not listed as such in the database.[23] On the other hand, the presence of old women is hard to establish in the sources and the majority of old women, it can be assumed, simply went unrecorded.

One problem in prising old women out of the Anglo-Saxon documentary record is the fact that dates of birth were very rarely recorded. As a result, there is often no way to reconstruct a woman's age. Even the birth year of one of the most powerful women of the Anglo-Saxon period, Emma of Normandy (d. 1052), is unknown, despite her marriage to two successive kings and a chronicle bearing her name, the *Encomium Emmae Reginae*, which was commissioned in her honour. In cases where

---

[19] The absence of women from the cultural record is discussed by Lees and Overing, *Double Agents*, 1–14; J. T. Rosenthal, 'Anglo-Saxon Attitudes: Men's Sources, Women's History', in *Medieval Women and the Sources of Medieval History*, ed. J. T. Rosenthal (Athens, 1990), 259–84.

[20] *PASE*.

[21] Rosenthal, 'Anglo-Saxon Attitudes'.

[22] Anonymous 286 is labelled as "Æbbe 4's old nurse" and Anonymous 287 is labelled as "Old nun of Wimborne". 'Anonymous 286' and 'Anonymous 287', *PASE*.

[23] For example, Hildelith (fl. c.700), abbess of Barking, is mentioned by Bede as having become "ad ultimam senectutem" [extremely old], but *PASE* labels her simply as "abbess of Barking". Bede, *HE*, IV.10; 'Hildelith 1', *PASE*.

someone's specific date of birth was recorded, there often was a particular reason to do so. The eleventh-century hagiographer Goscelin, for example, recorded that one Brihtgifu was born thirty days after the death of St Edith in 984 and that, inspired by the same saint, she had grabbed a burning wax taper during her baptism. The same Brihtgifu became the third abbess of St Edith's community at Wilton and, as Goscelin records, died in the year 1063, at the venerable age of seventy-nine.[24] Similarly, a woman's specific age at death would typically be recorded only when the number of years carried some significance. For instance, Bede reports that St Hild (614–680) died at the age of sixty-six, having spent thirty-three years as a lay woman and an equal number of years at the monastery of Strensall-Whitby.[25] Consequently, rather than relying on the age threshold by which one was considered old by the Anglo-Saxons (fifty years of age, as established in chapter 1), other factors need to be taken into account to trace old women.

Sporadically, women are labelled as 'old' in personal correspondence, chronicles and saints' lives. The letter from Boniface (d. 754) to Abbess Bugga is a case in point: it aims to console her in her "beautiful old age". The letter reveals little about Bugga's experience of old age, other than that, as Boniface tells her, God "desires to adorn the beauty of [her] soul with labour and sorrow".[26] The letter provides no further insight into what exactly ailed Bugga or how old she actually was. In chronicles and saints' lives, old women are occasionally named as witnesses to miracles, as witches or companions of saints. In such instances, it is often impossible to establish whether the women mentioned in these narrative sources represent actual, historical individuals or whether they are fictional *topoi* and thus reflect how the Anglo-Saxons expected an old woman to behave.[27]

In administrative and legal documents, old women can be identified only by deduction, since the label 'old woman' is not used in

---

[24] Goscelin, *Vita Edithe*, trans. M. Wright and K. Loncar, in *Writing the Wilton Women: Goscelin's Legend of Edith and Liber confortatorius*, ed. S. Hollis (Turnhout, 2004), ch. 26.

[25] Bede, *HE*, IV.23.

[26] *Letters of Boniface*, trans. Emerton, letter no. 77.

[27] The stories of two elderly Anglo-Saxon witches (see list, nos. 23 and 30), in particular, are problematic, since they occur in texts written after the Norman Conquest and most likely represent Norman (and not Anglo-Saxon) imagination. A. Davies, 'Witches in Anglo-Saxon England: Five Case Histories', in *Superstition and Popular Medicine in Anglo-Saxon England*, ed. D. G. Scragg (Manchester, 1989), 42–8; A. L. Meaney, 'Women, Witchcraft and Magic in Anglo-Saxon England', in *Superstition*, ed. Scragg, 30, identifies those working witchcraft in Anglo-Saxon England as "young women looking for lovers, wives trying to win the favour of their husbands, or to produce a live baby, or mothers anxious for the health of their children", rather than the alleged witches of later centuries, "old, lame, blear-eyed, pale, foul and full of wrinkles".

any charter or law code. A mention of grandchildren in a will, for example, is a clear indication that a woman was older, albeit that one might become a grandmother well before the age of fifty. The various widows that can be traced in the Anglo-Saxon documentary record may well have been old and widowhood is a conceivable aspect of the life of an old woman.[28] However, while some of these widows were certainly old, such as the royal widows Eadgifu (b. in or before 904, d. in or after 966) and Emma of Normandy, others need not have been elderly at all: Judith of Flanders, widow to Kings Æthelwulf (d. 858) and Æthelbald (d. 860), had already been widowed twice while still in her teens.[29] As such, widowhood does not necessarily imply old age. As it stands, it may well be that the actions and deeds of various old women were in fact recorded in charters, wills and other legal documents; however, there is often no way to identify these women beyond any doubt as being old.

Nevertheless, with some effort, old women can be traced in the Anglo-Saxon cultural record. The list below contains thirty-two women who can be classified as old: because it can be established that they lived beyond the age of fifty, because they are labelled 'old' in a narrative source or because they are mentioned as grandmothers.

List 4. Identifiably old women in Anglo-Saxon England

1. Hild (614–680), abbess of Strensall-Whitby[30]
2. Eanflæd (b. 626, d. after 685), queen in Northumbria, consort of King Oswiu, retired to the monastery of Strensall-Whitby[31]
3. Seaxburh (b. in or before 655, d. c.700), queen of Kent, consort of King Eorcenberht, abbess of Ely[32]
4. Ælfflæd (654–714), abbess of Strensall-Whitby[33]
5. Hildelith (fl. c.700), abbess of Barking[34]

---

[28] For widows in Anglo-Saxon England, see Bremmer, 'Widows'; J. Crick, 'Men, Women and Widows: Widowhood in Pre-Conquest England', in *Widowhood in Medieval and Early Modern Europe*, ed. S. Cavallo and L. Warner (Harlow, 1999), 24–36.
[29] Bremmer, 'Widows', 64.
[30] A. Thacker, 'Hild (614–680)', *ODNB*.
[31] A. Thacker, 'Eanflæd [St Eanflæd] (b. 626, d. after 685)', *ODNB*.
[32] D. Rollason, 'Seaxburh (b. in or before 655, d. c.700)', *ODNB*. According to the *Liber Eliensis*, trans. Fairweather, I.35, Seaxburh "brought her last day to a close at a good, late age".
[33] A. Thacker, 'Ælfflæd (654–714)', *ODNB*.
[34] M. Lapidge, 'Hildelith (fl. c.700)', *ODNB*. According to Bede, *HE*, IV.10, Hildelith "multisque annis, id est usque ad ultimam senectutem, eidem monasterio strenuissime" [presided over the monastery for many years until she was extremely old].

Old Women

6. Bugga (d. 759x65), abbess, correspondent of St Boniface[35]
7. Eangyth (fl. c.700), abbess, correspondent of St Boniface, mother of Bugga[36]
8. Sister of Eangyth (fl. c.700)[37]
9. Walburg (c.710–779?), abbess of Heidenheim[38]
10. Old mother of St Cuthman (fl. 8th c.)[39]
11. Leoba (d. 782), abbess of Tauberbischofsheim[40]
12. Æbba (8th c.), mother of St Leoba[41]
13. Old nurse (8th c.), who interprets dream of Æbba[42]
14. Old nun (8th c.), who interprets dream of St Leoba[43]
15. Dunne (8th c.), testatrix, leaves minster at Withington to granddaughter[44]
16. Eadgifu (b. in or before 904, d. in or after 966), queen of the Anglo-Saxons, consort of Edward the Elder[45]
17. Wynflæd (fl. c.950), testatrix, leaves lands, goods and horses to grandchildren[46]
18. Æthelthryth (fl. 964), abbess of Nunnaminster[47]
19. Ælfthryth (d. 999x1001), grandmother of Æthelstan and Edmund Ironside, retires to nunnery in Wherwell[48]

---

[35] B. Yorke, 'Bugga (d. 759x65)', *ODNB*; *Letters of Boniface*, trans. Emerton, letter no. 77.
[36] Eangyth describes herself as "more advanced in years and guilty of more offenses in my life". *Letters of Boniface*, trans. Emerton, letter no. 6.
[37] Eangyth describes this sister in her letter to Boniface as "a very aged mother". *Letters of Boniface*, trans. Emerton, letter no. 6.
[38] C. Larrington, 'Walburg (c.710–779?)', *ODNB*.
[39] *Vita s. Cuthmanni*, ed. Blair, 'Saint Cuthman', ch. 3–5. Cuthman's mother is paralysed because of her old age.
[40] Rudolf, *Vita s. Leoba*, trans. Talbot, *Missionaries*, 223, records that Leoba at the end of her life "was an old woman and became decrepit through age".
[41] Rudolf, *Vita s. Leoba*, trans. Talbot, *Missionaries*, 210, describes how "the onset of old age had deprived them [Æbba and her husband] of all hope of offspring".
[42] Rudolf, *Vita s. Leoba*, trans. Talbot, *Missionaries*, 210.
[43] Rudolf, *Vita s. Leoba*, trans. Talbot, *Missionaries*, 212.
[44] S 1255; S 1429.
[45] P. Stafford, 'Eadgifu (b. in or before 904, d. in or after 966)', *ODNB*.
[46] S 1539.
[47] According Wulfstan of Winchester, she was "moribus et aetate maturam" [ripe in years and experience]. Wulfstan of Winchester, *Life of Æthelwold*, trans. Lapidge and Winterbottom, ch. 2.
[48] P. Stafford, 'Ælfthryth (d. 999x1001)', *ODNB*.

20. Æthelflæd of Damerham (10th c.), second wife of King Edmund the Elder (920/21–946)[49]
21. Emma of Normandy (d. 1052), queen of England[50]
22. Brihtgifu (984–1065), abbess of Wilton[51]
23. Old witch (fl. 1017–1034) who makes a love potion for Thorkell's wife, during the episcopate of Æthelric, bishop of Dorchester (1016)[52]
24. Gytha (fl. c.1022–1068), mother of Harold Godwinson[53]
25. Vulfrunna/Judith (fl. c.1000–c.1087), nun at Barking[54]
26. Mother of St Wulfstan (10th/11th c.), retired to Worcester nunnery in old age[55]
27. Ælflæd (10th/11th c.), old nun at Wilton, witnesses a lamb come out of the tomb of St Wulfthryth[56]
28. Ælfwen (11th c.), aged recluse at St Benet's at Hulme[57]
29. Ælfwen (11th c.), aged recluse at St Stephen's, Hackington[58]
30. Old witch (11th c.) who curses Hereward the Wake for William the Conqueror[59]
31. Old, deaf and blind woman (???), whose youth, hearing and sight are restored by St Birinus[60]

---

[49] Æthelflæd left a will dated to 962x991 (S 1494), meaning she may have outlived her husband by as long as forty-five years. According to the *Liber Eliensis*, Æthelflæd "remained perpetually in widowhood, following the example of the blessed Anna". *Liber Eliensis*, trans. Fairweather, II.64.

[50] S. Keynes, 'Emma (d. 1052)', *ODNB*. Emma is called "seo ealde hlæfdige" [the old lady] in MS C of *The Anglo-Saxon Chronicle*. *The Anglo-Saxon Chronicle: A Collaborative Edition. Vol. 5: MS C*, ed. K. O'Brien O'Keeffe (Cambridge, 2001), s.a. 1051.

[51] Goscelin, *Vita Edithe*, trans. Wright and Loncar, ch. 26.

[52] *Chronicon abbatiae Rameseiensis*, ed. W. D. Macray (London, 1886), ch. 74. Lived during the episcopate of Æthelric, bishop of Dorchester (1017–1034).

[53] A. Williams, 'Godwine, earl of Wessex (d. 1053)', *ODNB*.

[54] Goscelin, *Vita et virtutes sanctae Vulfildae virginis*, ed. M. L. Colker, 'Texts of Jocelyn of Canterbury which Relate to the History of Barking Abbey', *Studia Monastica* 7 (1965), 383–460, prol., ch. 13, 15.

[55] William of Malmesbury, *Vita s. Wulfstani*, trans. Winterbottom and Thomson, I.2.

[56] Goscelin, *Translatio Edithe*, trans. M. Wright and K. Loncar, in *Writing*, ed. Hollis, ch. 8.

[57] Herman, *Miracula sancti Eadmundi*, ed. T. Arnold, *Memorials of St Edmund's Abbey. Vol. 1* (London, 1890), ch. 8.

[58] Goscelin, *Translatio s. Mildrethe*, ed. D. W. Rollason, 'Goscelin of Canterbury's Account of the Translation and Miracles of St Mildrith (*BHL* 5961/4): An Edition with Notes', *Mediaeval Studies* 48 (1986), 139–211, ch. 30.

[59] *Gesta Herewardi*, trans. M. Swanton, *Robin Hood and Other Outlaw Tales*, ed. S. Knight and T. H. Olgren (Kalamazoo, 2000), ch. 24–5.

[60] *Vita s. Birini*, ed. and trans. R. C. Love, *Three Eleventh-Century Anglo-Latin Saints' Lives* (Oxford, 1996), ch. 15–16.

32. Old, blind woman (???), whose sight is restored at the altar of St Augustine[61]

Quantitatively, the results remain poor and this select group of elderly female individuals cannot claim any sort of representativeness, if only because noble and clerical women are generally overrepresented in the sources. Moreover, the disparate nature and dates of these sources, ranging from wills to chronicles, dating from the eighth to the thirteenth centuries, make it impossible to draw a single, monolithic picture of the old woman in Anglo-Saxon England. Nevertheless, there is some value in bringing these old women to light; their lives may at least partially represent a general experience of old age for Anglo-Saxon women.

The remainder of this chapter examines the roles some of these old Anglo-Saxon women played as political figures, grandmothers and sources of cultural knowledge. Overall, there appear to be no grounds for assuming that these old women enjoyed a particularly low status or were considered socially valueless; rather, some of them appear as well-respected 'culture bearers', a term familiar from anthropological studies on old women.

Crones at court: Old women as political figures

Minois, musing on Eleanor of Aquitaine (1122/24–1204) who remained politically active until well into her eighties, remarked that "[i]n an age when giving birth was more deadly than participating in battle, only the strongest mothers would reach the menopause, and they would then expend their surplus energy in politics".[62] In Carolingian Francia, as Garver has shown, the latter certainly was the case and old women, in their capacities as royal widows, abbesses or landowners, still exerted a level of political influence that must not be underestimated.[63] Although the Anglo-Saxon period did not produce a woman equal to Eleanor, a number of elderly women certainly left their mark on the political history of Anglo-Saxon England.

Gytha of Wessex (fl. c.1022–1068), a prominent player in the aftermath of the Norman Conquest, was one such woman. Widow of the once powerful Earl Godwine (d. 1053) and mother of the fallen King Harold Godwinson (d. 1066), Gytha had become a focal point of rebellion against the Norman usurpers. Despite the fact that she was aged over sixty, William the Conqueror considered her enough of a political

---

[61] Goscelin, *Historia translationis s. Augustini*, PL 155, I.20.
[62] Minois, *History of Old Age*, 195.
[63] Garver, 'Old Age and Women', 133–4.

threat to conduct a pre-emptive strike against Exeter, one of Gytha's strongholds. William besieged the town for eighteen days and forced it to surrender during the winter of 1068, causing Gytha to flee to Flanders where she died the following year.[64] William had good reason to fear the old lady: she had powerful political connections, such as her nephew King Swein of Denmark,[65] and, as one of the richest lay landholders in the south-west of England, she was able to rally the support of many men who had been and still were her tenants.[66]

Two other Anglo-Saxon noblewomen remained active within the political sphere despite their old age and, like Gytha, were ousted from their positions. The royal widows Eadgifu (b. in or before 904, d. in or after 966) and Emma of Normandy (d. 1052) are both examples of Pauline Stafford's claim that "[m]any queens reach the height of their careers not as wives of royal husbands but as mothers and regents for young royal sons".[67] Eadgifu was the widow of Edward the Elder (d. 924) and had a prominent position at court during the successive reigns of her sons Edmund the Elder (r. 939–946) and Eadred (r. 946–955), as demonstrated by the fact that she signed various charters as "mater regis" [mother of the king]. When her grandson, Eadwig (r. 955–959), became king in 955, he seems to have considered his grandmother a political opponent and deprived her of her lands.[68] However, as soon as her other grandson Edgar (r. 959–975) took to the throne, Eadgifu's possessions were restored and she began to sign charters as "ava regis" [grandmother of the king]. Later, Eadgifu left the court and probably retired to a religious house.[69] Emma of Normandy, widow of Æthelred the Unready (d. 1016) and Cnut the Great (d. 1035), was probably aged in her fifties and sixties, when she was actively involved in the rise to royal power of her sons Harthacnut (r. 1040–1042) and Edward the Confessor (r. 1042–1066). While the first allowed his aged mother to exercise considerable political control,[70] the latter, upon his ascension to the throne, terminated Emma's political pretensions. MS D of *The Anglo-Saxon Chronicle* reports that Edward did so because his mother had not supported him enough in the past:

---

[64] Mason, *House of Godwine*, 180; J. O. Prestwich, *The Place of War in English History 1066-1214*, ed. M. Prestwich (Woodbridge, 2004), 28–31.
[65] Prestwich, *Place of War*, 29.
[66] Mason, *House of Godwine*, 180–1; P. Stafford, 'Chronicle D, 1067 and Women: Gendering Conquest in Eleventh-Century England', in *Anglo-Saxons: Studies Presented to Cyril Roy Hart*, ed. S. Keynes and A. P. Smyth (Scarborough, 2006), 219–20.
[67] Stafford, *Queens, Concubines*, 146.
[68] Stafford, 'Eadgifu'.
[69] Bremmer, 'Widows', 65.
[70] P. Stafford, *Queen Emma and Queen Edith: Queenship and Women's Power in Eleventh-Century England* (Oxford, 1997), 247.

Her wæs Eadward gehalgod to cynge æt Wincestre on forman Easterdæg. 7 þæs geres .xiiii. nihton ær Andreas mæssan, man gerædde þan cynge þæt he rad of Gleawcestre 7 Leofric eorl 7 Godwine eorl 7 Sigwarð eorl mid heora genge to Wincestre on unwær on þa hlæfdian, 7 bereafedan hi æt eallon þan gærsaman þe heo ahte, þa wæron unatellendlice, for þan þe heo wæs æror þam cynge hire suna swiðe heard, þæt heo him læsse dyde þonne he wolde, ær þam þe he cyng wære 7 eac syððan, 7 leton hi þær siððan binnan sittan.[71]

[In this year (1043) Edward was consecrated as king at Winchester on the first day of Easter and in that year, fourteen nights before the Mass of St Andrew, the king was advised to ride from Gloucester, as well as earls Leofric, Godwine and Siward with their retinue, to Winchester in secret to the lady (Emma), and they robbed her of all the riches that she owned, which were uncountable, because she had been very tough on her son the king, in that she did less for him than he wanted her to, before he was king and also afterwards, and they allowed her to remain in there since.]

Although Emma was allowed to return to court in 1044, she, like Eadgifu, spent the last years of her life away from court, dying at Winchester in 1052, in her sixties or early seventies.[72] The fact that it took a king and three prominent earls to deprive Emma of her possessions is testimony to the powerful political position Emma still held in her old age.[73]

Whether they did so willingly or not, most elderly royal widows in the early Middle Ages retired to monastic communities, often founded by themselves on their dower lands.[74] For Anglo-Saxon England, this route appears to have been taken voluntarily by former queens Ælfthryth (d. 999x1001), who retired to a nunnery in Wherwell,[75] Eanflæd (b. 626, d. after 685), who entered the monastery of Strensall-Whitby,[76] and Seaxburh (b. in or before 655, d. c.700), who became abbess of Ely.[77] Life in a monastery presented these elderly royal widows with the opportunity to live out their lives in peace and religious reflection, away from politics.

Some elderly nuns still played their part at court, however, as advisors to kings. For example, it seems the political influence of St Hild (614–680), abbess of Strensall-Whitby and one of the "dominant figures

---

[71] *The Anglo-Saxon Chronicle: A Collaborative Edition. Vol. 6: MS D*, ed. G. P. Cubbin (Cambridge, 1996), s.a. 1043.
[72] Stafford, *Queen Emma*, 253.
[73] H. O'Brien, *Queen Emma and the Vikings: The Woman Who Shaped the Events of 1066* (London, 2005), 208.
[74] Stafford, *Queens, Concubines*, 175–82.
[75] Stafford, 'Ælfthryth'.
[76] Thacker, 'Eanflæd'.
[77] Rollason, 'Seaxburh'.

in the early English Church",[78] peaked in her later years. She hosted the Synod of Whitby (664), an important meeting which decided the future course of the English Church, when she was fifty years old. Furthermore, Bede reports that Hild, despite suffering an illness in the last six years of her life, maintained an active role in ecclesiastical politics until her death.[79] At the age of sixty-four, Hild was still politically involved enough to attempt to get her former pupil Wilfrid expelled from the see of York, albeit unsuccessfully.[80] Hild's successor as abbess of Strensall-Whitby, Ælfflæd (654–714), took part in another matter concerning Wilfrid and was consulted as one of four senior ecclesiastics, alongside three archbishops. Ælfflæd was aged fifty-two at the time and is described by Wilfrid's biographer as "semper totius provinciae consolatrix optimaque consiliatrix" [always the comforter and best counsellor of the whole province].[81] Ælfflæd's words carried weight and, in the words of historian Alan Thacker, she "could make and unmake bishops".[82]

As was the case for Carolingian women, the political influence of Anglo-Saxon women did not necessarily waver with the onset of old age. Royal widows, such as Gytha, Eadgifu and Emma, were still considered political threats in their later years, and elderly abbesses, such as Hild and Ælfflæd, were treasured for their insights and had the ear of kings.

From child bearers to culture bearers: The cultural role of old women

As outlined above, anthropologists have found that old women in non-industrial societies can take on the role of culture bearers: grandmothers involved in rearing grandchildren, religious role models and sources of cultural knowledge. Some of the old women who appear in the Anglo-Saxon cultural record can be described in similar terms, suggesting that in Anglo-Saxon England, too, the role of some old women was that of culture bearer.

---

[78] P. Wormald, 'Hilda, Saint and Scholar (614–680)', in *The Times of Bede: Studies in Early English Christian Society and Its Historian*, ed. S. Baxter (Malden, 2006), 267.

[79] Bede, *HE*, IV.23, describes how Hild was "[p]ercussa etenim febribus acri coepit ardore fatigari" [attacked by a fever which tortured her with its burning heat]. R. Smith, 'Glimpses of Some Anglo-Saxon Women', in *A Wyf Ther Was: Essays in Honour of Paule Mertens-Fonck*, ed. J. Dor (Liège, 1992), 258, has suggested that these fevers may have been "nothing more than the hot flushes of the menopause".

[80] Thacker, 'Hild'.

[81] Stephen of Ripon, *Life of Wilfrid*, ed. and trans. Colgrave, ch. 60.

[82] Thacker, 'Ælfflæd'.

As grandmothers, old women could act as mentors for their grandchildren or could provide them with valuable connections.[83] Ælfthryth, widow to King Edgar (d. 975), was responsible for rearing her grandson Æthelstan (d. 1014), as is evidenced by the latter's will. In this document, Æthelstan declared that everything he had granted to God and the Church was to benefit not only the souls of himself and his father (Æthelred the Unready), but also that of "Ælfþryðe minre ealdemodor þe me afedde" [Ælfthryth my grandmother, who brought me up].[84] Another royal widow, Eadgifu, as noted above, actively participated in the governmental activities of her grandson Edgar.

Two other Anglo-Saxon wills provide further evidence of grandmothers taking an interest in the well-being of their children's children. In her will dated to c.950, the noblewoman Wynflaed left considerable wealth to her grandchildren Eadwold and Eadgifu, such as lands, slaves and "hyre taman hors" [her tame horses].[85] A gift specifically intended for her grandson shows Wynflæd's consideration for his stature and ornamental display: "goldfagan teowena[n] cuppan þæt he ice his beah mid þam golde" [a gold-adorned wooden cup in order that he (Eadwold) may enlarge his armlet with the gold].[86] Likewise, her granddaughter Eadgifu may have had a special place in Wynflæd's heart, as she bequeathed the girl the very best of her linen:

> … hyre betsþe bedwahrift 7 linnenne ruwan 7 eal þæt bedref þe þærto gebyreð 7 [gap in manuscript] hyre betstan dunnan tunecan 7 hyre beteran mentel 7 hyre twa treowenan gesplottude cuppan 7 hyre ealdan gewiredan preon is an VI mancussum.[87]
>
> [… her best bed-curtain and a linen covering and all the bed-clothing which goes with it and … her best dun tunic, and the better of her cloaks, and her two wooden cups ornamented with dots, and her old filigree brooch which is worth six *mancuses*.]

Another example of a gift from a grandmother to her granddaughter is recorded in the will of Wulfric Spott, made between 1002 and 1004. Wulfric gave his goddaughter "ðo[ne] bule þe wæs hire ealdermodor" [the brooch which was her grandmother's].[88] Wynflæd's and Wulfric's bequests are unique among the extant corpus of sixty-eight Anglo-Saxon wills in that they are the only ones to feature bequests by a grandparent to a grandchild.[89]

---

[83] Garver, 'Old Age and Women', 135–6.
[84] *Anglo-Saxon Wills*, ed. and trans. D. Whitelock (Cambridge, 1930), 62, line 9.
[85] *Wills*, ed. and trans. Whitelock, 10–16.
[86] *Wills*, ed. and trans. Whitelock, 12, lines 19–20.
[87] *Wills*, ed. and trans. Whitelock, 14, lines 9–12.
[88] *Wills*, ed. and trans. Whitelock, 50, line 16.
[89] The corpus of sixty-eight Anglo-Saxon wills is provided in L. Tollerton, *Wills and Will-Making in Anglo-Saxon England* (York, 2011), 285–8. J. Crick, 'Women,

Another administrative document demonstrates that, on occasion, a grandmother could even favour her grandchild over her own daughter. A charter made during the episcopate of Archbishop Nothhelm (735–739) relates the details of a case brought before the episcopal court, concerning the bequest of a monastery at Withington by a grandmother, Dunne, to her grandchild Hrothwaru:

> But the aforesaid handmaid of God, Dunne, granted indisputably the monastery which had been built on the aforesaid estate [Withington], with its lands and also the charter descriptive of the land, over which she at that time alone presided, into the possession of her daughter's daughter [Hrothwaru], when herself on the point of death. But because this grand-daughter was still young in age, she entrusted the keeping of the charter of the enrolled land, and also all the charge of the monastery until she should reach a riper age, to the girl's mother, a married woman. When the grand-daughter asked that the charter should be given back, her mother, not wishing to give it back, replied that it had been stolen.[90]

The episcopal court ruled in favour of Hrothwaru and condemned the laywoman who had falsely tried to claim her daughter's inheritance.[91] The charter reveals that Dunne was able to exert control independently over her possessions and could, if she wished, bypass her own daughter in favour of her grandchild. In this case, the rationale behind Dunne's action may have been that she, as a nun, had not approved of her daughter's marriage and that she intended her bequest of the monastery to Hrothwaru as an incentive for the latter to take her vows. At any rate, Hrothwaru followed in the footsteps of her grandmother and entered the monastery, where she later became an abbess.[92] In this way, the case of Dunne and Hrothwaru shows not only a grandmother's interest in the welfare of her granddaughter but also an old woman acting as a religious role model.

By no means was Dunne the only old woman who can be regarded as setting a religious example. Much the same can be said for the ten elderly women in the list above who lived out their days as mother superiors of religious houses. These aged abbesses would by virtue of their position act as exemplars for the younger members of their communities. Although several abbesses in Anglo-Saxon England never reached old age, and senectitude was thus not a prerequisite for the position, there is some circumstantial evidence, in the

---

Posthumous Benefaction, and Family Strategy in Pre-Conquest England', *Journal of British Studies* 38 (1999), 405, has noted that children are rarely mentioned in wills; the same, apparently, applies to grandchildren.

[90] S 1429. *English Historical Documents*, ed. and trans. Whitelock, 454–5.

[91] This case is also discussed by Foot, *Veiled Women*, I, 57; Lees and Overing, *Double Agents*, 68.

[92] S 1255. *English Historical Documents*, ed. and trans. Whitelock, 463–4.

form of two post-Conquest anecdotes, that old age could at least have been regarded as an advantage for the position of abbess. The first anecdote is found in Geoffrey of Burton's *Vita s. Moduenne uirginis*, a twelfth-century saint's life written in England about the seventh-century Irish saint Modwenna who was also venerated in Anglo-Saxon England. Geoffrey reports that Modwenna appointed one of the younger nuns, Orbila, to become the new mother superior of a convent. Orbila, rather than gladly accepting her new role, burst into tears and complained:

> 'Quomodo possum obtemperare his iussis, domina, cum sim iuuencula corpore et imbecillis animo et timeam etati mee et pulcritudini ne, si forte absque te remansero, capiar a turbinibus procellarum et iuuenes seculares propter formositatem corporis et speciem capillorum conentur me furari Deo et abstrahere a proposito sanctitatis.'

> [How can I obey these commands, mistress, since I am young in body and weak in mind? My youth and my beauty make me fearful that if I stay here without you, I shall be snatched up by the whirlwind and, because of the beauty of my body and the loveliness of my hair, young men from the secular world will try to steal me from God and divert me from my holy purpose.][93]

In other words, Orbila argued that a young woman is unfit for the position of abbess. Fortunately, Saint Modwenna had a solution to this problem. When she girded her own belt around the young Orbila's waist, "statimque est caput eius albefactum decora canitie et facies eius inmutata est in aliam effigiem, quasi esset seuere etatis et uenerabilis senectutis" [straightaway the hair of her (Orbila's) head became white and her face changed into that of a grave and venerable old woman].[94] After this miraculous transformation, the newly aged woman now felt fit to serve as an abbess, which she did until the end of her life. Hence, for Orbila at least, old age represented freedom from the social constraints and worldly threats that govern the lives of younger women. The second anecdote suggests that having a young, attractive abbess could indeed prove problematic for a nunnery. In his *De nugis curialium* [Courtiers' Trifles], the twelfth-century author Walter Map describes how the young abbess of a convent in Berkeley, along with several of her sisters, was seduced by the handsome nephew of Earl Godwine (d. 1052). Once the abbess and the other members of the nunnery were visibly pregnant, Godwine reported their wantonness to King Edward the Confessor (d. 1066), who then granted the nunnery and its lands to

---

[93] Geoffrey of Burton, *Life and Miracles of St Modwenna*, ed. and trans. R. Bartlett (Oxford, 2002), ch. 10.
[94] Geoffrey of Burton, *Life of St Modwenna*, ed. and trans. Bartlett, ch. 10.

the earl.⁹⁵ Thus, while not every abbess was old and not every old nun was an abbess, the Anglo-Saxons may have been aware that there were some advantages to having an elderly mother superior, if only because their barrenness would eliminate the risk of forced eviction as a result of pregnancy.

In general, old women appear to have been drawn to an ecclesiastical life; more than three quarters of the women listed above are abbesses, nuns, vowesses or recluses. On the one hand, this is a direct consequence of the nature of the source material for the Anglo-Saxon period, which favours ecclesiastical women over laywomen. On the other hand, some reasons can be brought forward why cloisters were a typical place to find old women. First and foremost, entering a monastery dramatically increased one's chances of reaching old age, as childbirth was one of the main causes of early death. Further, elderly widows in particular choose to enter cloisters: Hild, Seaxburh, Eanflæd and Ælfthryth all retired to nunneries to live out their lives in peace and religious reflection. They may have been inspired to do so by the example of Anna, the biblical prophetess who remained a pious widow until the age of eighty-four. The example of Anna was certainly invoked by various Anglo-Saxon preachers, including Bede.⁹⁶ Archbishop Wulfstan was the most explicit in this and gave the following advice to widows in his *Institutes of Polity*:

> It is right that widows should earnestly follow the example of Anna. She was in the temple day and night diligently serving. She fasted greatly and attended to prayers and called on Christ with mourning spirit, and distributed alms over and again, and ever propitiated God as far as she could by word and deed, and has now heavenly bliss for a reward. So shall a good widow obey her Lord.⁹⁷

Even when married, a woman approaching old age could still decide to retire to a monastery. One telling example is provided by William of Malmesbury, who reports how both parents of Wulfstan of Worcester devoted their life to religious service in old age.⁹⁸ Thus, aside from being a place of religious devotion, a nunnery could also provide a safe environment for a woman in widowhood and old age. Within such convents, elderly women could play exemplary roles.

While a number of Anglo-Saxon old women thus functioned as grandmothers and religious role models, some of them also embod-

---

⁹⁵ Walter Map, *De nugis curialium*, ed. and trans. M. R. James, rev. C. N. L. Brooke and R. A. B. Mynors (Oxford, 1983), V.3.
⁹⁶ Foot, *Veiled Women*, 115, 128–32.
⁹⁷ Wulfstan, *Institutes of Polity*, 18, trans. M. Swanton, *Anglo-Saxon Prose* (London, 1975).
⁹⁸ William of Malmesbury, *Vita s. Wulfstani*, trans. Winterbottom and Thomson, I.2.

ied the third aspect of the anthropological notion of culture bearers; they conveyed cultural knowledge. For one thing, elderly women who functioned as abbesses would also play a role in educating the members of their religious houses. Hild, for example, gained great renown as a teacher and no fewer than five of her students would later become bishops: Bosa (York), Ætla (Dorchester), Oftfor (Worcester), John of Beverley (Hexham and York) and Wilfrid (York).[99] A possible non-monastic example of an elderly woman as a teacher may be traced in the Domesday Book's entry for Oakley, Buckinghamshire. Here, a woman named Ælfgyth is said to have received half a hide of land from "Godric vicecomes" [Godric the sheriff] in exchange for teaching his daughter to embroider with gold.[100] Ælfgyth has been identified as the mother of a man named Godwine Ælfgyth's son, who owned land in Dawley, Middlesex.[101] Therefore, she may at least have reached an age at which her adult son had left his family's home.[102] Chapter 3 already established that the elderly were expected to instruct and teach the young; the examples above show that this notion applied not only to men but also to women.

In addition to teachers, a number of Anglo-Saxon old women occur in the sources as 'remembrancers', people who were called upon to report stories of local history.[103] Some of these women feature prominently in the writings of Goscelin, a Flemish hagiographer who travelled around England from 1058 onwards and earned his living by composing lives of Anglo-Saxon saints.[104] In his *vita* of Edith of Wilton, for instance, Goscelin explains that much of his narrative relies on the testimony of older nuns who had known Edith herself, tapping into a history which stretched back over a hundred years.[105] In other works, too, he reports the stories that were told to him by elderly women, such as Vulfrunna, a nun at Barking, and Ælfwen, an aged recluse at St Stephen's, Hackington.[106] Another elderly recluse

---

[99] Thacker, 'Hild'.
[100] *Domesday Book. Vol. 13: Buckinghamshire*, ed. and trans. J. Morris (Chichester, 1978), 149b.
[101] A. Williams, *The World before Domesday: The English Aristocracy 900–1066* (London, 2008), 206, n. 151.
[102] One possible argument against viewing Ælfgyth as an elderly woman, or even as the mother of Godwine Ælfgyth's son, is the fact that the Domesday Book entry for Oakley, Buckinghamshire, calls her "puella" [a girl] and does not mention any son. Cf. Williams, *World before Domesday*, 120.
[103] The role of women in the memorial tradition of the Middle Ages is discussed by E. van Houts, *Memory and Gender in Medieval Europe 900–1200* (Basingstoke, 1999).
[104] van Houts, *Memory and Gender*, 50–2.
[105] Goscelin, *Vita Edithe*, trans. Wright and Loncar, prol.
[106] See list, above, nos. 25, 29.

named Ælfwen, at St Benet's at Hulme,[107] had been interviewed by a contemporary of Goscelin, the hagiographer Herman, who used her testimony in his *Miracula sancti Eadmundi*.[108] The fact that both Goscelin and Herman mention the age of these women suggests that they may have felt that the age of their sources added to the credibility of their stories.

Apart from knowledge about local history, old women were also called upon for the interpretation of dreams. In his *Vita s. Leoba*, Rudolf describes how both Leoba and her mother Æbba turned to elderly women for explication of their dreams. The latter, having dreamt about bearing a church bell in her bosom, was told by "her old nurse" that the dream announced the birth of her daughter, Leoba.[109] When Leoba herself dreamt that a purple thread issued from her mouth, she too turned to an older woman, albeit hesitantly:

> Now there was in the same monastery an aged nun who was known to possess the spirit of prophecy, because other things that she had foretold had always been fulfilled. As Leoba was diffident about revealing the dream to her, she told it to one of her disciples just as it had occurred and asked her to go to the old nun and describe it to her as a personal experience and learn from her the meaning of it.[110]

The old nun, after angrily noting that the dream was Leoba's and not her disciple's, announced that the purple thread symbolised Leoba's wise counsels. In another saint's life, the *Vita s. Æthelwoldi* by Wulfstan of Winchester, Æthelthryth, "moribus et aetate maturam" [ripe in years and experience], explains to the saint's mother that her dream of a golden eagle leaping forth from her mouth announced the birth of her son.[111] A last anecdote suggests that the association of old women with prophetic dreams may have been typically Anglo-Saxon. In his *Historia ecclesiastica*, Orderic Vitalis (1075–c.1142) reports how the abbot of Gloucester sent a letter to King William Rufus (r. 1087–1100) warning him, on the basis of a dream, to amend his ways. The king replied: "Num prosequi me ritum autumat Anglorum, qui pro sternutatione et somnio uetularum dimittunt iter suum seu negotium?" [Does he (the abbot) think I act after the fashion of the English, who put off their journeys and business on account of the snores and dreams of little old women?].[112]

---

[107] For these and other recluses in Anglo-Saxon England, see T. Licence, 'Evidence of Recluses in Eleventh-Century England', *ASE* 36 (2007), 221–34.
[108] Herman, *Miracula*, ed. Arnold, ch. 8.
[109] Rudolf, *Vita s. Leoba*, trans. Talbot, *Missionaries*, 210.
[110] Rudolf, *Vita s. Leoba*, trans. Talbot, *Missionaries*, 212.
[111] Wulfstan of Winchester, *Life of Æthelwold*, trans. Lapidge and Winterbottom, ch. 2.
[112] Orderic Vitalis, *Historia ecclesiastica*, ed. and trans. M. Chibnall (Oxford, 1975), X.15.

Old Women

In summary, in their roles as grandmothers, abbesses, teachers, remembrancers and explainers of dreams, the old women discussed above share several aspects with the culture bearers described by anthropologists. While some archaeologists have claimed that the value of an Anglo-Saxon woman derived mainly from her ability to bear children, the examples above show that many old women seized opportunities to make valuable cultural contributions to their communities.

Conclusion

The Anglo-Saxon evidence, fragmented, ambiguous and anecdotal though it is, suggests that the transition to old age for women did not necessarily result in a reduced social status, as has been claimed on the basis of archaeological evidence. In the case of royal widows and abbesses, old age frequently involved 'empowerment' and freedom from the social constraints that governed the lives of younger women. Generally, old women still played important roles in the Church, politics and the household; they were culture bearers, individuals charged with the responsibility of teaching the young and respected sources of historical knowledge and dream divination.

Despite the generally optimistic tone of this chapter, I would not go so far as to herald the Anglo-Saxon period as a 'golden age for old women' – there is no way to prove such sweeping statements, although in the past they have been made with regard to both women and the elderly.[113] If not a golden age, the scanty written records do reveal at the very least that for an old woman the Anglo-Saxon period need not have been the worst of times.

---

[113] For a refutation of the claim that Anglo-Saxon England was a golden age for women, see P. Stafford, 'Women and the Norman Conquest', *Transactions of the Royal Historical Society* 4 (1994), 221–8. For claims that the Anglo-Saxon period was a heyday for the elderly, see the introduction to this book.

Conclusion

This book comprises a detailed study of the Anglo-Saxon cultural conceptualisation of old age as manifested and reflected by texts and artwork of the inhabitants of early medieval England. A synthesis of the most noteworthy results of the investigation is provided below. The remainder of the conclusion then proposes some areas for future research.

This book started with the question of how the Anglo-Saxons themselves defined old age in relation to other stages of life. Chapter 1 drew on more than twenty-five different schematisations of the life cycle, most of which had been overlooked in the previous overviews. It appeared that Anglo-Saxon scholars and artists typically broke up the human lifespan into three parts: childhood, middle age and old age. Each element of this underlying tripartite structure allowed for further subdivisions, resulting in schemes of four, five or even six ages of man. Each of these schematisations was connected with concepts from the fields of early Christian learning, such as the Three Magi and the Six Ages of the World, or of natural philosophy, such as the four bodily humours. Significantly, old age was only rarely subdivided, contrary to what has been argued for the early Middle Ages as a whole.[1] Rather than distinguishing between a 'green' and a 'grey' old age, Anglo-Saxon authors generally framed old age as a single phase that started around the age of fifty.

As shown in chapters 2 and 3, Anglo-Saxon poets and homilists approached senescence with mixed feelings. On the one hand, growing old was associated with the accumulation of wisdom and respect; on the other, Anglo-Saxon writings demonstrate an awareness of the social, mental and physical drawbacks of age. The cultural conceptualisation of the merits of senescence is reflected in Old English words such as *frōd*, 'old and wise', the role of elderly narrators as venerable advisors in poems such as *Precepts*, and the homiletic appeal to the old to exhibit clearly their spiritual superiority. This correlation between old age and wisdom, respect and piety, however, was not entirely unambiguous. Anglo-Saxon homilists in particular worried about ungodly elderly and deemed it necessary to remind the aged of their impending death, impelling them to part from their foolish ways if they had not done so already. Thus, old age did not inherently imply wisdom and devout behaviour, nor was respect granted to the elderly solely on account of their years. The idea of an Anglo-Saxon predilection for old age over other age categories, as had been proposed by various scholars, was

---

[1] Cochelin, 'Introduction: Pre-Thirteenth-Century Definitions', 11–14.

Conclusion

further challenged by the analysis of the recurring concerns over the disadvantages of growing old. Horrific descriptions of foul-smelling, aging bodies without teeth and hair clearly illustrate the Anglo-Saxon association of old age with bodily decline. Moreover, the aged often appear as sad and gloomy in the Anglo-Saxon cultural record, as reflected in the image of the mourning old man in wisdom poems, such as *The Wanderer*. Associated with the loss of friends, social standing and bodily aptitude, Anglo-Saxon poets utilised the old man as a metaphor for the transience of earthly pleasures. This metaphor was used to the same effect in the pastoral literature of early medieval England, serving as a reminder that nothing in this terrestrial life is eternal and one's attention should be turned towards Heaven instead. More dramatically, Anglo-Saxon homilists defined senescence as one of the horrors of Hell, whilst presenting Paradise as a place without age. Thus, rather than a preference for old age, the cultural conceptualisation of the downsides of growing old seems to reflect a sense of *gerontophobia*, 'fear of old age'.

The literary representation of, and the cultural roles attributed to, elderly individuals were the central concerns of chapters 4 to 7. Chapters 4 and 5, first of all, established how Anglo-Saxon authors of such divergent genres as hagiography and heroic poetry presented role models for the elderly. The elderly saints identified in chapter 4, for instance, exhibited all the merits of old age, acting as wise and venerable examples to the younger members of their communities. Their declining health, revealed by poor eyesight, inability to walk and tendency to fall asleep, was presented as an obstacle, albeit not an insurmountable one. In fact, Anglo-Saxon hagiographers typically focused on the saint's ability to overcome his decrepitude in order to call attention to his unalleviated asceticism and piety. As such, the saint's behaviour in old age became instead a marker of sanctity and provided a model worthy of emulation. In this respect, these aged saints were no different from the elderly warriors of the heroic poetry described in chapter 5. Like their saintly counterparts, old heroes were depicted as wise and venerable advisors to the younger members in their following and, despite the waning of their bodies, they ideally remained active, leading by example. The old warrior's uncompromising courage, in this sense, has much in common with the elderly saint's unrelenting devotion. Indeed, the words uttered by the old warrior Byrhtwold in *The Battle of Maldon* not only encapsulate the heroic spirit demanded from aged warriors, they are equally applicable to elderly saints: "Hige sceal þe heardra, heorte þe cenre, / mod sceal þe mare, þe ure mægen lytlað" [Spirit must be the harder, heart the bolder, courage must be the greater, as our strength diminishes].[2]

---

[2] *Battle of Maldon*, lines 312–19.

Aged saint and warrior alike inspired an Anglo-Saxon audience to persevere in spite of the disadvantages of old age. If they managed to do so, they often enjoyed a special status, as demonstrated by active elderly clergymen, such as Bishop Wilfrid and Archbishop Dunstan, who were celebrated as saints. Similarly, real-life elderly warriors, such as Ealdorman Byrhtnoth and Earl Siward, were remembered as heroes. For the Anglo-Saxons, then, old people could still be champions, both spiritually and martially. However, elderly individuals did not always meet these ideals and one should be wary to misconstrue the high expectations Anglo-Saxons had of old people as widespread appreciation.

In actual fact, failing to live up to these expectations could pose a real problem for an old person, especially when he was a king, as chapter 6 has shown. In the early Middle Ages, a king's power still depended on his martial prowess and, once declined in old age, aged rulers suffered politically. This problem of old kings was of central concern to the *Beowulf* poet and found its most poignant expression in his characterisation of the aged, passive and disillusioned King Hrothgar. The contrast that the poet draws between Hrothgar and the heroic old King Beowulf, as well as the various references to active, elderly warrior kings of Germanic legend, serve as reminders that an Anglo-Saxon audience would expect an old king to continue to stand up for his ideals, rather than cower passively under his bedding. As such, the poem is best read as a mirror of elderly kings, advocating active kingship, even in old age. Subsequently, I argued that the poem may well have been written at the behest of an aged ruler and a case was made for King Offa of Mercia, an active, old ruler who would have been well aware of the political problems of aged kings.

While chapters 4 to 6 mostly concentrated on Anglo-Saxon views on elderly men, the last chapter was an attempt to analyse the position of old women. Given the almost negligible presence of aged women in the pastoral, hagiographic and heroic literature of the Anglo-Saxons, this chapter turned to a more socio-historical approach in order to evaluate whether or not the transition to old age resulted in a decrease of social status for old women, as had been suggested on the basis of archaeological research. The analysis resulted in the identification of a group of over thirty old women, whose lives and deeds were recorded in chronicles, letters and wills. Most of these old women had managed to make themselves useful to those around them and functioned as respected 'culture bearers' in their roles as grandmother, abbess, witness and explicator of dreams. As long as they proved their worth, it seems, aged women, like their male counterparts, need not have feared being relegated to the margins of their communities.

With respect to the Anglo-Saxon cultural conceptualisation of old age, there are still some opportunities for further research that have

Conclusion

yet to be undertaken. For instance, early medieval English texts on old age might be studied within the broader context of disability studies, as one factor of many that affected a person's capabilities and status. Another viable route for future research is a comparative analysis with contemporary societies, such as early medieval Wales, Ireland and Francia, in order to establish what was truly distinctive about how the Anglo-Saxons conceptualised old age.[3] Such a comparison might also reveal more about how certain cultures may have influenced each other; in this book, I have already highlighted how Anglo-Saxon homilists adopted Hiberno-Latin traditions with regard to the place of old age in the afterlife. Given the range of interactions between early medieval England, the Continent and Ireland, more cultural transfer may have taken place.[4] Aside from comparing the Anglo-Saxons with other contemporary cultures, it will be worthwhile to study how the cultural conceptualisation of old age in medieval England has changed over time. Cultural conceptualisations are not static, but constantly negotiated and renegotiated.[5] Whereas I have found little variation between the earlier and later sources discussed in this book, notable differences do exist with the period after the Norman Conquest of 1066. Middle English, spoken between c.1100 and c.1500, was influenced by Anglo-Norman French and developed and acquired new words to denote the aged, such as *hagge* 'ugly old woman and witch' and *veillar* 'old man, villain'; the literature developed, too, and only later medieval English texts feature such stereotypes as the *senex amans* 'the old lover' (the old man lusting after a young girl) and the old woman as a 'go-between' and expert on sexual matters;[6] the influx of Arabic medical literature in the twelfth century further led to the introduction of new kinds of publications on old age, including the works of the philosopher and Franciscan friar Roger Bacon (c.1214–1292?) which described the physiological process of aging and its remedies.[7]

---

[3] Early Welsh poetry, in particular, features intriguing parallels to Old English material, including the motif of a mourning old narrator. See F. Le Saux, '*Canu Llywarch Hen*: La vieillesse dans les Englynion Gallois', in *Vieillesse et vieillissement au Moyen Âge*, ed. N. Coulet *et al.* (Aix-en-Provence, 1987), 181–98.

[4] See, e.g., *Anglo-Saxon England and the Continent*, ed. H. Sauer and J. Story (Tempe, 2011); Wright, *Irish Tradition*.

[5] Sharifian, *Cultural Conceptualisations*, 3–17.

[6] On the *senex amans*, see Burrow, *Ages of Man*, 135. A fine example of the old woman as a 'go-between' and sexual expert is the titular character of the Middle English poem *Dame Sirith*, see, e.g., Mieszkowski, 'Old Age and Medieval Misogyny', 299–319; for the obscenity of old women in later medieval literature in general, see J. M. Ziolkowski, 'The Obscenities of Old Women, Vetulary and Vernacularity', in *Obscenity, Social Control and Artistic Creation in the European Middle Ages*, ed. J. M. Ziolkowski (Leiden, 1998), 73–89.

[7] Minois, *History of Old Age*, 175–9; J. T. Freeman, 'Medical Perspectives in Aging (12th–19th Century)', *The Gerontologist* 5 (1965), 1–24.

Christine Fell, in a pioneering study, has shown how the Norman Conquest and its aftermath greatly affected the position and image of women in English culture;[8] it is not unlikely, therefore, that ideas about the elderly were similarly affected. Further research could establish whether the Norman Conquest was a watershed moment in the English cultural conceptualisation of old age as well.

With this book, I hope to have offered a balanced analysis of the cultural conceptualisation of old age by the Anglo-Saxons. Whereas prior scholarship had singled out the Anglo-Saxon period as a time when old age enjoyed a particularly positive status, this book demonstrates a more nuanced view that arises from the Anglo-Saxon cultural record. Anglo-Saxon poets and homilists did not only associate old age with wisdom, but also highlighted the disadvantages of longevity in order to demonstrate the futility of loving life on Earth, warn for impending death, or fuel the fear of Hell. Every old person – man or woman; saint, warrior or king – was still expected to meet certain standards of behaviour and, ideally, had to find some way to overcome the physical repercussions of age. On the whole, Anglo-Saxons were aware of the opportunities provided by senescence, but, at the same time, they were afraid of the consequences; they looked up to those elderly people who managed to remain active despite their age, but denounced those who could not. In that respect, the way Anglo-Saxons reflected on old age may not be too different from our own.

---

[8] Fell, *Women in Anglo-Saxon England*.

Bibliography

Primary sources

Ælfric, *Ælfric's Catholic Homilies: The First Series*, ed. P. Clemoes, EETS ss 17 (Oxford, 1997)
——, *Ælfric's Catholic Homilies: The Second Series*, ed. M. Godden, EETS ss 5 (London, 1979)
——, *Ælfrics Grammatik und Glossar*, ed. J. Zupitza (Berlin, 1880)
——, *Die Hirtenbriefe Ælfrics in altenglischer und lateinischer Fassung*, ed. B. Fehr (Hamburg, 1914)
——, *Homilies of Ælfric: A Supplementary Collection*, ed. J. C. Pope, EETS os 259–60 (Oxford, 1967–8)
——, *The Anglo-Saxon Version of the Hexameron of St Basil*, ed. and trans. H. W. Norman (London, 1848)
——, *Two Ælfric Texts: The Twelve Abuses and The Vices and Virtues*, ed. and trans. M. Clayton (Cambridge, 2013)
Æthelwulf, *De Abbatibus*, ed. and trans. A. Campbell (Oxford, 1967)
Alcuin, *Commentarii in s. Joannis evangelium*, PL 100, cols. 733–1008c
——, *Disputatio puerorum per interrogationes et responsiones*, ed. L. E. Felsen, '"Disputatio puerorum": Analysis and Critical Edition', unpublished PhD dissertation, University of Oregon, 2003
——, *Epistolae*, PL 100, cols. 139c–512b
——, *His Life and Letters*, trans. S. Allott (York, 1974)
——, *Propositiones ad acuendos iuvenes*, trans. J. Hadley and D. Singmaster, 'Problems to Sharpen the Young', *The Mathematical Gazette* 76 (1992), 102–26
Aldhelm, *The Poetic Works*, trans. M. Lapidge and J. L. Rosier (Cambridge, 1985)
——, *The Prose Works*, trans. M. Lapidge and M. W. Herren (Cambridge, 1979)
Anlezark, D., ed. and trans., *The Old English Dialogues of Solomon and Saturn* (Cambridge, 2009)
Arngart, O. S., 'The Durham Proverbs', *Speculum* 56 (1982), 288–300
Arnold, T., ed., *Memorials of St Edmund's Abbey. Vol. 1* (London, 1890)
Ashdown, M., ed. and trans., *English and Norse Documents: Relating to the Reign of Ethelred the Unready* (Cambridge, 1930)
Assmann, B., ed., *Angelsächsische Homilien und Heiligenleben* (Kassel, 1889)
Athanasius, *The Life of Saint Anthony*, trans. R. T. Meyer (London, 1950)
Augustine, *De diversis quaestionibus octaginta tribus*, ed. A. Mutzenbecher, CCSL 44 A (Turnhout, 1975)

——, *The City of God against the Pagans*, ed. and trans. R. W. Dyson (Cambridge, 1998)

Barlow, F., ed. and trans., *The Life of King Edward Who Rests at Westminster: Attributed to a Monk of Saint-Bertin*, 2nd ed. (Oxford, 1992)

Bately, J. M., ed., *The Anglo-Saxon Chronicle: A Collaborative Edition. Vol. 3: MS A* (Cambridge, 1986)

Bayless, M., and M. Lapidge, eds and trans., *Collectanea Pseudo-Bedae* (Dublin, 1998)

Bazire, J., and J. E. Cross, eds, *Eleven Old English Rogationtide Homilies* (Toronto, 1982)

Bede, *A Biblical Miscellany*, trans. W. Trent Foley and A. G. Holder (Liverpool, 1999)

——, *Bedas metrische Vita sancti Cuthberti*, ed. W. Jaager (Leipzig, 1935)

——, *Bede's Ecclesiastical History of the English People*, ed. and trans. B. Colgrave and R. A. B. Mynors (Oxford, 1969; rpt. 1992)

——, *De temporibus*, ed. C. W. Jones, *Opera didascalica*, CCSL 123 C (Turnhout, 1980)

——, *De temporum ratione*, ed. C. W. Jones, *Opera didascalica*, CCSL 123 B (Turnhout, 1977); trans. F. Wallis, *Bede: The Reckoning of Time* (Liverpool, 2012)

——, *In Lucam evangelium expositio*, ed. D. Hurst, CCSL 120 (Turnhout, 1960)

——, *In s. Joannis evangelium expositio*, PL 92, 633–938a

——, *On Genesis*, trans. C. B. Kendall (Liverpool, 2008)

——, *The Ecclesiastical History of the English People, The Greater Chronicle, Bede's Letter to Egbert*, ed. and trans. J. McClure and R. Collins (Oxford, 1994)

Bjork, R. E., ed. and trans., *Old English Shorter Poems. Volume II: Wisdom and Lyric*, DOML 32 (Cambridge, MA, 2014)

Blair, J., 'Saint Cuthman, Steyning and Bosham', *Sussex Archaeological Collections* 135 (1997), 173–92

Blake, N. F., ed., *The Phoenix* (Exeter, 1990)

——, trans., *The Saga of the Jomsvikings* (London, 1962)

Bradley, S. A. J., ed. and trans., *Anglo-Saxon Poetry* (London, 1982)

Broszinski, H., ed. and trans., *Hildebrandlied*, 3rd ed. (Kassel, 2004)

Buma, W. J., and W. Ebel, eds, *Das Fivelgoer Recht* (Göttingen, 1972)

Buma, W. J., P. Gerbenzon and M. Tragter-Schubert, eds, *Codex Aysma, die altfriesischen Texte* (Assen, 1993)

Byrhtferth, *Byrhtferth's Enchiridion*, ed. and trans. P. S. Baker and M. Lapidge, EETS ss 15 (London, 1995)

——, *De concordia mensium atque elementorum. On the Concord of the Months and the Elements. Also Known as his Diagram of the Physical and Physiological Fours*, ed. P. S. Baker, http://web.archive.org/web/19961025235309/http://www.engl.virginia.edu/OE/Editions/Decon.pdf

Bibliography

——, *The Lives of St Oswald and St Ecgwine*, ed. and trans. M. Lapidge (Oxford, 2009)

Caie, G. D., ed. and trans., *The Old English Poem Judgement Day II* (Cambridge, 2000)

Campbell, A., ed., *The Battle of Brunanburh* (London, 1938)

Carnicelli, T. A., ed., *King Alfred's Version of St Augustine's Soliloquies* (Cambridge, MA, 1969)

Chickering, H. D., Jr, ed. and trans., *Beowulf: A Dual-Language Edition* (New York, 1977)

Clayton, M., ed. and trans., *The Apocryphal Gospels of Mary in Anglo-Saxon England* (Cambridge, 1998)

Cockayne, T. O., ed., *Leechdoms, Wortcunning and Starcraft of Early England* (London, 1864–6)

Colgrave, B., ed. and trans., *Two Lives of Saint Cuthbert* (Cambridge, 1985)

Columbanus, *Sancti Columbani opera*, ed. G. S. M. Walker (Dublin, 1957)

Cox, R. S., 'The Old English Dicts of Cato', *Anglia* 90 (1972), 1–42

Crawford, S. J., ed., *The Old English Version of the Heptateuch*, EETS os 160 (London, 1922)

Cubbin, G. P., ed., *The Anglo-Saxon Chronicle: A Collaborative Edition. Vol. 6: MS D* (Cambridge, 1996)

Cynewulf, *Elene*, ed. P. O. A. Gradon (New York, 1966)

Doane, A. N., ed., *Genesis A: A New Edition, Revised* (Tempe, 2013)

——, ed., *The Saxon Genesis: An Edition of the West Saxon Genesis B and the Old Saxon Vatican Genesis* (Madison, 1991)

Dobbie, E. v. K., ed., *The Anglo-Saxon Minor Poems*, ASPR 6 (New York, 1942)

Dodwell, C. R. and P. Clemoes, eds, *The Old English Illustrated Hexateuch: British Museum Cotton Claudius B. iv*, Early English Manuscripts in Facsimile 18 (Copenhagen, 1974)

Eadmer of Canterbury, *Lives and Miracles of Saints Oda, Dunstan, and Oswald*, ed. and trans. A. J. Turner and B. J. Muir (Oxford, 2006)

Eastman, D. L., ed. and trans., *The Ancient Martyrdom Accounts of Peter and Paul* (Atlanta, 2015)

Emerton, E., trans., *The Letters of Saint Boniface* (New York, 1940)

Fairweather, J., trans., *Liber Eliensis* (Woodbridge, 2005)

Faricius, *Vita s. Aldhelmi*, ed. M. Winterbottom, 'An Edition of Faricius, Vita s. Aldhelmi', *Journal of Medieval Latin* 15 (2005), 93–147

Felix, *Life of Saint Guthlac*, ed. and trans. B. Colgrave (Cambridge, 1956)

Finch, R. G., ed. and trans., *The Saga of the Volsungs* (London, 1965)

Förster, M., 'A New Version of the Apocalypse of Thomas in Old English', *Anglia* 73 (1955), 6–36

——, 'Die altenglischen Beigaben des Lambeth-Psalters', *Archiv* 132 (1914), 328–35

Fowler, R., 'A Late Old English Handbook for the Use of a Confessor', *Anglia* 83 (1965), 1–34

Fulk, R. D., ed. and trans., *The Beowulf Manuscript. Complete Texts and The Fight at Finnsburg*, DOML 3 (Cambridge, MA, 2010)

——, R. E. Bjork and J. D. Niles, eds, *Klaeber's Beowulf*, 4th ed. (Toronto, 2008)

Garmonsway, G. N., and J. Simpson, ed. and trans., *Beowulf and Its Analogues* (London, 1980)

Geoffrey of Burton, *Life and Miracles of St Modwenna*, ed. and trans. R. Bartlett (Oxford, 2002)

Godman, P., ed. and trans., *Poetry of the Carolingian Renaissance* (London, 1985)

Gonser, P., ed., *Das angelsächsische Prosa-Leben des heiligen Guthlac* (Heidelberg, 1909)

Gordon, E. V., ed., *The Battle of Maldon*, with a supplement by D. G. Scragg (Manchester, 1976)

Goscelin, *Historia translationis s. Augustini*, PL 155, cols. 13–46d

——, *Translatio s. Mildrethe*, ed. D. W. Rollason, 'Goscelin of Canterbury's Account of the Translation and Miracles of St Mildrith (*BHL* 5961/4): An Edition with Notes', *Mediaeval Studies* 48 (1986), 139–211

——, *Vita et virtutes sanctae Vulfildae virginis*, ed. M. L. Colker, 'Texts of Jocelyn of Canterbury which Relate to the History of Barking Abbey', *Studia Monastica* 7 (1965), 383–460

Gregory, *Dialogues*, ed. A. de Vogüé (Paris, 1978–80)

——, *Homiliae in evangelia*, ed. R. Étaix, CCSL 141 (Turnhout, 1999); trans. D. Hurst, *Gregory the Great: Forty Gospel Homilies* (Kalamazoo, 1990)

Grocock, C. W., and I. N. Wood, eds and trans., *Abbots of Wearmouth and Jarrow* (Oxford, 2013)

Haymo, *Homiliae aliquot de sanctis*, PL 118, cols. 747–804b

——, *Homiliae de tempore*, PL 118, cols. 11–746

Hecht, H., *Bischof Wærferths von Worcester Übersetzung der Dialoge Gregors des Grossen über das Leben und die Wundertaten italienischer Väter und über die Unsterblichkeit der Seelen* (Leipzig, 1900–7; rpt. Darmstadt, 1965)

Henry of Huntingdon, *Historia Anglorum*, ed. and trans. D. E. Greenway (Oxford, 1996)

Hollis, S., ed., *Writing the Wilton Women: Goscelin's Legend of Edith and Liber confortatorius* (Turnhout, 2004)

Irvine, S., ed., *Old English Homilies from MS Bodley 343*, EETS os 302 (Oxford, 1993)

Irving, E. B., Jr, ed., *Exodus* (New Haven, 1953)

Isidore, *Differentiae*, PL 83, cols. 9–98

——, *Isidore of Seville's Etymologies*, trans. P. Throop (Charlotte, 2013)

Bibliography

——, *Isidore of Seville's Synonyms and Differences*, trans. P. Throop (Charlotte, 2012)
——, *Isidorus Hispalensis: Etymologiae XI*, ed. F. Gasti (Paris, 2010)
Jerome, *Epistolae*, PL 22, cols. 325–1224
Keynes, S., and M. Lapidge, trans., *Alfred the Great: Asser's Life of King Alfred and Other Contemporary Sources* (Harmondsworth, 1983)
Klinck, A. L., ed., *The Old English Elegies: A Critical Edition and Genre Study* (Montreal, 1992)
Knight, S., and T. H. Olgren, eds, *Robin Hood and Other Outlaw Tales* (Kalamazoo, 2000)
Krapp, G. P., ed., *The Vercelli Book*, ASPR 2 (New York, 1932)
——, and E. v. K. Dobbie, eds, *The Exeter Book*, ASPR 3 (New York, 1936)
Kuypers, A. B., ed., *The Prayer Book of Aedeluald the Bishop, Commonly Called the Book of Cerne* (Cambridge, 1902)
Langefeld, B., ed. and trans., *The Old English Version of the Enlarged Rule of Chrodegang*, (Frankfurt am Main, 2003)
Lapidge, M., ed. and trans., *The Cult of St Swithun* (Oxford, 2003)
Lindelöf, U. L., ed., *Rituale ecclesiae Dunelmensis: The Durham Collectar* (Durham, 1927)
Logeman, H., 'Anglo-Saxonica Minora, I', *Anglia* 11 (1889), 97–120
Love, R. C., ed. and trans., *Three Eleventh-Century Anglo-Latin Saints' Lives* (Oxford, 1996)
Lucas, P. J., ed., *Exodus* (London, 1977)
Macray, W. D., ed., *Chronicon abbatiae Rameseiensis* (London, 1886)
Magennis, H., ed. and trans., *The Old English Life of St Mary of Egypt* (Exeter, 2002)
Malone, K., ed., *Widsith* (Copenhagen, 1962)
Miller, T. A., ed., *The Old English Version of Bede's Ecclesiastical History of the English People*, EETS os 95, 96, 110 and 111 (London, 1890–8)
Morris, J., ed. and trans., *Domesday Book. Vol. 13: Buckinghamshire* (Chichester, 1978)
Morris, R., ed., *The Blickling Homilies of the Tenth Century*, EETS os 58, 63, 73 (London, 1874–80)
Napier, A. S., 'Altenglische Kleinigkeiten', *Anglia* 11 (1889), 1–10
——, ed., *Wulfstan; Sammlung der ihm zugeschriebenen Homilien nebst Untersuchungen über ihre Echtheit* (Berlin, 1883)
O'Brien O'Keeffe, K., *Manuscripts Containing the Anglo-Saxon Chronicle, Works by Bede, and Other Texts*. Anglo-Saxon Manuscripts in Microfiche Facsimile 10 (Tempe, 2003)
——, ed., *The Anglo-Saxon Chronicle: A Collaborative Edition. Vol. 5: MS C* (Cambridge, 2001)
Orchard, A., *Pride and Prodigies: Studies in the Monsters of the Beowulf-Manuscript* (Cambridge, 1995)

Orderic Vitalis, *Historia ecclesiastica*, ed. and trans. M. Chibnall (Oxford, 1975)
Óskarsdóttir, Svanhildur, ed., *Egil's Saga*, trans. B. Scudder (London, 2004)
Ovid, *Amores*, ed. E. J. Kenney, 2nd ed. (Oxford, 1994)
Prudentius, *Psychomachia*, ed. and trans. H. J. Thomson (Cambridge, MA, 2015)
Pseudo-Basil, *De admonitio ad filium spiritualem*, ed. P. Lehmann (Munich, 1955); trans. J. F. LePree, 'Pseudo-Basil's *De admonitio ad filium spiritualem*: A New English Translation', *HA* 13 (2010)
Pseudo-Cyprian, *De duodecim abusiuis*, ed. S. Hellmann, *Texte under Untersuchungen zur Geschichte der altchristlichen Literatur*, Reihe 3, Band 4, Heft 1 (Leipzig, 1909); trans. P. Throop, *Vincent of Beauvais, The Moral Instruction of a Prince, and Pseudo-Cyprian, The Twelve Abuses of the World* (Charlotte, 2011)
Pulsiano, P., ed., 'The Old English Life of St Pantaleon', in *Via crucis: Essays on Early Medieval Sources and Ideas in Memory of J. E. Cross*, ed. T. N. Hall, T. D. Hill and C. D. Wright (Morgantown, 2002), 61–103
Rau, R., ed., *Bonifatii epistulae. Willibaldi vita Bonifatii* (Darmstadt, 1968)
Rauer, C., ed. and trans., *The Old English Martyrology* (Cambridge, 2013)
Ritter-Schaumburg, H., ed., *Die Thidrekssaga oder Dietrich von Bern und die Niflungen*, trans. F. H. von der Hagen (St Goar, 1989)
Robinson, F. C., 'The Rewards of Piety: "Two" Old English Poems in Their Manuscript Context', in *The Editing of Old English*, ed. F. C. Robinson (Oxford, 1994), 180–95
——, 'The Rewards of Piety: Two Old English Poems in Their Manuscript Context', in *Hermeneutics and Medieval Culture*, ed. P. J. Gallacher and H. Damico (New York, 1989), 193–200
Roeder, F., ed., *Der altenglische Regius-Psalter. Eine Interlinearversion in Hs. Royal 2. B. 5 des brit. Mus.* (Halle, 1904)
Rose, V., ed., *Theodori Prisciani Euporiston libri III* (Leipzig, 1894)
Rosier, J. L., '*Instructions for Christians*: A Poem in Old English', *Anglia* 82 (1964), 4–22
Sauer, H., ed., *Theodulfi Capitula in England. Die altenglischen Übersetzungen, zusammen mit dem lateinischen Text* (Munich, 1978)
Saxo Grammaticus, *History of the Danes*, ed. H. Ellis Davidson, trans. P. Fisher (Cambridge, 1979)
Schröer, A., ed., *Die angelsächsischen Prosabearbeitungen der Benediktinerregel* (Kassel, 1885)
Scragg, D. G., ed. and trans., 'The Battle of Maldon', in *Battle of Maldon*, ed. Scragg, 1–36
——, ed., *The Vercelli Homilies and Related Texts*, EETS os 300 (London, 1992)
Shippey, T. A., ed. and trans., *Poems of Wisdom and Learning in Old English* (Cambridge, 1976)

Skeat, W. W., ed., *Ælfric's Lives of Saints*, EETS os 76, 82, 94, 114 (London, 1881–1900)
Snorri Sturluson, *Edda*, ed. and trans. A. Faulkes (London, 1987)
——, *Heimskringla*, trans. A. Finlay and A. Faulkes (London, 2011)
Stephen of Ripon, *The Life of Bishop Wilfrid*, ed. and trans. B. Colgrave (Cambridge, 1927)
Stettiner, R., ed., *Die illustrierten Prudentiushandschriften* (Berlin, 1895–1905)
Sulpicius Severus, *Vita s. Martini*, ed. K. Smolak (Eisenstadt, 1997)
Swanton, M., trans., *Anglo-Saxon Prose* (London, 1975)
——, ed. and trans., *Beowulf* (Manchester, 1978)
——, ed. and trans., *The Anglo-Saxon Chronicles*, rev. ed. (London, 2000)
——, ed. and trans., *The Lives of Two Offas* (Crediton, 2010)
Tacitus, *Germania*, ed. and trans. H. W. Benario (Warminster, 1999)
Talbot, C. H., trans., *The Anglo-Saxon Missionaries in Germany* (London, 1954)
Thorpe, B., ed., *Ancient Laws and Institutes of England* (London, 1840)
Treharne, E. M., ed. and trans., *Old English Life of St Nicholas with the Old English Life of St Giles* (Leeds, 1997)
Twain, M., *The Science Fiction of Mark Twain*, ed. D. Ketterer (Hamden, 1984)
Van Caenegem, R. C., ed. and trans., *English Lawsuits from William I to Richard I. Volume I: William I to Stephen* (London, 1990)
Walter Map, *De nugis curialium*, ed. and trans. M. R. James, rev. C. N. L. Brooke and R. A. B. Mynors (Oxford, 1983)
Whitelock, D., ed. and trans., *Anglo-Saxon Wills* (Cambridge, 1930)
——, ed. and trans., *English Historical Documents. Volume 1: c. 500–1042* (London, 1955)
William of Malmesbury, *Gesta pontificum Anglorum*, ed. and trans. M. Winterbottom (Oxford, 2007)
——, *Gesta regum Anglorum*, ed. and trans. R. A. B. Mynors, R. M. Thomson and M. Winterbottom (Oxford, 1998–9)
——, *Saints' Lives. Lives of ss. Wulfstan, Dunstan, Patrick, Benignus and Indract*, ed. and trans. M. Winterbottom and R. M. Thomson (Oxford, 2002)
Wilson, D. M., *The Bayeux Tapestry: The Complete Tapestry in Colour* (London, 1985)
Winterbottom, M., and M. Lapidge, eds and trans., *The Early Lives of St Dunstan* (Oxford, 2012)
Wrenn, C. L., *Beowulf with the Finnesburg Fragment*, 2nd rev. ed. (London, 1958)
Wulfstan of Winchester, *The Life of St Æthelwold*, ed. and trans. M. Lapidge and M. Winterbottom (Oxford, 1991)
Wulfstan, *Canons of Edgar*, ed. R. Fowler, EETS os 266 (London, 1972)
——, *The Homilies of Wulfstan*, ed. D. Bethurum (Oxford, 1957)

Bibliography

——, *Wulfstan's Eschatological Homilies*, ed. and trans. J. T. Lionarons (2000), http://webpages.ursinus.edu/jlionarons/wulfstan/Wulfstan.html

Yerkes, D., ed., *The Old English Life of Machutus* (Toronto, 1984)

Secondary sources

Abels, R., 'Army', in *Blackwell Encyclopaedia*, ed. Lapidge *et al.*, 47–8

——, 'Byrhtnoth (d. 991)', *ODNB*

——, 'What Has Weland To Do with Christ? The Franks Casket and the Acculturation of Christianity in Anglo-Saxon England', *Speculum* 84 (2009), 549–81

——, *Lordship and Military Obligation in Anglo-Saxon England* (London, 1988)

Achenbaum, W. A., 'Foreword: Literature's Value in Gerontological Research', in *Perceptions of Aging*, ed. von Dorotka Bagnell and Soper, xiii–xxii

Alexander, J. J. G., *Insular Manuscripts, 6th to the 9th Century* (London, 1978)

Amos, A. C., 'Old English Words for Old', in *Aging and the Aged*, ed. Sheehan, 95–106

Anderson, E. R., *Cynewulf: Structure, Style, and Theme in His Poetry* (London, 1983)

——, *Understanding* Beowulf *as an Indo-European Epic: A Study in Comparative Mythology* (Lewiston, 2010)

Anderson, S. M., 'Old Age', in *Handbook of Medieval Culture*, ed. A. Classen (Berlin, 2015), 1281–1323

Atherton, M., 'Mentions of Offa in *The Anglo-Saxon Chronicle*, *Beowulf* and *Widsith*', in *Æthelbald and Offa*, ed. Hill and Worthington, 65–74

Baker, P. S., *Honour, Exchange and Violence in* Beowulf (Cambridge, 2013)

——, ed., *The* Beowulf *Reader* (New York, 2000)

Bar-Itzhak, H., 'Old Jewish Moroccan Women Relate in an Israeli Context', in her *Israeli Folk Narratives: Settlement, Immigration, Ethnicity* (Detroit, 2005), 97–152

Barlow, F., *Edward the Confessor* (London, 1970)

Barnhouse, R., and B. C. Withers, 'Introduction: Aspects and Approaches', in *The Old English Hexateuch: Aspects and Approaches*, ed. R. Barnhouse and B. C. Withers (Kalamazoo, 2000), 1–13

Bately, J. M., 'The Anglo-Saxon Chronicle', in *Battle of Maldon*, ed. Scragg, 37–50

Bazelmans, J., *By Weapons Made Worthy: Lords, Retainers and Their Relationship in* Beowulf (Amsterdam, 1999)

Beckwith, J., *The Adoration of the Magi in Whalebone* (London, 1966)

Bernstein, D. J., *The Mystery of the Bayeux Tapestry* (London, 1986)

Berschin, W., *Biographie und Epochenstil im lateinischen Mittelalter* (Stuttgart, 1991)

Bibliotheca Hagiographica Latina, ed. Bollandists, 2 vols (Brussels, 1899–1901)

Biggam, C. P., *Grey in Old English: An Interdisciplinary Semantic Study* (London, 1998)

Biggs, F. M., '*Beowulf* and Some Fictions of the Geatish Succession', *ASE* 32 (2003), 55–77

——, 'The Politics of Succession in *Beowulf* and Anglo-Saxon England', *Speculum* 80 (2005), 709–41

——, T. D. Hill and P. E. Szarmach, eds, *Sources of Anglo-Saxon Literary Culture: A Trial Version* (Binghamton, 1990)

Bjork, R. E., ed., *The Cynewulf Reader* (New York, 2001)

Blair, J., 'A Handlist of Anglo-Saxon Saints', in *Local Saints*, ed. Thacker and Sharpe, 495–566

Bloomfield, M. W., 'Understanding Old English Poetry', *Annuale mediaevale* 9 (1968), 5–25, repr. in *Essays and Explorations: Studies in Ideas, Language and Literature* (Cambridge, MA, 1970), 59–82

——, and C. W. Dunn, *The Role of the Poet in Early Societies* (Cambridge, 1989)

Boll, F., 'Die Lebensalter. Ein Beitrag zur antiken Ethologie und zur Geschichte der Zahlen', in *Kleine Schriften zur Sternkunde des Altertums*, ed. V. Stegemann (Leipzig, 1950), 156–225

Bonjour, A., *The Digressions in* Beowulf (Oxford, 1950)

Bouwer, H., *Studien zum Wortfeld um eald und niwe im Altenglischen* (Heidelberg, 2004)

Boyer, R., 'An Attempt To Define the Typology of Medieval Hagiography', in *Hagiography and Medieval Literature: A Symposium*, ed. H. Bekker-Nielsen, P. Foote, J. Hojgaard Jorgensen and T. Nyberg (Odense, 1981), 27–36

Brandt, H., *Wird auch silbern mein Haar: Eine Geschichte des Alters in der Antike* (Munich, 2002)

Breeze, A., '*Exodus, Elene*, and the *Rune Poem*: milpæþ "Army Road, Highway"', *NQ* ns 38 (1991), 436–8

Bremmer, R. H., Jr, *An Introduction to Old Frisian* (Amsterdam, 2011)

——, 'Across Borders: Anglo-Saxon England and the Germanic World', in *The Cambridge History of Early Medieval English Literature*, ed. C. A. Lees (Cambridge, 2013), 185–208

——, 'Leiden, Universiteitsbibliotheek, Vossianus Latinus Q. 69 (Part 2): Schoolbook or Proto-Encyclopaedic Miscellany?', in *Practice in Learning: The Transfer of Encyclopaedic Knowledge in the Early Middle Ages*, ed. R. H. Bremmer Jr and K. Dekker (Paris, 2010), 19–54

——, 'Old English Heroic Literature', in *Readings in Medieval Literature. Interpreting Old and Middle English Literature*, ed. D. F. Johnson and E. M. Treharne (Oxford, 2006), 75–90

——, 'The Germanic Context of Cynewulf and Cyneheard Revisited', *Neophilologus* 81 (1997), 445–65
——, 'The Importance of Kinship: Uncle and Nephew in *Beowulf*', *Amsterdamer Beiträge zur Älteren Germanistik* 15 (1980), 21–38
——, 'Widows in Anglo-Saxon England', in *Between Poverty and the Pyre: Moments in the History of Widowhood*, ed. J. Bremmer and L. van den Bosch (London, 1995), 58–88
Brodeur, A. G., 'The Structure and the Unity of Beowulf', *PMLA* 68 (1953)
Brooks, N., 'The Social and Political Background', in *Cambridge Companion*, ed. Godden and Lapidge, 1–18
Brooks, N. P., and H. E. Walker, 'The Authority and Interpretation of the Bayeux Tapestry', *Anglo-Norman Studies* 1 (1978), 1–35
Brown, M. P., *The Book of Cerne: Prayer, Patronage and Power in Ninth-Century England* (London, 1996)
Bruce, A. M., 'An Education in the Mead-Hall', *HA* 5 (2001)
Budny, M., 'The Byrhtnoth Tapestry or Embroidery', in *Battle of Maldon*, ed. Scragg, 262–78
Burrow, J. A., *The Ages of Man: A Study in Medieval Writing and Thought* (Oxford, 1986)
Caie, G. D., 'Codicological Clues: Reading Old English Christian Poetry in Its Manuscript Context', in *The Christian Tradition in Anglo-Saxon England*, ed. P. Cavill (Cambridge, 2004), 3–14
Cameron, M. L., *Anglo-Saxon Medicine* (Cambridge, 1993)
Campbell, J. J., 'Knowledge of Rhetorical Figures in Anglo-Saxon England', *JEGP* 66 (1967), 1–20
Carp, T. C., '*Puer senex* in Roman and Medieval Thought', *Latomus* 39 (1980), 736–9
Carruthers, L. M., ed., *Heroes and Heroines in Medieval English Literature: A Festschrift Presented to André Crépin on the Occasion of His Sixty-Fifth Birthday* (Cambridge, 1994)
——, 'Kingship and Heroism in *Beowulf*', in *Heroes and Heroines*, ed. Carruthers, 19–29
Cave, C., and M. Oxenham, 'Identification of the Archaeological "Invisible Elderly": An Approach Illustrated with an Anglo-Saxon Example', *International Journal of Osteoarchaeology* 26 (2016), 163–75
——, 'Sex and the Elderly: Attitudes to Long-Lived Women and Men in Early Anglo-Saxon England', *Journal of Anthropological Archaeology* 48 (2017), 207–16
Cavill, P., 'Maxims in *The Battle of Maldon*', *Neophilologus* 82 (1988), 631–44
——, *Maxims in Old English Poetry* (Cambridge, 1999)
Cayton, H., 'Some Contributions from the Written Sources', in *East Anglian Archaeology Report No. 9: North Elmham. Vol. 2*, ed. P. Wade-Martins (Gressenhall, 1980), 303–14

Chadwick Hawkes, S., ed., *Weapons and Warfare in Anglo-Saxon England* (Oxford, 1989)
Chase, C., 'Opinions on the Date of *Beowulf*, 1815–1980', in *The Dating of Beowulf*, ed. C. Chase (Toronto, 1981), 3–8
Chojnacka, M., and M. E. Wiesner-Hanks, eds, *Ages of Woman, Ages of Man: Sources in European Social History, 1400–1750* (London, 2002)
Clark, G., 'The Hero of Maldon: *Vir pius et strenuus*', *Speculum* 54 (1979), 257–82
Clarke, H. B., 'The Identity of the Designer of the Bayeux Tapestry', *Anglo-Norman Studies* 35 (2013), 119–40
Classen, A., 'Old Age in the Middle Ages and the Renaissance: Also an Introduction', in *Old Age in the Middle Ages*, ed. Classen, 1–84
——, ed., *Old Age in the Middle Ages and the Renaissance: Interdisciplinary Approaches to a Neglected Topic* (Berlin, 2007)
Clayton, M., '*De Duodecim Abusiuis*, Lordship and Kingship in Anglo-Saxon England', in *Saints and Scholars. New Perspectives on Anglo-Saxon Literature and Culture in Honour of Hugh Magennis*, ed. S. McWilliams (Cambridge, 2012), 153–63
——, 'Of Mice and Men: Ælfric's Second Homily for the Feast of a Confessor', *Leeds Studies in English* ns 24 (1993), 1–26
Clemoes, P., *Interactions of Thought and Language in Old English Poetry* (Cambridge, 1995)
Clover, C. J., 'Regardless of Sex: Men, Women and Power in Early Northern Europe', *Speculum* 68 (1993), 363–87
Coatsworth, E., 'Byrhtnoth's Tomb', in *Battle of Maldon*, ed. Scragg, 279–88
Cochelin, I., '*In senectute bona*: pour une typologie de la vieillesse dans l'hagiographie monastique des XIIe et XIIIe siècles', in *Les âges de la vie au Moyen âge: actes du colloque du Département d'études médiévales de l'Université de Paris-Sorbonne et de l'Université Friedrich-Wilhelm de Bonn*, ed. H. Dubois and M. Zink (Paris, 1992), 119–38
——, 'Introduction: Pre-Thirteenth-Century Definitions of the Life Cycle', in *Medieval Life Cycles*, ed. Cochelin and Smyth, 1–54
——, and K. E. Smyth, eds, *Medieval Life Cycles: Continuity and Change* (Turnhout, 2013)
Coffman, G. R., 'Old Age from Horace to Chaucer. Some Literary Affinities and Adventures of an Idea', *Speculum* 9 (1934), 249–77
Conner, P. W., 'On Dating Cynewulf', in *Cynewulf Reader*, ed. Bjork, 23–56
Conrad, C., and H.-J. von Kondratowitz, eds, *Zur Kulturgeschichte des Alterns. Toward a Cultural History of Aging* (Berlin, 1993)
Cooke, W., 'Hrothulf: A Richard III, or an Alfred the Great?', *SiP* 104 (2007), 175–98
——, 'Who Cursed Whom, and When? The Cursing of the Hoard and Beowulf's Fate', *Medium Ævum* 76 (2007), 207–24

Covey, H. C., *Images of Older People in Western Art and Society* (New York, 1991)
——, 'Old Age Portrayed by the Ages-of-Life Models from the Middle Ages to the 16th Century', *The Gerontologist* 29 (1989), 692–8
Craig, D. J., 'Oswiu (611/12–670)', *ODNB*
Crawford, S., *Childhood in Anglo-Saxon England* (Stroud, 1999)
——, '*Gomol is snoterost*: Growing Old in Anglo-Saxon England', in *Collectanea Antiqua: Essays in Memory of Sonia Chadwick Hawkes*, ed. M. Henig and T. J. Smith (Oxford, 2007), 53–9
Crick, J., 'Men, Women and Widows: Widowhood in Pre-Conquest England', in *Widowhood in Medieval and Early Modern Europe*, ed. S. Cavallo and L. Warner (Harlow, 1999), 24–36
——, 'Women, Posthumous Benefaction, and Family Strategy in Pre-Conquest England', *Journal of British Studies* 38 (1999), 399–422
Croon, J. H., ed., *De lastige ouderdom: De senex in de literatuur* (Muiderberg, 1981)
Cross, J. E., *The Literate Anglo-Saxon – On Sources and Disseminations* (London, 1972)
Cubitt, C., 'Memory and Narrative in the Cult of Early Anglo-Saxon Saints', in *The Uses of the Past in the Early Middle Ages*, ed. Y. Hen and M. Innes (Cambridge, 2000), 29–66
——, 'Universal and Local Saints in Anglo-Saxon England', in *Local Saints*, ed. Thacker and Sharpe, 423–53
Dales, D., *Alcuin: His Life and Legacy* (Cambridge, 2012)
Daunt, M., 'Minor Realism and Contrast in *Beowulf*', in *Mélanges de linguistique et de philologie. Fernand Mossé in memoriam* (Paris, 1959), 87–94
Davies, A., 'Witches in Anglo-Saxon England: Five Case Histories', in *Superstition*, ed. Scragg, 41–56
De Bonis, G. D., 'The Birth of Saint John the Baptist: A Source Comparison between Blickling Homily XIV and Ælfric's Catholic Homily I.xxv', in *Hagiography in Anglo-Saxon England: Adopting and Adapting Saints' Lives into Old English Prose (c.950–1150)*, ed. L. Lazzari, P. Lendinara and C. Di Sciacca (Barcelona, 2014), 255–91
De Looze, L. N., 'Frame Narratives and Fictionalization: Beowulf as Narrator', *Texas Studies in Literature and Language* 26 (1984), 145–56
DeGregorio, S., 'Theorizing Irony in *Beowulf*: The Case of Hrothgar', *Exemplaria* 11 (1999), 309–43
Dekker, K., 'Anglo-Saxon Encyclopaedic Notes: Tradition and Function', in *Foundations of Learning: The Transfer of Encyclopaedic Knowledge in the Early Middle Ages*, ed. R. H. Bremmer Jr and K. Dekker (Paris, 2007), 279–315
——, 'The Organisation and Structure of Old English Encyclopaedic Notes', *Filologia Germanica – Germanic Philology* 5 (2013), 95–130

Di Sciacca, C., *Finding the Right Words: Isidore's Synonyma in Anglo-Saxon England* (Toronto, 2008)

Dickerson-Putman, J., 'Old Women at the Top: An Exploration of Age Stratification among Bena Bena Women', *Journal of Cross-Cultural Gerontology* 9 (1994), 193–205

Dictionary of Old English: A to H online, ed. A. Cameron, A. C. Amos, A. diPaolo Healey et al. (Toronto, 2016), http://www.doe.utoronto.ca/index.html

Dinkelacker, W., 'Der alte Held. Belege aus mittelalterlicher Heldendichtung und ihr kulturhistorischer Quellenwert', in *Alterskulturen des Mittelalters und der frühen Neuzeit*, ed. E. Vavra (Vienna, 2008), 183–202

Dorotka Bagnell, P. von, and P. S. Soper, eds, *Perceptions of Aging in Literature: A Cross-Cultural Study* (New York, 1989)

Dove, M., *The Perfect Age of Man's Life* (Cambridge, 1986)

Drijvers, J. W., *Helena Augusta: The Mother of Constantine the Great and the Legend of Her Finding of the True Cross* (Leiden, 1992)

Drout, M. D. C., 'Possible Instructional Effects of the Exeter Book "Wisdom Poems": A Benedictine Reform Context', in *Form and Content of Instruction in Anglo-Saxon England in the Light of Contemporary Manuscript Evidence: Papers Presented at the International Conference, Udine, 6–8 April 2006*, ed. P. Lendinara, L. Lazzari and M. A. D'Aronco (Turnhout, 2007), 447–66

Dutton, P. E., 'Beyond the Topos of Senescence: The Political Problems of Aged Carolingian Rulers', in *Aging and the Aged*, ed. Sheehan, 75–94

——, *Charlemagne's Mustache and Other Cultural Clusters of a Dark Age* (New York, 2004), 151–68

Earl, J. W., 'Typology and Iconographic Styles in Early Medieval Hagiography', *Studies in the Literary Imagination* 8 (1975), 15–47

Einarsson, S., and N. E. Eliason, eds, *Studies in Heroic Legend and in Current Speech by Kemp Malone* (Copenhagen, 1959)

Elliott, R. W. V., 'Cynewulf's Runes in *Christ II* and *Elene*', in *Cynewulf Reader*, ed. Bjork, 281–93

——, 'Hildebrand and Byrhtnoth: A Study in Heroic Technique', *Comparative Literature* 14 (1962), 53–70

Ellis Davidson, H., 'The Training of Warriors', in *Weapons and Warfare*, ed. Chadwick Hawkes, 11–24

Emerson, O., 'Notes on Old English', *Modern Language Review* 14 (1919), 205–9

Enright, M. J., 'Charles the Bald and Æthelwulf of Wessex: The Alliance of 856 and Strategies of Royal Succession', *Journal of Medieval History* 5 (1979), 291–302

Evans, R. J., *In Defence of History*, rev. ed. (London, 2000)

Fallis, R. C., '"Grow Old with Me": Images of Older People in British and American Literature', in *Perceptions of Aging*, ed. von Dorotka Bagnell and Soper, 35–50

Farmer, D. H., ed., *The Oxford Dictionary of Saints*, 5th rev. ed. (Oxford, 2011)

Farrar, R. S., 'Structure and Function in Representative Old English Saints' Lives', *Neophilologus* 57 (1973), 83–93

Fell, C., with C. Clark and E. Williams, *Women in Anglo-Saxon England and the Impact of 1066* (London, 1984)

Fera, R. M., 'Metaphors for the Five Senses in Old English Prose', *RES* ns 63 (2012), 709–31

Ferreiro, A., *Simon Magus in Patristic, Medieval and Early Modern Traditions* (Leiden, 2005)

Fontes Anglo-Saxonici Project, ed., *Fontes Anglo-Saxonici: World Wide Web Register*, http://fontes.english.ox.ac.uk/

Foot, S., *Veiled Women: Female Religious Communities in England, 871–1066* (Aldershot, 2000)

Foxhall Forbes, H., M. Ammon, E. Boyle, C. T. Doyle, P. D. Evan, R. M. Fera, P. Gazzoli, H. Imhoff, A. Matheson, S. Rixon and L. Roach, 'Anglo-Saxon and Related Entries in the *Oxford Dictionary of National Biography* (2004)', *ASE* 37 (2008), 183–232

Frank, R., 'The *Battle of Maldon* and Heroic Literature', in *Battle of Maldon*, ed. Scragg, 196–207

Frantzen, A. J., *The Literature of Penance in Anglo-Saxon England* (New Brunswick, 1983)

Freedman, R., 'Sufficiently Decayed: Gerontophobia in English Literature', in *Aging and the Elderly: Humanistic Perspectives in Gerontology*, ed. S. F. Spicker, K. M. Woodward and D. D. van Tassel (Atlantic Highlands, 1978), 49–61

Freeman, J. T., 'Medical Perspectives in Aging (12th–19th Century)', *The Gerontologist* 5 (1965), 1–24

——, *Aging: Its History and Literature* (New York, 1979)

Frese, D. W., 'The Art of Cynewulf's Runic Signatures', in *Cynewulf Reader*, ed. Bjork, 323–46

Friis-Jensen, K., *Saxo Grammaticus as Latin Poet: Studies in the Verse Passages of the Gesta Danorum* (Rome, 1987)

Fulk, R. D., 'Cynewulf: Canon, Dialect, and Date', in *Cynewulf Reader*, ed. Bjork, 3–22

——, *History of Old English Meter* (Philadelphia, 1992)

——, ed., *Interpretations of* Beowulf*: A Critical Anthology* (Bloomington, 1991)

Garde, J., 'Christian and Folkloric Tradition in *Beowulf*: Death and the Dragon Episode', *Literature & Theology* 11 (1997), 325–46

Garmonsway, G. N., 'Anglo-Saxon Heroic Attitudes', in *Franciplegius: Medieval and Linguistic Studies in Honor of Francis*

Peabody Magoun, Jr, ed. J. B. Bessinger Jr and R. P. Creed (New York, 1965), 139–46

Garrison, M., '"Quid Hinieldus cum Christo?"', in *Latin Learning and English Lore: Studies in Anglo-Saxon Literature for Michael Lapidge*, ed. K. O'Brien O'Keeffe and A. Orchard (Toronto, 2005), I, 237–59

Garver, V. L., 'Old Age and Women in the Carolingian World', in Classen, *Old Age in the Middle Ages*, 121–41

Gatch, M. McC., *Preaching and Theology in Anglo-Saxon England: Ælfric and Wulfstan* (Toronto, 1977)

——, 'The Unknowable Audience of the Blickling Homilies', *ASE* 18 (1989), 99–115

Georgianna, L., 'King Hrethel's Sorrow and the Limits of Heroic Action in *Beowulf*', *Speculum* 62 (1987), 829–50

Gilchrist, R., *Medieval Life: Archaeology and the Life Course* (Woodbridge, 2012)

Gilleard, C., 'Old Age in the Dark Ages: The Status of Old Age During the Early Middle Ages', *Ageing & Society* 29 (2009), 1065–84

Gneuss, H., '*The Battle of Maldon* 89: Byrthnoð's *ofermod* Again', *SiP* 73 (1976), 117–37

——, and M. Lapidge, *Anglo-Saxon Manuscripts: A Bibliographical Handlist of Manuscripts and Manuscript Fragments Written or Owned in England up to 1100* (Toronto, 2014)

Godden, M., *Ælfric's Catholic Homilies: Introduction, Commentary and Glossary*, EETS ss 18 (Oxford, 2000)

——, and M. Lapidge, eds, *The Cambridge Companion to Old English Literature*, 2nd ed. (Cambridge, 2013)

Godman, P., 'Alcuin's Poetic Style and the Authenticity of *O mea cella*', *Studi Medievali* 20 (1979), 555–83

Goodich, M., *From Birth to Old Age: The Human Life Cycle in Medieval Thought, 1250–1350* (Lanham, 1989)

——, 'The Death of a Saint: A Hagiographical Topos', in *Hoping for Continuity. Childhood, Education and Death in Antiquity and the Middle Ages*, ed. K. Mustakallio, J. Hanska, H.-L. Sainio and V. Vuolanto (Rome, 2005), 227–38

Gowland, R., 'Age, Ageism and Osteological Bias: The Evidence from Late Roman Britain', *Journal of Roman Archaeology* ss 65 (2007), 153–69

——, 'Ageing the Past: Examining Age Identity from Funerary Evidence', in *Social Archaeology of Funerary Remains*, ed. R. Gowland and C. Knüsel (Oxford, 2006), 143–54

Grmek, M. D., *On Ageing and Old Age: Basic Problems and Historic Aspects of Gerontology and Geriatrics* (The Hague, 1958)

Gurevich, A., 'Historical Anthropology and the Science of History', in *Historical Anthropology of the Middle Ages*, ed. J. Howlett (Cambridge, 1992), 3–20

Gwara, S., 'A Metaphor in *Beowulf* 2487a: *guðhelm toglad*', *SiP* 93 (1996), 333–48
——, *Heroic Identity in the World of* Beowulf (Leiden, 2008)
Halbrooks, J., 'Byrhtnoth's Great-Hearted Mirth, or Praise and Blame in *The Battle of Maldon*', *Philological Quarterly* 82 (2003), 235–55
Hall, A., 'Hygelac's Only Daughter: A Present, a Potentate and a Peaceweaver in *Beowulf*', *Studia Neophilologica* 78 (2006), 81–7
Halsall, G., 'Female Status and Power in Early Merovingian Central Austrasia: The Burial Evidence', *Early Medieval Europe* 5 (1996), 1–24
——, *Warfare and Society in the Barbarian West, 450–900* (London, 2003)
Hamerow, H., D. A. Hinton and S. Crawford, eds, *The Oxford Handbook of Anglo-Saxon Archaeology* (Oxford, 2011)
Härke, H., 'Changing Symbols in a Changing Society: The Anglo-Saxon Weapon Burial Rite in the Seventh Century', in *The Age of Sutton Hoo: The Seventh Century in North-Western Europe*, ed. M. O. H. Carver (Woodbridge, 1992), 149–66
——, 'Warrior Graves? The Background of the Anglo-Saxon Weapon Burial Rite', *Past and Present* 126 (1990), 22–43
Harris, R. M., 'The Marginal Drawings of the Bury St. Edmunds Psalter (Rome, Vatican Library MS Reg. Lat. 12)', unpublished PhD dissertation, Princeton University, 1960
Heimann, A., 'Three Illustrations from the Bury St. Edmunds Psalter and Their Prototypes. Notes on the Iconography of Some Anglo-Saxon Drawings', *Journal of the Warburg and Courtauld Institutes* 29 (1966), 39–59
Hendricks, J., and C. A. Leedham, 'Making Sense: Interpreting Historical and Cross-Cultural Literature on Aging', in *Perceptions of Aging*, ed. von Dorotka Bagnell and Soper, 1–16
Herlihy, D., *Women, Family and Society in Medieval Europe: Historical Essays, 1978–1991* (Providence, 1995)
Heuchan, V., 'All Things to All Men: Representations of the Apostle Paul in Anglo-Saxon Literature', unpublished PhD dissertation, University of Toronto, 2010
Hill, D., and M. Worthington, eds, *Æthelbald and Offa: Two Eighth-Century Kings of Mercia* (Oxford, 2005)
Hill, J. M., *The Anglo-Saxon Warrior Ethic: Reconstructing Lordship in Early English Literature* (Gainesville, 2000)
——, *The Cultural World in* Beowulf (Toronto, 1995)
Hill, J., 'Ælfric and Haymo Revisited', in *Intertexts: Studies in Anglo-Saxon Culture Presented to Paul E. Szarmach*, ed. V. Blanton and H. Scheck (Tempe, 2008), 331–48
Hill, T. D., 'History and Heroic Ethic in Maldon', *Neophilologus* 54 (1970), 291–6
——, '*Imago Dei*: Genre, Symbolism, and Anglo-Saxon Hagiography', in *Holy Men*, ed. Szarmach, 35–50

Bibliography

——, 'Saturn's Time Riddle: An Insular Latin Analogue for *Solomon and Saturn II* Lines 282–291', *RES* ns 39 (1988), 273–6
——, 'The Failing Torch: The Old English *Elene*, 1256–1259', *NQ* ns 52 (2005), 155–60
——, 'The Seven Joys of Heaven in *Christ III* and Old English Homiletic Texts', *NQ* ns 16 (1969), 165–6
——, '"When the Leader Is Brave...": An Old English Proverb and Its Vernacular Context', *Anglia* 119 (2001), 232–6
Hollis, S., *Anglo-Saxon Women and the Church: Sharing a Common Fate* (Woodbridge, 1992)
——, 'Beowulf and the Succession', *Parergon* 1 (1983), 39–54
Hooper, N., 'The Aberlemno Stone and Cavalry in Anglo-Saxon England', *Northern History* 29 (1993), 188–96
——, 'The Anglo-Saxons at War', in *Weapons and Warfare*, ed. Chadwick Hawkes, 191–201
Horst, K. van der, and F. Ankersmit, *The Utrecht Psalter: Picturing the Psalms of David*, CD-ROM (Utrecht, 1996)
Horstmanshoff, H. F. J., 'De drempel van de ouderdom; medische en sociale zorg voor de oudere mens in de Grieks-Romeinse Oudheid', in *Verpleeghuiskunde. Een vak van doen en laten*, ed. J. F. Hoek, N. F. de Pijper, M. W. Ribbe and J. A. Stoop (Utrecht, 1996), 315–23
——, A. M. Luyendijk-Elshout, F. G. Schlesinger, H. Beukers, J. G. de Bie Leuveling Tjeenk-Brands, M. A. P. van der Geest, R. H. van Gent, G. T. Haneveld, Ch. L. Heesakkers, H. M. E. de Jong, Th. Laurentius and D. O. Wijnands, eds, *The Four Seasons of Human Life: Four Anonymous Engravings from the Trent Collection* (Rotterdam, 2002)
Houts, E. van, *Memory and Gender in Medieval Europe 900–1200* (Basingstoke, 1999)
Hume, R. D., *Reconstructing Contexts: The Aims and Principles of Archaeo-Historicism* (Oxford, 1999)
Irving, E. B., Jr, 'Heroic Role-Models: Beowulf and Others', in *Heroic Poetry in the Anglo-Saxon Period: Studies in Honor of Jess B. Bessinger, Jr*, ed. H. Damico and J. Leyerle (Kalamazoo, 1993), 347–72
——, 'The Text of Fate', in *Interpretations of* Beowulf, ed. Fulk, 168–93
——, 'What To Do with Old Kings', in *Comparative Research on Oral Traditions: A Memorial for Milman Parry*, ed. J. M. Foley (Columbus, 1987), 259–68
Janssen, A., *Grijsaards in zwart-wit. De verbeelding van de ouderdom in de Nederlandse prentkunst (1550–1650)* (Zutphen, 2007)
Johnson, D. F., 'The Five Horrors of Hell: An Insular Homiletic Motif', *English Studies* 74 (1993), 414–31
Johnson, P., 'Historical Readings of Old Age and Ageing', in *Old Age*, ed. Johnson and Thane, 1–18

——, and P. Thane, eds, *Old Age from Antiquity to Post-Modernity* (London, 1998)

Jong, M. de, *In Samuel's Image: Child Oblation in the Early Medieval West* (Leiden, 1996)

——, 'The Foreign Past: Medieval Historians and Cultural Anthropology', *Tijdschrift voor Geschiedenis* 109 (1996), 326–42

Karasawa, K., 'Wise Old *Ceorl(as)* in *Beowulf* and Its Original Meaning', *English Studies* 97 (2016), 227–37

Kaske, R. E., '*Sapientia et fortitudo* as the Controlling Theme of *Beowulf*', in *Anthology of Beowulf Criticism*, ed. Nicholson, 269–310. First published 1958

Kennedy, A., 'Byrhtnoth's Obits and Twelfth-Century Accounts of the Battle of Maldon', in *Battle of Maldon*, ed. Scragg, 59–78

Ker, N. R., *Catalogue of Manuscripts Containing Anglo-Saxon* (Oxford, 1957)

Ker, W. P., *Epic and Romance: Essays on Medieval Literature*, 2nd rev. ed. (New York, 1957)

Kershaw, P. J. E., *Peaceful Kings: Peace, Power, and the Early Medieval Political Imagination* (Oxford, 2011)

Keynes, S., 'Emma (d. 1052)', *ODNB*

——, 'Rulers of the English, c.450–1066', in *Blackwell Encyclopaedia*, ed. Lapidge *et al.*, 500–20

——, 'The Kingdom of the Mercians in the Eighth Century', in *Æthelbald and Offa*, ed. Hill and Worthington, 1–26

Kiff, J., 'Images of War: Illustrations of Warfare in Early Eleventh-Century England', *Anglo-Norman Studies* VII (1984), 177–94

Kirby, I. J., 'In Defence of Byrhtnoth', *Florilegium* 11 (1992), 53–60

Knight Bostock, J., *A Handbook of Old High German Literature*, 2nd rev. ed., ed. K. C. King and D. R. McLintock (Oxford, 1976)

Lapidge, M., *Anglo-Latin Literature. Vol. 1: 600–899* (London, 1996)

——, *Anglo-Latin Literature. Vol. 2: 900–1066* (London, 1993)

——, 'Hildelith (fl. c.700)', *ODNB*

——, *The Anglo-Saxon Library* (Oxford, 2006)

——, 'The Career of Archbishop Theodore', in *Archbishop Theodore: Commemorative Studies on his Life and Influence*, ed. M. Lapidge (Cambridge, 1995), 1–29

——, 'The *Life of St Oswald*', in *Battle of Maldon*, ed. Scragg, 51–8

——, 'The Origin of the *Collectanea*', in *Collectanea*, ed. and trans. Bayless and Lapidge, 1–12

——, J. Blair, S. Keynes and D. G. Scragg, *The Blackwell Encyclopaedia of Anglo-Saxon England* (Oxford, 1999)

Larrington, C., *A Store of Common Sense: Gnomic Theme and Style in Old Icelandic and Old English Wisdom Poetry* (Oxford, 1993)

——, 'Walburg (c.710–779?)', *ODNB*

Laslett, P., 'Necessary Knowledge: Age and Ageing in the Societies of the Past', in *Aging in the Past: Demography, Society and Old Age*, ed. D. I. Kertzer and P. Laslett (Berkeley, 1995), 3–80

Lavelle, R., *Alfred's Wars: Sources and Interpretations of Anglo-Saxon Warfare in the Viking Age* (Woodbridge, 2010)

Lazda-Cazers, R., 'Old Age in Wolfram von Eschenbach's *Parzival* and *Titurel*', in *Old Age in the Middle Ages*, ed. Classen, 201–18

Le Saux, F., '*Canu Llywarch Hen*: La vieillesse dans les Englynion Gallois', in *Vieillesse et vieillissement au Moyen Âge*, ed. N. Coulet *et al.* (Aix-en-Provence, 1987), 181–98

Lee, C., 'Body and Soul: Disease and Impairment', in *The Material Culture of Daily Living in the Anglo-Saxon World*, ed. M. Clegg Hyer and G. Owen-Crocker (Exeter, 2011), 293–309

——, 'Disease', in *Oxford Handbook*, ed. Hamerow, Hinton and Crawford, 704–23

Lees, C. A., and G. R. Overing, *Double Agents: Women and Clerical Culture in Anglo-Saxon England* (Philadelphia, 2001)

Lehmann, R. P. M., 'The Old English *Riming Poem*: Interpretation, Text and Translation', *JEGP* 69 (1970), 437–49

Leneghan, F., 'The Poetic Purpose of the Offa-Digression in *Beowulf*', *RES* ns 60 (2009), 538–60

Lewis, M., 'The Bayeux Tapestry and Eleventh-Century Material Culture', in *King Harold II and the Bayeux Tapestry*, ed. G. R. Owen-Crocker (Woodbridge, 2005), 179–94

Lewis-Simpson, S., 'Old Age in Viking-Age Britain', in *Youth and Age*, ed. Lewis-Simpson, 243–60

——, ed., *Youth and Age in the Medieval North* (Leiden, 2008)

Leyerle, J., 'Beowulf: The Hero and the King', *Medium Ævum* 34 (1965), 89–102

Licence, T., 'Evidence of Recluses in Eleventh-Century England', *ASE* 36 (2007), 221–34

Liuzza, R. M., 'On the Dating of *Beowulf*', in Beowulf *Reader*, ed. Baker, 281–302

——, 'The Sense of Time in Anglo-Saxon England', *Bulletin of the John Rylands Library* 89:2 (2013), 131–51

Locherbie-Cameron, M. A., 'From Caesarea to Eynsham: A Consideration of the Proposed Route(s) of the *Admonition to a Spiritual Son* to Anglo-Saxon England', *HA* 3 (2000)

——, 'The Men Named in the Poem', in *Battle of Maldon*, ed. Scragg, 238–49

Malina, B. J., *The New Testament World: Insights from Cultural Anthropology*, 4th ed. (Louisville, 2001)

Malone, K., 'The Daughter of Healfdene', in *Studies in Heroic Legend*, ed. Einarsson and Eliason, 124–41

——, 'The Tale of Ingeld', in *Studies in Heroic Legend*, ed. Einarsson and Eliason, 1–62

Mason, E., *The House of Godwine: The History of a Dynasty* (London, 2004)

Mathiesen, K., 'Seven New Species of Miniature Frogs Discovered in Cloud Forests of Brazil', *The Guardian*, 4 June 2015

McCord, L. R., 'A Probable Source for the *ubi sunt* Passage in Blickling Homily V', *Neuphilologische Mitteilungen* 82 (1981), 360–1

McFadden, B., 'Sleeping after the Feast: Deathbeds, Marriage Beds, and the Power Structure of Heorot', *Neophilologus* 84 (2000), 631–48

McKinnell, J., 'A Farewell to Old English Elegy: The Case of *Vainglory*', *Parergon* 9 (1991), 67–89

McNamara, M., *The Apocrypha in the Irish Church* (Dublin, 1975)

Meaney, A. L., 'Women, Witchcraft and Magic in Anglo-Saxon England', in *Superstition*, ed. Scragg, 9–40

Mieszkowski, G., 'Old Age and Medieval Misogyny: The Old Woman', in *Old Age in the Middle Ages*, ed. Albrecht Classen, 299–319

Millar, E. G., *English Illuminated Manuscripts from the Xth to the XIIIth Century* (Paris, 1926)

Minois, G., *History of Old Age from Antiquity to the Renaissance*, trans. Sarah Hanbury Tenison (Oxford, 1989)

Naumann, H., *Germanisches Gefolgschaftswesen* (Leipzig, 1939)

Neidorf, L., 'Germanic Legend, Scribal Errors, and Cultural Change', in *Dating of* Beowulf, ed. Neidorf, 37–57

——, 'On the Epistemology of Old English Scholarship', *Neophilologus* 99 (2015), 631–47

——, ed., *The Dating of* Beowulf: *A Reassessment* (Cambridge, 2015)

——, 'The Dating of *Widsið* and the Study of Germanic Antiquity', *Neophilologus* 97 (2013), 165–183

Newlands, C., 'Alcuin's Poem of Exile: *O mea cella*', *Mediaevalia* 11 (1985), 19–45

Newton, S., *The Origins of* Beowulf *and the Pre-Viking Kingdom of East Anglia* (Cambridge, 1993)

Nicholson, L. E., ed., *An Anthology of* Beowulf *Criticism* (New York, 1963)

Nijst, U., 'The Magi in Anglo-Saxon England', in *Feestnummer aangeboden aan prof. dr. Aurelius Pompen O.F.M. op zijn zestigsten verjaardag* (Tilburg, 1939), 129–37

Niles, J. D., Beowulf: *The Poem and Its Tradition* (Cambridge, MA, 1983)

Noel, W., 'The Utrecht Psalter in England: Continuity and Experiment', in *The Utrecht Psalter in Medieval Art: Picturing the Psalms of David*, ed. K. van der Horst, W. Noel and W. C. M. Wüstefeld (Tuurdijk, 1996), 121–65

——, *The Harley Psalter* (Cambridge, 1995)

O'Brien O'Keeffe, K., 'Heroic Values and Christian Ethics', in *Cambridge Companion*, ed. Godden and Lapidge, 101–19
O'Brien, H., *Queen Emma and the Vikings: The Woman Who Shaped the Events of 1066* (London, 2005)
O'Neill, P., 'Latin Learning at Winchester in the Early Eleventh Century: The Evidence of the Lambeth Psalter', *ASE* 20 (1991), 143–66
Ogilvy, J. D. A., *Books Known to the English, 597–1066* (Cambridge, MA, 1967)
Ohlgren, T. H., *Insular and Anglo-Saxon Illuminated Manuscripts: An Iconographic Catalogue, c. A.D. 625 to 1100* (New York, 1986)
Onians, R. B., *The Origins of European Thought: About the Body, the Mind, the Soul, the World, Time and Fate* (Cambridge, 1951)
Orchard, A., *A Critical Companion to* Beowulf (Cambridge, 2003)
——, 'Conspicuous Heroism: Abraham, Prudentius, and the Old English Verse *Genesis*', in *Heroes and Heroines*, ed. Carruthers, 45–58
Overing, G. R., 'The Women of *Beowulf*: A Context for Interpretation', in Beowulf *Reader*, ed. Baker, 219–60
Oxford Dictionary of National Biography (Oxford, 2004), http://www.oxforddnb.com
Oxford English Dictionary Online, http://www.oed.com
Painter, S., *William Marshal: Knight-Errant, Baron and Regent of England* (Baltimore, 1933)
Parker, E., 'Siward the Dragon-Slayer: Mythmaking in Anglo-Scandinavian England', *Neophilologus* 98 (2014), 481–93
Pelle, S., 'Sources and Analogues for Blickling Homily V and Vercelli Homily XI', *NQ* ns 59 (2012), 8–13
Peters, E., *The Shadow King: Rex Inutilis in Medieval Law and Literature, 751–1327* (New Haven, 1970)
Peters, H., 'Jupiter and Saturn: Medieval Ideals of "Elde"', in *Old Age in the Middle Ages*, ed. Classen, 375–91
Peterson, J. W., 'Age of Wisdom: Elderly Black Women in Family and Church', in *Cultural Context of Aging*, ed. Sokolovsky, 276–92
Phillips, J., *The Fourth Crusade and the Sack of Constantinople* (London, 2004)
Poortinga, Y., *De Palmridder fan Lissabon* (Ljouwert, 1965)
Pope, J. C., 'Beowulf's Old Age', in *Philological Essays: Studies in Old and Middle English Language and Literature in Honour of Herbert Dean Meritt*, ed. J. L. Rosier (The Hague, 1970), 55–64
——, review of Wulfstan, *Homilies*, ed. Bethurum, *MLN* 74 (1959), 338–9
Porck, T., 'Growing Old among the Anglo-Saxons: The Cultural Conceptualisation of Old Age in Early Medieval England', unpublished PhD dissertation, Leiden University, 2016
——, 'Treasures in a Sooty Bag? A Note on *Durham Proverb 7*', *NQ* ns 62 (2015), 203–6

———, 'Two Notes on an Old English Confessional Prayer in Vespasian D. xx', *NQ* ns 60 (2013), 493–8

———, 'Vergrijzing in een Oudengels heldendicht. De rol van oude koningen in de *Beowulf*', *Madoc* 26 (2012), 66–76

Powell, K., 'Meditating on Men and Monsters: A Reconsideration of the Thematic Unity of the *Beowulf* Manuscript', *RES* ns 57 (2006), 1–15

Prestwich, J. O., *The Place of War in English History 1066-1214*, ed. M. Prestwich (Woodbridge, 2004)

Prosopography of Anglo-Saxon England, http://www.pase.ac.uk

Rasmussen, S. J., 'From Childbearers to Culture-Bearers: Transition to Postchildbearing among Tuareg Women', *Medical Anthropology: Cross-Cultural Studies in Health and Illness* 19 (2000), 91–116

Raw, B. C., *The Art and Background of Old English Poetry* (London, 1978)

Remley, P. G., *Old English Biblical Verse: Studies in Genesis, Exodus and Daniel* (Cambridge, 1996)

Roberts, J., 'The English Saints Remembered in the Old English Anonymous Homilies', in *Old English Prose*, ed. Szarmach, 433–61

Roisman, H. M., 'Nestor the Good Counsellor', *The Classical Quarterly* ns 51 (2005), 17–38

Rollason, D., 'Seaxburh (b. in or before 655, d. c.700)', *ODNB*

Rosenthal, J. T., 'Anglo-Saxon Attitudes: Men's Sources, Women's History', in *Medieval Women and the Sources of Medieval History*, ed. J. T. Rosenthal (Athens, 1990), 259–84

———, *Old Age in Late Medieval England* (Philadelphia, 1997)

Rosivach, V., '*Anus*: Some Older Women in Latin Literature', *The Classical World* 88 (1994), 107–17

Rothauser, B. C. L., 'Winter in Heorot: Looking at Anglo-Saxon Perceptions of Age and Kingship through the Character of Hrothgar', in *Old Age in the Middle Ages*, ed. Classen, 103–20

Rumble, A. R., 'Church Leadership and the Anglo-Saxons', in *Leaders of the Anglo-Saxon Church: From Bede to Stigand*, ed. A. R. Rumble (Woodbridge, 2012), 1–24

Sánchez-Martí, J., 'Age Matters in Old English Literature', in *Youth and Age*, ed. Lewis-Simpson, 205–25

Sandidge, M., 'Forty Years of Plague: Attitudes toward Old Age in the Tales of Boccaccio and Chaucer', in *Old Age in the Middle Ages*, ed. Classen, 357–74

Sauer, H., and J. Story, eds, *Anglo-Saxon England and the Continent* (Tempe, 2011)

Sawyer, P. H., *Anglo-Saxon Charters: An Annotated List and Bibliography* (London, 1968)

Schiller, G., *Iconography of Christian Art* (London, 1971)

Schücking, L. L., 'Das Königsideal im *Beowulf*', *MHRA Bulletin* 3 (1929), 143–54, translated as 'The Ideal of Kingship in *Beowulf*', in *Anthology of* Beowulf *Criticism*, ed. Nicholson, 35–50
——, 'Wann entstand der Beowulf? Glossen, Zweifel und Fragen', *BGdSL* 42 (1917), 347–410
Schürr, D., 'Hiltibrants Gottvertrauen', *Amsterdamer Beiträge zur älteren Germanistik* 68 (2011), 1–25
Schwab, U., *Die Sternrune im Wessobrunner Gebet* (Amsterdam, 1973)
Scragg, D. G., 'Napier's "Wulfstan" Homily XXX: Its Sources, Its Relationship to the Vercelli Book and Its Style', *ASE* 6 (1977), 197–211
——, ed., *Superstition and Popular Medicine in Anglo-Saxon England* (Manchester, 1989)
——, ed., *The Battle of Maldon, AD 991* (Oxford, 1991)
——, 'The Corpus of Vernacular Homilies and Prose Saints' Lives before Ælfric', in *Old English Prose*, ed. Szarmach, 73–150
Sears, E., *The Ages of Man: Medieval Interpretations of the Life Cycle* (Princeton, 1986)
See, K. von, B. La Farge, E. Picard and K. Schulz, *Kommentar zu den Liedern der Edda. Bd. 3: Götterlieder* (Heidelberg, 2000)
Semper, P., '*Byð se ealda man ceald and snoflig*: Stereotypes and Subversions of the Last Stages of the Life Cycle in Old English Texts and Anglo-Saxon Contexts', in *Medieval Life Cycles*, ed. Cochelin and Smyth, 287–318
Shahar, S., *Growing Old in the Middle Ages: 'Winter Clothes us in Shadow and Pain'* (London, 1997)
——, 'Old Age in the High and Late Middle Ages: Image, Expectation and Status', in *Old Age*, ed. Johnson and Thane, 43–63
——, 'The Middle Ages and Renaissance', in *Long History*, ed. Thane, 77–111
——, 'Who Were Old in the Middle Ages?', *Social History of Medicine* 6 (1993), 313–41
Sharifian, F., *Cultural Conceptualisations and Language: Theoretical Framework and Applications* (Amsterdam, 2011)
Sheehan, M. M., 'Afterword', in *Aging and the Aged*, ed. Sheehan, 201–7
——, ed., *Aging and the Aged in Medieval Europe* (Toronto, 1990)
Sheerin, D. J., 'John Leland and Milred of Worcester', *Manuscripta* 21 (1977), 172–80
Shippey, T. A., '*The Wanderer* and *The Seafarer* as Wisdom Poetry', in *A Companion to Old English Literature*, ed. H. Aertsen and R. H. Bremmer Jr (Amsterdam, 1994), 145–58
Sims-Williams, P., *Religion and Literature in Western England, 600–800* (Cambridge, 1990)
Sisam, K., *The Structure of* Beowulf (Oxford, 1965)
Smetana, C. L., 'Ælfric and the Homiliary of Haymo of Halberstadt', *Traditio* 17 (1961), 457–69

Smith, R., 'Glimpses of Some Anglo-Saxon Women', in *A Wyf Ther Was: Essays in Honour of Paule Mertens-Fonck*, ed. J. Dor (Liège, 1992), 256–63

Smithers, G. V., 'The Meaning of *The Seafarer* and *The Wanderer*', *Medium Ævum* 28 (1959), 1–22

Sokolovsky, J., 'Status of Older People: Tribal Societies', in *Encyclopedia of Aging*, ed. D. J. Ekerdt (New York, 2002), 1341–6

——, ed., *The Cultural Context of Aging: Worldwide Perspectives*, 2nd ed. (Westport, 1997)

Soper, H., '*Eald æfensceop*: Poetic Composition and the Authority of the Aged in Old English Verse', *Quaestio Insularis* 17 (2016), 74–100

——, 'Reading the Exeter Book Riddles as Life-Writing', *RES* 68 (2017), 841–65

Speirs, N., 'The Two Armies of the Old English *Exodus*: *twa þusendo*, Line 184b, and *cista*, Lines 229b and 230a', *NQ* ns 34 (1987), 145–6

Spencer, P., ed., *Anthropology and the Riddle of the Sphinx: Paradoxes of Change in the Life Course* (London, 1990)

Stafford, P., 'Ælfthryth (d. 999x1001)', *ODNB*

——, 'Chronicle D, 1067 and Women: Gendering Conquest in Eleventh-Century England', in *Anglo-Saxons: Studies Presented to Cyril Roy Hart*, ed. S. Keynes and A. P. Smyth (Scarborough, 2006), 208–23

——, 'Eadgifu (b. in or before 904, d. in or after 966)', *ODNB*

——, *Queen Emma and Queen Edith: Queenship and Women's Power in Eleventh-Century England* (Oxford, 1997)

——, *Queens, Concubines and Dowagers: The King's Wife in the Early Middle Ages* (London, 1983)

——, 'Women and the Norman Conquest', *Transactions of the Royal Historical Society* 4 (1994), 221–49

Stanley, E. G., '*Beowulf*: Lordlessness in Ancient Times Is the Theme, as Much as the Glory of Kings, if not More', *NQ* ns 52 (2005), 267–81

——, *In the Foreground:* Beowulf (Cambridge, 1994)

Stearns, P. N., *Old Age in Preindustrial Society* (New York, 1982)

Stephens, G. R., and W. D. Stephens, 'Cuthman: A Neglected Saint', *Speculum* 13 (1938), 448–53

Stephenson, I. P., *The Late Anglo-Saxon Army* (Stroud, 2007)

Stokes, P. A., 'The Digital Dictionary', *Florilegium* 26 (2009), 37–66

Stoodley, N., 'Childhood to Old Age', in *Oxford Handbook*, ed. Hamerow, Hinton and Crawford, 641–66

——, 'From the Cradle to the Grave: Age Organization and the Early Anglo-Saxon Burial Rite', *World Archaeology* 31 (2000), 456–72

Swanton, M., *Crisis and Development in Germanic Society 700–800:* Beowulf *and the Burden of Kingship* (Göppingen, 1982)

Szarmach, P. E., ed., *Holy Men and Holy Women: Old English Prose Saints' Lives and Their Contexts* (New York, 1996)

——, ed., *Old English Prose: Basic Readings* (New York, 2000)

Ţăranu, C., 'The Elusive Nature of Germanic Heroic Poetry: A Rhizomatic Model', *Neighbours and Networks* 1 (2013), 44–66

Thacker, A., 'Ælfflæd (654–714)', *ODNB*

——, 'Eanflæd [St Eanflæd] (b. 626, d. after 685)', *ODNB*

——, 'Hild (614–680)', *ODNB*

——, and R. Sharpe, eds, *Local Saints and Local Churches in the Early Medieval West* (Oxford, 2002)

Thane, P., *Old Age in English History: Past Experiences, Present Issues* (Oxford, 2000)

——, 'Old Age in English History', in *Zur Kulturgeschichte des Alterns*, ed. Conrad and von Kondratowitz, 17–35

——, 'The Age of Old Age', in *Long History*, ed. Thane, 9–29

——, ed., *The Long History of Old Age* (London, 2005)

Thormann, J., 'Enjoyment of Violence and Desire for History in Beowulf', in *The Postmodern* Beowulf: *A Critical Casebook*, ed. E. A. Joy and M. K. Ramsey (Morgantown, 2006), 287–318

Timmers, J. J. M., *A Handbook of Romanesque Art* (New York, 1976)

Tolkien, J. R. R.,*'Beowulf*: The Monsters and the Critics', in *Interpretations of* Beowulf, ed. Fulk, 14–44. First published 1937

——, 'Ofermod', in *Tree and Leaf, Including the Poem Mythopoeia. The Homecoming of Beorhtnoth* (London, 2001), 143–50. First published 1953

Tollerton, L., *Wills and Will-Making in Anglo-Saxon England* (York, 2011)

Tosh, J., *The Pursuit of History: Aims, Methods and New Directions in the Study of Modern History*, 4th ed. (Harlow, 2006)

Tripp, R. P., 'The Exemplary Role of Hrothgar and Heorot', *Philological Quarterly* 56 (1977), 123–7

Tristram, H. L. C., *Sex aetates mundi: Die Weltzeitalter bei den Angelsachsen und den Iren. Untersuchungen und Texte* (Heidelberg, 1985)

——, 'Stock Descriptions of Heaven and Hell in Old English Prose and Poetry', *Neuphilologische Mitteilungen* 79 (1978), 102–13

Troyansky, D. G., 'The Older Person in the Western World: From the Middle Ages to the Industrial Revolution', in *Handbook of the Humanities and Aging*, ed. T. R. Cole, D. D. van Tassel and R. Kastenbaum (New York, 1992), 40–61

Tuttle Hansen, E., 'Hrothgar's "Sermon" in *Beowulf* as Parental Wisdom', *ASE* 10 (1981), 53–67

——, '*Precepts*: An Old English Instruction', *Speculum* 56 (1981), 1–16

——, *The Solomon Complex: Reading Wisdom in Old English Poetry* (Toronto, 1988)

Vidal, T., 'Houses and Domestic Life in the Viking Age and Medieval Period: Material Perspectives from Sagas and Archaeology', unpublished PhD dissertation, University of Nottingham, 2013

Bibliography

Waldman, G. A., 'Excerpts from a Little Encyclopaedia – the *Wessobrunn Prayer* Manuscript Clm. 22053', *Allegorica* 2 (1977), 9–26

Wallace-Hadrill, J. M., *Early Germanic Kingship in England and on the Continent* (Oxford, 1971)

Watson, C., 'Old English Hagiography: Recent and Future Research', *Literature Compass* 1 (2004), 1–14

Weinstein, D., and R. M. Bell, *Saints and Society: The Two Worlds of Western Christendom, 1000–1700* (Chicago, 1982)

Weiskott, E., 'The Meter of *Widsith* and the Distant Past', *Neophilologus* 99 (2015), 143–50

Wentersdorf, K. P., 'The Old English *Rhyming Poem*: A Ruler's Lament', *SiP* 82 (1985), 265–94

Whatley, E. G., 'An Introduction to the Study of Old English Prose Hagiography: Sources and Resources', in *Holy Men*, ed. Szarmach, 3–32

Whitbread, L., '"Wulfstan" Homilies XXIX, XXX and Some Related Texts', *Anglia* 81 (1963), 347–64

Whitelock, D., 'Anglo-Saxon Poetry and the Historian', *Transactions of the Royal Historical Society* 31 (1949), 75–94

——, *The Audience of* Beowulf (Oxford, 1951)

Wieland, G. R., 'The Anglo-Saxon Manuscripts of Prudentius's *Psychomachia*', *ASE* 16 (1987), 213–31

——, 'The Origin and Development of the Anglo-Saxon *Psychomachia* Illustrations', *ASE* 26 (1997), 169–86

Williams, A., 'Æthelred (d. after 704)', *ODNB*

——, 'Godwine, earl of Wessex (d. 1053)', *ODNB*

——, *The World before Domesday: The English Aristocracy 900–1066* (London, 2008)

Williams, G., 'Military Obligations and Mercian Supremacy in the Eighth Century', in *Æthelbald and Offa*, ed. Hill and Worthington, 103–8

Williamson, P., *Medieval Ivory Carvings: Early Christian to Romanesque* (London, 2010)

Wood, H. H., *The Battle of Hastings: The Fall of Anglo-Saxon England* (London, 2008)

Wormald, F., *The Utrecht Psalter* (Utrecht, 1953)

Wormald, P., 'Hilda, Saint and Scholar (614–680)', in *The Times of Bede: Studies in Early English Christian Society and Its Historian*, ed. S. Baxter (Malden, 2006), 267–76

Wright, C. D., *The Irish Tradition in Anglo-Saxon England* (Cambridge, 1993)

Wright, C. E., *The Cultivation of Saga in Anglo-Saxon England* (Edinburgh, 1939)

Wyatt, A. J., *An Anglo-Saxon Reader* (Cambridge, 1919)

Yorke, B., 'Bugga (d. 759x65)', *ODNB*

Bibliography

Ziolkowski, J. M., 'The Obscenities of Old Women, Vetularity and Vernacularity', in *Obscenity, Social Control and Artistic Creation in the European Middle Ages*, ed. J. M. Ziolkowski (Leiden, 1998), 73–89

Zwikstra, C. J., '*Wintrum frod*: *frod* and the Aging Mind in Old English Poetry', *SiP* 108 (2011), 133–64

Index

Abbo of Fleury, abbot 57
Aberlemno Stone 138
Abraham 19, 28–9, 38, 46, 66 n.61, 130 n.111, 139–41, 166–8
Acta Sanctorum 61 n.42
adolescentia 20, 23, 32, 35–43, 45, 50–1
Æbba, mother of St Leoba 130, 216 n.22, 219, 230
Ælfflæd, abbess 3, 218, 224
Ælfflæd, noblewoman 151
Ælfgyth, teacher of gold embroidery 229
Ælflæd, nun 220
Ælfric of Eynsham, abbot 3, 10, 104, 108
  Admonitio ad filium spiritualem 94, 97–8
  De duodecim abusiuis 64–5
  Grammar 55, 192
  homilies 20 n.22, 22 n.29, 26
    ÆCHom I, hom. 4 124–5
    ÆCHom I, hom. 8 19
    ÆCHom I, hom. 16 105
    ÆCHom I, hom. 26 24
    ÆCHom I, hom. 29 123
    ÆCHom I, hom. 32 74–5
    ÆCHom I, hom. 40 98–9
    ÆCHom II, hom. 5 37–8, 51
    ÆCHom II, hom. 6 65–6, 213
    ÆCHom II, hom. 13 46 n.133
    ÆCHom II, hom. 17 118
    ÆCHom II, hom. 19 60 n.40
    ÆCHom II, hom. 25 60 n.40
    ÆCHom II, hom. 34 128 n.101
    Assmann, hom. 2 65–6, 213
    Assmann, hom. 4 21–2, 50
    Pope, hom. 11 22, 50, 105
    Pope, hom. 19 63–4
    Pope, hom. 23 119–20
  Letter to Sigefyrth 65, 213
  Letter to Sigeweard 213 n.8
  Letter to Wulfsige 68
  Letter to Wulfstan 68
  Life of St Swithun 113 n.14, 117 n.46
  Lives of Saints 111, 114
    ÆLS, no. 3 (Basil) 114 n.18
    ÆLS, no. 6 (Maurus) 114 n.18, 118
    ÆLS, no. 7 (Agnes) 119–20
    ÆLS, no. 15 (Mark) 114 n.18
    ÆLS, no. 25 (Maccabees) 114 n.18, 122–3
    ÆLS, no. 28 (Maurice) 114 n.18
    ÆLS, no. 31 (Martin) 114 n.18, 128
    ÆLS, no. 32 (Edmund) 57
    ÆLS, no. 34 (Cecilia) 110
  Old English Hexateuch 141 n.30 *see also* London, British Library, Cotton Claudius B. iv *under* manuscripts
  Vita s. Æthelwoldi 116 n.36
Ælfthryth, queen 219, 223, 225, 228
Ælfwald of East Anglia, king 183
Ælfweard, king 209
Ælfwen, recluse at St Benet's at Hulme 220, 230
Ælfwen, recluse at St Stephen's, Hackington 220, 229
Ælfwine, abbot 58
Æthelbald of Mercia, king 183–4, 209–10
Æthelbald of Wessex, king 182, 184, 218
Æthelberht of East Anglia, king 211
Æthelflæd of Damerham 220
Æthelgar, bishop 127 n.93
Æthelhun, monk 2
Æthelred of Mercia, king 182–3

Index

Æthelred of Northumbria, king 85 n.37
Æthelred the Unready, king 182–3, 209, 222, 225
Æthelric, bishop of Chichester 58
Æthelric, bishop of Dorchester 220
Æthelstan, ætheling 219, 225
Æthelstan, king 57, 168
Æthelthryth, abbess 219, 230
Æthelwold, abbot and bishop 3, 58, 116, 120, 122, 125–6, 132
Æthelwulf
    De abbatibus 122
Æthelwulf of Wessex, king 182, 184, 218
Ætla, bishop 229
ageism 12, 88 n.55
ages of man *see* life cycle
ages of the world 38–41
Agnes, saint 119
Alchfrith of Deira, king 184
Alcuin, scholar 3, 5 n.20, 38, 43, 44 n.124, 55–6, 60, 79, 93, 139 n. 25, 158, 211
    Commentaria in s. Joannis euangelium 17 n.9, 40–1, 46, 51
    Disputatio puerorum per interrogationes et responsiones 39–40, 45, 51
    letters 56, 60, 79, 84, 93, 158, 211
    poetry 88, 90–1
    De rerum humanarum vicissitudine et clade Lindisfarnensis monasterii 83–5, 87
    O mea cella 83, 85–6
    Propositiones ad acuendos iuvenes 74 n.98
    Vita Willibrordi 117, 119, 132
Aldhelm, bishop and scholar 116, 122, 129 n.106
    Carmen de Virginitate 106, 114–15
    De laude virginitatis 114–15, 124
Aldwulf of East Anglia, king 183
Alexander, saint 119

Alexander the Great 84, 186 n.38
Alfred the Great, king 148, n.49, 182–3, 209
Amalarius
    De regula canonicorum 55 n.15
Anglo-Saxon Chronicle 48 n.141, 58–9, 150, 152–3, 154, 168 n.136, 181, 220 n.50, 222–3
animals
    caterpillar 57 n.27
    dragon 148, 152 *see also under Beowulf*
    frog 8, 12–13
    goat 20 n.22
    horse 20 n.22, 90, 138 n.20, 140, 145, 163 n.121, 190, 194, 219, 225
    lamb 220
    lion 20 n.22, 130–1
    mule 180–1 n.17
    polar bear 152
    snake 20 n.22
    wolf 76, 92
Anthimus of Nicomedia, martyr 123–4
Anthony the Hermit 114 n.17, 124, 125 n.84
anthropology 10–11, 55, 59, 214–15
archaeology 5, 7, 77, 136–8, 153, 214–15
Aristotle 20, 47
    De anima 20
    Ars rhetorica 20
Árni Audunarson 155
art 26–9, 138–48, 153
Asser, bishop
    Vita Ælfredi 182, 184
Athanasius
    The Life of Saint Anthony 124, 125 n.84
Augustine of Hippo 38–9, 43, 74 n.100, 191
    De civitate Dei 66 n.61
    De diversis quaestionibus octaginta tribus 41
    Soliloquies 104–5, 108

Augustine, saint 221
Bald's *Leechbook* 47–8, 77–8, 187 n.41
Basil, saint 114 n.18
Battle of Brunanburh 154, 168–9, 173–5
Battle of Maldon 135–6, 151, 154–6, 159–64, 166, 173–5, 233
   Byrhtwold 135–6, 160–1, 164, 166, 170, 233
   Dunnere 135–6, 173
   see also Byrhtnoth, ealdorman
Bayeux Tapestry 145–8, 151, 153, 173
beard 25, 27–9, 116 n.25, 122, 138–40, 142–4, 146–8
Bede, monk and scholar 3, 25, 69 n.77, 213 n.8, 228
   Biblical Miscellany 63
   death 56
   De die iudicii 105
   De temporibus 17 n.9, 38–40, 44 n.27, 51
   De temporum ratione 17 n.9, 31–4, 38–40, 50–1, 70 n.80, 78, 126, 176
   Historia abbatum 78, 116 n.38, 117 n.40, 119, 122, 127
   Historia ecclesiastica 2, 44, 56, 57, 79, 182, 191–2, 216 n.23, 217, 218 n.34, 224
   Homilia in natale s. Benedicti 116 n.38, 122, 127–8
   In Epistolas Septem Catholicas 69 n.77
   In Lucam evangelium expositio 21 n.23, 50, 66
   In s. Joannis evangelium expositio 46
   Letter to Ecgberht 149
   On Genesis 66 n.61
   Vita s. Cuthberti 41, 44 n.27, 120
Benedict Biscop, abbot 3, 115–16, 119, 122, 126–7
Benedict of Nursia, saint 119
Beowulf 58, 76–7 n.3, 82 n.25, 149 n.54, 154–6, 164
   Æschere 186, 193–4, 204
   as a mirror of princes 177–9, 201–7
   audience 177–9, 209–11
Beowulf
   childhood 46 n.132
   as a young man 68 n.72, 154, 178, 188, 190, 193–4, 198
   as an old king 48, 83 n.32, 164, 166, 174, 187–90, 197–208
   dragon 169, 187, 198–201, 206–7
   Ecgtheow 169, 195–6
   Finnsburg episode (ll. 1063–1159) 196
   Grendel 169, 190, 193, 195, 201, 203–4
   Grendel's mother 48, 187, 190, 212
   Healfdene 164, 186, 199, 206
   Heremod 177, 191
   Hrethel 186–7, 200, 205
   Hrothgar 48, 83, 154, 158, 164, 166, 169–70, 174, 187–98, 201–8
   Hrothgar's 'sermon' (ll. 1700–84) 54 n.8, 70–1, 81, 192–3
   Hrothulf 158, 195, 203
   Hygelac 165, 177, 200 n.82, 207
   Ingeld episode (ll. 2024b–2069a) 83 n.32, 159, 164, 186, 196
   Lament of the old father (ll. 2444–2463a) 83 n.32, 186–7, 200, 205
   Ongentheow 83 n.32, 164, 165–6, 186, 200, 206
   wife 186, 200, 212
   Scyld Scefing 177, 186
   Unferth 203
   Wealhtheow 195
   Weohstan 186
   Wiglaf 178, 188, 197–8, 199–200, 207–8
   see also Heime; Ingeld; Offa of Angeln; Sigemund; Volsung; Wermund of Angeln
Berhtwald, archbishop 2, 3
Biblical figures

Index

Adam 38, 82
Anna 228
David 38
Elijah and Elisha 126
Eve 82
Holofernes 169
Isaac 19, 29, 66 n.61, 130 n.111
Jacob 19, 29
John the Apostle 114 n.16, 115–16, 125
John the Baptist, parents of (Elizabeth and Zachary) 23, 114 n.17, 130 n.111
Lot 139–42, 166
Luke the Apostle 114 ns.16–17, 116
Magi, adoration of the 25–8, 31, 50
Mary 27, 120, 130 n.111
Moses 170
Noah 38, 68
Paul the Apostle 23, 24, 93, 213
Peter the Apostle 23, 24
Philip the Apostle 116, 118
Rachel 74
Rebecca 74, 130 n.111
Samson, parents of 130 n.111
Samuel and Daniel 61
Sarah 66 n.61, 74, 130 n.111
Sem 68
Solomon 48, 91–2, 191–2
Tobias 60
see also Abraham; Christ
Biblical passages
1 John 3 69 n.77
1 Pet. 1:24 95
2 Cor. 12:10 93
Deut. 5:16 60
Eccles. 11:9 21
Eccles. 12:1–4 89 n.56
Eph. 5:6 74
Eph. 6:1–3 60
Eph. 6:14–17 152 n.68
Exod. 12:37 171
Exod. 20:12 60
Gen. 14:13 (War of the Kings) 139, 142–3, 166
Gen. 18:11 66 n.61
Isa. 65:20 63
James 1:11 95
John 4:6 40
John 8:57 46
Lev. 19:32 59
Luke 12:36–8 (Parable of the Three Vigils) 20–1, 31, 66
Matt. 2:1–12 25
Matt. 8:11 19
Matt. 20:1–16 (Parable of the Vineyard) 37–8
Numbers 1 171
Numbers 8:24–8 46
Ps. 7:8, 13 144
Ps. 71:10–11 27
Ps. 89:10 36, 43
Ps. 104 28–9
Ps. 108 79–80 n.16
Ps. 109 79–80 n.16
Titus 2:3–5 213
Tob. 10:4 60
Tob. 14:15 63
Wisd. 4:8–9 63
Birinus, saint 220
Blickling Homilies
  hom. 5 95–7, 106 n.120
  hom. 8 106 n.120
  hom. 14 22–3, 50
  hom. 15 24
bona senectute 63
Boniface, missionary 3, 37, 117, 120 n.64, 132
  correspondence 74, 79, 93, 217, 219
  health 79, 125, 127
Bonifacius, bishop of Ferenti 57 n.27
Bosa, bishop 229
Brendan, saint 67
Brihtgifu, abbess 217, 220
Brihtwold, archbishop 73
Brorda, ealdorman 211
Bugga, abbess 93, 217–18

Index

Byrhtferth of Ramsey, monk and scholar 17 n.9, 31
  De concordia mensium atque elementorum (Diagram) 34–6, 45, 50
  Enchiridion 32–4, 50, 69–70 n.80, 78
  Vita s. Ecgwini 36–7, 50, 114, 117, 129, 134, 173
  Vita s. Oswaldi 36, 117, 129, 130, 149–50
Byrhtnoth, ealdorman 149–54, 173, 234
  in *Battle of Maldon* 135–6, 154, 160–4, 166–8, 170, 174
  ofermōd 163
Calepodius, saint 114 n.17
care for the elderly 1, 59–62, 125
Catechesis Celtica 99–103, 106 n.119
Cecilia, saint 110
Ceolfrith, abbot 3, 78–9, 114 n.17, 117, 122, 124, 127, 191–2
Charlemagne 55–6, 79, 93, 179–81, 211
Charles the Bald 181
charters *see* Sawyer number
Chaucer, Geoffrey 212
childhood, characteristics of 32–6, 40, 121 *see also* life cycle; *puer senex*; *puer centum annorum*
children 44–5, 107, 119–21
  and warfare 137–8
  care for parents 1, 60–1
  grandchildren 215, 218, 219, 224–6
Christ 38, 41, 74, 86, 95, 105, 123, 158, 228
Christ III 106
Chronicon abbatiae Rameseiensis 220
Cnut the Great, king 58, 151, 209, 222
Coenwulf of Mercia, king 183
Coleman, monk 117 n.50
Collectanea Pseudo-Bedae 25, 38, 39, 45, 50–1, 73 n.95, 92 n.67, 100 n.93, 106 n.119
Columbanus
  De mundi transitu 107–8

Constantine II of Scotland, king 154, 168–9, 173–4
councilors 58–9
Crusades 135–6, 156 n.92
cultural conceptualisation 8–13
Cuthbert, saint 120, 138
Cuthman, saint 1, 60–1, 219
Cynewulf, poet 88
  Christ II 88
  Elene 54 n.8, 84, 86, 88–91, 212
  Fates of the Apostles 88
  Juliana 88
Cynewulf of Wessex, king 183
  and Cyneheard 154
Dame Sirith 235 n.6
Das jüngere Hildebrandlied 166
De duodecim abusiuis see under Pseudo-Cypran
death
  anticipated 2, 89, 126, 131–2, 175, 198
  average age at death 4
  contrasted to life 18, 81, 106
  effect on body 96–8, 132–3
  fear 80
  inevitability 18, 64–5, 71, 94, 99–100, 103–4, 193
  kept secret 180
  prefiguration of Hell 101
  saintly death 130–3
  three types 22
  warrior's death 151–2, 154, 163
Death of Edgar 58–9, 153
decrepitas 39–40, 42, 51
decrepitude *see* health
demography 4
Dicts of Cato 55
disability *see* health
disease *see* health
Domesday Book 229
dream interpretation 219, 230
duguþ 149
Dunne, testatrix 219, 226

Index

Dunstan, archbishop 57–8, 117, 121–2, 125–6, 127 n.93, 128–9, 131, 132, 234
Durham Proverbs 72–3
Durham Ritual 74
Eadgifu, queen 3, 218, 219, 222–4, 225
Eadmer of Canterbury
  Vita s. Oswaldi 62–3
Eadred, king 222
Eadwig, king 209, 222
Eanflæd, queen 218, 223, 228
Eangyth, abbess 219
Ecgberht, bishop 149
Ecgberht, church reformer 3, 57
Ecgberht of Wessex, king 182–3
Ecgfrith of Mercia, king 60, 184 n.29, 211
Ecgwine, bishop 36, 114, 117, 129, 134, 173
Edgar the Peaceful, king 152
Edith of Wilton, saint 217, 229
Edmund Ironside 219
Edmund of East Anglia, king 57
Edmund the Elder, king 168, 220, 222
Edward the Confessor, king 3, 117, 130, 183, 184, 222–3, 227
Edward the Elder, king 183, 219, 222
Egbert, monk 2
Egil Skallagrímsson 168
Egil Ulserk 152, 155, 156 n.90
Egils saga 151, 168, 180 n.16
Eilmer, pioneer of man-powered flight 3, 61
Eleanor of Aquitaine, queen 221
Eleazar, chief scribe and martyr 114, 116, 122–3
elements 31–5
Emma of Normandy 216, 218, 220, 222–4
Encomium Emmae Reginae 216
encyclopaedic notes 41–3, 45, 51
Enrico Dandolo, doge 135–6
Eventius, martyr 116

exemptions 78
Exhortation to Christian Living see *Rewards of Piety*
Exodus 170–2
family 76, 214
  aged parents 1, 23, 130, 228
  children's care for parents 1, 60–1
  father and daughter 94, 177
  father and son 71–2, 74 n.98, 157, 162, 181–2, 184 n.27, 195–6, 200, 210–11
  grandchildren 215, 218, 219, 224–6
  grandmothers 121, 215, 218, 222, 224–5
  mother and son 1, 60–1, 212, 221–3
Faricius
  Vita s. Aldhelmi 116
Felix
  Life of Saint Guthlac 120 n.64, 121
Felix, saint 114 n.17
Finnsburg Fragment 155
Forthhere, bishop 74
Fortunes of Men 76–7, 109
Franks Casket 26–7, 50
Frederick I Barbarossa, emperor 135
Froda, king 157
Frodo III, king 180
Genesis A 166–8
Genesis B 82, 166 n.128
Geoffrey of Burton
  Vita s. Moduenne virginis 227
gerontophobia 6, 52, 109, 233
Gesta Fresonum 156
Gesta Herewardi 220
Godric, sheriff 229
Godwine, earl 221, 223, 227–8
Goscelin, hagiographer 217, 229–30
  Historia translationis s. Augustini 221
  Translatio Edithe 220
  Translatio s. Mildrethe 220
  Vita Edithe 217, 220, 229
  Vita et virtutes sanctae Vulfildae virginis 220

269

grauitas 35, 40–1, 51
Gregory the Great, pope 21, 38
  Dialogi 46–7, 57 n.27, 119, 187 n.41
  Homiliae in Evangelia 21, 98–9
Guthlac, saint 120 n.64, 121, 138
Guthlac B 88 n.52
Guthorm 177
Gytha, noblewoman 220–2, 224
Hadding, king 177
Hadrian, abbot 3, 56 n.22
Hagen 155
hagiography 110–34
  Life of King Edward 117, 130
  OE prose life of Guthlac 18
  OE *Life of Machutus* 67, 120 n.64, 130
  OE *Life of St Mary of Egypt* 114–15 n.18, 116, 124, 129–31, 212 n.3
  OE *Life of St Nicholas* 48–9 n.145
  OE *Life of St Pantaleon* 123–4
  Passio sanctorum apostolum Petri et Pauli 24
  Vita Ceolfrithi 78–9 n.12, 117, 122 n.73
  Vita s. Birini 220
  Vita s. Cuthmanni 1 n.2, 61, 219
  Vita s. Dunstani 117, 122, 127 n.93, 128–9, 132
  Vita Tertia (of St Patrick) 80 n.19, 103 n.104
  see also saints' lives indexed under the authors' names
hair
  falling out 99–102
  grey 24, 33, 58–9, 63, 82, 87, 94, 100–1, 135, 153–4, 160, 164–8, 171, 174–5, 188
  red 25
  white 25, 80, 116 n.30, 117 n.46, 130–1, 139, 144, 146–8, 150, 153, 161, 212 n.3, 227
Hálfs saga 155

Harald Fairhair 180 n.16
Harold Godwinson, king 146–8, 184, 220–1
Harthacnut, king 222
Hathagat 155
Haymo, homilist 19, 22
health 61, 77–80, 93–8, 124–8, 235
  ankles, swollen 99–100
  blindness 103 n.104, 135, 210, 220–1
  breathing problems 98–102
  cancer 77
  eyesight, poor 77, 79–80, 84, 99–103, 125
  forgetfulness 32–4, 78
  'half-dead disease' 47–8, 77–8
  headache 80
  hearing, impaired 80 n.19, 99–103, 193, 220
  indigestion 77
  limbs, afflicted 80, 84, 94, 98–102, 125
  menopause 224 n.79
  osteoarthritis 77
  seizure 125
  sleepiness 32–4, 78, 84, 125–6, 130, 176, 193–4
  speech, impaired 80 n.19, 84, 98–103
  swelling up 98
  teeth fall out 77, 80, 94, 99–100
  teeth turn yellow 101
  unaffected by age 124–5
  wrinkles 94, 98–9
  see also hair
Heaven 85, 88, 91, 94, 104–8, 110, 128–9, 133, 157, 174
Heime 155, 164
Helena, saint 88, 89, 212
Hell 7, 100–4, 108–9
Henry of Bonn, crusader 156 n.92
Henry of Huntingdon 152 n.68
  Historia Anglorum 151–2
Hereward the Wake 220
Herfast, bishop 58

Index

Herman, hagiographer 230
  Miracula sancti Eadmundi 220, 230
heroic poetry 153–73 *see also*
  individual poems such as
  Battle of Maldon and *Beowulf*
Hilarion, saint 114 ns.16–7, 115,
  131–2
Hilary of Arles
  De vita S. Honorati 37
Hild, abbess 2, 3, 114 n.17, 217, 218,
  223–4, 228, 229
Hildebrand 155, 156 n.91, 162, 166
Hildebrandlied 155, 156 n.91, 162
Hildelith, abbess 2, 216 n.23, 218
Hjálmgunnar 155
homilies 53, 60, 62–7, 93–108, 213
  Assmann, hom. 14 106 n.120
  Bazire and Cross, hom. 1 106
    n.120
  Bazire and Cross, hom. 4 106
    n.120, 108
  Bazire and Cross, hom. 7 60 n.40,
    65
  Bazire and Cross, hom. 10 66–7
  'Be heofonwarum 7 be
    helwarum' 108
  'Geherað nu mæn ða leofestan hu
    us godes bec' 106 n.120
  Irvine, hom. 7 107
  Napier, hom. 29 106 n.120
  Napier, hom. 30 101, 102–4
  see also Blickling Homilies; homilies
    under Ælfric; homilies *under*
    Wulfstan of York; *Vercelli
    Homilies*
Hrothgar *see under Beowulf*
Hrothwaru, abbess 226
humours 31–5
Huneberc
  Hodoeporicon 117, 118
Ine of Wessex, king 58, 79, 182,
  183
Ingulf, abbot 3
infantia 22, 35, 37–46, 50–1
Ingeld 157–9, 161, 196

Innstein 155
Instructions for Christians 67
Isidore of Seville 20 n.22, 36, 44
  n.127
  Etymologiae 20, n.22, 35, 38–43, 68
    n.71
  De natura rerum 33
  Differentiae 35, 38–43
  iuuentus 17, 20–3, 30, 32, 35–43, 45,
    49–51
Jerome
  Epistolae 93–4
John of Beverley, bishop 2, 229
John the Hermit 114 n.16, 115
Jomsvikings 148–9, 171
Judgement Day 80, 91, 104–5, 108
Judgement Day II 105
Judith 169
Judith of Flanders, princess 182,
  218
Julian of Toledo
  Prognosticon futuri saeculi 22, 105
    n.111
kingship
  ideals 177–8, 190–201
  problems of old rulers 179–86
Kudrun 156
Lantfred of Winchester
  *Translatio et miracula s.
    Swithuni* 117
law texts 48–9, 57–8, 138 n.20, 218
Lawrence, saint 123
Leofric, earl 223
Letter of Alexander to Aristotle 186
  n.38
letters 73–4, 93–4, 149, 191–2, 219,
  230
  by Ælfric 65, 68, 213
  by Alcuin 56, 60, 79, 84, 93, 158,
    211
  by Boniface 80, 93, 217
Leoba, saint 74, 117, 130, 219, 230
Liber de Numeris 106 n.119
Liber Eliensis 150–1, 218 n.32, 220
  n.49

271

Index

life cycle 16–52
  age limits 35–6, 39–43, 44–9
  two ages of man 18–20
  three ages of man 16–17, 20–31
  four ages of man 31–7
  five ages of man 37–8
  six ages of man 38–43
  seven ages of man 43–4
life expectancy 4
Lindisfarne *Liber Vitae* 88
longevity 74–5
Lothair II, king 191 n.52
Louis the German 179, 181
Louis the Pious 179, 181
Lul, archbishop 3
Machutus, saint 67, 120 n.64, 130
manuscripts
  Antwerp, Museum Plantin-Moretus, M. 17.4 ('Antwerp Sedulius') 28, 50
  Cambridge, Corpus Christi College, 23 140–1, 145
  Cambridge, Corpus Christi College, 183 42, 51
  Cambridge, Corpus Christi College, 303 48–9 n.145
  Cambridge, Corpus Christi College, 320 42, 51
  Cambridge, Trinity College Library, R.17.1 ('Eadwine Psalter') 28, 29, 144, 145 n.38
  Cambridge, University Library, MS L1.1.10 ('Book of Cerne') 29–31, 50, 100 n.97
  Durham, Cathedral Library, B. III. 32 73 n.93
  Exeter, Cathedral Library, 3501 ('Exeter Book') 69 n.74, 71, 76, 82
  Leiden, Universiteitsbibliotheek, Voss. Lat. Q. 69 66 n.61
  London, British Library, Add. 24199 140
  London, British Library, Add. 49598 ('Benedictional of St Æthelwold') 28 n.53
  London, British Library, Cotton Claudius B. iv ('Old English Hexateuch') 141–3, 145, 153, 172
  London, British Library, Cotton Cleopatra C. viii 140
  London, British Library, Cotton Otho A. xii 160 n.106
  London, British Library, Cotton Tiberius A. iii 68
  London, British Library, Cotton Tiberius B. i 72 n.92
  London, British Library, Cotton Tiberius C. i 30–1, 42, 45, 51
  London, British Library, Cotton Vespasian B. vi 42, 45, 51
  London, British Library, Cotton Vespasian D. xx 30, 37, 50
  London, British Library, Cotton Vitellius A. xix 41, 51
  London, British Library, Harley 603 ('Harley Psalter') 28–9, 50, 144–5
  London, British Library, Harley 1117 41 n.116
  London, British Library, Harley 3667 34
  London, British Library, Royal 2 B. v ('Royal Psalter') 42, 51, 81
  London, Lambeth Palace Library, 427 ('Lambeth Psalter') 79–80
  Munich, Bayerische Staatsbibliothek, clm. 22053 ('*Wessobrunn Prayer* manuscript') 26
  Munich, Bayerische Staatsbibliothek, clm. 29336/1 140
  Oxford, Bodleian Library, Bodley 109 41 n.116
  Oxford, Bodleian Library, Bodley 343 107

Index

Oxford, Bodleian Library, Hatton 115 101 n.98, 103 n.105
Oxford, Bodleian Library, Junius 11 ('Junius Manuscript') 143 n.35, 166 n.128, 170 n.143
Oxford, Bodleian Library, Junius 85/86 106 n.120
Oxford, St John's College 17 34
Paris, Bibliothèque nationale de France, lat. 2825 42, 51
Paris, Bibliothèque nationale de France, lat. 8846 ('Paris Psalter') 28, 29 n.59, 144, 145 n.38
Rome, Vatican City, Biblioteca Apostolica Vaticana, Reg. lat. 12 ('Bury St Edmunds Psalter') 27, 50
Rome, Vatican City, Biblioteca Apostolica Vaticana, Reg. lat. 204 41, 51
Rouen, Bibliothèque municipale, 274 (Y.6) ('Sacramentary of Robert of Jumièges') 28 n.53
Utrecht, Universiteitsbibliotheek 32 ('Utrecht Psalter') 28, 29, 144, 145 n.38
Vercelli, Biblioteca Capitolare, CXVII ('Vercelli Book') 7, 101 n.98, 102–4
Martin of Tours, saint 114–16, 128–9, 133 n.126
martyrdom, old age as 128
Mary of Egypt, saint 114–15 n.18, 116, 124, 129–31, 212 n.3
masculinity 169–70, 204
Maurice, saint 114 n.18, 157
Maurus, saint 114, 116, 118
Maximianus, emperor 123–4
Maxims I 82
Maxims II 18–19, 54 n.8, 72–3, 81, 154, 187 n.42
middle age 20–30, 50

miracles 44, 129–30
  barren couples conceive 130, 134, 219 n.41
  caterpillars leave vegetable garden 57 n.27
  child resurrected 44
  health restored 220–1
  lamb comes out of tomb 220
  levitating chair 125–6
  lion helps with burial 130–1
  mill runs on its own 130
  young woman turns old 227
  youth restored 132–3, 220
mockery 1, 168–9, 180–1 n.17
Modwenna, saint 227
Nestor 161–2
Nibelungenlied 155
Nothhelm, archbishop 226
Odo of Bayeux, bishop 145
Offa of Angeln, king 210–11
Offa of Mercia, king 60, 183, 184 n.29, 209–11, 234
Oftfor, bishop 229
Olaf Tryggvason, king 149, 171
old age
  chronological definition 2–4
  contrasted to youth *see* youth
  cultural definition 5–7
  functional definition 2, 5
  physical characteristics *see* health
  threshold of old age 13, 44–9
Old English Gospel of Pseudo-Matthew 120
Old English Heptateuch 59
Old English Hexateuch *see* London, British Library, Cotton Claudius B. iv *under* manuscripts
Old English Martyrology 26, 82 n.29, 111, 113 n.13, 114, 115, 121, 124, 130, 131–2
Orbila, abbess 227
Orderic Vitalis
  Historia ecclesiastica 230
Origen, church father 38

273

Index

Oslac, earl 58–9, 152–3
Oswald of Worcester 36, 62–3, 117, 129, 130
Oswiu of Northumbria, king 183–4, 218
Ovid 212
  Amores 172
Pantaleon, saint 123–4
Paul the Hermit 114 ns.16–17, 124
Paulinus of Aquileia
  Liber exhortationis 66
Pepin the Hunchback 181
personification 92–3
Peter the Apostle 23, 24
Peter Chrysologus, bishop 23
Petrocellus
  Pratica Petrocelli Salernitani 48
Philip the Apostle 116, 118
Phoenix 105–6
Popta, Frisian warrior 156–7
Porus, king 186 n.38
prayers 30–1, 79–80
Precepts 54 n.8, 71–2, 232
Prosopography of Anglo-Saxon England 216
proverbs 72–3, 81, 143 n.34, 154, 161, 181 *see also Dicts of Cato; Durham Proverbs; Maxims I; Maxims II*
Prudentius
  Psychomachia 139–41, 153, 167 n.130, 172
Pseudo-Basil
  De admonitio ad filium spiritualem 94–9
Pseudo-Cyprian
  De duodecim abusiuis 64, 99–104
puer centum annorum 63–4, 67
puer senex 62–3, 67, 68 n.72, 112, 118–21, 198 n.75
pueritia 17, 20–1, 23, 35–43, 45–6, 49–51
Pythagoras, philosopher 31
queens 213–14 n.9, 215
Raymond of St Gilles, crusader 135

Raynald of Châtillon, crusader 135
remembrancers *see* witnesses
respect for the elderly 59–62
retirement 78–9, 126–7, 164, 168, 182, 212–3, 218, 228
Rewards of Piety 174–6
Riddle 43 82
riddles 16, 82, 91–2
Riming Poem 69–71, 84, 86–8, 185–6
Robert, bishop 133
Roger Bacon, scholar 235
Rudolf
  Vita s. Leoba 117, 130, 219, 230
Rule of Chrodegang 55 n.15, 60–1, 72, 78
Rule of St Benedict 60
runes 27, 90–1
sadness 82–91, 110, 200, 205–7
saints 110–34
  death 131–3
  spiritual guides 121–4
  suffering from old age 124–31
  youth 118–21
Saturn 48, 91
Sawyer number (charters)
  S 1255 219, 226
  S 1429 219, 226
  S 1494 220 n.49
  S 1503 219, 225
  S 1536 225
  S 1539 219, 225
Saxo Grammaticus
  Gesta Danorum 155, 157–8, 161, 177, 180, 180–1 n.17, 210
Seafarer 69–71, 81–2, 84, 86–8
seasons 31–5
Seaxburh, abbess 218, 223, 228
Sedulius Scottus
  De rectoribus christianis 191 n.52
senectus 17, 20–3, 30, 35–43, 45, 49–51
senex amans 235
senex sine religione 64–5, 67, 99–100
senium 22, 35, 39, 41–3, 45, 51
sexual activity 65–6, 213, 235
Sicgfrith, abbot 127

Index

Sigemund 155, 164, 199, 206
Simeon Stylites, saint 114 n.17, 121
Simon Magus 23–4
Siward, earl 150–3, 156 n.90, 173, 223, 234
Sixtus II, pope and martyr 116, 123
Snorri Sturluson
   Prose Edda 93 n.71
   Heimskringla 149, 152, 155
Solomon and Saturn II 48, 54 n.8, 91–3, 187 n.41
sleep *see* health
Speusippus, Eleusippus and Meleusippus, saints 121
spiritual superiority 62–7
Starkad 152, 155, 156 n.90, 157–9, 161, 164, 180–1 n. 17
Stephen of Ripon 3
   Vita s. Wilfrithi 44, 46, 111, 120, 125, 132, 224
Sturlunga saga 155
Sulpicius Severus
   Vita s. Martini 128, 129 n.103, 133 n.126
Summons to Prayer see Rewards of Piety
Swein, king 222
Swithun, saint 113 n.14, 117
symptoms of old age *see* health
Tacitus
   Germania 191
teachers 47, 55–6, 70–2, 123–4, 192, 229
Theodore of Tarsus, archbishop 2, 3, 56
Theodulf, bishop
   Theodulfi Capitula 59
theoretical framework 8–13
Thidrekssaga 155, 162, 164
Thor 93 n.71
Tostig Godwinson, earl 184
Tranquillinus, saint 114 n.17
transience 83–99
ubi sunt motif 86, 95, 97
Ulvild, princess 177

Vainglory 69, 71
Vercelli Homilies
   hom. 9 7, 101–4, 106–7
   hom. 18 116, 128
   hom. 19 106
   hom. 21 106
Vergil
   Eclogue 85 n.38
Vindicianus
   Epistola ad Pentadium 33
Vitae Offarum duorum 210
Volsung 155, 164, 199–200, 206
Völsunga saga 155, 164, 199
Vulfrunna, nun 220, 229
Walburg, abbess 3, 219
Waldere 155
Wanderer 54 n.8, 69–71, 83–4, 86, 88, 233
Walter Map
   De nugis curialium 227–8
warriors, old 135–73
   active 162–8
   advisors 156–62
   depictions of 138–48
   exclusion of 170–2
   retired 168–70
Wate 156
Wergild 59
Wermund of Angeln, king 210–11
widows 1, 215, 218, 221–4
Widsith 155, 158, 210 n.7
Widukind
   Res gestae Saxonicae 155
Wihtred of Kent, king 183
Wilfrid, bishop 3, 44, 46, 117, 120 n.64, 125, 132, 138, 184 n.27, 224, 229, 234
William Marshall, knight 136 n.7
William of Malmesbury
   Gesta pontificum Anglorum 116, 122, 129 n.106
   Gesta regum Anglorum 61
   Vita Dunstani 117, 125–6
   Vita s. Wulfstani 117, 126, 129, 132–3, 220, 228

William Rufus, king 230
William the Conqueror 57–8, 146, 184, 220, 221–2
Willibald, bishop 117
    Vita Bonifatii 37, 117, 120 n.64, 125, 127, 132
Willibrord, missionary 2, 3, 117, 119, 127, 132
wills 225
Wimbert, abbot of Nursling 127
Winnoc, abbot of Wormhout 114 n.17, 130
winter 32–4, 69–70 n.80, 85
wisdom 52–9, 64, 68–74, 89, 93, 119–20, 156, 161, 188, 191–3, 196, 198, 200, 202–3
wisdom poetry 53–4, 68–73, 81–93, 185
witches 217 n.27, 220
witnesses 57–8, 113 n.14, 229–30
women, old 212–31
  in Francia 214–15
  as culture bearers 224–31
  as political figures 221–4
Wulfric Spott 225
Wulfstan of Winchester
    Narratio metrica de s. Swithuno 117, 125, 131

Vita s. Æthelwoldi 116, 120, 122, 125, 131–2, 219 n.47, 230
Wulfstan of Worcester, bishop 117, 126, 129, 132–3, 220, 228
Wulfstan of York, archbishop 68, 120, 213 n.8
    Canons of Edgar 55
    homilies
      Bethurum, hom. 8c 66
      Bethurum, hom. 10a 55
      Bethurum, hom. 10c 55
      'De temporibus Anticristi' 23–5, 50
      Napier, hom. 50 78
    Institutes of Polity 228
Wulfthryth, saint 220
Wynflæd, noblewoman 219, 225
youth 170
  contrasted to old age 18–20, 63–4, 76, 81, 85, 87, 89 n.56, 90–1, 98–9, 106–8, 110, 163, 169, 185, 187–8, 199–200 *see also puer centum annorum; puer senex*
  fear of 227
  loss of 84, 90, 96
  restoration of 105, 131–3, 200
  see also life cycle
Zosimus, saint 114–15 n.18, 116, 129–31, 212 n.3

ANGLO-SAXON STUDIES

Volume 1: The Dramatic Liturgy of Anglo-Saxon England,
M. Bradford Bedingfield

Volume 2: The Art of the Anglo-Saxon Goldsmith: Fine Metalwork in Anglo-Saxon England: its Practice and Practitioners,
Elizabeth Coatsworth and Michael Pinder

Volume 3: The Ruler Portraits of Anglo-Saxon England, *Catherine E. Karkov*

Volume 4: Dying and Death in Later Anglo-Saxon England, *Victoria Thompson*

Volume 5: Landscapes of Monastic Foundation: The Establishment of Religious Houses in East Anglia, c. 650-1200, *Tim Pestell*

Volume 6: Pastoral Care in Late Anglo-Saxon England,
edited by Francesca Tinti

Volume 7: Episcopal Culture in Late Anglo-Saxon England,
Mary Frances Giandrea

Volume 8: Elves in Anglo-Saxon England: Matters of Belief, Health, Gender and Identity, *Alaric Hall*

Volume 9: Feasting the Dead: Food and Drink in Anglo-Saxon Burial Rituals,
Christina Lee

Volume 10: Anglo-Saxon Button Brooches: Typology, Genealogy, Chronology,
Seiichi Suzuki

Volume 11: Wasperton: A Roman, British and Anglo-Saxon Community in Central England, *edited by Martin Carver with Catherine Hills and Jonathan Scheschkewitz*

Volume 12: A Companion to Bede, *George Hardin Brown*

Volume 13: Trees in Anglo-Saxon England: Literature, Lore and Landscape,
Della Hooke

Volume 14: The Homiletic Writings of Archbishop Wulfstan,
Joyce Tally Lionarons

Volume 15: The Archaeology of the East Anglian Conversion, *Richard Hoggett*

Volume 16: The Old English Version of Bede's *Historia Ecclesiastica*,
Sharon M. Rowley

Volume 17: Writing Power in Anglo-Saxon England: Texts, Hierarchies, Economies, *Catherine A.M. Clarke*

Volume 18: Cognitive Approaches to Old English Poetry, *Antonina Harbus*

Volume 19: Environment, Society and Landscape in Early Medieval England: Time and Topography, *Tom Williamson*

Volume 20: Honour, Exchange and Violence in *Beowulf*, *Peter S. Baker*

Volume 21: *John the Baptist's Prayer* or *The Descent into Hell* from the Exeter Book: Text, Translation and Critical Study, *M.R. Rambaran-Olm*

Volume 22: Food, Eating and Identity in Early Medieval England, *Allen J. Frantzen*

Volume 23: Capital and Corporal Punishment in Anglo-Saxon England, *edited by Jay Paul Gates and Nicole Marafioti*

Volume 24: The Dating of *Beowulf*: A Reassessment, *edited by Leonard Neidorf*

Volume 25: The Cruciform Brooch and Anglo-Saxon England, *Toby F. Martin*

Volume 26: Trees in the Religions of Early Medieval England, *Michael D.J. Bintley*

Volume 27: The Peterborough Version of the Anglo-Saxon Chronicle: Rewriting Post-Conquest History, *Malasree Home*

Volume 28: The Anglo-Saxon Chancery: The History, Language and Production of Anglo-Saxon Charters from Alfred to Edgar, *Ben Snook*

Volume 29: Representing Beasts in Early Medieval England and Scandinavia, *edited by Michael D.J. Bintley and Thomas J.T. Williams*

Volume 30: Direct Speech in *Beowulf* and Other Old English Narrative Poems, *Elise Louviot*

Volume 31: Old English Philology: Studies in Honour of R.D. Fulk, *edited by Leonard Neidorf, Rafael J. Pascual and Tom Shippey*

Volume 32: 'Charms', Liturgies, and Secret Rites in Early Medieval England, *Ciaran Arthur*

Volume 33: Old Age in Early Medieval England: A Cultural History, *Thijs Porck*

Volume 34: Priests and their Books in Late Anglo-Saxon England, *Gerald P. Dyson*

Volume 35: Burial, Landscape and Identity in Early Medieval Wessex, *Kate Mees*

Volume 36: The Sword in Early Medieval Northern Europe: Experience, Identity, Representation, *Sue Brunning*

Volume 37: The Chronology and Canon of Ælfric of Eynsham, *Aaron J Kleist*

Volume 38: Medical Texts in Anglo-Saxon Literary Culture, *Emily Kesling*

Volume 39: The Dynastic Drama of *Beowulf*, *Francis Leneghan*

Volume 40: Old English Lexicology and Lexicography: Essays in Honor of Antonette diPaolo Healey, *edited by Maren Clegg Hyer, Haruko Momma and Samantha Zacher*

Volume 41: Debating with Demons: Pedagogy and Materiality in Early English Literature, *Christina M. Heckman*

www.ingramcontent.com/pod-product-compliance
Lightning Source LLC
Chambersburg PA
CBHW051605230426
43668CB00013B/1982